FREE Study Skills Videos/DVD Offer

Dear Customer,

Thank you for your purchase from Mometrix! We consider it an honor and a privilege that you have purchased our product and we want to ensure your satisfaction.

As part of our ongoing effort to meet the needs of test takers, we have developed a set of Study Skills Videos that we would like to give you for <u>FREE</u>. These videos cover our *best practices* for getting ready for your exam, from how to use our study materials to how to best prepare for the day of the test.

All that we ask is that you email us with feedback that would describe your experience so far with our product. Good, bad, or indifferent, we want to know what you think!

To get your FREE Study Skills Videos, you can use the **QR code** below, or send us an **email** at studyvideos@mometrix.com with *FREE VIDEOS* in the subject line and the following information in the body of the email:

- The name of the product you purchased.
- Your product rating on a scale of 1-5, with 5 being the highest rating.
- Your feedback. It can be long, short, or anything in between. We just want to know your impressions and experience so far with our product. (Good feedback might include how our study material met your needs and ways we might be able to make it even better. You could highlight features that you found helpful or features that you think we should add.)

If you have any questions or concerns, please don't hesitate to contact me directly.

Thanks again!

Sincerely,

Jay Willis
Vice President
jay.willis@mometrix.com
1-800-673-8175

GRE

Test Prep 2023-2024

3 Full-Length Practice Exams

GRE Study Book Secrets
with Step-by-Step
Video Tutorials

7th Edition

Written and edited by Mometrix Test Prep

Printed in the United States of America

This paper meets the requirements of ANSI/NISO Z39.48-1992 (Permanence of Paper).

Mometrix offers volume discount pricing to institutions. For more information or a price quote, please contact our sales department at sales@mometrix.com or 888-248-1219.

Paperback
ISBN 13: 978-1-5167-2265-5
ISBN 10: 1-5167-2265-5

DEAR FUTURE EXAM SUCCESS STORY

First of all, **THANK YOU** for purchasing Mometrix study materials!

Second, congratulations! You are one of the few determined test-takers who are committed to doing whatever it takes to excel on your exam. **You have come to the right place.** We developed these study materials with one goal in mind: to deliver you the information you need in a format that's concise and easy to use.

In addition to optimizing your guide for the content of the test, we've outlined our recommended steps for breaking down the preparation process into small, attainable goals so you can make sure you stay on track.

We've also analyzed the entire test-taking process, identifying the most common pitfalls and showing how you can overcome them and be ready for any curveball the test throws you.

Standardized testing is one of the biggest obstacles on your road to success, which only increases the importance of doing well in the high-pressure, high-stakes environment of test day. Your results on this test could have a significant impact on your future, and this guide provides the information and practical advice to help you achieve your full potential on test day.

Your success is our success

We would love to hear from you! If you would like to share the story of your exam success or if you have any questions or comments in regard to our products, please contact us at **800-673-8175** or **support@mometrix.com**.

Thanks again for your business and we wish you continued success!

Sincerely,
The Mometrix Test Preparation Team

Need more help? Check out our flashcards at:
http://mometrixflashcards.com/GRE

TABLE OF CONTENTS

Introduction

Thank you for purchasing this resource! You have made the choice to prepare yourself for a test that could have a huge impact on your future, and this guide is designed to help you be fully ready for test day. Obviously, it's important to have a solid understanding of the test material, but you also need to be prepared for the unique environment and stressors of the test, so that you can perform to the best of your abilities.

For this purpose, the first section that appears in this guide is the **Secret Keys**. We've devoted countless hours to meticulously researching what works and what doesn't, and we've boiled down our findings to the five most impactful steps you can take to improve your performance on the test. We start at the beginning with study planning and move through the preparation process, all the way to the testing strategies that will help you get the most out of what you know when you're finally sitting in front of the test.

We recommend that you start preparing for your test as far in advance as possible. However, if you've bought this guide as a last-minute study resource and only have a few days before your test, we recommend that you skip over the first two Secret Keys since they address a long-term study plan.

If you struggle with **test anxiety**, we strongly encourage you to check out our recommendations for how you can overcome it. Test anxiety is a formidable foe, but it can be beaten, and we want to make sure you have the tools you need to defeat it.

Secret Key #1 – Plan Big, Study Small

There's a lot riding on your performance. If you want to ace this test, you're going to need to keep your skills sharp and the material fresh in your mind. You need a plan that lets you review everything you need to know while still fitting in your schedule. We'll break this strategy down into three categories.

Information Organization

Start with the information you already have: the official test outline. From this, you can make a complete list of all the concepts you need to cover before the test. Organize these concepts into groups that can be studied together, and create a list of any related vocabulary you need to learn so you can brush up on any difficult terms. You'll want to keep this vocabulary list handy once you actually start studying since you may need to add to it along the way.

Time Management

Once you have your set of study concepts, decide how to spread them out over the time you have left before the test. Break your study plan into small, clear goals so you have a manageable task for each day and know exactly what you're doing. Then just focus on one small step at a time. When you manage your time this way, you don't need to spend hours at a time studying. Studying a small block of content for a short period each day helps you retain information better and avoid stressing over how much you have left to do. You can relax knowing that you have a plan to cover everything in time. In order for this strategy to be effective though, you have to start studying early and stick to your schedule. Avoid the exhaustion and futility that comes from last-minute cramming!

Study Environment

The environment you study in has a big impact on your learning. Studying in a coffee shop, while probably more enjoyable, is not likely to be as fruitful as studying in a quiet room. It's important to keep distractions to a minimum. You're only planning to study for a short block of time, so make the most of it. Don't pause to check your phone or get up to find a snack. It's also important to **avoid multitasking**. Research has consistently shown that multitasking will make your studying dramatically less effective. Your study area should also be comfortable and well-lit so you don't have the distraction of straining your eyes or sitting on an uncomfortable chair.

 The time of day you study is also important. You want to be rested and alert. Don't wait until just before bedtime. Study when you'll be most likely to comprehend and remember. Even better, if you know what time of day your test will be, set that time aside for study. That way your brain will be used to working on that subject at that specific time and you'll have a better chance of recalling information.

Finally, it can be helpful to team up with others who are studying for the same test. Your actual studying should be done in as isolated an environment as possible, but the work of organizing the information and setting up the study plan can be divided up. In between study sessions, you can discuss with your teammates the concepts that you're all studying and quiz each other on the details. Just be sure that your teammates are as serious about the test as you are. If you find that your study time is being replaced with social time, you might need to find a new team.

2

Secret Key #3 – Practice the Right Way

Your success on test day depends not only on how many hours you put into preparing, but also on whether you prepared the right way. It's good to check along the way to see if your studying is paying off. One of the most effective ways to do this is by taking practice tests to evaluate your progress. Practice tests are useful because they show exactly where you need to improve. Every time you take a practice test, pay special attention to these three groups of questions:

- The questions you got wrong
- The questions you had to guess on, even if you guessed right
- The questions you found difficult or slow to work through

This will show you exactly what your weak areas are, and where you need to devote more study time. Ask yourself why each of these questions gave you trouble. Was it because you didn't understand the material? Was it because you didn't remember the vocabulary? Do you need more repetitions on this type of question to build speed and confidence? Dig into those questions and figure out how you can strengthen your weak areas as you go back to review the material.

 Additionally, many practice tests have a section explaining the answer choices. It can be tempting to read the explanation and think that you now have a good understanding of the concept. However, an explanation likely only covers part of the question's broader context. Even if the explanation makes perfect sense, **go back and investigate** every concept related to the question until you're positive you have a thorough understanding.

As you go along, keep in mind that the practice test is just that: practice. Memorizing these questions and answers will not be very helpful on the actual test because it is unlikely to have any of the same exact questions. If you only know the right answers to the sample questions, you won't be prepared for the real thing. **Study the concepts** until you understand them fully, and then you'll be able to answer any question that shows up on the test.

It's important to wait on the practice tests until you're ready. If you take a test on your first day of study, you may be overwhelmed by the amount of material covered and how much you need to learn. Work up to it gradually.

On test day, you'll need to be prepared for answering questions, managing your time, and using the test-taking strategies you've learned. It's a lot to balance, like a mental marathon that will have a big impact on your future. Like training for a marathon, you'll need to start slowly and work your way up. When test day arrives, you'll be ready.

Start with the strategies you've read in the first two Secret Keys—plan your course and study in the way that works best for you. If you have time, consider using multiple study resources to get different approaches to the same concepts. It can be helpful to see difficult concepts from more than one angle. Then find a good source for practice tests. Many times, the test website will suggest potential study resources or provide sample tests.

Secret Key #2 – Make Your Studying Count

You're devoting a lot of time and effort to preparing for this test, so you want to be absolutely certain it will pay off. This means doing more than just reading the content and hoping you can remember it on test day. It's important to make every minute of study count. There are two main areas you can focus on to make your studying count.

Retention

It doesn't matter how much time you study if you can't remember the material. You need to make sure you are retaining the concepts. To check your retention of the information you're learning, try recalling it at later times with minimal prompting. Try carrying around flashcards and glance at one or two from time to time or ask a friend who's also studying for the test to quiz you.

To enhance your retention, look for ways to put the information into practice so that you can apply it rather than simply recalling it. If you're using the information in practical ways, it will be much easier to remember. Similarly, it helps to solidify a concept in your mind if you're not only reading it to yourself but also explaining it to someone else. Ask a friend to let you teach them about a concept you're a little shaky on (or speak aloud to an imaginary audience if necessary). As you try to summarize, define, give examples, and answer your friend's questions, you'll understand the concepts better and they will stay with you longer. Finally, step back for a big picture view and ask yourself how each piece of information fits with the whole subject. When you link the different concepts together and see them working together as a whole, it's easier to remember the individual components.

Finally, practice showing your work on any multi-step problems, even if you're just studying. Writing out each step you take to solve a problem will help solidify the process in your mind, and you'll be more likely to remember it during the test.

Modality

Modality simply refers to the means or method by which you study. Choosing a study modality that fits your own individual learning style is crucial. No two people learn best in exactly the same way, so it's important to know your strengths and use them to your advantage.

For example, if you learn best by visualization, focus on visualizing a concept in your mind and draw an image or a diagram. Try color-coding your notes, illustrating them, or creating symbols that will trigger your mind to recall a learned concept. If you learn best by hearing or discussing information, find a study partner who learns the same way or read aloud to yourself. Think about how to put the information in your own words. Imagine that you are giving a lecture on the topic and record yourself so you can listen to it later.

For any learning style, flashcards can be helpful. Organize the information so you can take advantage of spare moments to review. Underline key words or phrases. Use different colors for different categories. Mnemonic devices (such as creating a short list in which every item starts with the same letter) can also help with retention. Find what works best for you and use it to store the information in your mind most effectively and easily.

Secret Key #5 – Have a Plan for Guessing

When you're taking the test, you may find yourself stuck on a question. Some of the answer choices seem better than others, but you don't see the one answer choice that is obviously correct. What do you do?

The scenario described above is very common, yet most test takers have not effectively prepared for it. Developing and practicing a plan for guessing may be one of the single most effective uses of your time as you get ready for the exam.

In developing your plan for guessing, there are three questions to address:

- When should you start the guessing process?
- How should you narrow down the choices?
- Which answer should you choose?

When to Start the Guessing Process

Unless your plan for guessing is to select C every time (which, despite its merits, is not what we recommend), you need to leave yourself enough time to apply your answer elimination strategies. Since you have a limited amount of time for each question, that means that if you're going to give yourself the best shot at guessing correctly, you have to decide quickly whether or not you will guess.

Of course, the best-case scenario is that you don't have to guess at all, so first, see if you can answer the question based on your knowledge of the subject and basic reasoning skills. Focus on the key words in the question and try to jog your memory of related topics. Give yourself a chance to bring the knowledge to mind, but once you realize that you don't have (or you can't access) the knowledge you need to answer the question, it's time to start the guessing process.

It's almost always better to start the guessing process too early than too late. It only takes a few seconds to remember something and answer the question from knowledge. Carefully eliminating wrong answer choices takes longer. Plus, going through the process of eliminating answer choices can actually help jog your memory.

Summary: Start the guessing process as soon as you decide that you can't answer the question based on your knowledge.

How to Narrow Down the Choices

The next chapter in this book (**Test-Taking Strategies**) includes a wide range of strategies for how to approach questions and how to look for answer choices to eliminate. You will definitely want to read those carefully, practice them, and figure out which ones work best for you. Here though, we're going to address a mindset rather than a particular strategy.

Your odds of guessing an answer correctly depend on how many options you are choosing from.

Number of options left	5	4	3	2	1
Odds of guessing correctly	20%	25%	33%	50%	100%

You can see from this chart just how valuable it is to be able to eliminate incorrect answers and make an educated guess, but there are two things that many test takers do that cause them to miss out on the benefits of guessing:

 big mistake

- Accidentally eliminating the correct answer
- Selecting an answer based on an impression

We'll look at the first one here, and the second one in the next section.

To avoid accidentally eliminating the correct answer, we recommend a thought exercise called **the $5 challenge**. In this challenge, you only eliminate an answer choice from contention if you are willing to bet $5 on it being wrong. Why $5? Five dollars is a small but not insignificant amount of money. It's an amount you could afford to lose but wouldn't want to throw away. And while losing

$5 once might not hurt too much, doing it twenty times will set you back $100. In the same way, each small decision you make—eliminating a choice here, guessing on a question there—won't by itself impact your score very much, but when you put them all together, they can make a big difference. By holding each answer choice elimination decision to a higher standard, you can reduce the risk of accidentally eliminating the correct answer.

The $5 challenge can also be applied in a positive sense: If you are willing to bet $5 that an answer choice *is* correct, go ahead and mark it as correct.

Summary: Only eliminate an answer choice if you are willing to bet $5 that it is wrong.

Which Answer to Choose

You're taking the test. You've run into a hard question and decided you'll have to guess. You've eliminated all the answer choices you're willing to bet $5 on. Now you have to pick an answer. Why do we even need to talk about this? Why can't you just pick whichever one you feel like when the time comes?

The answer to these questions is that if you don't come into the test with a plan, you'll rely on your impression to select an answer choice, and if you do that, you risk falling into a trap. The test writers know that everyone who takes their test will be guessing on some of the questions, so they intentionally write wrong answer choices to seem plausible. You still have to pick an answer though, and if the wrong answer choices are designed to look right, how can you ever be sure that you're not falling for their trap? The best solution we've found to this dilemma is to take the decision out of your hands entirely. Here is the process we recommend:

Once you've eliminated any choices that you are confident (willing to bet $5) are wrong, select the first remaining choice as your answer.

Whether you choose to select the first remaining choice, the second, or the last, the important thing is that you use some preselected standard. Using this approach guarantees that you will not be enticed into selecting an answer choice that looks right, because you are not basing your decision on how the answer choices look.

> X This is wrong.
> X Also wrong.
> C. Maybe?
> D. Maybe?

This is not meant to make you question your knowledge. Instead, it is to help you recognize the difference between your knowledge and your impressions. There's a huge difference between thinking an answer is right because of what you know, and thinking an answer is right because it looks or sounds like it should be right.

Summary: To ensure that your selection is appropriately random, make a predetermined selection from among all answer choices you have not eliminated.

The strategy eliminates bias!!!!!

9

Test-Taking Strategies

This section contains a list of test-taking strategies that you may find helpful as you work through the test. By taking what you know and applying logical thought, you can maximize your chances of answering any question correctly!

It is very important to realize that every question is different and every person is different: no single strategy will work on every question, and no single strategy will work for every person. That's why we've included all of them here, so you can try them out and determine which ones work best for different types of questions and which ones work best for you.

Question Strategies

☑ READ CAREFULLY

Read the question and the answer choices carefully. Don't miss the question because you misread the terms. You have plenty of time to read each question thoroughly and make sure you understand what is being asked. Yet a happy medium must be attained, so don't waste too much time. You must read carefully and efficiently.

☑ CONTEXTUAL CLUES

Look for contextual clues. If the question includes a word you are not familiar with, look at the immediate context for some indication of what the word might mean. Contextual clues can often give you all the information you need to decipher the meaning of an unfamiliar word. Even if you can't determine the meaning, you may be able to narrow down the possibilities enough to make a solid guess at the answer to the question.

☑ PREFIXES

If you're having trouble with a word in the question or answer choices, try dissecting it. Take advantage of every clue that the word might include. Prefixes can be a huge help. Usually, they allow you to determine a basic meaning. *Pre-* means before, *post-* means after, *pro-* is positive, *de-* is negative. From prefixes, you can get an idea of the general meaning of the word and try to put it into context.

☑ HEDGE WORDS

Watch out for critical hedge words, such as *likely, may, can, sometimes, often, almost, mostly, usually, generally, rarely,* and *sometimes.* Question writers insert these hedge phrases to cover every possibility. Often an answer choice will be wrong simply because it leaves no room for exception. Be on guard for answer choices that have definitive words such as *exactly* and *always.* ~~onpound~~

☑ SWITCHBACK WORDS

Stay alert for *switchbacks.* These are the words and phrases frequently used to alert you to shifts in thought. The most common switchback words are *but, although,* and *however.* Others include *nevertheless, on the other hand, even though, while, in spite of, despite,* and *regardless of.* Switchback words are important to catch because they can change the direction of the question or an answer choice.

10

⊘ FACE VALUE

When in doubt, use common sense. Accept the situation in the problem at face value. Don't read too much into it. These problems will not require you to make wild assumptions. If you have to go beyond creativity and warp time or space in order to have an answer choice fit the question, then you should move on and consider the other answer choices. These are normal problems rooted in reality. The applicable relationship or explanation may not be readily apparent, but it is there for you to figure out. Use your common sense to interpret anything that isn't clear.

Answer Choice Strategies

⊘ ANSWER SELECTION

If you can

The most thorough way to pick an answer choice is to identify and eliminate wrong answers until only one is left, then confirm it is the correct answer. Sometimes an answer choice may immediately seem right, but be careful. The test writers will usually put more than one reasonable answer choice on each question, so take a second to read all of them and make sure that the other choices are not equally obvious. As long as you have time left, it is better to read every answer choice than to pick the first one that looks right without checking the others.

⊘ ANSWER CHOICE FAMILIES

An answer choice family consists of two (in rare cases, three) answer choices that are very similar in construction and cannot all be true at the same time. If you see two answer choices that are direct opposites or parallels, one of them is usually the correct answer. For instance, if one answer choice says that quantity x increases and another either says that quantity x decreases (opposite) or says that quantity y increases (parallel), then those answer choices would fall into the same family. An answer choice that doesn't match the construction of the answer choice family is more likely to be incorrect. Most questions will not have answer choice families, but when they do appear, you should be prepared to recognize them. ✗

⊘ ELIMINATE ANSWERS

Eliminate answer choices as soon as you realize they are wrong, but make sure you consider all possibilities. If you are eliminating answer choices and realize that the last one you are left with is also wrong, don't panic. Start over and consider each choice again. There may be something you missed the first time that you will realize on the second pass.

⊘ AVOID FACT TRAPS

Don't be distracted by an answer choice that is factually true but doesn't answer the question. You are looking for the choice that answers the question. Stay focused on what the question is asking for so you don't accidentally pick an answer that is true but incorrect. Always go back to the question and make sure the answer choice you've selected actually answers the question and is not merely a true statement.

⊘ EXTREME STATEMENTS

In general, you should avoid answers that put forth extreme actions as standard practice or proclaim controversial ideas as established fact. An answer choice that states the "process should be used in certain situations, if..." is much more likely to be correct than one that states the "process should be discontinued completely." The first is a calm rational statement and doesn't even make a definitive, uncompromising stance, using a hedge word *if* to provide wiggle room, whereas the second choice is far more extreme.

⦸ BENCHMARK

As you read through the answer choices and you come across one that seems to answer the question well, mentally select that answer choice. This is not your final answer, but it's the one that will help you evaluate the other answer choices. The one that you selected is your benchmark or standard for judging each of the other answer choices. Every other answer choice must be compared to your benchmark. That choice is correct until proven otherwise by another answer choice beating it. If you find a better answer, then that one becomes your new benchmark. Once you've decided that no other choice answers the question as well as your benchmark, you have your final answer.

⦸ PREDICT THE ANSWER

Before you even start looking at the answer choices, it is often best to try to predict the answer. When you come up with the answer on your own, it is easier to avoid distractions and traps because you will know exactly what to look for. The right answer choice is unlikely to be word-for-word what you came up with, but it should be a close match. Even if you are confident that you have the right answer, you should still take the time to read each option before moving on.

General Strategies

⦸ TOUGH QUESTIONS

If you are stumped on a problem or it appears too hard or too difficult, don't waste time. Move on! Remember though, if you can quickly check for obviously incorrect answer choices, your chances of guessing correctly are greatly improved. Before you completely give up, at least try to knock out a couple of possible answers. Eliminate what you can and then guess at the remaining answer choices before moving on.

⦸ CHECK YOUR WORK

Since you will probably not know every term listed and the answer to every question, it is important that you get credit for the ones that you do know. Don't miss any questions through careless mistakes. If at all possible, try to take a second to look back over your answer selection and make sure you've selected the correct answer choice and haven't made a costly careless mistake (such as marking an answer choice that you didn't mean to mark). This quick double check should more than pay for itself in caught mistakes for the time it costs.

⦸ PACE YOURSELF

It's easy to be overwhelmed when you're looking at a page full of questions; your mind is confused and full of random thoughts, and the clock is ticking down faster than you would like. Calm down and maintain the pace that you have set for yourself. Especially as you get down to the last few minutes of the test, don't let the small numbers on the clock make you panic. As long as you are on track by monitoring your pace, you are guaranteed to have time for each question.

⦸ DON'T RUSH

It is very easy to make errors when you are in a hurry. Maintaining a fast pace in answering questions is pointless if it makes you miss questions that you would have gotten right otherwise. Test writers like to include distracting information and wrong answers that seem right. Taking a little extra time to avoid careless mistakes can make all the difference in your test score. Find a pace that allows you to be confident in the answers that you select.

⊘ KEEP MOVING

Panicking will not help you pass the test, so do your best to stay calm and keep moving. Taking deep breaths and going through the answer elimination steps you practiced can help to break through a stress barrier and keep your pace.

Final Notes

The combination of a solid foundation of content knowledge and the confidence that comes from practicing your plan for applying that knowledge is the key to maximizing your performance on test day. As your foundation of content knowledge is built up and strengthened, you'll find that the strategies included in this chapter become more and more effective in helping you quickly sift through the distractions and traps of the test to isolate the correct answer.

Now that you're preparing to move forward into the test content chapters of this book, be sure to keep your goal in mind. As you read, think about how you will be able to apply this information on the test. If you've already seen sample questions for the test and you have an idea of the question format and style, try to come up with questions of your own that you can answer based on what you're reading. This will give you valuable practice applying your knowledge in the same ways you can expect to on test day.

Good luck and good studying!

Analytical Writing

Parts of Speech

THE EIGHT PARTS OF SPEECH

(1) NOUNS

When you talk about a person, place, thing, or idea, you are talking about a **noun**. The two main types of nouns are **common** and **proper** nouns. Also, nouns can be abstract (i.e., general) or concrete (i.e., specific).

COMMON NOUNS

Common nouns are generic names for people, places, and things. Common nouns are not usually capitalized.

Examples of common nouns:

> *People*: boy, girl, worker, manager

> *Places*: school, bank, library, home

> *Things*: dog, cat, truck, car

> **Review Video: What is a Noun?**
> Visit mometrix.com/academy and enter code: 344028

PROPER NOUNS

Proper nouns name specific people, places, or things. All proper nouns are capitalized.

Examples of proper nouns:

> *People*: Abraham Lincoln, George Washington, Martin Luther King, Jr.

> *Places*: Los Angeles, California; New York; Asia

> *Things*: Statue of Liberty, Earth, Lincoln Memorial

Note: When referring to the planet that we live on, capitalize *Earth*. When referring to the dirt, rocks, or land, lowercase *earth*.

GENERAL AND SPECIFIC NOUNS

General nouns are the names of conditions or ideas. **Specific nouns** name people, places, and things that are understood by using your senses.

General nouns:

> *Condition*: beauty, strength

> *Idea*: truth, peace

15

Specific nouns:

People: baby, friend, father

Places: town, park, city hall

Things: rainbow, cough, apple, silk, gasoline

COLLECTIVE NOUNS

Collective nouns are the names for a group of people, places, or things that may act as a whole. The following are examples of collective nouns: *class, company, dozen, group, herd, team,* and *public.* Collective nouns usually require an article, which denotes the noun as being a single unit. For instance, a choir is a group of singers. Even though there are many singers in a choir, the word choir is grammatically treated as a single unit. If we refer to the members of the group, and not the group itself, it is no longer a collective noun.

Incorrect: The *choir are* going to compete nationally this year.

Correct: The *choir is* going to compete nationally this year.

Incorrect: The *members* of the choir *is* competing nationally this year.

Correct: The *members* of the choir *are* competing nationally this year.

2 PRONOUNS

Pronouns are words that are used to stand in for nouns. A pronoun may be classified as personal, intensive, relative, interrogative, demonstrative, indefinite, and reciprocal.

Personal: *Nominative* is the case for nouns and pronouns that are the subject of a sentence. *Objective* is the case for nouns and pronouns that are an object in a sentence. *Possessive* is the case for nouns and pronouns that show possession or ownership.

Singular

	Nominative	Objective	Possessive
First Person	I	me	my, mine
Second Person	you	you	your, yours
Third Person	he, she, it	him, her, it	his, her, hers, its

Plural

	Nominative	Objective	Possessive
First Person	we	us	our, ours
Second Person	you	you	your, yours
Third Person	they	them	their, theirs

Intensive: I myself, you yourself, he himself, she herself, the (thing) itself, we ourselves, you yourselves, they themselves

Relative: which, who, whom, whose

Interrogative: what, which, who, whom, whose

Demonstrative: this, that, these, those

Indefinite: all, any, each, everyone, either/neither, one, some, several

Reciprocal: each other, one another

> **Review Video: Nouns and Pronouns**
> Visit mometrix.com/academy and enter code: 312073

VERBS

If you want to write a sentence, then you need a verb. Without a verb, you have no sentence. The verb of a sentence indicates action or being. In other words, the verb shows something's action or state of being or the action that has been done to something.

TRANSITIVE AND INTRANSITIVE VERBS

A **transitive verb** is a verb whose action (e.g., drive, run, jump) indicates a receiver (e.g., car, dog, kangaroo). **Intransitive verbs** do not indicate a receiver of an action. In other words, the action of the verb does not point to a subject or object. *verb does not point to an action receiver*

> **Transitive**: He plays the piano. | The piano was played by him.

> **Intransitive**: He plays. | John plays well. *no*

A dictionary will tell you whether a verb is transitive or intransitive. Some verbs can be transitive and intransitive.

can be an entire sentence!

ACTION VERBS AND LINKING VERBS

Action verbs show what the subject is doing. In other words, an action verb shows action. Unlike most types of words, a single action verb, in the right context, can be an entire sentence. **Linking verbs** link the subject of a sentence to a noun or pronoun, or they link a subject with an adjective. You always need a verb if you want a complete sentence. However, linking verbs on their own cannot be a complete sentence. *cannot complete a sentence on its own*

Common linking verbs include *appear, be, become, feel, grow, look, seem, smell, sound*, and *taste*. However, any verb that shows a condition and connects to a noun, pronoun, or adjective that describes the subject of a sentence is a linking verb.

Action: He sings. | Run! | Go! | I talk with him every day. | She reads.

Linking:

> Incorrect: I am

> Correct: I am John. | The roses smell lovely. | I feel tired.

Note: Some verbs are followed by words that look like prepositions, but they are a part of the verb and a part of the verb's meaning. These are known as phrasal verbs, and examples include *call off, look up*, and *drop off.*

> **Review Video: Action Verbs and Linking Verbs**
> Visit mometrix.com/academy and enter code: 743142

VOICE

Transitive verbs come in active or passive **voice**. If something does an action or is acted upon, then you will know whether a verb is active or passive. When the subject of the sentence is doing the action, the verb is in **active voice**. When the subject is acted upon, the verb is in **passive voice**.

When the subject is doing action **Active**: Jon <u>drew</u> the picture. (The subject *Jon* is doing the action of *drawing a picture*.)

Passive: The picture is drawn by Jon. (The subject *picture* is receiving the action from Jon.)

Subject is acted upon ## VERB TENSES

A verb <u>tense</u> shows the different form of a verb to point to the time of an action. The present and past tense are indicated by the verb's form. An action in the present, *I talk*, can change form for the past: *I talked*. However, for the other tenses, an auxiliary (i.e., helping) verb is needed to show the change in form. These helping verbs include *am, are, is | have, has, had | was, were, will* (or *shall*).

Auxiliary

Present: I talk	Present perfect: I have talked
Past: I talked	Past perfect: I had talked
Future: I will talk	Future perfect: I will have talked

Present: The action happens at the current time.

Example: He *walks* to the store every morning.

To show that something is happening right now, use the progressive present tense: I *am walking*.

Past: The action happened in the past.

Example: He *walked* to the store an hour ago.

Future: The action is going to happen later.

Example: I *will walk* to the store tomorrow.

Present perfect: The action started in the past and continues into the present or took place previously at an unspecified time.

Example: I *have walked* to the store three times today.

Past perfect: The second action happened in the past. The first action came before the second.

Example: Before I walked to the store (Action 2), I *had walked* to the library (Action 1).

Future perfect: An action that uses the past and the future. In other words, the action is complete before a future moment.

This I don't really understand Example: When she comes for the supplies (future moment), I *will have walked* to the store (action completed before the future moment).

> **Review Video: <u>Present Perfect, Past Perfect, and Future Perfect Verb Tenses</u>**
> Visit mometrix.com/academy and enter code: 269472

CONJUGATING VERBS

congeyute hus to do with tense

When you need to change the form of a verb, you are **conjugating** a verb. The key forms of a verb are singular, present tense (dream); singular, past tense (dreamed); and the past participle (have dreamed). Note: the past participle needs a helping verb to make a verb tense. For example, I *have dreamed* of this day. The following tables demonstrate some of the different ways to conjugate a verb:

Singular

Tense	First Person	Second Person	Third Person
Present	I dream	You dream	He, she, it dreams
Past	I dreamed	You dreamed	He, she, it dreamed
Past Participle	I have dreamed	You have dreamed	He, she, it has dreamed

Plural

Tense	First Person	Second Person	Third Person
Present	We dream	You dream	They dream
Past	We dreamed	You dreamed	They dreamed
Past Participle	We have dreamed	You have dreamed	They have dreamed

MOOD

There are three **moods** in English: the indicative, the imperative, and the subjunctive.

The **indicative mood** is used for facts, opinions, and questions.

Fact: You can do this.

Opinion: I think that you can do this.

Question: Do you know that you can do this?

The **imperative** is used for orders or requests.

Order: You are going to do this!

Request: Will you do this for me?

The **subjunctive mood** is for wishes and statements that go against fact.

Wish: I wish that I were famous.

Statement against fact: If I were you, I would do this. (This goes against fact because I am not you. You have the chance to do this, and I do not have the chance.)

4 ADJECTIVES

An **adjective** is a word that is used to modify a noun or pronoun. An adjective answers a question: *Which one? What kind?* or *How many?* Usually, adjectives come before the words that they modify, but they may also come after a linking verb.

Which one? The *third* suit is my favorite.

What kind? This suit is *navy blue*.

How many? I am going to buy *four* pairs of socks to match the suit.

> **Review Video: Descriptive Text**
> Visit mometrix.com/academy and enter code: 174903

ARTICLES

Articles are adjectives that are used to distinguish nouns as definite or indefinite. **Definite** nouns are preceded by the article *the* and indicate a specific person, place, thing, or idea. **Indefinite** nouns are preceded by *a* or *an* and do not indicate a specific person, place, thing, or idea. *A, an,* and *the* are the only articles. Note: *An* comes before words that start with a vowel sound. For example, "Are you going to get an **u**mbrella?"

(handwritten: "The" indicates specific nouns)

(handwritten: "a" "an" do not indicate specific noun)

Definite: I lost *the* bottle that belongs to me.

Indefinite: Does anyone have *a* bottle to share?

(handwritten: only 3 Articles "A", "An", "The")

> **Review Video: Function of Articles**
> Visit mometrix.com/academy and enter code: 449383

COMPARISON WITH ADJECTIVES

Some adjectives are relative and other adjectives are absolute. Adjectives that are **relative** can show the comparison between things. **Absolute** adjectives can also show comparison, but they do so in a different way. Let's say that you are reading two books. You think that one book is perfect, and the other book is not exactly perfect. It is not possible for one book to be more perfect than the other. Either you think that the book is perfect, or you think that the book is imperfect. In this case, perfect and imperfect are absolute adjectives. *(handwritten: There is no middle ground)*

Relative adjectives will show the different **degrees** of something or someone to something else or someone else. The three degrees of adjectives include positive, comparative, and superlative.

The **positive** degree is the normal form of an adjective.

Example: This work is *difficult*. | She is *smart*.

The **comparative** degree compares one person or thing to another person or thing.

Example: This work is *more difficult* than your work. | She is *smarter* than me.

The **superlative** degree compares more than two people or things.

Example: This is the *most difficult* work of my life. | She is the *smartest* lady in school.

5 ADVERBS

An **adverb** is a word that is used to **modify** a verb, adjective, or another adverb. Usually, adverbs answer one of these questions: *When? Where? How?* and *Why?* The negatives *not* and *never* are considered adverbs. Adverbs that modify adjectives or other adverbs **strengthen** or **weaken** the words that they modify. *Two sides to the modification*

not & never = adverbs

The word that doesn't necesary need to be in the sentence or endin -ly

Examples:

adverb

He walks *quickly* through the crowd.

The water flows *smoothly* on the rocks.

Note: Adverbs are usually indicated by the morpheme *-ly*, which has been added to the root word. For instance, *quick* can be made into an adverb by adding *-ly* to construct *quickly*. Some words that end in *-ly* do not follow this rule and can behave as other parts of speech. Examples of adjectives ending in *-ly* include: *early, friendly, holy, lonely, silly*, and *ugly*. To know if a word that ends in *-ly* is an adjective or adverb, check your dictionary. Also, while many adverbs end in *-ly*, you need to remember that not all adverbs end in *-ly*.

I can't do that during ates

Examples:

He is *never* angry.

You walked *across* the bridge.

COMPARISON WITH ADVERBS

The rules for comparing adverbs are the same as the rules for adjectives. *Same degress as adjectives*

The **positive** degree is the standard form of an adverb.

Example: He arrives *soon*. | She speaks *softly* to her friends.

The **comparative** degree compares one person or thing to another person or thing. *Same compares two thing*

Example: He arrives *sooner* than Sarah. | She speaks *more softly* than him.

The **superlative** degree compares more than two people or things. *compares more than two things*

Example: He arrives *soonest* of the group. | She speaks the *most softly* of any of her friends.

6 PREPOSITIONS *Placed before noun that shows a relationship*

A **preposition** is a word placed before a noun or pronoun that shows the relationship between an object and another word in the sentence.

Common prepositions:

about	before	during	on	under
after	beneath	for	over	until
against	between	from	past	up
among	beyond	in	through	with
around	by	of	to	within
at	down	off	toward	without

Examples:

The napkin is *in* the drawer. *(noun)*

The Earth rotates *around* the Sun. *(nun)*

The needle is *beneath* the haystack. *(noun)*

Can you find "me" *among* the words? *(noun)*

> **Review Video: Prepositions**
> Visit mometrix.com/academy and enter code: 946763

7 CONJUNCTIONS

Conjunctions join words, phrases, or clauses and they show the connection between the joined pieces. **Coordinating conjunctions** connect equal parts of sentences. **Correlative conjunctions** show the connection between pairs. **Subordinating conjunctions** join subordinate (i.e., dependent) clauses with independent clauses. ?

COORDINATING CONJUNCTIONS

The **coordinating conjunctions** include: *and, but, yet, or, nor, for,* and *so*] *examples*

Examples:

The rock was small, *but* it was heavy.

She drove in the night, *and* he drove in the day.

22

CORRELATIVE CONJUNCTIONS

The **correlative conjunctions** are: *either...or* | *neither...nor* | *not only...but also*

Examples:

Either you are coming *or* you are staying.

He *not only* ran three miles *but also* swam 200 yards.

> **Review Video: Coordinating and Correlative Conjunctions**
> Visit mometrix.com/academy and enter code: 390329
>
> **Review Video: Adverb Equal Comparisons**
> Visit mometrix.com/academy and enter code: 231291

SUBORDINATING CONJUNCTIONS   *(handwritten) join subordinate*

Common **subordinating conjunctions** include:

after	since	whenever
although	so that	where
because	unless	wherever
before	until	whether
in order that	when	while

Examples:

I am hungry *because* I did not eat breakfast.

He went home *when* everyone left.

> **Review Video: Subordinating Conjunctions**
> Visit mometrix.com/academy and enter code: 958913

8 INTERJECTIONS

(handwritten) I kind of understand but not really

Interjections are words of exclamation (i.e., audible expression of great feeling) that are used alone or as a part of a sentence. Often, they are used at the beginning of a sentence for an introduction. Sometimes, they can be used in the middle of a sentence to show a change in thought or attitude.

Common Interjections: Hey! | Oh, | Ouch! | Please! | Wow!

100%

CHAPTER QUIZ

1. Which of the following is NOT considered a type of mood?

    a. Indicative
    b. Imperative
    c. Subjunctive
    d. Conjunctive

2. How many different degrees of relative adjectives are there?

    a. Two
    b. Three
    c. Four
    d. Five

3. In general, adverbs may modify all of the following, EXCEPT:

    a. Another adverb.
    b. Adjectives.
    c. Proper nouns.
    d. Verbs.

CHAPTER QUIZ ANSWER KEY

1. D: There are three moods in English: the indicative, the imperative, and the subjunctive.

2. B: Relative adjectives will show the different degrees of something or someone to something else or someone else. The three degrees of adjectives include positive, comparative, and superlative.

3. C: An adverb is a word that is used to modify a verb, adjective, or another adverb. Usually, adverbs answer one of the questions: *When? Where? How?* and *Why?* The negatives *not* and *never* are considered adverbs. Adverbs that modify adjectives or other adverbs strengthen or weaken the words that they modify.

not make flashcards
when you gethome

Agreement and Sentence Structure

SUBJECTS AND PREDICATES ✗

SUBJECTS — *names who or what the sentence is about*

The **subject** of a sentence names who or what the sentence is about. The subject may be directly stated in a sentence, or the subject may be the implied *you*. The **complete subject** includes the simple subject and all of its modifiers. To find the complete subject, ask *Who* or *What* and insert the verb to complete the question. The answer, including any modifiers (adjectives, prepositional phrases, etc.), is the complete subject. To find the **simple subject**, remove all of the modifiers in the complete subject. Being able to locate the subject of a sentence helps with many problems, such as those involving sentence fragments and subject-verb agreement.

complete subject
ask who or what

simple subject
remove all modifies

Examples:

simple subject

The small, red car is the one that he wants for Christmas.
complete subject   Predicate

simple subject

The young artist is coming over for dinner.
complete subject   Predicate

> **Review Video: Subjects in English**
> Visit mometrix.com/academy and enter code: 444771

In **imperative** sentences, the verb's subject is understood (e.g., [You] Run to the store), but is not actually present in the sentence. Normally, the subject comes before the verb. However, the subject comes after the verb in sentences that begin with *There are* or *There was*.

Direct:

John knows the way to the park.	Who knows the way to the park?	John
The cookies need ten more minutes.	What needs ten minutes?	The cookies
By five o'clock, Bill will need to leave.	Who needs to leave?	Bill
✗There are five letters on the table for him.	What is on the table?	Five letters
✗There were coffee and doughnuts in the house.	What was in the house?	Coffee and doughnuts

Implied:

Go to the post office for me.	Who is going to the post office?	You
Come and sit with me, please?	Who needs to come and sit?	You

PREDICATES

In a sentence, you always have a predicate and a subject. The subject tells what the sentence is about, and the **predicate** explains or describes the subject.

25

Think about the sentence *He sings*. In this sentence, we have a subject (He) and a predicate (sings). This is all that is needed for a sentence to be complete. Most sentences contain more information, but if this is all the information that you are given, then you have a complete sentence.

Now, let's look at another sentence: *John and Jane sing on Tuesday nights at the dance hall*.

[handwritten: sub, Pred]

subject   predicate

John and Jane sing on Tuesday nights at the dance hall.

SUBJECT-VERB AGREEMENT

Verbs **agree** with their subjects in number. In other words, singular subjects need singular verbs. Plural subjects need plural verbs. **Singular** is for **one** person, place, or thing. **Plural** is for **more than one** person, place, or thing. Subjects and verbs must also share the same point of view, as in first, second, or third person. The present tense ending *-s* is used on a verb if its subject is third person singular; otherwise, the verb's ending is not modified.

[handwritten left margin: Singular subjects + need singular verbs]

> **Review Video: Subject-Verb Agreement**
> Visit mometrix.com/academy and enter code: 479190

NUMBER AGREEMENT EXAMPLES:

[handwritten right margin: Third person Singular = -S endings]

singular subject   singular verb

Single Subject and Verb: Dan calls home.

Dan is one person. So, the singular verb *calls* is needed.

[handwritten right margin: Calls = present Singular; Call = Plural]

plural subject   plural verb

Plural Subject and Verb: Dan and Bob call home.

More than one person needs the plural verb *call*.

PERSON AGREEMENT EXAMPLES:

First Person: I *am* walking.

Second Person: You *are* walking.

Third Person: He *is* walking.

COMPLICATIONS WITH SUBJECT-VERB AGREEMENT

WORDS BETWEEN SUBJECT AND VERB

Words that come between the simple subject and the verb have no bearing on subject-verb agreement.

Examples:

singular subject   singular verb

The joy of my life returns home tonight.

The phrase *of my life* does not influence the verb *returns*.

singular
subject

singular
verb

The question that still remains unanswered is "Who are you?"

Don't let the phrase "*that still remains…*" trouble you. The subject *question* goes with *is*.

COMPOUND SUBJECTS

A compound subject is formed when two or more nouns joined by *and*, *or*, or *nor* jointly act as the subject of the sentence.

JOINED BY AND

When a compound subject is joined by *and*, it is treated as a plural subject and requires a plural verb.

Examples:

plural
subject

plural
verb

You and Jon are invited to come to my house.

plural
subject

plural
verb

The pencil and paper belong to me.

JOINED BY OR/NOR

Plu/sing

For a compound subject joined by *or* or *nor*, the verb must agree in number with the part of the subject that is closest to the verb (italicized in the examples below).

Examples:

subject

verb

Today or tomorrow is the day.

subject

verb Plural sing

Stan or Phil wants to read the book.

subject

verb

Neither the pen nor the book is on the desk.

subject

verb

Either the blanket or pillows arrive this afternoon.

INDEFINITE PRONOUNS AS SUBJECT

An indefinite pronoun is a pronoun that does not refer to a specific noun. Different indefinite pronouns may only function as a singular noun, only function as a plural noun, or change depending on how they are used. I don't understand ?

ALWAYS SINGULAR

Pronouns such as *each, either, everybody, anybody, somebody,* and *nobody* are always singular.

Examples:

singular
subject   singular
verb

Each of the runners has a different bib number.

singular singular
verb   subject

Is either of you ready for the game?

Note: The words *each* and *either* can also be used as adjectives (e.g., *each* person is unique). When one of these adjectives modifies the subject of a sentence, it is always a singular subject.

singular
subject   singular
verb

Everybody grows a day older every day.

singular singular
subject   verb

Anybody is welcome to bring a tent.

ALWAYS PLURAL

Pronouns such as *both, several,* and *many* are always plural.

Examples:

plural
subject   plural
verb

Both of the siblings were too tired to argue.

plural plural
subject verb

Many have tried , but none have succeeded.

DEPEND ON CONTEXT

Pronouns such as *some, any, all, none, more,* and *most* can be either singular or plural depending on what they are representing in the context of the sentence.

Examples:

singular
subject   singular
verb

All of my dog's food was still there in his bowl.

plural
subject   plural
verb

By the end of the night, all of my guests were already excited about coming to my next party.

OTHER CASES INVOLVING PLURAL OR IRREGULAR FORM

Some nouns are **singular in meaning but plural in form**: news, mathematics, physics, and economics.

> The *news is* coming on now.

> *Mathematics is* my favorite class.

Some nouns are plural in form and meaning, and have **no singular equivalent**: scissors and pants.

> Do these *pants come* with a shirt?

> The *scissors are* for my project.

Mathematical operations are **irregular** in their construction, but are normally considered to be **singular in meaning**.

> *One plus one is* two.

> *Three times three is* nine.

Note: Look to your **dictionary** for help when you aren't sure whether a noun with a plural form has a singular or plural meaning.

COMPLEMENTS

A complement is a noun, pronoun, or adjective that is used to give more information about the subject or verb in the sentence.

DIRECT OBJECTS

A direct object is a noun or pronoun that takes or receives the **action** of a verb. (Remember: a complete sentence does not need a direct object, so not all sentences will have them. A sentence needs only a subject and a verb.) When you are looking for a direct object, find the verb and ask *who* or *what*.

Examples:

> I took *the blanket.*

> Jane read *books.*

[handwritten note: direct object]

[handwritten note: Sentence only need a ~~direct~~ subject & averb]

INDIRECT OBJECTS

An indirect object is a word or group of words that show how an action had an **influence** on someone or something. If there is an indirect object in a sentence, then you always have a direct object in the sentence. When you are looking for the indirect object, find the verb and ask *to/for whom or what.*

[handwritten note: if you have a direct object You Always have a Indirect object]

Examples:

$$\underbrace{\text{indirect}}_{\text{object}} \quad \underbrace{\text{direct}}_{\text{object}}$$

We taught the old dog a new trick.

$$\underbrace{\text{indirect}}_{\text{object}} \quad \underbrace{\text{direct}}_{\text{object}}$$

I gave them a math lesson.

> **Review Video: Direct and Indirect Objects**
> Visit mometrix.com/academy and enter code: 817385

PREDICATE NOMINATIVES AND PREDICATE ADJECTIVES

As we looked at previously, verbs may be classified as either action verbs or linking verbs. A linking verb is so named because it links the subject to words in the predicate that describe or define the subject. These words are called predicate nominatives (if nouns or pronouns) or predicate adjectives (if adjectives).

Examples:

$$\underbrace{\text{subject}} \quad \underbrace{\text{predicate}}_{\text{nominative}}$$

My father is a lawyer.

$$\underbrace{\text{subject}} \quad \underbrace{\text{predicate}}_{\text{adjective}}$$

Your mother is patient.

PRONOUN USAGE

boy, girl　*andrao/andraina*

The **antecedent** is the noun that has been replaced by a pronoun. A pronoun and its antecedent **agree** when they have the same number (singular or plural) and gender (male, female, or neutral).

Examples: *I don't fully understand*

$$\underbrace{\text{antecedent}} \qquad \underbrace{\text{pronoun}}$$

Singular agreement: John came into town, and he played for us.

$$\underbrace{\text{antecedent}} \qquad \underbrace{\text{pronoun}}$$

Plural agreement: John and Rick came into town, and they played for us.

To determine which is the correct pronoun to use in a compound subject or object, try each pronoun **alone** in place of the compound in the sentence. Your knowledge of pronouns will tell you which one is correct.

Example:

Bob and (I, me) will be going.

Test: (1) *I will be going* or (2) *Me will be going*. The second choice cannot be correct because *me* cannot be used as the subject of a sentence. Instead, *me* is used as an object.

Answer: Bob and I will be going.

When a pronoun is used with a noun immediately following (as in "we boys"), try the sentence **without the added noun**.

[handwritten: Person]

Example:

> (We/Us) boys played football last year.
>
> Test: (1) *We played football last year* or (2) *Us played football last year*. Again, the second choice cannot be correct because *us* cannot be used as a subject of a sentence. Instead, *us* is used as an object.
>
> **Answer**: We boys played football last year.

A pronoun should point clearly to the **antecedent**. Here is how a pronoun reference can be unhelpful if it is puzzling or not directly stated.

[handwritten: what does that mean]

>   antecedent   pronoun
> **Unhelpful**: Ron and Jim went to the store, and he bought sodas
>
> *[handwritten: They]*
>
> Who bought soda? Ron or Jim?

>   antecedent   pronoun
> **Helpful**: Jim went to the store, and he bought soda.
>
> The sentence is clear. Jim bought the soda.

Some pronouns change their form by their placement in a sentence. A pronoun that is a **subject** in a sentence comes in the **subjective case**. Pronouns that serve as **objects** appear in the **objective case**. Finally, the pronouns that are used as **possessives** appear in the **possessive case**.

Examples:

> **Subjective case**: *He* is coming to the show.
>
> The pronoun *He* is the subject of the sentence.
>
> **Objective case**: Josh drove *him* to the airport.
>
> The pronoun *him* is the object of the sentence.
>
> **Possessive case**: The flowers are *mine*.
>
> The pronoun *mine* shows ownership of the flowers.

[handwritten: great break down]

The word *who* is a subjective-case pronoun that can be used as a **subject**. The word *whom* is an objective-case pronoun that can be used as an **object**. The words *who* and *whom* are common in subordinate clauses or in questions.

Examples:

He knows who wants to come. *Siy*
(subject: who, verb: wants)

He knows the man whom we want at the party. *Siny*
(object: whom, verb: want)

CLAUSES

A clause is a group of words that contains both a subject and a predicate (verb). There are two types of clauses: independent and dependent. An **independent clause** contains a complete thought, while a **dependent (or subordinate) clause** does not. A dependent clause includes a subject and a verb, and may also contain objects or complements, but it cannot stand as a complete thought without being joined to an independent clause. Dependent clauses function within sentences as adjectives, adverbs, or nouns.

[handwritten: depen clause cannot stand on its own]

[handwritten: Clause = group of ward including subject & predicat]

Example:

I am running (independent clause) because I want to stay in shape. (dependent clause)

The clause *I am running* is an independent clause: it has a subject and a verb, and it gives a complete thought. The clause *because I want to stay in shape* is a dependent clause: it has a subject and a verb, but it does not express a complete thought. It adds detail to the independent clause to which it is attached.

> **Review Video: What is a Clause?**
> Visit mometrix.com/academy and enter code: 940170
>
> **Review Video: Independent and Dependent Clauses**
> Visit mometrix.com/academy and enter code: 556903

TYPES OF DEPENDENT CLAUSES

ADJECTIVE CLAUSES

An **adjective clause** is a dependent clause that modifies a noun or a pronoun. Adjective clauses begin with a relative pronoun (*who, whose, whom, which,* and *that*) or a relative adverb (*where, when,* and *why*).

Also, adjective clauses come after the noun that the clause needs to explain or rename. This is done to have a clear connection to the independent clause.

Examples:

I learned the reason (independent clause) why I won the award. (adjective clause)

This is the place (independent clause) where I started my first job. (adjective clause)

An adjective clause can be an essential or nonessential clause. An essential clause is very important to the sentence. **Essential clauses** explain or define a person or thing. **Nonessential clauses** give

32

more information about a person or thing but are not necessary to define them. Nonessential clauses are set off with commas while essential clauses are not.

[handwritten: none has commas]

Examples:

essential
clause
A person who works hard at first can often rest later in life.

nonessential
clause *[handwritten: not needed]*
Neil Armstrong, who walked on the moon, is my hero.

> **Review Video: Adjective Clauses and Phrases**
> Visit mometrix.com/academy and enter code: 520888

ADVERB CLAUSES

An **adverb clause** is a dependent clause that modifies a verb, adjective, or adverb. In sentences with multiple dependent clauses, adverb clauses are usually placed immediately before or after the independent clause. An adverb clause is introduced with words such as *after, although, as, before, because, if, since, so, unless, when, where,* and *while.*

Examples:

adverb
clause
When you walked outside, I called the manager.

adverb
clause
I will go with you unless you want to stay.

NOUN CLAUSES

A **noun clause** is a dependent clause that can be used as a subject, object, or complement. Noun clauses begin with words such as *how, that, what, whether, which, who,* and *why.* These words can also come with an adjective clause. Unless the noun clause is being used as the subject of the sentence, it should come after the verb of the independent clause.

[handwritten: Don't fully understand ?]

Examples:

noun
clause
The real mystery is how you avoided serious injury.

noun
clause
What you learn from each other depends on your honesty with others.

SUBORDINATION

When two related ideas are not of equal importance, the ideal way to combine them is to make the more important idea an independent clause and the less important idea a dependent or subordinate clause. This is called **subordination**.

[handwritten: Don't fully undstand]

Example:

Separate ideas: The team had a perfect regular season. The team lost the championship.

Subordinated: Despite having a perfect regular season, *the team lost the championship*.

PHRASES

A phrase is a group of words that functions as a single part of speech, usually a noun, adjective, or adverb. A **phrase** is not a complete thought, but it adds detail or explanation to a sentence, or renames something within the sentence.

not a complete thought

PREPOSITIONAL PHRASES

a
most common
Phrase

One of the most common types of phrases is the prepositional phrase. A **prepositional phrase** begins with a preposition and ends with a noun or pronoun that is the object of the preposition. Normally, the prepositional phrase functions as an **adjective** or an **adverb** within the sentence.

Examples:

prepositional
phrase

The picnic is on the blanket.

prepositional
phrase

I am sick with a fever today.

prepositional
phrase

Among the many flowers, John found a four-leaf clover.

VERBAL PHRASES

does not function as a verb

A **verbal** is a word or phrase that is formed from a verb but does not function as a verb. Depending on its particular form, it may be used as a noun, adjective, or adverb. A verbal does **not** replace a verb in a sentence.

So verbal

Examples:

verb

Correct: Walk a mile daily.

This is a complete sentence with the implied subject *you*.

verbal

Incorrect: To walk a mile. *not a sentence*

This is not a sentence since there is no functional verb.

There are three types of verbal: **participles**, **gerunds**, and **infinitives**. Each type of verbal has a corresponding **phrase** that consists of the verbal itself along with any complements or modifiers.

34

Types of Verbal Phrases

PARTICIPLES

A **participle** is a type of verbal that always functions as an adjective. The present participle always ends with *-ing.* Past participles end with *-d, -ed, -n,* or *-t.*

Examples:

verb	present participle	past participle
dance	dancing	danced

Participial phrases most often come right before or right after the noun or pronoun that they modify.

Examples:

participial phrase

Shipwrecked on an island, the boys started to fish for food.

verb

participial phrase

Having been seated for five hours, we got out of the car to stretch our legs.

verb

participial phrase

Praised for their work, the group accepted the first-place trophy.

verb

GERUNDS

A **gerund** is a type of verbal that always functions as a **noun**. Like present participles, gerunds always end with *-ing,* but they can be easily distinguished from one another by the part of speech they represent (participles always function as adjectives). Since a gerund or gerund phrase always functions as a noun, it can be used as the subject of a sentence, the predicate nominative, or the object of a verb or preposition.

always functions as a noun.

found in th object or subject

Examples:

gerund

We want to be known for teaching the poor.

object of preposition

gerund

Coaching this team is the best job of my life.

subject

gerund

We like practicing our songs in the basement.

object of verb

INFINITIVES

An **infinitive** is a type of verbal that can function as a noun, an adjective, or an adverb. An infinitive is made of the word *to* and the basic form of the verb. As with all other types of verbal phrases, an infinitive phrase includes the verbal itself and all of its complements or modifiers.

to + verb

Examples:

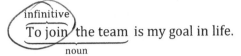

To join the team is my goal in life.

infinitive
noun

The animals have enough food to eat for the night.

infinitive
adjective

People lift weights to exercise their muscles.

infinitive
adverb

> **Review Video: Gerunds, Infinitives, and Participles**
> Visit mometrix.com/academy and enter code: 634263

APPOSITIVE PHRASES

An **appositive** is a word or phrase that is used to explain or rename nouns or pronouns. Noun phrases, gerund phrases, and infinitive phrases can all be used as appositives.

Examples:

rename nouns & pronouns

appositive

Terriers, hunters at heart, have been dressed up to look like lap dogs.

The noun phrase _hunters at heart_ renames the noun _terriers_.

appositive

His plan, to save and invest his money, was proven as a safe approach.

The infinitive phrase explains what the plan is.

Appositive phrases can be **essential** or **nonessential**. An appositive phrase is essential if the person, place, or thing being described or renamed is too general for its meaning to be understood without the appositive.

Examples:

good examples

essential

Two of America's Founding Fathers, George Washington and Thomas Jefferson, served as presidents.

nonessential

George Washington and Thomas Jefferson, two Founding Fathers, served as presidents.

ABSOLUTE PHRASES

type of verbal

An absolute phrase is a phrase that consists of **a noun followed by a participle**. An absolute phrase provides **context** to what is being described in the sentence, but it does not modify or explain any particular word; it is essentially independent.

Examples:

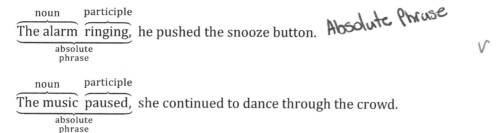

noun   participle
The alarm ringing, he pushed the snooze button.   *Absolute Phrase* ✓
absolute
phrase

noun   participle
The music paused, she continued to dance through the crowd.
absolute
phrase

PARALLELISM

When multiple items or ideas are presented in a sentence in series, such as in a list, the items or ideas must be stated in grammatically equivalent ways. In other words, if one idea is stated in gerund form, the second cannot be stated in infinitive form. For example, to write, *I enjoy reading and to study* would be incorrect. An infinitive and a gerund are not equivalent. Instead, you should write *I enjoy reading and studying*. In lists of more than two, all items must be parallel.

Example:

> **Incorrect**: He stopped at the office, grocery store, and the pharmacy before heading home.

> The first and third items in the list of places include the article *the*, so the second item needs it as well.

> **Correct**: He stopped at the office, *the* grocery store, and the pharmacy before heading home.

Example:

> **Incorrect**: While vacationing in Europe, she went biking, skiing, and climbed mountains. *reverse*

> The first and second items in the list are gerunds, so the third item must be as well.

> **Correct**: While vacationing in Europe, she went biking, skiing, and *mountain climbing.*

> **Review Video: Parallel Sentence Construction**
> Visit mometrix.com/academy and enter code: 831988

SENTENCE PURPOSE

There are four types of sentences: declarative, imperative, interrogative, and exclamatory.

A **declarative** sentence states a fact and ends with a period.

> *The football game starts at seven o'clock.*

An **imperative** sentence tells someone to do something and generally ends with a period. An urgent command might end with an exclamation point instead.

> *Don't forget to buy your ticket.*

An **interrogative** sentence asks a question and ends with a question mark.

> *Are you going to the game on Friday?*

✗ An **exclamatory** sentence <u>shows strong emotion and ends</u> with an exclamation point.

I can't believe we won the game!

> **Review Video: <u>Functions of a Sentence</u>**
> Visit mometrix.com/academy and enter code: 475974

SENTENCE STRUCTURE

Sentences are classified by structure based on the type and number of clauses present. The four classifications of sentence structure are the following:

✓ **Simple**: A simple sentence has one independent clause with <u>no dependent clauses</u>. A simple sentence <u>may have **compound elements**</u> (i.e., compound subject or verb).

Examples:

— no dependent clause

single single
subject verb
Judy watered the lawn.

What is a compound verb?

compound single
subject verb
Judy and Alan watered the lawn.

single compound *same word* compound
subject verb verb
Judy watered the lawn and pulled weeds.

compound compound compound
subject verb verb
Judy and Alan watered the lawn and pulled weeds.

✗ **Compound**: A compound sentence has <u>two or more independent clauses</u> with <u>no dependent clauses.</u> Usually, the independent clauses are joined with a comma and a coordinating conjunction or with a semicolon.

Two independent clauses } They can stand alone

Examples:

independent independent
clause clause
The time has come, and we are ready.

independent independent
clause clause
I woke up at dawn; the sun was just coming up.

✗ **Complex**: A complex sentence has one independent clause and at <u>least one dependent clause.</u>

has both independent & dependent

Examples:

dependent independent
clause clause
Although he had the flu, Harry went to work.

independent dependent
clause clause
Marcia got married, after she finished college.

38

Compound-Complex: A compound-complex sentence has at least two independent clauses and at least one dependent clause.

[handwritten: X]

Examples:

independent clause	dependent clause	independent clause
John is my friend	who went to India,	and he brought back souvenirs.

independent clause	independent clause	dependent clause
You may not realize this,	but we heard the music	that you played last night.

> **Review Video: Sentence Structure**
> Visit mometrix.com/academy and enter code: 700478

[handwritten left margin: writing technique]

Sentence variety is important to consider when writing an essay or speech. A variety of sentence lengths and types creates rhythm, makes a passage more engaging, and gives writers an opportunity to demonstrate their writing style. Writing that uses the same length or type of sentence without variation can be boring or difficult to read. To evaluate a passage for effective sentence variety, it is helpful to note whether the passage contains diverse sentence structures and lengths. It is also important to pay attention to the way each sentence starts and avoid beginning with the same words or phrases.

[handwritten: Don't write with only one sentence type!!]

SENTENCE FRAGMENTS

Recall that a group of words must contain at least one **independent clause** in order to be considered a sentence. If it doesn't contain even one independent clause, it is called a **sentence fragment**.

[handwritten: no independent clause, no sentence]

The appropriate process for **repairing** a sentence fragment depends on what type of fragment it is. If the fragment is a dependent clause, it can sometimes be as simple as removing a subordinating word (e.g., when, because, if) from the beginning of the fragment. Alternatively, a dependent clause can be incorporated into a closely related neighboring sentence. If the fragment is missing some required part, like a subject or a verb, the fix might be as simple as adding the missing part.

[handwritten right margin: repair fragment]

Examples:

Fragment: Because he wanted to sail the Mediterranean.

Removed subordinating word: He wanted to sail the Mediterranean.

Combined with another sentence: Because he wanted to sail the Mediterranean, he booked a Greek island cruise.

RUN-ON SENTENCES

Run-on sentences consist of multiple independent clauses that have not been joined together properly. Run-on sentences can be corrected in several different ways:

[handwritten right margin: Can be fixed with commas]

Join clauses properly: This can be done with a comma and coordinating conjunction, with a semicolon, or with a colon or dash if the second clause is explaining something in the first.

Example:

> **Incorrect**: I went on the trip, we visited lots of castles.

> **Corrected**: I went on the trip, and we visited lots of castles.

correction 2 **Split into separate sentences**: This correction is most effective when the independent clauses are very long or when they are not closely related.

Example:

> **Incorrect**: The drive to New York takes ten hours, my uncle lives in Boston.

> **Corrected**: The drive to New York takes ten hours. My uncle lives in Boston.

Correction 3 **Make one clause dependent**: This is the easiest way to make the sentence correct and more interesting at the same time. It's often as simple as adding a subordinating word between the two clauses or before the first clause. *easiest way.*

Example:

> **Incorrect**: I finally made it to the store and I bought some eggs.

> **Corrected**: When I finally made it to the store, I bought some eggs.

Correction 4 **Reduce to one clause with a compound verb**: If both clauses have the same subject, remove the subject from the second clause, and you now have just one clause with a compound verb.

Example:

> **Incorrect**: The drive to New York takes ten hours, it makes me very tired.

> *↓ replace*

> **Corrected**: The drive to New York takes ten hours and makes me very tired.

Note: While these are the simplest ways to correct a run-on sentence, often the best way is to completely reorganize the thoughts in the sentence and rewrite it.

> **Review Video: Fragments and Run-on Sentences**
> Visit mometrix.com/academy and enter code: 541989

DANGLING AND MISPLACED MODIFIERS
DANGLING MODIFIERS *Bad !!*

A dangling modifier is a dependent clause or verbal phrase that does not have a clear logical connection to a word in the sentence.

Example:

Incorrect: <u>Reading each magazine article,</u> the stories caught my attention.
(dangling modifier)

The word *stories* cannot be modified by *Reading each magazine article.* People can read, but stories cannot read. Therefore, the subject of the sentence must be a person.

Corrected: <u>Reading each magazine article,</u> I was entertained by the stories.
(dependent clause)

Example:

Incorrect: <u>Ever since childhood,</u> my grandparents have visited me for Christmas.
(dangling modifier) — *no clear subject*

The speaker in this sentence can't have been visited by her grandparents when *they* were children, since she wouldn't have been born yet. Either the modifier should be clarified or the sentence should be rearranged to specify whose childhood is being referenced.

Clarified: <u>Ever since I was a child,</u> my grandparents have visited for Christmas.
(dependent clause) — *clear subject*

Rearranged: I have enjoyed my grandparents visiting for Christmas, <u>ever since childhood.</u>
clear subject — *(dependent clause)*

MISPLACED MODIFIERS

Because modifiers are grammatically versatile, they can be put in many different places within the structure of a sentence. The danger of this versatility is that a modifier can accidentally be placed where it is modifying the wrong word or where it is not clear which word it is modifying.

Example:

Incorrect: She read the book to a crowd <u>that was filled with beautiful pictures.</u>   *good*
(modifier)

The book was filled with beautiful pictures, not the crowd.

Corrected: She read the book <u>that was filled with beautiful pictures</u> to a crowd.
(modifier)

41

Example:

unclear

Ambiguous: Derek saw a bus nearly hit a man $\overbrace{\text{on his way to work}}^{\text{modifier}}$.

Was Derek on his way to work or was the other man?

Derek: $\overbrace{\text{On his way to work,}}^{\text{modifier}}$ Derek saw a bus nearly hit a man.

The other man: Derek saw a bus nearly hit a man $\overbrace{\text{who was on his way to work}}^{\text{modifier}}$.

SPLIT INFINITIVES

A split infinitive occurs when a modifying word comes between the word *to* and the verb that pairs with *to*.

Example: To *clearly* explain vs. *To explain* clearly | To *softly* sing vs. *To sing* softly

Though considered improper by some, split infinitives may provide better clarity and simplicity in some cases than the alternatives. As such, avoiding them should not be considered a universal rule.

DOUBLE NEGATIVES

Standard English allows **two negatives** only when a **positive** meaning is intended. For example, *The team was not displeased with their performance.* Double negatives to emphasize negation are not used in standard English.

positive

Negative modifiers (e.g., never, no, and not) should not be paired with other negative modifiers or negative words (e.g., none, nobody, nothing, or neither). The modifiers *hardly, barely*, and *scarcely* are also considered negatives in standard English, so they should not be used with other negatives.

80%

CHAPTER QUIZ

1. Which of the following is an imperative statement?
- a. John knows the way to the park.
- b. There are five letters on the table for him.
- (c.) Go to the post office for me.
- d. The cookies need to cook for a few more minutes.

2. Which of the following is NOT a word used to combine nouns to make a compound subject?
- a. Or
- b. Nor
- c. And
- (d.) Also ✗

3. Which of the following is always singular?
- (a) Each
- b. Both ✗
- c. Several ✗
- d. Many ✗

4. Identify the indirect object of the following sentence: "We taught the old dog a new trick."

Ind subject
- a. We
- b. Taught
- (c.) The old dog
- d. A new trick

5. Identify the infinitive of the following sentence: "The animals have enough food to eat for the night."
- a. The animals
- b. Have enough food
- (c.) To eat
- d. For the night

6. How many types of sentences are there?
- a. Three
- (b) Four
- c. Five
- d. Six

7. Which of the following sentences correctly expresses the idea of parallelism?
- a. He stopped at the office, grocery store, and the pharmacy before heading home. ✗
- b. While vacationing in Europe, she went biking, skiing, and climbed mountains. ✗
- (c) The crowd jumped and cheered, roared and hollered, and whistled as the game concluded.
- d. The flurry of blows left him staggered, discombobulated, and overwhelmed before falling.

43

8. Identify the phrase, "The music paused," in the following sample sentence:

"The music paused, she continued to dance through the crowd."

a. Subordinate phrase
b. Essential appositive
c. Nonessential appositive
d. Absolute phrase

CHAPTER QUIZ ANSWER KEY

1. C: In an imperative sentence, the verb's subject is understood without actually appearing or being named in the sentence itself. For example, in the imperative sentence, "Run to the store," the subject is the person being told to run.

2. D: A compound subject is formed when two or more nouns joined by *and, or,* or *nor* jointly act as the subject of the sentence.

3. A: Pronouns such as *each, either, everybody, anybody, somebody,* and *nobody* are always singular.

4. C: An indirect object is a word or group of words that show how an action had an influence on someone or something. If there is an indirect object in a sentence, then there will always be a direct object in the sentence. When looking for the indirect object, find the verb and ask *to, for whom,* or *what.*

We taught the old dog a new trick.
indirect object — the old dog
direct object — a new trick

5. C: An infinitive is a type of verbal that can function as a noun, an adjective, or an adverb. An infinitive is made of the word *to* and the basic form of the verb. As with all other types of verbal phrases, an infinitive phrase includes the verbal itself and all of its complements or modifiers.

The animals have enough food to eat for the night.
infinitive — to eat
adjective

6. B: There are four types of sentences: declarative, imperative, interrogative, and exclamatory.

7. D: When multiple items or ideas are presented in a sentence in series, such as in a list, the items or ideas must be stated in grammatically equivalent ways. In other words, if one idea is stated in gerund form, the second cannot be stated in infinitive form. For example, writing "I enjoy *reading* and *to study*" would be incorrect. An infinitive and a gerund are not equivalent. Instead, the sentence should be, "I enjoy *reading* and *studying*." In lists of more than two, all items must be parallel.

Example:

Incorrect: He stopped at the office, grocery store, and the pharmacy before heading home.

(The first and third items in the list of places include the article *the*, so the second item needs it as well.)

Correct: He stopped at the office, *the* grocery store, and the pharmacy before heading home.

8. D: An absolute phrase is a phrase that consists of a noun followed by a participle. An absolute phrase provides context to what is being described in the sentence, but it does not modify or explain any particular word; it is essentially independent.

noun   participle

The music paused, she continued to dance through the crowd.

absolute
phrase

- what I know
- what I Don't know
- what I kinda know

Punctuation

END PUNCTUATION

PERIODS

Use a period to end all sentences except direct questions and exclamations. Periods are also used for abbreviations.

Examples: 3 p.m. | 2 a.m. | Mr. Jones | Mrs. Stevens | Dr. Smith | Bill, Jr. | Pennsylvania Ave.

Note: An abbreviation is a shortened form of a word or phrase.

QUESTION MARKS

Question marks should be used following a **direct question**. A polite request can be followed by a period instead of a question mark.

Direct Question: What is for lunch today? | How are you? | Why is that the answer?

Polite Requests: Can you please send me the item tomorrow. | Will you please walk with me on the track.

> **Review Video: Question Marks**
> Visit mometrix.com/academy and enter code: 118471

EXCLAMATION MARKS

Exclamation marks are used after a word group or sentence that shows much feeling or has special importance. Exclamation marks should not be overused. They are saved for proper **exclamatory interjections.**

Example: We're going to the finals! | You have a beautiful car! | "That's crazy!" she yelled.

> **Review Video: Exclamation Points**
> Visit mometrix.com/academy and enter code: 199367

COMMAS

The comma is a punctuation mark that can help you understand connections in a sentence. Not every sentence needs a comma. However, if a sentence needs a comma, you need to put it in the right place. A comma in the wrong place (or an absent comma) will make a sentence's meaning unclear. These are some of the rules for commas:

Use Case	Example
Before a **coordinating conjunction** joining independent clauses.	Bob caught three fish, and I caught two fish.
After an **introductory phrase**	After the final out, we went to a restaurant to celebrate.
After an **adverbial clause**	Studying the stars, I was awed by the beauty of the sky.
Between **items in a series**	I will bring the turkey, the pie, and the coffee.
For **interjections**	Wow, you know how to play this game.
After *yes* and *no* responses	No, I cannot come tomorrow.
Separate **nonessential modifiers**	John Frank, who coaches the team, was promoted today.
Separate **nonessential appositives**	Thomas Edison, an American inventor, was born in Ohio.
Separate **nouns of direct address**	You, John, are my only hope in this moment.
Separate **interrogative tags**	This is the last time, correct?
Separate **contrasts**	You are my friend, not my enemy.
Writing **dates**	July 4, 1776, is an important date to remember.
Writing **addresses**	He is meeting me at 456 Delaware Avenue, Washington, D.C., tomorrow morning.
Writing **geographical names**	Paris, France, is my favorite city.
Writing **titles**	John Smith, PhD, will be visiting your class today.
Separate **expressions like** *he said*	"You can start," she said, "with an apology."

Also, you can use a comma **between coordinate adjectives** not joined with *and*. However, not all adjectives are coordinate (i.e., equal or parallel).

What is a coordinate adjective?

not coord adjec

Incorrect: The kind, brown dog followed me home.

Correct: The kind, loyal dog followed me home.

There are two simple ways to know if your adjectives are coordinate. One, you can join the adjectives with *and*: *The kind and loyal dog.* Two, you can change the order of the adjectives: *The loyal, kind dog.*

Review Video: When to Use a Comma
Visit mometrix.com/academy and enter code: 786797

SEMICOLONS

The semicolon is used to connect major sentence pieces of equal value. Some rules for semicolons include:

Can you use a coordinating conjunction to substitut

Use Case	Example
Between closely connected independent clauses **not connected with a coordinating conjunction**	You are right; we should go with your plan.
Between independent clauses **linked with a transitional word**	I think that we can agree on this; however, I am not sure about my friends.
Between items in a **series that has internal punctuation**	I have visited New York, New York; Augusta, Maine; and Baltimore, Maryland.

Review Video: How to Use Semicolons
Visit mometrix.com/academy and enter code: 370605

47

COLONS

The colon is used to call attention to the words that follow it. A colon must come after a **complete independent clause**. The rules for colons are as follows:

[handwritten: most →]

Use Case	Example
After an independent clause to **make a list**	I want to learn many languages: Spanish, German, and Italian.
For **explanations**	There is one thing that stands out on your resume: responsibility.
To give a **quote**	He started with an idea: "We are able to do more than we imagine."
After the **greeting in a formal letter**	To Whom It May Concern:
Show **hours and minutes**	It is 3:14 p.m.
Separate a **title and subtitle**	The essay is titled "America: A Short Introduction to a Modern Country."

> **Review Video: Colons**
> Visit mometrix.com/academy and enter code: 868673

PARENTHESES

Parentheses are used for additional information. Also, they can be used to put labels for letters or numbers in a series. Parentheses should be not be used very often. If they are overused, parentheses can be a distraction instead of a help.

[handwritten: ? Do not over use]

Examples:

Extra Information: The rattlesnake (see Image 2) is a dangerous snake of North and South America.

Series: Include in the email (1) your name, (2) your address, and (3) your question for the author.

> **Review Video: Parentheses**
> Visit mometrix.com/academy and enter code: 947743

QUOTATION MARKS

Use quotation marks to close off **direct quotations** of a person's spoken or written words. Do not use quotation marks around indirect quotations. An indirect quotation gives someone's message without using the person's exact words. Use **single quotation marks** to close off a quotation inside a quotation.

[handwritten: Don't]

Direct Quote: Nancy said, "I am waiting for Henry to arrive."

Indirect Quote: Henry said that he is going to be late to the meeting.

Quote inside a Quote: The teacher asked, "Has everyone read 'The Gift of the Magi'?"

Quotation marks should be used around the titles of **short works**: newspaper and magazine articles, poems, short stories, songs, television episodes, radio programs, and subdivisions of books or websites.

Examples:

"Rip Van Winkle" (short story by Washington Irving)

"O Captain! My Captain!" (poem by Walt Whitman)

Although it is not standard usage, quotation marks are sometimes used to highlight **irony** or the use of words to mean something other than their dictionary definition. This type of usage should be employed sparingly, if at all.

Examples:

The boss warned Frank that he was walking on "thin ice."	Frank is not walking on real ice. Instead, he is being warned to avoid mistakes.
The teacher thanked the young man for his "honesty."	The quotation marks around *honesty* show that the teacher does not believe the young man's explanation.

[handwritten: Term for In trouble]
[handwritten: He lied]

> **Review Video: Quotation Marks**
> Visit mometrix.com/academy and enter code: 884918

Periods and commas are put **inside** quotation marks. Colons and semicolons are put **outside** the quotation marks. Question marks and exclamation points are placed inside quotation marks when they are part of a quote. When the question or exclamation mark goes with the whole sentence, the mark is left outside of the quotation marks.

[handwritten: ? " ! = inside when apart of quots , ") = inside ; = outside]

Examples:

Period and comma	We read "The Gift of the Magi," "The Skylight Room," and "The Cactus."
Semicolon	They watched "The Nutcracker"; then, they went home.
Exclamation mark that is a part of a quote	The crowd cheered, "Victory!"
Question mark that goes with the whole sentence	Is your favorite short story "The Tell-Tale Heart"?

APOSTROPHES

An apostrophe is used to show **possession** or the **deletion of letters in contractions**. An apostrophe is not needed with the possessive pronouns *his, hers, its, ours, theirs, whose,* and *yours.*

Singular Nouns: David's car | a book's theme | my brother's board game

Plural Nouns that end with -*s*: the scissors' handle | boys' basketball ✗

Plural Nouns that end without -*s*: Men's department | the people's adventure

> **Review Video: When to Use an Apostrophe**
> Visit mometrix.com/academy and enter code: 213068
>
> **Review Video: Punctuation Errors in Possessive Pronouns**
> Visit mometrix.com/academy and enter code: 221438

HYPHENS

Hyphens are used to **separate compound words**. Use hyphens in the following cases:

Use Case	Example
Compound numbers from 21 to 99 when written out in words	This team needs twenty-five points to win the game.
Written-out fractions that are used as adjectives	The recipe says that we need a three-fourths cup of butter.
Compound adjectives that come before a noun	The well-fed dog took a nap.
Unusual compound words that would be hard to read or easily confused with other words	This is the best anti-itch cream on the market.

Note: This is not a complete set of the rules for hyphens. A dictionary is the best tool for knowing if a compound word needs a hyphen.

> **Review Video: Hyphens**
> Visit mometrix.com/academy and enter code: 981632

DASHES

Dashes are used to show a **break** or a **change in thought** in a sentence or to act as parentheses in a sentence. When typing, use two hyphens to make a dash. Do not put a space before or after the dash. The following are the functions of dashes:

Use Case	Example
Set off parenthetical statements or an **appositive with internal punctuation**	The three trees—oak, pine, and magnolia—are coming on a truck tomorrow.
Show a **break or change in tone or thought**	The first question—how silly of me—does not have a correct answer.

ELLIPSIS MARKS

The ellipsis mark has **three** periods (…) to show when **words have been removed** from a quotation. If a **full sentence or more** is removed from a quoted passage, you need to use **four periods** to show the removed text and the end punctuation mark. The ellipsis mark should not be used at the beginning of a quotation. The ellipsis mark should also not be used at the end of a quotation unless some words have been deleted from the end of the final sentence.

Example:

Do not use at begining of quote or end of a quote unless words were deleted

"Then he picked up the groceries…paid for them…later he went home."

BRACKETS

There are two main reasons to use brackets:

Use Case	Example
Placing **parentheses inside of parentheses**	The hero of this story, Paul Revere (a silversmith and industrialist [see Ch. 4]), rode through towns of Massachusetts to warn of advancing British troops.
Adding **clarification or detail to a quotation** that is not part of the quotation	The father explained, "My children are planning to attend my alma mater [State University]."

Review Video: Brackets
Visit mometrix.com/academy and enter code: 727546

100%.

CHAPTER QUIZ

1. Which of the following correctly implements the use of parentheses?

    a. The rattlesnake (see Image 2) is a dangerous snake of North and South America.
    b. The rattlesnake see (Image 2) is a dangerous snake of North and South America.
    c. The rattlesnake see Image (2) is a dangerous snake of North and South America.
    d. The rattlesnake (see Image) (2) is a dangerous snake of North and South America.

2. Which of the following correctly describes the placement of punctuation in reference to quotations?

    a. Periods and commas are put outside quotation marks; colons and semicolons go inside.
    b. Periods and colons are put outside quotation marks; commas and semicolons go inside.
    c. Periods and commas are put inside quotation marks; colons and semicolons go outside.
    d. Periods and colons are put inside quotation marks; commas and semicolons go outside.

3. Which of the following correctly implements the use of commas?

    a. He is meeting me at, 456 Delaware Avenue, Washington, D.C., tomorrow morning.
    b. He is meeting me at 456 Delaware Avenue, Washington, D.C., tomorrow morning.
    c. He is meeting me at 456 Delaware Avenue Washington, D.C. tomorrow morning.
    d. He is meeting me at 456 Delaware Avenue, Washington, D.C. tomorrow morning.

CHAPTER QUIZ ANSWER KEY

1. A: Parentheses are used for additional information. Also, they can be used to put labels for letters or numbers in a series. Parentheses should be not be used very often because their overuse can become a distraction.

2. C: Periods and commas are put inside quotation marks, while colons and semicolons are put outside quotation marks. Question marks and exclamation points are placed inside quotation marks when they are part of a quote. When the question mark or exclamation point is not part of a quoted section but instead part of an entire sentence, then it is left outside of the quotation marks.

3. B: These are some of the rules for commas:

Use Case	Example
Before a **coordinating conjunction** joining independent clauses	Bob caught three fish, and I caught two fish.
After an **introductory phrase**	After the final out, we went to a restaurant to celebrate.
After an **adverbial clause**	Studying the stars, I was awed by the beauty of the sky.
Between **items in a series**	I will bring the turkey, the pie, and the coffee.
For **interjections**	Wow, you know how to play this game.
After *yes* and *no* responses	No, I cannot come tomorrow.
Separate **nonessential modifiers**	John Frank, who coaches the team, was promoted today.
Separate **nonessential appositives**	Thomas Edison, an American inventor, was born in Ohio.
Separate **nouns of direct address**	You, John, are my only hope in this moment.
Separate **interrogative tags**	This is the last time, correct?
Separate **contrasts**	You are my friend, not my enemy.
Writing **dates**	July 4, 1776, is an important date to remember.
Writing **addresses**	He is meeting me at 456 Delaware Avenue, Washington, D.C., tomorrow morning.
Writing **geographical names**	Paris, France, is my favorite city.
Writing **titles**	John Smith, PhD, will be visiting your class today.
Separate **expressions like "he said"**	"You can start," she said, "with an apology."

Common Usage Mistakes

WORD CONFUSION
WHICH, THAT, AND WHO
The words *which*, *that*, and *who* can act as **relative pronouns** to help clarify or describe a noun.

Which is used for things only.

> Example: Andrew's car, *which is old and rusty,* broke down last week.

That is used for people or things. *That* is usually informal when used to describe people.

> Example: Is this the only book *that Louis L'Amour wrote?*

> Example: Is Louis L'Amour the author *that wrote Western novels?*

Who is used for people or for animals that have an identity or personality.

> Example: Mozart was the composer *who wrote those operas.*

> Example: John's dog, *who is called Max,* is large and fierce.

HOMOPHONES
Homophones are words that sound alike (or similar) but have different **spellings** and **definitions**. A homophone is a type of **homonym**, which is a pair or group of words that are pronounced or spelled the same, but do not mean the same thing.

TO, TOO, AND TWO
To can be an adverb or a preposition for showing direction, purpose, and relationship. See your dictionary for the many other ways to use *to* in a sentence.

> Examples: I went to the store. | I want to go with you.

Too is an adverb that means *also, as well, very, or in excess.*

> Examples: I can walk a mile too. | You have eaten too much.

Two is a number.

> Example: You have two minutes left.

THERE, THEIR, AND THEY'RE
There can be an adjective, adverb, or pronoun. Often, *there* is used to show a place or to start a sentence.

> Examples: I went there yesterday. | There is something in his pocket.

Their is a pronoun that is used to show ownership.

> Examples: He is their father. | This is their fourth apology this week.

They're is a contraction of *they are.*

> Example: Did you know that they're in town?

54

KNEW AND NEW

Knew is the past tense of *know*.

> Example: I knew the answer.

New is an adjective that means something is current, has not been used, or is modern.

> Example: This is my new phone.

THEN AND THAN

Then is an adverb that indicates sequence or order:

> Example: I'm going to run to the library and then come home.

Than is special-purpose word used only for comparisons:

> Example: Susie likes chips more than candy.

ITS AND IT'S

Its is a pronoun that shows ownership.

> Example: The guitar is in its case.

It's is a contraction of *it is*.

> Example: It's an honor and a privilege to meet you.

Note: The *h* in honor is silent, so *honor* starts with the vowel sound *o*, which must have the article *an*.

YOUR AND YOU'RE

Your is a pronoun that shows ownership.

> Example: This is your moment to shine.

You're is a contraction of *you are*.

> Example: Yes, you're correct.

SAW AND SEEN

Saw is the past-tense form of *see*.

> Example: I saw a turtle on my walk this morning.

Seen is the past participle of *see*.

> Example: I have seen this movie before.

AFFECT AND EFFECT

There are two main reasons that *affect* and *effect* are so often confused: 1) both words can be used as either a noun or a verb, and 2) unlike most homophones, their usage and meanings are closely related to each other. Here is a quick rundown of the four usage options:

Affect (n): feeling, emotion, or mood that is displayed

Example: The patient had a flat *affect.* (i.e., his face showed little or no emotion)

Affect (v): to alter, to change, to influence

Example: The sunshine *affects* the plant's growth.

Effect (n): a result, a consequence

Example: What *effect* will this weather have on our schedule?

Effect (v): to bring about, to cause to be

Example: These new rules will *effect* order in the office.

The noun form of *affect* is rarely used outside of technical medical descriptions, so if a noun form is needed on the test, you can safely select *effect*. The verb form of *effect* is not as rare as the noun form of *affect*, but it's still not all that likely to show up on your test. If you need a verb and you can't decide which to use based on the definitions, choosing *affect* is your best bet.

HOMOGRAPHS

Homographs are words that share the same spelling, but have different meanings and sometimes different pronunciations. To figure out which meaning is being used, you should be looking for context clues. The context clues give hints to the meaning of the word. For example, the word *spot* has many meanings. It can mean "a place" or "a stain or blot." In the sentence "After my lunch, I saw a spot on my shirt," the word *spot* means "a stain or blot." The context clues of "After my lunch" and "on my shirt" guide you to this decision. A homograph is another type of homonym.

I knew that

BANK

(noun): an establishment where money is held for savings or lending

(verb): to collect or pile up

CONTENT

(noun): the topics that will be addressed within a book

(adjective): pleased or satisfied

(verb): to make someone pleased or satisfied

FINE

(noun): an amount of money that acts a penalty for an offense

(adjective): very small or thin

(adverb): in an acceptable way

(verb): to make someone pay money as a punishment

INCENSE

(noun): a material that is burned in religious settings and makes a pleasant aroma

(verb): to frustrate or anger

LEAD

(noun): the first or highest position

(noun): a heavy metallic element

(verb): to direct a person or group of followers

(adjective): containing lead

OBJECT

(noun): a lifeless item that can be held and observed

(verb): to disagree

PRODUCE

(noun): fruits and vegetables

(verb): to make or create something

REFUSE

(noun): garbage or debris that has been thrown away

(verb): to not allow

SUBJECT

(noun): an area of study

(verb): to force or subdue

TEAR

(noun): a fluid secreted by the eyes

(verb): to separate or pull apart

01.

CHAPTER QUIZ

1. Which of the following correctly implements the word "affect"?

   a. These new rules will affect order in the office.
   b. What affect will this weather have on our schedule?
   c. The patient had a flat affect during her examination.
   d. His narcissism had a detrimental affect on everyone around him.

2. "Affect" and "effect" would be considered which of the following?

   a. Homographs
   b. Synonyms
   c. Antonyms
   d. Homophones

CHAPTER QUIZ ANSWER KEY

1. C: There are two main reasons that *affect* and *effect* are so often confused: 1) both words can be used as either a noun or a verb; and 2) unlike most homophones, their usage and meanings are closely related to each other. Here is a quick rundown of the four usage options:

Affect (n): feeling, emotion, or mood that is displayed

> Example: The patient had a flat *affect* (i.e., his face showed little or no emotion).

Affect (v): to alter, to change, to influence

> Example: The sunshine *affects* the plant's growth.

Effect (n): a result, a consequence

> Example: What *effect* will this weather have on our schedule?

Effect (v): to bring about, to cause to be

> Example: These new rules will *effect* order in the office.

The noun form of *affect* is rarely used outside of technical medical descriptions, so if a noun form is needed on the test, *effect* is a safe selection. The verb form of *effect* is not as rare as the noun form of *affect*, but it's still not likely to show up on a test. If a verb is needed and the definitions aren't enough of an indicator for which one to use, choosing *affect* is the safest option.

2. D: Homophones are words that sound alike (or similar) but have different spellings and definitions. A homophone is a type of homonym, which is a pair or group of words that are pronounced or spelled the same, but do not mean the same thing.

The Writing Process

BRAINSTORMING

free association to create ideas

Brainstorming is a technique that is used to find a creative approach to a subject. This can be accomplished by simple **free-association** with a topic. For example, with paper and pen, write every thought that you have about the topic in a word or phrase. This is done without critical thinking. You should put everything that comes to your mind about the topic on your scratch paper. Then, you need to read the list over a few times. Next, look for patterns, repetitions, and clusters of ideas. This allows a variety of fresh ideas to come as you think about the topic.

FREE WRITING

Free writing is a more structured form of brainstorming. The method involves taking a limited amount of time (e.g., 2 to 3 minutes) to write everything that comes to mind about the topic in complete sentences. When time expires, review everything that has been written down. Many of your sentences may make little or no sense, but the insights and observations that can come from free writing make this method a valuable approach. Usually, free writing results in a fuller expression of ideas than brainstorming because thoughts and associations are written in complete sentences. However, both techniques can be used to complement each other.

timed Brainstorming

Complete thoughts

PLANNING

Planning is the process of organizing a piece of writing before composing a draft. Planning can include creating an outline or a graphic organizer, such as a Venn diagram, a spider-map, or a flowchart. These methods should help the writer identify their topic, main ideas, and the general organization of the composition. Preliminary research can also take place during this stage. Planning helps writers organize all of their ideas and decide if they have enough material to begin their first draft. However, writers should remember that the decisions they make during this step will likely change later in the process, so their plan does not have to be perfect.

Planning aids in organization

DRAFTING

Writers may then use their plan, outline, or graphic organizer to compose their first draft. They may write subsequent drafts to improve their writing. Writing multiple drafts can help writers consider different ways to communicate their ideas and address errors that may be difficult to correct without rewriting a section or the whole composition. Most writers will vary in how many drafts they choose to write, as there is no "right" number of drafts. Writing drafts also takes away the pressure to write perfectly on the first try, as writers can improve with each draft they write.

Hard to do with a time limit

REVISING, EDITING, AND PROOFREADING

maybe I should start

Once a writer completes a draft, they can move on to the revising, editing, and proofreading steps to improve their draft. These steps begin with making broad changes that may apply to large sections of a composition and then making small, specific corrections. **Revising** is the first and broadest of these steps. Revising involves ensuring that the composition addresses an appropriate audience, includes all necessary material, maintains focus throughout, and is organized logically. Revising may occur after the first draft to ensure that the following drafts improve upon errors from the first draft. Some revision should occur between each draft to avoid repeating these errors. The **editing** phase of writing is narrower than the revising phase. Editing a composition should include steps such as improving transitions between paragraphs, ensuring each paragraph is on topic, and improving the flow of the text. The editing phase may also include correcting grammatical errors that cannot be fixed without significantly altering the text. **Proofreading** involves fixing misspelled words, typos, other grammatical errors, and any remaining surface-level flaws in the composition.

I know all of this but have never applied them well!!

(handwritten note in margin: Do the priveous section again)

RECURSIVE WRITING PROCESS

However you approach writing, you may find comfort in knowing that the revision process can occur in any order. The **recursive writing process** is not as difficult as the phrase may make it seem. Simply put, the recursive writing process means that you may need to revisit steps after completing other steps. It also implies that the steps are not required to take place in any certain order. Indeed, you may find that planning, drafting, and revising can all take place at about the same time. The writing process involves moving back and forth between planning, drafting, and revising, followed by more planning, more drafting, and more revising until the writing is satisfactory.

> **Review Video: Recursive Writing Process**
> Visit mometrix.com/academy and enter code: 951611

TECHNOLOGY IN THE WRITING PROCESS

(handwritten note in margin: wont help on the GRE)

Modern technology has yielded several tools that can be used to make the writing process more convenient and organized. Word processors and online tools, such as databases and plagiarism detectors, allow much of the writing process to be completed in one place, using one device.

TECHNOLOGY FOR PLANNING AND DRAFTING

For the planning and drafting stages of the writing process, word processors are a helpful tool. These programs also feature formatting tools, allowing users to create their own planning tools or create digital outlines that can be easily converted into sentences, paragraphs, or an entire essay draft. Online databases and references also complement the planning process by providing convenient access to information and sources for research. Word processors also allow users to keep up with their work and update it more easily than if they wrote their work by hand. Online word processors often allow users to collaborate, making group assignments more convenient. These programs also allow users to include illustrations or other supplemental media in their compositions.

TECHNOLOGY FOR REVISING, EDITING, AND PROOFREADING

(handwritten note in margin: Grammerly)

Word processors also benefit the revising, editing, and proofreading stages of the writing process. Most of these programs indicate errors in spelling and grammar, allowing users to catch minor errors and correct them quickly. There are also websites designed to help writers by analyzing text for deeper errors, such as poor sentence structure, inappropriate complexity, lack of sentence variety, and style issues. These websites can help users fix errors they may not know to look for or may have simply missed. As writers finish these steps, they may benefit from checking their work for any plagiarism. There are several websites and programs that compare text to other documents and publications across the internet and detect any similarities within the text. These websites show the source of the similar information, so users know whether or not they referenced the source and unintentionally plagiarized its contents.

TECHNOLOGY FOR PUBLISHING

Technology also makes managing written work more convenient. Digitally storing documents keeps everything in one place and is easy to reference. Digital storage also makes sharing work easier, as documents can be attached to an email or stored online. This also allows writers to publish their work easily, as they can electronically submit it to other publications or freely post it to a personal blog, profile, or website.

CHAPTER QUIZ

1. Which of the following is a more structured form of brainstorming?

100%.
a. Free writing
b. Planning
c. Drafting
d. Proofreading

CHAPTER QUIZ ANSWER KEY

1. A: Free writing is a more structured form of brainstorming. The method involves taking a limited amount of time (e.g., two to three minutes) to write everything that comes to mind about the topic in complete sentences. When time expires, review everything that has been written down. Many of the sentences may make little or no sense, but the insights and observations that can come from free writing make this method a valuable approach. Usually, free writing results in a fuller expression of ideas than brainstorming because thoughts and associations are written in complete sentences. However, both techniques can be used to complement each other.

Outlining and Organizing Ideas

Main Ideas, Supporting Details, and Outlining a Topic

A writer often begins the first paragraph of a paper by stating the **main idea** or point, also known as the **topic sentence**. The rest of the paragraph supplies particular details that develop and support the main point. One way to visualize the relationship between the main point and supporting information is by considering a table: the tabletop is the main point, and each of the table's legs is a supporting detail or group of details. Both professional authors and students can benefit from planning their writing by first making an outline of the topic. Outlines facilitate quick identification of the main point and supporting details without having to wade through the additional language that will exist in the fully developed essay, article, or paper. Outlining can also help readers to analyze a piece of existing writing for the same reason. The outline first summarizes the main idea in one sentence. Then, below that, it summarizes the supporting details in a numbered list. Writing the paper then consists of filling in the outline with detail, writing a paragraph for each supporting point, and adding an introduction and conclusion.

Introduction

The purpose of the introduction is to capture the reader's attention and announce the essay's main idea. Normally, the introduction contains 50-80 words, or 3-5 sentences. An introduction can begin with an interesting quote, a question, or a strong opinion—something that will **engage** the reader's interest and prompt them to keep reading. If you are writing your essay to a specific prompt, your introduction should include a **restatement or summarization** of the prompt so that the reader will have some context for your essay. Finally, your introduction should briefly state your **thesis or main idea**: the primary thing you hope to communicate to the reader through your essay. Don't try to include all of the details and nuances of your thesis, or all of your reasons for it, in the introduction. That's what the rest of the essay is for!

> **Review Video: Introduction**
> Visit mometrix.com/academy and enter code: 961328

Thesis Statement

The thesis is the main idea of the essay. A temporary thesis, or working thesis, should be established early in the writing process because it will serve to keep the writer focused as ideas develop. This temporary thesis is subject to change as you continue to write.

The temporary thesis has two parts: a **topic** (i.e., the focus of your essay based on the prompt) and a **comment**. The comment makes an important point about the topic. A temporary thesis should be interesting and specific. Also, you need to limit the topic to a manageable scope. These three questions are useful tools to measure the effectiveness of any temporary thesis:

- Does the focus of my essay have enough interest to hold an audience?
- Is the focus of my essay specific enough to generate interest?
- Is the focus of my essay manageable for the time limit? Too broad? Too narrow?

The thesis should be a generalization rather than a fact because the thesis prepares readers for facts and details that support the thesis. The process of bringing the thesis into sharp focus may help in outlining major sections of the work. Once the thesis and introduction are complete, you can address the body of the work. *Valid*

Review Video: Thesis Statements
Visit mometrix.com/academy and enter code: 691033

SUPPORTING THE THESIS

body Paraghraph

Throughout your essay, the thesis should be **explained clearly and supported** adequately by additional arguments. The thesis sentence needs to contain a clear statement of the purpose of your essay and a comment about the thesis. With the thesis statement, you have an opportunity to state what is noteworthy of this particular treatment of the prompt. Each sentence and paragraph should build on and support the thesis. *How do you build well though*

When you respond to the prompt, use parts of the passage to support your argument or defend your position. Using supporting evidence from the passage strengths your argument because readers can see your attention to the entire passage and your response to the details and facts within the passage. You can use facts, details, statistics, and direct quotations from the passage to uphold your position. Be sure to point out which information comes from the original passage and base your argument around that evidence. *Cite your sorce*

use parts of prompt to defend thesis

BODY

In an essay's introduction, the writer establishes the thesis and may indicate how the rest of the piece will be structured. In the body of the piece, the writer **elaborates** upon, **illustrates**, and **explains** the **thesis statement**. How writers arrange supporting details and their choices of paragraph types are development techniques. Writers may give examples of the concept introduced in the thesis statement. If the subject includes a cause-and-effect relationship, the author may explain its causality. A writer will explain or analyze the main idea of the piece throughout the body, often by presenting arguments for the veracity or credibility of the thesis statement. Writers may use development to define or clarify ambiguous terms. Paragraphs within the body may be organized using natural sequences, like space and time. Writers may employ **inductive reasoning**, using multiple details to establish a generalization or causal relationship, or **deductive reasoning**, proving a generalized hypothesis or proposition through a specific example or case. *use this*

Review Video: Drafting Body Paragraphs
Visit mometrix.com/academy and enter code: 724590

PARAGRAPHS

After the introduction of a passage, a series of body paragraphs will carry a message through to the conclusion. Each paragraph should be **unified around a main point.** Normally, a good topic sentence summarizes the paragraph's main point. A topic sentence is a general sentence that gives an introduction to the paragraph.

The sentences that follow support the topic sentence. However, though it is usually the first sentence, the topic sentence can come as the final sentence to the paragraph if the earlier sentences give a clear explanation of the paragraph's topic. This allows the topic sentence to function as a concluding sentence. Overall, the paragraphs need to stay true to the main point. This means that any unnecessary sentences that do not advance the main point should be removed. *try that*

The main point of a paragraph requires adequate development (i.e., a substantial paragraph that covers the main point). A paragraph of two or three sentences does not cover a main point. This is

63

especially true when the main point of the paragraph gives strong support to the argument of the thesis. An occasional short paragraph is fine as a transitional device. However, a well-developed argument will have paragraphs with more than a few sentences.

METHODS OF DEVELOPING PARAGRAPHS

Common methods of adding substance to paragraphs include examples, illustrations, analogies, and cause and effect.

- **Examples** are supporting details to the main idea of a paragraph or a passage. When authors write about something that their audience may not understand, they can provide an example to show their point. When authors write about something that is not easily accepted, they can give examples to prove their point.
- **Illustrations** are extended examples that require several sentences. Well-selected illustrations can be a great way for authors to develop a point that may not be familiar to their audience. *use lots of adjectives*
- **Analogies** make comparisons between items that appear to have nothing in common. Analogies are employed by writers to provoke fresh thoughts about a subject. These comparisons may be used to explain the unfamiliar, to clarify an abstract point, or to argue a point. Although analogies are effective literary devices, they should be used carefully in arguments. Two things may be alike in some respects but completely different in others.
- **Cause and effect** is an excellent device to explain the connection between an action or situation and a particular result. One way that authors can use cause and effect is to state the effect in the topic sentence of a paragraph and add the causes in the body of the paragraph. This method can give an author's paragraphs structure, which always strengthens writing.

Try it

TYPES OF PARAGRAPHS

A **paragraph of narration** tells a story or a part of a story. Normally, the sentences are arranged in chronological order (i.e., the order that the events happened). However, flashbacks (i.e., an anecdote from an earlier time) can be included.

A **descriptive paragraph** makes a verbal portrait of a person, place, or thing. When specific details are used that appeal to one or more of the senses (i.e., sight, sound, smell, taste, and touch), authors give readers a sense of being present in the moment.

A **process paragraph** is related to time order (i.e., First, you open the bottle. Second, you pour the liquid, etc.). Usually, this describes a process or teaches readers how to perform a process.

Comparing two things draws attention to their similarities and indicates a number of differences. When authors contrast, they focus only on differences. Both comparing and contrasting may be done point-by-point, noting both the similarities and differences of each point, or in sequential paragraphs, where you discuss all the similarities and then all the differences, or vice versa.

BREAKING TEXT INTO PARAGRAPHS

For most forms of writing, you will need to use multiple paragraphs. As such, determining when to start a new paragraph is very important. Reasons for starting a new paragraph include:

- To mark off the introduction and concluding paragraphs
- To signal a shift to a new idea or topic
- To indicate an important shift in time or place
- To explain a point in additional detail
- To highlight a comparison, contrast, or cause and effect relationship

PARAGRAPH LENGTH

Most readers find that their comfort level for a paragraph is between 100 and 200 words. Shorter paragraphs cause too much starting and stopping and give a choppy effect. Paragraphs that are too long often test the attention span of readers. Two notable exceptions to this rule exist. In scientific or scholarly papers, longer paragraphs suggest seriousness and depth. In journalistic writing, constraints are placed on paragraph size by the narrow columns in a newspaper format.

The first and last paragraphs of a text will usually be the introduction and conclusion. These special-purpose paragraphs are likely to be shorter than paragraphs in the body of the work. Paragraphs in the body of the essay follow the subject's outline (e.g., one paragraph per point in short essays and a group of paragraphs per point in longer works). Some ideas require more development than others, so it is good for a writer to remain flexible. A paragraph of excessive length may be divided, and shorter ones may be combined.

COHERENT PARAGRAPHS

A smooth flow of sentences and paragraphs without gaps, shifts, or bumps will lead to paragraph **coherence**. Ties between old and new information can be smoothed using several methods:

- **Linking ideas clearly**, from the topic sentence to the body of the paragraph, is essential for a smooth transition. The topic sentence states the main point, and this should be followed by specific details, examples, and illustrations that support the topic sentence. The support may be direct or indirect. In **indirect support**, the illustrations and examples may support a sentence that in turn supports the topic directly.
- The **repetition of key words** adds coherence to a paragraph. To avoid dull language, variations of the key words may be used.
- **Parallel structures** are often used within sentences to emphasize the similarity of ideas and connect sentences giving similar information.
- Maintaining a **consistent verb tense** throughout the paragraph helps. Shifting tenses affects the smooth flow of words and can disrupt the coherence of the paragraph.

> **Review Video: How to Write a Good Paragraph**
> Visit mometrix.com/academy and enter code: 682127

SEQUENCE WORDS AND PHRASES

When a paragraph opens with the topic sentence, the second sentence may begin with a phrase like *first of all*, introducing the first supporting detail or example. The writer may introduce the second supporting item with words or phrases like *also*, *in addition*, and *besides*. The writer might introduce succeeding pieces of support with wording like, *another thing, moreover, furthermore,* or *not only that, but.* The writer may introduce the last piece of support with *lastly, finally,* or *last but not least.* Writers get off the point by presenting off-target items not supporting the main point. For example, a main point *my dog is not smart* is supported by the statement, *he's six years old and still doesn't answer to his name.* But *he cries when I leave for school* is not supportive, as it does not indicate lack of intelligence. Writers stay on point by presenting only supportive statements that are directly relevant to and illustrative of their main point.

TRANSITIONS

Transitions between sentences and paragraphs guide readers from idea to idea and indicate relationships between sentences and paragraphs. Writers should be judicious in their use of transitions, inserting them sparingly. They should also be selected to fit the author's purpose—transitions can indicate time, comparison, and conclusion, among other purposes. Tone is also important to consider when using transitional phrases, varying the tone for different audiences. For example, in a scholarly essay, *in summary* would be preferable to the more informal *in short.*

When working with transitional words and phrases, writers usually find a natural flow that indicates when a transition is needed. In reading a draft of the text, it should become apparent where the flow is disrupted. At this point, the writer can add transitional elements during the revision process. Revising can also afford an opportunity to delete transitional devices that seem heavy handed or unnecessary.

TYPES OF TRANSITIONAL WORDS

Time	Afterward, immediately, earlier, meanwhile, recently, lately, now, since, soon, when, then, until, before, etc.
Sequence	too, first, second, further, moreover, also, again, and, next, still, besides, finally
Comparison	similarly, in the same way, likewise, also, again, once more
Contrasting	but, although, despite, however, instead, nevertheless, on the one hand... on the other hand, regardless, yet, in contrast.
Cause and Effect	because, consequently, thus, therefore, then, to this end, since, so, as a result, if... then, accordingly
Examples	for example, for instance, such as, to illustrate, indeed, in fact, specifically
Place	near, far, here, there, to the left/right, next to, above, below, beyond, opposite, beside
Concession	granted that, naturally, of course, it may appear, although it is true that
Repetition, Summary, or Conclusion	as mentioned earlier, as noted, in other words, in short, on the whole, to summarize, therefore, as a result, to conclude, in conclusion
Addition	and, also, furthermore, moreover
Generalization	in broad terms, broadly speaking, in general

> **Review Video: <u>Transitional Words and Phrases</u>**
> Visit mometrix.com/academy and enter code: 197796
>
> **Review Video: <u>What are Transition Words?</u>**
> Visit mometrix.com/academy and enter code: 707563
>
> **Review Video: <u>How to Effectively Connect Sentences</u>**
> Visit mometrix.com/academy and enter code: 948325

CONCLUSION

<u>Two important principles to consider when writing a conclusion are strength and closure.</u> A strong conclusion gives the reader a sense that the author's main points are meaningful and important, and that the supporting facts and arguments are convincing, solid, and well developed. When a conclusion achieves closure, it gives the impression that the writer has stated all necessary information and points and completed the work, rather than simply stopping after a specified length. Some things to avoid when writing concluding paragraphs include:

- Introducing a completely new idea
- Beginning with obvious or unoriginal phrases like "In conclusion" or "To summarize"
- Apologizing for one's opinions or writing
- Repeating the thesis word for word rather than rephrasing it
- Believing that the conclusion must always summarize the piece

> **Review Video: <u>Drafting Conclusions</u>**
> Visit mometrix.com/academy and enter code: 209408

100% ✓

CHAPTER QUIZ

✓ **1. Which of the following is considered the main idea of an essay?**

   a. Topic
   b. Body
   c. Theme
   (d.) Thesis

✓ **2. Which of the following are supporting details to the main idea of a paragraph or a passage?**

   a. Analogies
   (b.) Examples
   c. Cause and effect
   d. Transitions

✓ **3. Which of the following is NOT a transitional word or phrase in the concession category?**

   a. Granted that
   b. Naturally
   (c.) Broadly speaking
   d. It may appear

CHAPTER QUIZ ANSWER KEY

1. D: The thesis is the main idea of an essay. A temporary thesis, or working thesis, should be established early in the writing process because it will serve to keep the writer focused as ideas develop. This temporary thesis is subject to change as writing continues. The thesis should be a generalization rather than a fact because the thesis prepares readers for facts and details that support the thesis. The process of bringing the thesis into sharp focus may help in outlining major sections of the work. Once the thesis and introduction are complete, the body of the work can be addressed.

2. B: Examples are supporting details to the main idea of a paragraph or a passage. When authors write about something that their audience may not understand or that is not easily accepted, they can provide an example to show their point.

3. C: Types of transitional words

Time	Afterward, immediately, earlier, meanwhile, recently, lately, now, since, soon, when, then, until, before, etc.
Sequence	Too, first, second, further, moreover, also, again, and, next, still, besides, finally
Comparison	Similarly, in the same way, likewise, also, again, once more
Contrasting	But, although, despite, however, instead, nevertheless, on the one hand... on the other hand, regardless, yet, in contrast.
Cause and effect	Because, consequently, thus, therefore, then, to this end, since, so, as a result, if... then, accordingly
Examples	For example, for instance, such as, to illustrate, indeed, in fact, specifically
Place	Near, far, here, there, to the left/right, next to, above, below, beyond, opposite, beside
Concession	Granted that, naturally, of course, it may appear, although it is true that
Repetition, summary, or conclusion	As mentioned earlier, as noted, in other words, in short, on the whole, to summarize, therefore, as a result, to conclude, in conclusion
Addition	And, also, furthermore, moreover
Generalization	In broad terms, broadly speaking, in general

Handwritten margin note (top left):
- Do not know
- kinda know
- know

Writing Style and Form

WRITING STYLE AND LINGUISTIC FORM

Linguistic form encodes the literal meanings of words and sentences. It comes from the phonological, morphological, syntactic, and semantic parts of a language. **Writing style** consists of different ways of encoding the meaning and indicating figurative and stylistic meanings. An author's writing style can also be referred to as his or her **voice**.

Writers' stylistic choices accomplish three basic effects on their audiences:

- They **communicate meanings** beyond linguistically dictated meanings,
- They communicate the **author's attitude**, such as persuasive or argumentative effects accomplished through style, and
- They communicate or **express feelings**.

Within style, component areas include:

- Narrative structure
- Viewpoint
- Focus
- Sound patterns?
- Meter and rhythm
- Lexical and syntactic repetition and parallelism ?
- Writing genre
- Representational, realistic, and mimetic effects ?
- Representation of thought and speech
- Meta-representation (representing representation) ?
- Irony
- Metaphor and other indirect meanings
- Representation and use of historical and dialectal variations
- Gender-specific and other group-specific speech styles, both real and fictitious ?
- Analysis of the processes for inferring meaning from writing

LEVEL OF FORMALITY

The relationship between writer and reader is important in choosing a **level of formality** as most writing requires some degree of formality. **Formal writing** is for addressing a superior in a school or work environment. Business letters, textbooks, and newspapers use a moderate to high level of formality. **Informal writing** is appropriate for private letters, personal emails, and business correspondence between close associates.

Handwritten margin note (left): on exam do this

For your exam, you will want to be aware of informal and formal writing. One way that this can be accomplished is to watch for shifts in point of view in the essay. For example, unless writers are using a personal example, they will rarely refer to themselves (e.g., "*I* think that *my* point is very clear.") to avoid being informal when they need to be formal.

Also, be mindful of an author who addresses his or her audience **directly** in their writing (e.g., "Readers, *like you*, will understand this argument.") as this can be a sign of informal writing. Good writers understand the need to be consistent with their level of formality. Shifts in levels of formality or point of view can confuse readers and cause them to discount the message.

Handwritten note (bottom center): Do not shif point of views

CLICHÉS

Clichés are phrases that have been **overused** to the point that the phrase has no importance or has lost the original meaning. These phrases have no originality and add very little to a passage. Therefore, most writers will avoid the use of clichés. Another option is to make changes to a cliché so that it is not predictable and empty of meaning.

Examples:

When life gives you lemons, make lemonade.

Every cloud has a silver lining.

Avoid them

JARGON

Jargon is **specialized vocabulary** that is used among members of a certain trade or profession. Since jargon is understood by only a small audience, writers will use jargon in passages that will only be read by a specialized audience. For example, medical jargon should be used in a medical journal but not in a New York Times article. Jargon includes exaggerated language that tries to impress rather than inform. Sentences filled with jargon are not precise and are difficult to understand.

Examples:

"He is going to *toenail* these frames for us." (Toenail is construction jargon for nailing at an angle.)

"They brought in a *kip* of material today." (Kip refers to 1000 pounds in architecture and engineering.) *Ya I wouldn't have known*

SLANG

Slang is an **informal** and sometimes private language that is understood by some individuals. Slang terms have some usefulness, but they can have a small audience. So, most formal writing will not include this kind of language.

Examples:

"Yes, the event was a blast!" (In this sentence, *blast* means that the event was a great experience.)

"That attempt was an epic fail." (By *epic fail*, the speaker means that his or her attempt was not a success.)

COLLOQUIALISM *Informal language*

A colloquialism is a word or phrase that is found in informal writing. Unlike slang, **colloquial language** will be familiar to a greater range of people. However, colloquialisms are still considered inappropriate for formal writing. Colloquial language can include some slang, but these are limited to contractions for the most part.

Examples:

"Can *y'all* come back another time?" (Y'all is a contraction of "you all.")

"Will you stop him from building this *castle in the air*?" (A "castle in the air" is an improbable or unlikely event.)

ACADEMIC LANGUAGE

In educational settings, students are often expected to use academic language in their schoolwork. Academic language is also commonly found in dissertations and theses, texts published by academic journals, and other forms of academic research. Academic language conventions may vary between fields, but general academic language is free of slang, regional terminology, and noticeable grammatical errors. Specific terms may also be used in academic language, and it is important to understand their proper usage. A writer's command of academic language impacts their ability to communicate in an academic or professional context. While it is acceptable to use colloquialisms, slang, improper grammar, or other forms of informal speech in social settings or at home, it is inappropriate to practice non-academic language in academic contexts.

Just right

TONE

Tone may be defined as the writer's **attitude** toward the topic, and to the audience. This attitude is reflected in the language used in the writing. The tone of a work should be **appropriate to the topic** and to the intended audience. While it may be fine to use slang or jargon in some pieces, other texts should not contain such terms. Tone can range from humorous to serious and any level in between. It may be more or less formal, depending on the purpose of the writing and its intended audience. All these nuances in tone can flavor the entire writing and should be kept in mind as the work evolves.

Choose your words wisely

WORD SELECTION

A writer's choice of words is a signature of their style. Careful thought about the use of words can improve a piece of writing. A passage can be an exciting piece to read when attention is given to the use of vivid or specific nouns rather than general ones.

Example:

pay attention to details

General: His kindness will never be forgotten.

more specific

Specific: His thoughtful gifts and bear hugs will never be forgotten.

Attention should also be given to the kind of verbs that are used in sentences. Active verbs (e.g., run, swim) are about an action. Whenever possible, an **active verb should replace a linking verb** to provide clear examples for arguments and to strengthen a passage overall. When using an active verb, one should be sure that the verb is used in the active voice instead of the passive voice. Verbs are in the active voice when the subject is the one doing the action. A verb is in the passive voice when the subject is the recipient of an action.

active verb = active voice

Example:

Passive: The winners were called to the stage by the judges.

Active: The judges called the winners to the stage.

CONCISENESS

Conciseness is writing that communicates a message in the fewest words possible. Writing concisely is valuable because short, uncluttered messages allow the reader to understand the author's message more easily and efficiently. Planning is important in writing concise messages. If you have in mind what you need to write beforehand, it will be easier to make a message short and to the point. Do not state the obvious. *always plan*

Revising is also important. After the message is written, make sure you have effective, pithy sentences that efficiently get your point across. When reviewing the information, imagine a conversation taking place, and concise writing will likely result.

APPROPRIATE KINDS OF WRITING FOR DIFFERENT TASKS, PURPOSES, AND AUDIENCES

When preparing to write a composition, consider the audience and purpose to choose the best type of writing. Three common types of writing are persuasive, expository, and narrative. **Persuasive**, or argumentative writing, is used to convince the audience to take action or agree with the author's claims. **Expository** writing is meant to inform the audience of the author's observations or research on a topic. **Narrative** writing is used to tell the audience a story and often allows more room for creativity. While task, purpose, and audience inform a writer's mode of writing, these factors also impact elements such as tone, vocabulary, and formality.

For example, students who are writing to persuade their parents to grant them some additional *argumentative* privilege, such as permission for a more independent activity, should use more sophisticated vocabulary and diction that sounds more mature and serious to appeal to the parental audience. However, students who are writing for younger children should use simpler vocabulary and sentence structure, as well as choose words that are more vivid and entertaining. They should treat their topics more lightly, and include humor when appropriate. Students who are writing for their classmates may use language that is more informal, as well as age-appropriate.

> **Review Video: Writing Purpose and Audience**
> Visit mometrix.com/academy and enter code: 146627

CHAPTER QUIZ

1. Which of the following would NOT be considered formal writing?

    a. Private letters
    b. Business letters
    c. Textbooks
    d. Newspapers

2. Which of the following sentences contains a verb in the passive voice?

    a. The judges called the winners to the stage for their awards. _Active_
    b. Each applicant must fill out all of the forms required.
    c. He raced through the copse of trees with the grace of a deer.
    d. I was told that there would be food available at the party.

CHAPTER QUIZ ANSWER KEY

1. A: The relationship between writer and reader is important in choosing a level of formality because most writing requires some degree of formality. Formal writing is for addressing a superior in a school or work environment. Business letters, textbooks, and newspapers use a moderate to high level of formality. Informal writing is appropriate for private letters, personal emails, and business correspondence between close associates.

2. D: Attention should also be given to the kind of verbs that are used in sentences. Active verbs (e.g., run, swim) are about an action. Whenever possible, an active verb should replace a linking verb to provide clear examples for arguments and to strengthen a passage overall. When using an active verb, one should be sure that the verb is used in the active voice instead of the passive voice. Verbs are in the active voice when the subject is the one doing the action. A verb is in the passive voice when the subject is the recipient of an action.

Modes of Writing

ESSAYS

Essays usually focus on one topic, subject, or goal. There are several types of essays, including informative, persuasive, and narrative. An essay's structure and level of formality depend on the type of essay and its goal. While narrative essays typically do not include outside sources, other types of essays often require some research and the integration of primary and secondary sources.

The basic format of an essay typically has three major parts: the introduction, the body, and the conclusion. The body is further divided into the writer's main points. Short and simple essays may have three main points, while essays covering broader ranges and going into more depth can have almost any number of main points, depending on length.

An essay's introduction should answer three questions:

1. What is the **subject** of the essay?

    If a student writes an essay about a book, the answer would include the title and author of the book and any additional information needed—such as the subject or argument of the book.

2. How does the essay **address** the subject?

    To answer this, the writer identifies the essay's organization by briefly summarizing main points and the evidence supporting them.

3. What will the essay **prove**?

    This is the thesis statement, usually the opening paragraph's last sentence, clearly stating the writer's message.

The body elaborates on all the main points related to the thesis, introducing one main point at a time, and includes supporting evidence with each main point. Each body paragraph should state the point in a topic sentence, which is usually the first sentence in the paragraph. The paragraph should then explain the point's meaning, support it with quotations or other evidence, and then explain how this point and the evidence are related to the thesis. The writer should then repeat this procedure in a new paragraph for each additional main point.

The conclusion reiterates the content of the introduction, including the thesis, to remind the reader of the essay's main argument or subject. The essay writer may also summarize the highlights of the argument or description contained in the body of the essay, following the same sequence originally used in the body. For example, a conclusion might look like: Point 1 + Point 2 + Point 3 = Thesis, or Point 1 → Point 2 → Point 3 → Thesis Proof. Good organization makes essays easier for writers to compose and provides a guide for readers to follow. Well-organized essays hold attention better and are more likely to get readers to accept their theses as valid.

INFORMATIVE VS. PERSUASIVE WRITING

Informative writing, also called explanatory or expository writing, begins with the basis that something is true or factual, while **persuasive** writing strives to prove something that may or may not be true or factual. Whereas argumentative text is written to **persuade** readers to agree with the author's position, informative text merely **provides information and insight** to readers. Informative writing concentrates on **informing** readers about why or how something is as it is. This can include offering new information, explaining how a process works, and developing a

75

concept for readers. To accomplish these objectives, the essay may name and distinguish various things within a category, provide definitions, provide details about the parts of something, explain a particular function or behavior, and give readers explanations for why a fact, object, event, or process exists or occurs.

NARRATIVE WRITING

Put simply, **narrative** writing tells a story. The most common examples of literary narratives are novels. Non-fictional biographies, autobiographies, memoirs, and histories are also narratives. Narratives should tell stories in such a way that the readers learn something or gain insight or understanding. Students can write more interesting narratives by describing events or experiences that were meaningful to them. Narratives should start with the story's actions or events, rather than long descriptions or introductions. Students should ensure that there is a point to each story by describing what they learned from the experience they narrate. To write an effective description, students should include sensory details, asking themselves what they saw, heard, felt or touched, smelled, and tasted during the experiences they describe. In narrative writing, the details should be **concrete** rather than **abstract**. Using concrete details enables readers to imagine everything that the writer describes.

> **Review Video: Narratives**
> Visit mometrix.com/academy and enter code: 280100

SENSORY DETAILS

Students need to use vivid descriptions when writing descriptive essays. Narratives should also include descriptions of characters, things, and events. Students should remember to describe not only the visual detail of what someone or something looks like, but details from other senses, as well. For example, they can contrast the feeling of a sea breeze to that of a mountain breeze, describe how they think something inedible would taste, and compare sounds they hear in the same location at different times of day and night. Readers have trouble visualizing images or imagining sensory impressions and feelings from abstract descriptions, so concrete descriptions make these more real.

CONCRETE VS. ABSTRACT DESCRIPTIONS IN NARRATIVE

Concrete language provides information that readers can grasp and may empathize with, while **abstract language**, which is more general, can leave readers feeling disconnected, empty, or even confused. "It was a lovely day" is abstract, but "The sun shone brightly, the sky was blue, the air felt warm, and a gentle breeze wafted across my skin" is concrete. "Ms. Couch was a good teacher" uses abstract language, giving only a general idea of the writer's opinion. But "Ms. Couch is excellent at helping us take our ideas and turn them into good essays and stories" uses concrete language, giving more specific examples of what makes Ms. Couch a good teacher. "I like writing poems but not essays" gives readers a general idea that the student prefers one genre over another, but not why. But when reading, "I like writing short poems with rhythm and rhyme, but I hate writing five-page essays that go on and on about the same ideas," readers understand that the student prefers the brevity, rhyme, and meter of short poetry over the length and redundancy of longer prose.

AUTOBIOGRAPHICAL NARRATIVES

Autobiographical narratives are narratives written by an author about an event or period in their life. Autobiographical narratives are written from one person's perspective, in first person, and often include the author's thoughts and feelings alongside their description of the event or period. Structure, style, or theme varies between different autobiographical narratives, since each narrative is personal and specific to its author and his or her experience.

REFLECTIVE ESSAY

A less common type of essay is the reflective essay. **Reflective essays** allow the author to reflect, or think back, on an experience and analyze what they recall. They should consider what they learned from the experience, what they could have done differently, what would have helped them during the experience, or anything else that they have realized from looking back on the experience. Reflection essays incorporate both objective reflection on one's own actions and subjective explanation of thoughts and feelings. These essays can be written for a number of experiences in a formal or informal context.

JOURNALS AND DIARIES

A **journal** is a personal account of events, experiences, feelings, and thoughts. Many people write journals to express their feelings and thoughts or to help them process experiences they have had. Since journals are **private documents** not meant to be shared with others, writers may not be concerned with grammar, spelling, or other mechanics. However, authors may write journals that they expect or hope to publish someday; in this case, they not only express their thoughts and feelings and process their experiences, but they also attend to their craft in writing them. Some authors compose journals to record a particular time period or a series of related events, such as a cancer diagnosis, treatment, surviving the disease, and how these experiences have changed or affected them. Other experiences someone might include in a journal are recovering from addiction, journeys of spiritual exploration and discovery, time spent in another country, or anything else someone wants to personally document. Journaling can also be therapeutic, as some people use journals to work through feelings of grief over loss or to wrestle with big decisions.

EXAMPLES OF DIARIES IN LITERATURE

The Diary of a Young Girl by Dutch Jew Anne Frank (1947) contains her life-affirming, nonfictional diary entries from 1942-1944 while her family hid in an attic from World War II's genocidal Nazis. *Go Ask Alice* (1971) by Beatrice Sparks is a cautionary, fictional novel in the form of diary entries by Alice, an unhappy, rebellious teen who takes LSD, runs away from home and lives with hippies, and eventually returns home. Frank's writing reveals an intelligent, sensitive, insightful girl, raised by intellectual European parents—a girl who believes in the goodness of human nature despite surrounding atrocities. Alice, influenced by early 1970s counterculture, becomes less optimistic. However, similarities can be found between them: Frank dies in a Nazi concentration camp while the fictitious Alice dies from a drug overdose. Both young women are also unable to escape their surroundings. Additionally, adolescent searches for personal identity are evident in both books.

> **Review Video: Journals, Diaries, Letters, and Blogs**
> Visit mometrix.com/academy and enter code: 432845

LETTERS

Letters are messages written to other people. In addition to letters written between individuals, some writers compose letters to the editors of newspapers, magazines, and other publications, while some write "Open Letters" to be published and read by the general public. Open letters, while intended for everyone to read, may also identify a group of people or a single person whom the letter directly addresses. In everyday use, the most-used forms are business letters and personal or friendly letters. Both kinds share common elements: business or personal letterhead stationery; the writer's return address at the top; the addressee's address next; a salutation, such as "Dear [name]" or some similar opening greeting, followed by a colon in business letters or a comma in personal letters; the body of the letter, with paragraphs as indicated; and a closing, like "Sincerely/Cordially/Best regards/etc." or "Love," in intimate personal letters.

EARLY LETTERS

The Greek word for "letter" is *epistolē*, which became the English word "epistle." The earliest letters were called epistles, including the New Testament's epistles from the apostles to the Christians. In ancient Egypt, the writing curriculum in scribal schools included the epistolary genre. Epistolary novels frame a story in the form of letters. Examples of noteworthy epistolary novels include:

- *Pamela* (1740), by 18th-century English novelist Samuel Richardson
- *Shamela* (1741), Henry Fielding's satire of *Pamela* that mocked epistolary writing.
- *Lettres persanes* (1721) by French author Montesquieu
- *The Sorrows of Young Werther* (1774) by German author Johann Wolfgang von Goethe
- *The History of Emily Montague* (1769), the first Canadian novel, by Frances Brooke
- *Dracula* (1897) by Bram Stoker
- *Frankenstein* (1818) by Mary Shelley
- *The Color Purple* (1982) by Alice Walker

BLOGS

The word "blog" is derived from "weblog" and refers to writing done exclusively on the internet. Readers of reputable newspapers expect quality content and layouts that enable easy reading. These expectations also apply to blogs. For example, readers can easily move visually from line to line when columns are narrow, while overly wide columns cause readers to lose their places. Blogs must also be posted with layouts enabling online readers to follow them easily. However, because the way people read on computer, tablet, and smartphone screens differs from how they read print on paper, formatting and writing blog content is more complex than writing newspaper articles. Two major principles are the bases for blog-writing rules: The first is while readers of print articles skim to estimate their length, online they must scroll down to scan; therefore, blog layouts need more subheadings, graphics, and other indications of what information follows. The second is onscreen reading can be harder on the eyes than reading printed paper, so legibility is crucial in blogs.

RULES AND RATIONALES FOR WRITING BLOGS

1. Format all posts for smooth page layout and easy scanning.
2. Column width should not be too wide, as larger lines of text can be difficult to read
3. Headings and subheadings separate text visually, enable scanning or skimming, and encourage continued reading.
4. Bullet-pointed or numbered lists enable quick information location and scanning.
5. Punctuation is critical, so beginners should use shorter sentences until confident in their knowledge of punctuation rules.
6. Blog paragraphs should be far shorter—two to six sentences each—than paragraphs written on paper to enable "chunking" because reading onscreen is more difficult.
7. Sans-serif fonts are usually clearer than serif fonts, and larger font sizes are better.
8. Highlight important material and draw attention with **boldface**, but avoid overuse. Avoid hard-to-read *italics* and ALL CAPITALS.
9. Include enough blank spaces: overly busy blogs tire eyes and brains. Images not only break up text but also emphasize and enhance text and can attract initial reader attention.
10. Use background colors judiciously to avoid distracting the eye or making it difficult to read.
11. Be consistent throughout posts, since people read them in different orders.
12. Tell a story with a beginning, middle, and end.

SPECIALIZED MODES OF WRITING

EDITORIALS

Editorials are articles in newspapers, magazines, and other serial publications. Editorials express an opinion or belief belonging to the majority of the publication's leadership. This opinion or belief generally refers to a specific issue, topic, or event. These articles are authored by a member, or a small number of members, of the publication's leadership and are often written to affect their readers, such as persuading them to adopt a stance or take a particular action.

RESUMES

Resumes are brief, but formal, documents that outline an individual's experience in a certain area. Resumes are most often used for job applications. Such resumes will list the applicant's work experience, certification, and achievements or qualifications related to the position. Resumes should only include the most pertinent information. They should also use strategic formatting to highlight the applicant's most impressive experiences and achievements, to ensure the document can be read quickly and easily, and to eliminate both visual clutter and excessive negative space.

REPORTS

Reports summarize the results of research, new methodology, or other developments in an academic or professional context. Reports often include details about methodology and outside influences and factors. However, a report should focus primarily on the results of the research or development. Reports are objective and deliver information efficiently, sacrificing style for clear and effective communication.

MEMORANDA

A memorandum, also called a memo, is a formal method of communication used in professional settings. Memoranda are printed documents that include a heading listing the sender and their job title, the recipient and their job title, the date, and a specific subject line. Memoranda often include an introductory section explaining the reason and context for the memorandum. Next, a memorandum includes a section with details relevant to the topic. Finally, the memorandum will conclude with a paragraph that politely and clearly defines the sender's expectations of the recipient.

CHAPTER QUIZ

1. The Greek word *epistolē* means:

    a. Pistol.
    b. Epistaxis.
    c. Essay.
    d. Letter.

2. What are the two major principles used to create an orderly blog?

    a. The content must be interesting with various fonts and color combinations, and it should take less than 10 minutes to read in its entirety.
    b. Blog layouts need more subheadings, graphics, and other indications of what information follows, and the content must be interesting with various fonts and color combinations.
    c. Legibility is crucial because onscreen reading is hard on the eyes, and it should take less than 10 minutes to read in its entirety.
    d. Blog layouts need more subheadings, graphics, and other indications of what information follows, and legibility is crucial because onscreen reading is hard on the eyes.

CHAPTER QUIZ ANSWER KEY

1. D: The Greek word for "letter" is *epistolē*, which became the English word "epistle." The earliest letters were called epistles, including the New Testament's epistles from the apostles to the Christians. In ancient Egypt, the writing curriculum in scribal schools included the epistolary genre. Epistolary novels frame a story in the form of letters.

2. D: There are two major principles that form the basis for blog-writing rules. The first is that while readers of print can skim articles to estimate their length, they must scroll down to scan something published online, meaning that blog layouts need more subheadings, graphics, and other indications of what information follows. The second principle is that onscreen reading can be harder on the eyes than reading printed paper, so legibility is crucial in blogs.

Verbal Reasoning

Informational Texts

TEXT FEATURES IN INFORMATIONAL TEXTS

The **title of a text** gives readers some idea of its content. The **table of contents** is a list near the beginning of a text, showing the book's sections and chapters and their coinciding page numbers. This gives readers an overview of the whole text and helps them find specific chapters easily. An **appendix**, at the back of the book or document, includes important information that is not present in the main text. Also at the back, an **index** lists the book's important topics alphabetically with their page numbers to help readers find them easily. **Glossaries**, usually found at the backs of books, list technical terms alphabetically with their definitions to aid vocabulary learning and comprehension. Boldface print is used to emphasize certain words, often identifying words included in the text's glossary where readers can look up their definitions. **Headings** separate sections of text and show the topic of each. **Subheadings** divide subject headings into smaller, more specific categories to help readers organize information. **Footnotes**, at the bottom of the page, give readers more information, such as citations or links. **Bullet points** list items separately, making facts and ideas easier to see and understand. A **sidebar** is a box of information to one side of the main text giving additional information, often on a more focused or in-depth example of a topic.

Illustrations and **photographs** are pictures that visually emphasize important points in text. The captions below the illustrations explain what those images show. Charts and tables are visual forms of information that make something easier to understand quickly. Diagrams are drawings that show relationships or explain a process. Graphs visually show the relationships among multiple sets of information plotted along vertical and horizontal axes. Maps show geographical information visually to help readers understand the relative locations of places covered in the text. Timelines are visual graphics that show historical events in chronological order to help readers see their sequence.

> **Review Video: Informative Text**
> Visit mometrix.com/academy and enter code: 924964

LANGUAGE USE

LITERAL AND FIGURATIVE LANGUAGE

As in fictional literature, informational text also uses both **literal language**, which means just what it says, and **figurative language**, which imparts more than literal meaning. For example, an informational text author might use a simile or direct comparison, such as writing that a racehorse "ran like the wind." Informational text authors also use metaphors or implied comparisons, such as "the cloud of the Great Depression." Imagery may also appear in informational texts to increase the reader's understanding of ideas and concepts discussed in the text.

EXPLICIT AND IMPLICIT INFORMATION

When informational text states something explicitly, the reader is told by the author exactly what is meant, which can include the author's interpretation or perspective of events. For example, a professor writes, "I have seen students go into an absolute panic just because they weren't able to complete the exam in the time they were allotted." This explicitly tells the reader that the students were afraid, and by using the words "just because," the writer indicates their fear was exaggerated out of proportion relative to what happened. However, another professor writes, "I have had

81

students come to me, their faces drained of all color, saying 'We weren't able to finish the exam.'" This is an example of implicit meaning: the second writer did not state explicitly that the students were panicked. Instead, he wrote a description of their faces being "drained of all color." From this description, the reader can infer that the students were so frightened that their faces paled.

> **Review Video: Explicit and Implicit Information**
> Visit mometrix.com/academy and enter code: 735771

TECHNICAL LANGUAGE

Technical language is more impersonal than literary and vernacular language. Passive voice makes the tone impersonal. For example, instead of writing, "We found this a central component of protein metabolism," scientists write, "This was found a central component of protein metabolism." While science professors have traditionally instructed students to avoid active voice because it leads to first-person ("I" and "we") usage, science editors today find passive voice dull and weak. Many journal articles combine both. Tone in technical science writing should be detached, concise, and professional. While one may normally write, "This chemical has to be available for proteins to be digested," professionals write technically, "The presence of this chemical is required for the enzyme to break the covalent bonds of proteins." The use of technical language appeals to both technical and non-technical audiences by displaying the author or speaker's understanding of the subject and suggesting their credibility regarding the message they are communicating.

TECHNICAL MATERIAL FOR NON-TECHNICAL READERS

Writing about **technical subjects** for **non-technical readers** differs from writing for colleagues because authors place more importance on delivering a critical message than on imparting the maximum technical content possible. Technical authors also must assume that non-technical audiences do not have the expertise to comprehend extremely scientific or technical messages, concepts, and terminology. They must resist the temptation to impress audiences with their scientific knowledge and expertise and remember that their primary purpose is to communicate a message that non-technical readers will understand, feel, and respond to. Non-technical and technical styles include similarities. Both should formally cite any references or other authors' work utilized in the text. Both must follow intellectual property and copyright regulations. This includes the author's protecting his or her own rights, or a public domain statement, as he or she chooses.

> **Review Video: Technical Passages**
> Visit mometrix.com/academy and enter code: 478923

NON-TECHNICAL AUDIENCES

Writers of technical or scientific material may need to write for many non-technical audiences. Some readers have no technical or scientific background, and those who do may not be in the same field as the authors. Government and corporate policymakers and budget managers need technical information they can understand for decision-making. Citizens affected by technology or science are a different audience. Non-governmental organizations can encompass many of the preceding groups. Elementary and secondary school programs also need non-technical language for presenting technical subject matter. Additionally, technical authors will need to use non-technical language when collecting consumer responses to surveys, presenting scientific or para-scientific material to the public, writing about the history of science, and writing about science and technology in developing countries.

Use of Everyday Language

Authors of technical information sometimes must write using non-technical language that readers outside their disciplinary fields can comprehend. They should use not only non-technical terms, but also normal, everyday language to accommodate readers whose native language is different than the language the text is written in. For example, instead of writing that "eustatic changes like thermal expansion are causing hazardous conditions in the littoral zone," an author would do better to write that "a rising sea level is threatening the coast." When technical terms cannot be avoided, authors should also define or explain them using non-technical language. Although authors must cite references and acknowledge their use of others' work, they should avoid the kinds of references or citations that they would use in scientific journals—unless they reinforce author messages. They should not use endnotes, footnotes, or any other complicated referential techniques because non-technical journal publishers usually do not accept them. Including high-resolution illustrations, photos, maps, or satellite images and incorporating multimedia into digital publications will enhance non-technical writing about technical subjects. Technical authors may publish using non-technical language in e-journals, trade journals, specialty newsletters, and daily newspapers.

Making Inferences About Informational Text

With informational text, reader comprehension depends not only on recalling important statements and details, but also on reader inferences based on examples and details. Readers add information from the text to what they already know to draw inferences about the text. These inferences help the readers to fill in the information that the text does not explicitly state, enabling them to understand the text better. When reading a nonfictional autobiography or biography, for example, the most appropriate inferences might concern the events in the book, the actions of the subject of the autobiography or biography, and the message the author means to convey. When reading a nonfictional expository (informational) text, the reader would best draw inferences about problems and their solutions, and causes and their effects. When reading a nonfictional persuasive text, the reader will want to infer ideas supporting the author's message and intent.

Structures or Organizational Patterns in Informational Texts

Informational text can be **descriptive**, appealing to the five senses and answering the questions what, who, when, where, and why. Another method of structuring informational text is sequence and order. **Chronological** texts relate events in the sequence that they occurred, from start to finish, while how-to texts organize information into a series of instructions in the sequence in which the steps should be followed. **Comparison-contrast** structures of informational text describe various ideas to their readers by pointing out how things or ideas are similar and how they are different. **Cause and effect** structures of informational text describe events that occurred and identify the causes or reasons that those events occurred. **Problem and solution** structures of informational texts introduce and describe problems and offer one or more solutions for each problem described.

Determining an Informational Author's Purpose

Informational authors' purposes are why they write texts. Readers must determine authors' motivations and goals. Readers gain greater insight into a text by considering the author's motivation. This develops critical reading skills. Readers perceive writing as a person's voice, not simply printed words. Uncovering author motivations and purposes empowers readers to know what to expect from the text, read for relevant details, evaluate authors and their work critically, and respond effectively to the motivations and persuasions of the text. The main idea of a text is what the reader is supposed to understand from reading it; the purpose of the text is why the

author has written it and what the author wants readers to do with its information. Authors state some purposes clearly, while other purposes may be unstated but equally significant. When stated purposes contradict other parts of a text, the author may have a hidden agenda. Readers can better evaluate a text's effectiveness, whether they agree or disagree with it, and why they agree or disagree through identifying unstated author purposes.

IDENTIFYING AUTHOR'S POINT OF VIEW OR PURPOSE

In some informational texts, readers find it easy to identify the author's point of view and purpose, such as when the author explicitly states his or her position and reason for writing. But other texts are more difficult, either because of the content or because the authors give neutral or balanced viewpoints. This is particularly true in scientific texts, in which authors may state the purpose of their research in the report, but never state their point of view except by interpreting evidence or data.

To analyze text and identify point of view or purpose, readers should ask themselves the following four questions:

1. With what main point or idea does this author want to persuade readers to agree?
2. How does this author's word choice affect the way that readers consider this subject?
3. How do this author's choices of examples and facts affect the way that readers consider this subject?
4. What is it that this author wants to accomplish by writing this text?

> **Review Video: <u>Understanding the Author's Intent</u>**
> Visit mometrix.com/academy and enter code: 511819
>
> **Review Video: <u>Author's Position</u>**
> Visit mometrix.com/academy and enter code: 827954

EVALUATING ARGUMENTS MADE BY INFORMATIONAL TEXT WRITERS

When evaluating an informational text, the first step is to identify the argument's conclusion. Then identify the author's premises that support the conclusion. Try to paraphrase premises for clarification and make the conclusion and premises fit. List all premises first, sequentially numbered, then finish with the conclusion. Identify any premises or assumptions not stated by the author but required for the stated premises to support the conclusion. Read word assumptions sympathetically, as the author might. Evaluate whether premises reasonably support the conclusion. For inductive reasoning, the reader should ask if the premises are true, if they support the conclusion, and if so, how strongly. For deductive reasoning, the reader should ask if the argument is valid or invalid. If all premises are true, then the argument is valid unless the conclusion can be false. If it can, then the argument is invalid. An invalid argument can be made valid through alterations such as the addition of needed premises.

USE OF RHETORIC IN INFORMATIONAL TEXTS

There are many ways authors can support their claims, arguments, beliefs, ideas, and reasons for writing in informational texts. For example, authors can appeal to readers' sense of **logic** by communicating their reasoning through a carefully sequenced series of logical steps to help "prove" the points made. Authors can appeal to readers' **emotions** by using descriptions and words that evoke feelings of sympathy, sadness, anger, righteous indignation, hope, happiness, or any other emotion to reinforce what they express and share with their audience. Authors may appeal to the **moral** or **ethical values** of readers by using words and descriptions that can convince readers that

something is right or wrong. By relating personal anecdotes, authors can supply readers with more accessible, realistic examples of points they make, as well as appealing to their emotions. They can provide supporting evidence by reporting case studies. They can also illustrate their points by making analogies to which readers can better relate.

CHAPTER QUIZ

1. Which of the following is the first step in evaluating an informational text?

    a. Read word assumptions sympathetically
    b. List all premises sequentially
    c. Determine if the premises are true
    d. Identify the argument's conclusion

2. Which of the following is NOT considered a type of appeal for an author to use?

    a. Logic
    b. Ethics
    c. Emotions
    d. Imagination

CHAPTER QUIZ ANSWER KEY

1. D: When evaluating an informational text, the first step is to identify the argument's conclusion. After that comes identifying the author's premises that support the conclusion. The reader should try to paraphrase premises for clarification and make the conclusion and premises fit. List all premises first, sequentially numbered, then finish with the conclusion. Identify any premises or assumptions not stated by the author but required for the stated premises to support the conclusion. Read word assumptions sympathetically, as the author might. Evaluate whether premises reasonably support the conclusion. For inductive reasoning, the reader should ask if the premises are true, if they support the conclusion, and how strong that support is. For deductive reasoning, the reader should ask if the argument is valid or invalid. If all premises are true, then the argument is valid unless the conclusion can be false. If it can, then the argument is invalid. An invalid argument can be made valid through alterations such as the addition of needed premises.

2. D: There are many ways authors can support their claims, arguments, beliefs, ideas, and reasons for writing in informational texts. For example, authors can appeal to readers' sense of logic by communicating their reasoning through a carefully sequenced series of logical steps to support their positions. Authors can appeal to readers' emotions by using descriptions and words that evoke feelings of sympathy, sadness, anger, righteous indignation, hope, happiness, or any other emotion to reinforce what they express and share with their audience. Authors may appeal to the moral or ethical values of readers by using words and descriptions that can convince readers that something is right or wrong. By relating personal anecdotes, authors can appeal to readers' emotions and supply them with more accessible, realistic examples of points they make. They can provide supporting evidence by reporting case studies. They can also illustrate their points by making analogies to which readers can better relate.

Persuasive Techniques

PERSUASIVE TECHNIQUES

To **appeal using reason**, writers present logical arguments, such as using "If... then... because" statements. To **appeal to emotions**, authors may ask readers how they would feel about something or to put themselves in another's place, present their argument as one that will make the audience feel good, or tell readers how they should feel. To **appeal to character**, **morality**, or **ethics**, authors present their points to readers as the right or most moral choices. Authors cite expert opinions to show readers that someone very knowledgeable about the subject or viewpoint agrees with the author's claims. **Testimonials**, usually via anecdotes or quotations regarding the author's subject, help build the audience's trust in an author's message through positive support from ordinary people. **Bandwagon appeals** claim that everybody else agrees with the author's argument and persuade readers to conform and agree, also. Authors **appeal to greed** by presenting their choice as cheaper, free, or more valuable for less cost. They **appeal to laziness** by presenting their views as more convenient, easy, or relaxing. Authors also anticipate potential objections and argue against them before audiences think of them, thereby depicting those objections as weak.

Authors can use **comparisons** like analogies, similes, and metaphors to persuade audiences. For example, a writer might represent excessive expenses as "hemorrhaging" money, which the author's recommended solution will stop. Authors can use negative word connotations to make some choices unappealing to readers, and positive word connotations to make others more appealing. Using **humor** can relax readers and garner their agreement. However, writers must take care: ridiculing opponents can be a successful strategy for appealing to readers who already agree with the author, but can backfire by angering other readers. **Rhetorical questions** need no answer, but create effect that can force agreement, such as asking the question, "Wouldn't you rather be paid more than less?" **Generalizations** persuade readers by being impossible to disagree with. Writers can easily make generalizations that appear to support their viewpoints, like saying, "We all want peace, not war" regarding more specific political arguments. **Transfer** and **association** persuade by example: if advertisements show attractive actors enjoying their products, audiences imagine they will experience the same. **Repetition** can also sometimes effectively persuade audiences.

> **Review Video: Using Rhetorical Strategies for Persuasion**
> Visit mometrix.com/academy and enter code: 302658

CLASSICAL AUTHOR APPEALS

In his *On Rhetoric,* ancient Greek philosopher Aristotle defined three basic types of appeal used in writing, which he called *pathos, ethos,* and *logos.* **Pathos** means suffering or experience and refers to appeals to the emotions (the English word *pathetic* comes from this root). Writing that is meant to entertain audiences, by making them either happy, as with comedy, or sad, as with tragedy, uses *pathos.* Aristotle's *Poetics* states that evoking the emotions of terror and pity is one of the criteria for writing tragedy. **Ethos** means character and connotes ideology (the English word *ethics* comes from this root). Writing that appeals to credibility, based on academic, professional, or personal merit, uses *ethos.* **Logos** means "I say" and refers to a plea, opinion, expectation, word or speech, account, opinion, or reason (the English word *logic* comes from this root.) Aristotle used it to mean persuasion that appeals to the audience through reasoning and logic to influence their opinions.

CRITICAL EVALUATION OF EFFECTIVENESS OF PERSUASIVE METHODS

First, readers should identify the author's **thesis**—what he or she argues for or against. They should consider the argument's content and the author's reason for presenting it. Does the author offer **solutions** to problems raised? If so, are they realistic? Note all central ideas and evidence supporting the author's thesis. Research any unfamiliar subjects or vocabulary. Readers should then outline or summarize the work in their own words. Identify which types of appeals the author uses. Readers should evaluate how well the author communicated meaning from the reader's perspective: Did they respond to emotional appeals with anger, concern, happiness, etc.? If so, why? Decide if the author's reasoning sufficed for changing the reader's mind. Determine whether the content and presentation were accurate, cohesive, and clear. Readers should also ask themselves whether they found the author believable or not, and why or why not.

EVALUATING AN ARGUMENT

Argumentative and persuasive passages take a stand on a debatable issue, seek to explore all sides of the issue, and find the best possible solution. Argumentative and persuasive passages should not be combative or abusive. The word *argument* may remind you of two or more people shouting at each other and walking away in anger. However, an argumentative or persuasive passage should be a calm and reasonable presentation of an author's ideas for others to consider. When an author writes reasonable arguments, his or her goal is not to win or have the last word. Instead, authors want to reveal current understanding of the question at hand and suggest a solution to a problem. The purpose of argument and persuasion in a free society is to reach the best solution.

EVIDENCE

The term **text evidence** refers to information that supports a main point or minor points and can help lead the reader to a conclusion about the text's credibility. Information used as text evidence is precise, descriptive, and factual. A main point is often followed by supporting details that provide evidence to back up a claim. For example, a passage may include the claim that winter occurs during opposite months in the Northern and Southern hemispheres. Text evidence for this claim may include examples of countries where winter occurs in opposite months. Stating that the tilt of the Earth as it rotates around the sun causes winter to occur at different times in separate hemispheres is another example of text evidence. Text evidence can come from common knowledge, but it is also valuable to include text evidence from credible, relevant outside sources.

> **Review Video: Textual Evidence**
> Visit mometrix.com/academy and enter code: 486236

Evidence that supports the thesis and additional arguments needs to be provided. Most arguments must be supported by facts or statistics. A fact is something that is known with certainty, has been verified by several independent individuals, and can be proven to be true. In addition to facts, examples and illustrations can support an argument by adding an emotional component. With this component, you persuade readers in ways that facts and statistics cannot. The emotional component is effective when used alongside objective information that can be confirmed.

CREDIBILITY

The text used to support an argument can be the argument's downfall if the text is not credible. A text is **credible**, or believable, when its author is knowledgeable and objective, or unbiased. The author's motivations for writing the text play a critical role in determining the credibility of the text and must be evaluated when assessing that credibility. Reports written about the ozone layer by an environmental scientist and a hairdresser will have a different level of credibility.

> **Review Video: Author Credibility**
> Visit mometrix.com/academy and enter code: 827257

APPEAL TO EMOTION

Sometimes, authors will appeal to the reader's emotion in an attempt to persuade or to distract the reader from the weakness of the argument. For instance, the author may try to inspire the pity of the reader by delivering a heart-rending story. An author also might use the bandwagon approach, in which he suggests that his opinion is correct because it is held by the majority. Some authors resort to name-calling, in which insults and harsh words are delivered to the opponent in an attempt to distract. In advertising, a common appeal is the celebrity testimonial, in which a famous person endorses a product. Of course, the fact that a famous person likes something should not really mean anything to the reader. These and other emotional appeals are usually evidence of poor reasoning and a weak argument.

> **Review Video: <u>Emotional Language in Literature</u>**
> Visit mometrix.com/academy and enter code: 759390

COUNTER ARGUMENTS

When authors give both sides to the argument, they build trust with their readers. As a reader, you should start with an undecided or neutral position. If an author presents only his or her side to the argument, then they are not exhibiting credibility and are weakening their argument.

Building common ground with readers can be effective for persuading neutral, skeptical, or opposed readers. Sharing values with undecided readers can allow people to switch positions without giving up what they feel is important. People who may oppose a position need to feel that they can change their minds without betraying who they are as a person. This appeal to having an open mind can be a powerful tool in arguing a position without antagonizing other views. Objections can be countered on a point-by-point basis or in a summary paragraph. Be mindful of how an author points out flaws in counter arguments. If they are unfair to the other side of the argument, then you should lose trust with the author.

RHETORICAL DEVICES

- An **anecdote** is a brief story authors may relate to their argument, which can illustrate their points in a more real and relatable way.
- **Aphorisms** concisely state common beliefs and may rhyme. For example, Benjamin Franklin's "Early to bed and early to rise / Makes a man healthy, wealthy, and wise" is an aphorism.
- **Allusions** refer to literary or historical figures to impart symbolism to a thing or person and to create reader resonance. In John Steinbeck's *Of Mice and Men,* protagonist George's last name is Milton. This alludes to John Milton, who wrote *Paradise Lost*, and symbolizes George's eventual loss of his dream.
- **Satire** exaggerates, ridicules, or pokes fun at human flaws or ideas, as in the works of Jonathan Swift and Mark Twain.
- A **parody** is a form of satire that imitates another work to ridicule its topic or style.
- A **paradox** is a statement that is true despite appearing contradictory.
- **Hyperbole** is overstatement using exaggerated language.
- An **oxymoron** combines seeming contradictions, such as "deafening silence."
- **Analogies** compare two things that share common elements.
- **Similes** (stated comparisons using the words *like* or *as*) and **metaphors** (stated comparisons that do not use *like* or *as*) are considered forms of analogy.
- When using logic to reason with audiences, **syllogism** refers either to deductive reasoning or a deceptive, very sophisticated, or subtle argument.

- **Deductive reasoning** moves from general to specific, **inductive reasoning** from specific to general.
- **Diction** is author word choice that establishes tone and effect.
- **Understatement** achieves effects like contrast or irony by downplaying or describing something more subtly than warranted.
- **Chiasmus** uses parallel clauses, the second reversing the order of the first. Examples include T. S. Eliot's "Has the Church failed mankind, or has mankind failed the Church?" and John F. Kennedy's "Ask not what your country can do for you; ask what you can do for your country."
- **Anaphora** regularly repeats a word or phrase at the beginnings of consecutive clauses or phrases to add emphasis to an idea. A classic example of anaphora was Winston Churchill's emphasis of determination: "[W]e shall fight on the beaches, we shall fight on the landing grounds, we shall fight in the fields and in the streets, we shall fight in the hills; we shall never surrender..."

CHAPTER QUIZ

1. Which of the following rhetorical devices exaggerates, ridicules, or pokes fun at human flaws or ideas?

   a. Allusions
   b. Satire
   c. Parody
   d. Hyperbole

2. An author arguing that his point is correct because everybody else already agrees with it is an example of which persuasive technique?

   a. Appeal to laziness
   b. Bandwagon appeal
   c. Testimonials
   d. Generalizations

CHAPTER QUIZ ANSWER KEY

1. B: Rhetorical devices:

- An anecdote is a brief story authors may relate to their argument, which can illustrate their points in a more real and relatable way.
- Aphorisms concisely state common beliefs and may rhyme. For example, Benjamin Franklin's "Early to bed and early to rise / Makes a man healthy, wealthy, and wise" is an aphorism.
- Allusions refer to literary or historical figures to impart symbolism to a thing or person and to create reader resonance. In John Steinbeck's *Of Mice and Men*, protagonist George's last name is Milton. This alludes to John Milton, who wrote *Paradise Lost*, and symbolizes George's eventual loss of his dream.
- Satire exaggerates, ridicules, or pokes fun at human flaws or ideas, as in the works of Jonathan Swift and Mark Twain.
- A parody is a form of satire that imitates another work to ridicule its topic or style.
- A paradox is a statement that is true despite appearing contradictory.
- Hyperbole is overstatement using exaggerated language.
- An oxymoron combines seeming contradictions, such as "deafening silence."
- Analogies compare two things that share common elements.
- Similes (stated comparisons using the words *like* or *as*) and metaphors (stated comparisons that do not use *like* or *as*) are considered forms of analogy.
- When using logic to reason with audiences, syllogism refers either to deductive reasoning or a deceptive, very sophisticated, or subtle argument.
- Deductive reasoning moves from general to specific, while inductive reasoning moves from specific to general.
- Diction is author word choice that establishes tone and effect.
- Understatement achieves effects like contrast or irony by downplaying or describing something more subtly than warranted.
- Chiasmus uses parallel clauses, with the second clause reversing the order of the first. Examples include T. S. Eliot's "Has the Church failed mankind, or has mankind failed the Church?" and John F. Kennedy's "Ask not what your country can do for you—ask what you can do for your country."

- Anaphora regularly repeats a word or phrase at the beginnings of consecutive clauses or phrases to add emphasis to an idea. A classic example of anaphora was Winston Churchill's emphasis of determination: "[W]e shall fight on the beaches, we shall fight on the landing grounds, we shall fight in the fields and in the streets, we shall fight in the hills; we shall never surrender..."

2. B: Bandwagon appeals claim that everybody else agrees with the author's argument and thus try to persuade readers to conform and agree as well.

Arguments and Logical Errors

AUTHOR'S ARGUMENT IN ARGUMENTATIVE WRITING

In argumentative writing, the argument is a belief, position, or opinion that the author wants to convince readers to believe as well. For the first step, readers should identify the **issue**. Some issues are controversial, meaning people disagree about them. Gun control, foreign policy, and the death penalty are all controversial issues. The next step is to determine the **author's position** on the issue. That position or viewpoint constitutes the author's argument. Readers should then identify the **author's assumptions**: things he or she accepts, believes, or takes for granted without needing proof. Inaccurate or illogical assumptions produce flawed arguments and can mislead readers. Readers should identify what kinds of **supporting evidence** the author offers, such as research results, personal observations or experiences, case studies, facts, examples, expert testimony and opinions, and comparisons. Readers should decide how relevant this support is to the argument.

> **Review Video: Argumentative Writing**
> Visit mometrix.com/academy and enter code: 561544

EVALUATING AN AUTHOR'S ARGUMENT

The first three reader steps to **evaluate an author's argument** are to identify the **author's assumptions**, identify the **supporting evidence**, and decide **whether the evidence is relevant**. For example, if an author is not an expert on a particular topic, then that author's personal experience or opinion might not be relevant. The fourth step is to assess the **author's objectivity**. For example, consider whether the author introduces clear, understandable supporting evidence and facts to support the argument. The fifth step is evaluating whether the author's **argument is complete**. When authors give sufficient support for their arguments and also anticipate and respond effectively to opposing arguments or objections to their points, their arguments are complete. However, some authors omit information that could detract from their arguments. If instead they stated this information and refuted it, it would strengthen their arguments. The sixth step in evaluating an author's argumentative writing is to assess whether the **argument is valid**. Providing clear, logical reasoning makes an author's argument valid. Readers should ask themselves whether the author's points follow a sequence that makes sense, and whether each point leads to the next. The seventh step is to determine whether the author's **argument is credible**, meaning that it is convincing and believable. Arguments that are not valid are not credible, so step seven depends on step six. Readers should be mindful of their own biases as they evaluate and should not expect authors to conclusively prove their arguments, but rather to provide effective support and reason.

EVALUATING AN AUTHOR'S METHOD OF APPEAL

To evaluate the effectiveness of an appeal, it is important to consider the author's purpose for writing. Any appeals an author uses in their argument must be relevant to the argument's goal. For example, a writer that argues for the reclassification of Pluto, but primarily uses appeals to emotion, will not have an effective argument. This writer should focus on using appeals to logic and support their argument with provable facts. While most arguments should include appeals to logic, emotion, and credibility, some arguments only call for one or two of these types of appeal. Evidence can support an appeal, but the evidence must be relevant to truly strengthen the appeal's effectiveness. If the writer arguing for Pluto's reclassification uses the reasons for Jupiter's classification as evidence, their argument would be weak. This information may seem relevant because it is related to the classification of planets. However, this classification is highly dependent on the size of the celestial object, and Jupiter is significantly bigger than Pluto. This use of evidence

93

is illogical and does not support the appeal. Even when appropriate evidence and appeals are used, appeals and arguments lose their effectiveness when they create logical fallacies.

OPINIONS, FACTS, AND FALLACIES

Critical thinking skills are mastered through understanding various types of writing and the different purposes of authors can have for writing different passages. Every author writes for a purpose. When you understand their purpose and how they accomplish their goal, you will be able to analyze their writing and determine whether or not you agree with their conclusions.

Readers must always be aware of the difference between fact and opinion. A **fact** can be subjected to analysis and proven to be true. An **opinion**, on the other hand, is the author's personal thoughts or feelings and may not be altered by research or evidence. If the author writes that the distance from New York City to Boston is about two hundred miles, then he or she is stating a fact. If the author writes that New York City is too crowded, then he or she is giving an opinion because there is no objective standard for overpopulation. Opinions are often supported by facts. For instance, an author might use a comparison between the population density of New York City and that of other major American cities as evidence of an overcrowded population. An opinion supported by facts tends to be more convincing. On the other hand, when authors support their opinions with other opinions, readers should employ critical thinking and approach the argument with skepticism.

> **Review Video: Fact or Opinion**
> Visit mometrix.com/academy and enter code: 870899

RELIABLE SOURCES

When you have an argumentative passage, you need to be sure that facts are presented to the reader from **reliable sources**. An opinion is what the author thinks about a given topic. An opinion is not common knowledge or proven by expert sources, instead the information is the personal beliefs and thoughts of the author. To distinguish between fact and opinion, a reader needs to consider the type of source that is presenting information, the information that backs-up a claim, and the author's motivation to have a certain point-of-view on a given topic. For example, if a panel of scientists has conducted multiple studies on the effectiveness of taking a certain vitamin, then the results are more likely to be factual than those of a company that is selling a vitamin and simply claims that taking the vitamin can produce positive effects. The company is motivated to sell their product, and the scientists are using the scientific method to prove a theory. Remember, if you find sentences that contain phrases such as "I think...", then the statement is an opinion.

BIASES

In their attempts to persuade, writers often make mistakes in their thought processes and writing choices. These processes and choices are important to understand so you can make an informed decision about the author's credibility. Every author has a point of view, but authors demonstrate a **bias** when they ignore reasonable counterarguments or distort opposing viewpoints. A bias is evident whenever the author's claims are presented in a way that is unfair or inaccurate. Bias can be intentional or unintentional, but readers should be skeptical of the author's argument in either case. Remember that a biased author may still be correct. However, the author will be correct in spite of, not because of, his or her bias.

A **stereotype** is a bias applied specifically to a group of people or a place. Stereotyping is considered to be particularly abhorrent because it promotes negative, misleading generalizations

about people. Readers should be very cautious of authors who use stereotypes in their writing. These faulty assumptions typically reveal the author's ignorance and lack of curiosity.

> **Review Video: <u>Bias and Stereotype</u>**
> Visit mometrix.com/academy and enter code: 644829

CHAPTER QUIZ

1. Which of the following is NOT one of the first three steps of evaluating an author's argument?

    a. Identify the author's assumptions
    b. Identify the supporting evidence
    c. Evaluate if the author's argument is complete
    d. Decide if the supporting evidence is relevant

CHAPTER QUIZ ANSWER KEY

1. C: The first three reader steps to evaluate an author's argument are to identify the author's assumptions, identify the supporting evidence, and decide whether the evidence is relevant. For example, if an author is not an expert on a particular topic, then that author's personal experience or opinion might not be relevant. The fourth step is to assess the author's objectivity. For example, consider whether the author introduces clear, understandable supporting evidence and facts to support the argument. The fifth step is evaluating whether the author's argument is complete. When authors give sufficient support for their arguments and also anticipate and respond effectively to opposing arguments or objections to their points, their arguments are complete. However, some authors omit information that could detract from their arguments. If instead they stated this information and refuted it, it would likely strengthen their arguments. The sixth step in evaluating an author's argumentative writing is to assess whether the argument is valid. Providing clear, logical reasoning makes an author's argument valid. Readers should ask themselves whether the author's points follow a sequence that makes sense, and whether each point leads to the next. The seventh step is to determine whether the author's argument is credible, meaning that it is convincing and believable. Arguments that are not valid are not credible, so step seven depends on step six. Readers should be mindful of their own biases as they evaluate and should not expect authors to conclusively prove their arguments, but rather to provide effective support and reason.

Vocabulary and Word Relationships

SYNONYMS AND ANTONYMS

When you understand how words relate to each other, you will discover more in a passage. This is explained by understanding **synonyms** (e.g., words that mean the same thing) and **antonyms** (e.g., words that mean the opposite of one another). As an example, *dry* and *arid* are synonyms, and *dry* and *wet* are antonyms.

There are many pairs of words in English that can be considered synonyms, despite having slightly different definitions. For instance, the words *friendly* and *collegial* can both be used to describe a warm interpersonal relationship, and one would be correct to call them synonyms. However, *collegial* (kin to *colleague*) is often used in reference to professional or academic relationships, and *friendly* has no such connotation.

If the difference between the two words is too great, then they should not be called synonyms. *Hot* and *warm* are not synonyms because their meanings are too distinct. A good way to determine whether two words are synonyms is to substitute one word for the other word and verify that the meaning of the sentence has not changed. Substituting *warm* for *hot* in a sentence would convey a different meaning. Although warm and hot may seem close in meaning, warm generally means that the temperature is moderate, and hot generally means that the temperature is excessively high.

Antonyms are words with opposite meanings. *Light* and *dark*, *up* and *down*, *right* and *left*, *good* and *bad*: these are all sets of antonyms. Be careful to distinguish between antonyms and pairs of words that are simply different. *Black* and *gray*, for instance, are not antonyms because gray is not the opposite of black. *Black* and *white*, on the other hand, are antonyms.

Not every word has an antonym. For instance, many nouns do not. What would be the antonym of *chair*? During your exam, the questions related to antonyms are more likely to concern adjectives. You will recall that adjectives are words that describe a noun. Some common adjectives include *purple*, *fast*, *skinny*, and *sweet*. From those four adjectives, *purple* is the item that lacks a group of obvious antonyms.

> **Review Video: <u>What Are Synonyms and Antonyms?</u>**
> Visit mometrix.com/academy and enter code: 105612

AFFIXES

Affixes in the English language are morphemes that are added to words to create related but different words. Derivational affixes form new words based on and related to the original words. For example, the affix *–ness* added to the end of the adjective *happy* forms the noun *happiness*. Inflectional affixes form different grammatical versions of words. For example, the plural affix *–s* changes the singular noun *book* to the plural noun *books*, and the past tense affix *–ed* changes the present tense verb *look* to the past tense *looked.* Prefixes are affixes placed in front of words. For example, *heat* means to make hot; *preheat* means to heat in advance. Suffixes are affixes placed at the ends of words. The *happiness* example above contains the suffix *–ness.* Circumfixes add parts both before and after words, such as how *light* becomes *enlighten* with the prefix *en-* and the suffix *–en.* Interfixes create compound words via central affixes: *speed* and *meter* become *speedometer* via the interfix *–o–*.

> **Review Video: <u>Affixes</u>**
> Visit mometrix.com/academy and enter code: 782422

WORD ROOTS, PREFIXES, AND SUFFIXES TO HELP DETERMINE MEANINGS OF WORDS

Many English words were formed from combining multiple sources. For example, the Latin *habēre* means "to have," and the prefixes *in-* and *im-* mean a lack or prevention of something, as in *insufficient* and *imperfect*. Latin combined *in-* with *habēre* to form *inhibēre*, whose past participle was *inhibitus*. This is the origin of the English word *inhibit*, meaning to prevent from having. Hence by knowing the meanings of both the prefix and the root, one can decipher the word meaning. In Greek, the root *enkephalo-* refers to the brain. Many medical terms are based on this root, such as encephalitis and hydrocephalus. Understanding the prefix and suffix meanings (*-itis* means inflammation; *hydro-* means water) allows a person to deduce that encephalitis refers to brain inflammation and hydrocephalus refers to water (or other fluid) in the brain.

> **Review Video: <u>Determining Word Meanings</u>**
> Visit mometrix.com/academy and enter code: 894894
>
> **Review Video: <u>Root Words in English</u>**
> Visit mometrix.com/academy and enter code: 896380

PREFIXES

While knowing prefix meanings helps ESL and beginning readers learn new words, other readers take for granted the meanings of known words. However, prefix knowledge will also benefit them for determining meanings or definitions of unfamiliar words. For example, native English speakers and readers familiar with recipes know what *preheat* means. Knowing that *pre-* means in advance can also inform them that *presume* means to assume in advance, that *prejudice* means advance judgment, and that this understanding can be applied to many other words beginning with *pre-*. Knowing that the prefix *dis-* indicates opposition informs the meanings of words like *disbar, disagree, disestablish,* and many more. Knowing *dys-* means bad, impaired, abnormal, or difficult informs *dyslogistic, dysfunctional, dysphagia,* and *dysplasia.*

SUFFIXES

In English, certain suffixes generally indicate both that a word is a noun, and that the noun represents a state of being or quality. For example, *-ness* is commonly used to change an adjective into its noun form, as with *happy* and *happiness, nice* and *niceness,* and so on. The suffix *–tion* is commonly used to transform a verb into its noun form, as with *converse* and *conversation or move* and *motion.* Thus, if readers are unfamiliar with the second form of a word, knowing the meaning of the transforming suffix can help them determine meaning.

PREFIXES FOR NUMBERS

Prefix	Definition	Examples
bi-	two	bisect, biennial
mono-	one, single	monogamy, monologue
poly-	many	polymorphous, polygamous
semi-	half, partly	semicircle, semicolon
uni-	one	uniform, unity

Prefixes for Time, Direction, and Space

Prefix	Definition	Examples
a-	in, on, of, up, to	abed, afoot
ab-	from, away, off	abdicate, abjure
ad-	to, toward	advance, adventure
ante-	before, previous	antecedent, antedate
anti-	against, opposing	antipathy, antidote
cata-	down, away, thoroughly	catastrophe, cataclysm
circum-	around	circumspect, circumference
com-	with, together, very	commotion, complicate
contra-	against, opposing	contradict, contravene
de-	from	depart
dia-	through, across, apart	diameter, diagnose
dis-	away, off, down, not	dissent, disappear
epi-	upon	epilogue
ex-	out	extract, excerpt
hypo-	under, beneath	hypodermic, hypothesis
inter-	among, between	intercede, interrupt
intra-	within	intramural, intrastate
ob-	against, opposing	objection
per-	through	perceive, permit
peri-	around	periscope, perimeter
post-	after, following	postpone, postscript
pre-	before, previous	prevent, preclude
pro-	forward, in place of	propel, pronoun
retro-	back, backward	retrospect, retrograde
sub-	under, beneath	subjugate, substitute
super-	above, extra	supersede, supernumerary
trans-	across, beyond, over	transact, transport
ultra-	beyond, excessively	ultramodern, ultrasonic

Negative Prefixes

Prefix	Definition	Examples
a-	without, lacking	atheist, agnostic
in-	not, opposing	incapable, ineligible
non-	not	nonentity, nonsense
un-	not, reverse of	unhappy, unlock

Copyright © Mometrix Media. You have been licensed one copy of this document for personal use only. Any other reproduction or redistribution is strictly prohibited. All rights reserved. This content is provided for test preparation purposes only and does not imply an endorsement by Mometrix of any particular political, scientific, or religious point of view.

EXTRA PREFIXES

Prefix	Definition	Examples
belli-	war, warlike	bellicose
bene-	well, good	benefit, benefactor
equi-	equal	equivalent, equilibrium
for-	away, off, from	forget, forswear
fore-	previous	foretell, forefathers
homo-	same, equal	homogenized, homonym
hyper-	excessive, over	hypercritical, hypertension
in-	in, into	intrude, invade
magn-	large	magnitude, magnify
mal-	bad, poorly, not	malfunction, malpractice
mis-	bad, poorly, not	misspell, misfire
mor-	death	mortality, mortuary
neo-	new	Neolithic, neoconservative
omni-	all, everywhere	omniscient, omnivore
ortho-	right, straight	orthogonal, orthodox
over-	above	overbearing, oversight
pan-	all, entire	panorama, pandemonium
para-	beside, beyond	parallel, paradox
phil-	love, like	philosophy, philanthropic
prim-	first, early	primitive, primary
re-	backward, again	revoke, recur
sym-	with, together	sympathy, symphony
vis-	to see	visage, visible

Below is a list of common suffixes and their meanings:

ADJECTIVE SUFFIXES

Suffix	Definition	Examples
-able (-ible)	capable of being	toler*able*, ed*ible*
-esque	in the style of, like	picturesque, grotesque
-ful	filled with, marked by	thankful, zestful
-ific	make, cause	terrific, beatific
-ish	suggesting, like	churlish, childish
-less	lacking, without	hopeless, countless
-ous	marked by, given to	religious, riotous

NOUN SUFFIXES

Suffix	Definition	Examples
-acy	state, condition	accuracy, privacy
-ance	act, condition, fact	acceptance, vigilance
-ard	one that does excessively	drunkard, sluggard
-ation	action, state, result	occupation, starvation
-dom	state, rank, condition	serfdom, wisdom
-er (-or)	office, action	teacher, elevator, honor
-ess	feminine	waitress, duchess
-hood	state, condition	manhood, statehood
-ion	action, result, state	union, fusion
-ism	act, manner, doctrine	barbarism, socialism
-ist	worker, follower	monopolist, socialist
-ity (-ty)	state, quality, condition	acidity, civility, twenty
-ment	result, action	Refreshment
-ness	quality, state	greatness, tallness
-ship	position	internship, statesmanship
-sion (-tion)	state, result	revision, expedition
-th	act, state, quality	warmth, width
-tude	quality, state, result	magnitude, fortitude

VERB SUFFIXES

Suffix	Definition	Examples
-ate	having, showing	separate, desolate
-en	cause to be, become	deepen, strengthen
-fy	make, cause to have	glorify, fortify
-ize	cause to be, treat with	sterilize, mechanize

DENOTATIVE VS. CONNOTATIVE MEANING

The **denotative** meaning of a word is the literal meaning. The **connotative** meaning goes beyond the denotative meaning to include the emotional reaction that a word may invoke. The connotative meaning often takes the denotative meaning a step further due to associations the reader makes with the denotative meaning. Readers can differentiate between the denotative and connotative meanings by first recognizing how authors use each meaning. Most non-fiction, for example, is fact-based and authors do not use flowery, figurative language. The reader can assume that the writer is using the denotative meaning of words. In fiction, the author may use the connotative meaning. Readers can determine whether the author is using the denotative or connotative meaning of a word by implementing context clues.

> **Review Video: <u>Connotation and Denotation</u>**
> Visit mometrix.com/academy and enter code: 310092

NUANCES OF WORD MEANING RELATIVE TO CONNOTATION, DENOTATION, DICTION, AND USAGE

A word's denotation is simply its objective dictionary definition. However, its connotation refers to the subjective associations, often emotional, that specific words evoke in listeners and readers. Two or more words can have the same dictionary meaning, but very different connotations. Writers use diction (word choice) to convey various nuances of thought and emotion by selecting synonyms for other words that best communicate the associations they want to trigger for readers. For example, a car engine is naturally greasy; in this sense, "greasy" is a neutral term. But when a person's smile, appearance, or clothing is described as "greasy," it has a negative connotation. Some words have even gained additional or different meanings over time. For example, *awful* used to be used to describe things that evoked a sense of awe. When *awful* is separated into its root word, awe, and suffix, -ful, it can be understood to mean "full of awe." However, the word is now commonly used to describe things that evoke repulsion, terror, or another intense, negative reaction.

> **Review Video: Word Usage in Sentences**
> Visit mometrix.com/academy and enter code: 197863

CONTEXT CLUES

Readers of all levels will encounter words that they have either never seen or have encountered only on a limited basis. The best way to define a word in **context** is to look for nearby words that can assist in revealing the meaning of the word. For instance, unfamiliar nouns are often accompanied by examples that provide a definition. Consider the following sentence: *Dave arrived at the party in hilarious garb: a leopard-print shirt, buckskin trousers, and bright green sneakers.* If a reader was unfamiliar with the meaning of garb, he or she could read the examples (i.e., a leopard-print shirt, buckskin trousers, and high heels) and quickly determine that the word means *clothing*. Examples will not always be this obvious. Consider this sentence: *Parsley, lemon, and flowers were just a few of the items he used as garnishes.* Here, the word *garnishes* is exemplified by parsley, lemon, and flowers. Readers who have eaten in a variety of restaurants will probably be able to identify a garnish as something used to decorate a plate.

> **Review Video: Context Clues**
> Visit mometrix.com/academy and enter code: 613660

USING CONTRAST IN CONTEXT CLUES

In addition to looking at the context of a passage, readers can use contrast to define an unfamiliar word in context. In many sentences, the author will not describe the unfamiliar word directly; instead, he or she will describe the opposite of the unfamiliar word. Thus, you are provided with some information that will bring you closer to defining the word. Consider the following example: *Despite his intelligence, Hector's low brow and bad posture made him look obtuse.* The author writes that Hector's appearance does not convey intelligence. Therefore, *obtuse* must mean unintelligent. Here is another example: *Despite the horrible weather, we were beatific about our trip to Alaska.* The word *despite* indicates that the speaker's feelings were at odds with the weather. Since the weather is described as *horrible*, then *beatific* must mean something positive.

SUBSTITUTION TO FIND MEANING

In some cases, there will be very few contextual clues to help a reader define the meaning of an unfamiliar word. When this happens, one strategy that readers may employ is **substitution**. A good reader will brainstorm some possible synonyms for the given word, and he or she will substitute these words into the sentence. If the sentence and the surrounding passage continue to make sense, then the substitution has revealed at least some information about the unfamiliar word. Consider the sentence: *Frank's admonition rang in her ears as she climbed the mountain.* A reader unfamiliar with *admonition* might come up with some substitutions like *vow, promise, advice, complaint*, or *compliment*. All of these words make general sense of the sentence, though their meanings are diverse. However, this process has suggested that an admonition is some sort of message. The substitution strategy is rarely able to pinpoint a precise definition, but this process can be effective as a last resort.

Occasionally, you will be able to define an unfamiliar word by looking at the descriptive words in the context. Consider the following sentence: *Fred dragged the recalcitrant boy kicking and screaming up the stairs.* The words *dragged*, *kicking*, and *screaming* all suggest that the boy does not want to go up the stairs. The reader may assume that *recalcitrant* means something like unwilling or protesting. In this example, an unfamiliar adjective was identified.

Additionally, using description to define an unfamiliar noun is a common practice compared to unfamiliar adjectives, as in this sentence: *Don's wrinkled frown and constantly shaking fist identified him as a curmudgeon of the first order.* Don is described as having a *wrinkled frown and constantly shaking fist*, suggesting that a *curmudgeon* must be a grumpy person. Contrasts do not always provide detailed information about the unfamiliar word, but they at least give the reader some clues.

WORDS WITH MULTIPLE MEANINGS

When a word has more than one meaning, readers can have difficulty determining how the word is being used in a given sentence. For instance, the verb *cleave*, can mean either *join* or *separate*. When readers come upon this word, they will have to select the definition that makes the most sense. Consider the following sentence: *Hermione's knife cleaved the bread cleanly.* Since a knife cannot join bread together, the word must indicate separation. A slightly more difficult example would be the sentence: *The birds cleaved to one another as they flew from the oak tree.* Immediately, the presence of the words *to one another* should suggest that in this sentence *cleave* is being used to mean *join*. Discovering the intent of a word with multiple meanings requires the same tricks as defining an unknown word: look for contextual clues and evaluate the substituted words.

CONTEXT CLUES TO HELP DETERMINE MEANINGS OF WORDS

If readers simply bypass unknown words, they can reach unclear conclusions about what they read. However, looking for the definition of every unfamiliar word in the dictionary can slow their reading progress. Moreover, the dictionary may list multiple definitions for a word, so readers must search the word's context for meaning. Hence context is important to new vocabulary regardless of reader methods. Four types of context clues are examples, definitions, descriptive words, and opposites. Authors may use a certain word, and then follow it with several different examples of what it describes. Sometimes authors actually supply a definition of a word they use, which is especially true in informational and technical texts. Authors may use descriptive words that elaborate upon a vocabulary word they just used. Authors may also use opposites with negation that help define meaning.

EXAMPLES AND DEFINITIONS

An author may use a word and then give examples that illustrate its meaning. Consider this text: "Teachers who do not know how to use sign language can help students who are deaf or hard of hearing understand certain instructions by using gestures instead, like pointing their fingers to indicate which direction to look or go; holding up a hand, palm outward, to indicate stopping; holding the hands flat, palms up, curling a finger toward oneself in a beckoning motion to indicate 'come here'; or curling all fingers toward oneself repeatedly to indicate 'come on', 'more', or 'continue.'" The author of this text has used the word "gestures" and then followed it with examples, so a reader unfamiliar with the word could deduce from the examples that "gestures" means "hand motions." Readers can find examples by looking for signal words "for example," "for instance," "like," "such as," and "e.g."

While readers sometimes have to look for definitions of unfamiliar words in a dictionary or do some work to determine a word's meaning from its surrounding context, at other times an author may make it easier for readers by defining certain words. For example, an author may write, "The company did not have sufficient capital, that is, available money, to continue operations." The author defined "capital" as "available money," and heralded the definition with the phrase "that is." Another way that authors supply word definitions is with appositives. Rather than being introduced by a signal phrase like "that is," "namely," or "meaning," an appositive comes after the vocabulary word it defines and is enclosed within two commas. For example, an author may write, "The Indians introduced the Pilgrims to pemmican, cakes they made of lean meat dried and mixed with fat, which proved greatly beneficial to keep settlers from starving while trapping." In this example, the appositive phrase following "pemmican" and preceding "which" defines the word "pemmican."

DESCRIPTIONS

When readers encounter a word they do not recognize in a text, the author may expand on that word to illustrate it better. While the author may do this to make the prose more picturesque and vivid, the reader can also take advantage of this description to provide context clues to the meaning of the unfamiliar word. For example, an author may write, "The man sitting next to me on the airplane was obese. His shirt stretched across his vast expanse of flesh, strained almost to bursting." The descriptive second sentence elaborates on and helps to define the previous sentence's word "obese" to mean extremely fat. A reader unfamiliar with the word "repugnant" can decipher its meaning through an author's accompanying description: "The way the child grimaced and shuddered as he swallowed the medicine showed that its taste was particularly repugnant."

OPPOSITES

Text authors sometimes introduce a contrasting or opposing idea before or after a concept they present. They may do this to emphasize or heighten the idea they present by contrasting it with something that is the reverse. However, readers can also use these context clues to understand familiar words. For example, an author may write, "Our conversation was not cheery. We sat and talked very solemnly about his experience and a number of similar events." The reader who is not familiar with the word "solemnly" can deduce by the author's preceding use of "not cheery" that "solemn" means the opposite of cheery or happy, so it must mean serious or sad. Or if someone writes, "Don't condemn his entire project because you couldn't find anything good to say about it," readers unfamiliar with "condemn" can understand from the sentence structure that it means the opposite of saying anything good, so it must mean reject, dismiss, or disapprove. "Entire" adds another context clue, meaning total or complete rejection.

SYNTAX TO DETERMINE PART OF SPEECH AND MEANINGS OF WORDS

Syntax refers to sentence structure and word order. Suppose that a reader encounters an unfamiliar word when reading a text. To illustrate, consider an invented word like "splunch." If this word is used in a sentence like "Please splunch that ball to me," the reader can assume from syntactic context that "splunch" is a verb. We would not use a noun, adjective, adverb, or preposition with the object "that ball," and the prepositional phrase "to me" further indicates "splunch" represents an action. However, in the sentence, "Please hand that splunch to me," the reader can assume that "splunch" is a noun. Demonstrative adjectives like "that" modify nouns. Also, we hand someone some*thing*—a thing being a noun; we do not hand someone a verb, adjective, or adverb. Some sentences contain further clues. For example, from the sentence, "The princess wore the glittering splunch on her head," the reader can deduce that it is a crown, tiara, or something similar from the syntactic context, without knowing the word.

SYNTAX TO INDICATE DIFFERENT MEANINGS OF SIMILAR SENTENCES

The syntax, or structure, of a sentence affords grammatical cues that aid readers in comprehending the meanings of words, phrases, and sentences in the texts that they read. Seemingly minor differences in how the words or phrases in a sentence are ordered can make major differences in meaning. For example, two sentences can use exactly the same words but have different meanings based on the word order:

- "The man with a broken arm sat in a chair."
- "The man sat in a chair with a broken arm."

While both sentences indicate that a man sat in a chair, differing syntax indicates whether the man's or chair's arm was broken.

DETERMINING MEANING OF PHRASES AND PARAGRAPHS

Like unknown words, the meanings of phrases, paragraphs, and entire works can also be difficult to discern. Each of these can be better understood with added context. However, for larger groups of words, more context is needed. Unclear phrases are similar to unclear words, and the same methods can be used to understand their meaning. However, it is also important to consider how the individual words in the phrase work together. Paragraphs are a bit more complicated. Just as words must be compared to other words in a sentence, paragraphs must be compared to other paragraphs in a composition or a section.

DETERMINING MEANING IN VARIOUS TYPES OF COMPOSITIONS

To understand the meaning of an entire composition, the type of composition must be considered. **Expository writing** is generally organized so that each paragraph focuses on explaining one idea, or part of an idea, and its relevance. **Persuasive writing** uses paragraphs for different purposes to organize the parts of the argument. **Unclear paragraphs** must be read in the context of the paragraphs around them for their meaning to be fully understood. The meaning of full texts can also be unclear at times. The purpose of composition is also important for understanding the meaning of a text. To quickly understand the broad meaning of a text, look to the introductory and concluding paragraphs. Fictional texts are different. Some fictional works have implicit meanings, but some do not. The target audience must be considered for understanding texts that do have an implicit meaning, as most children's fiction will clearly state any lessons or morals. For other fiction, the application of literary theories and criticism may be helpful for understanding the text.

ADDITIONAL RESOURCES FOR DETERMINING WORD MEANING AND USAGE

While these strategies are useful for determining the meaning of unknown words and phrases, sometimes additional resources are needed to properly use the terms in different contexts. Some words have multiple definitions, and some words are inappropriate in particular contexts or modes of writing. The following tools are helpful for understanding all meanings and proper uses for words and phrases.

- **Dictionaries** provide the meaning of a multitude of words in a language. Many dictionaries include additional information about each word, such as its etymology, its synonyms, or variations of the word.
- **Glossaries** are similar to dictionaries, as they provide the meanings of a variety of terms. However, while dictionaries typically feature an extensive list of words and comprise an entire publication, glossaries are often included at the end of a text and only include terms and definitions that are relevant to the text they follow.

- **Spell Checkers** are used to detect spelling errors in typed text. Some spell checkers may also detect the misuse of plural or singular nouns, verb tenses, or capitalization. While spell checkers are a helpful tool, they are not always reliable or attuned to the author's intent, so it is important to review the spell checker's suggestions before accepting them.
- **Style Manuals** are guidelines on the preferred punctuation, format, and grammar usage according to different fields or organizations. For example, the Associated Press Stylebook is a style guide often used for media writing. The guidelines within a style guide are not always applicable across different contexts and usages, as the guidelines often cover grammatical or formatting situations that are not objectively correct or incorrect.

CHAPTER QUIZ

1. Which of the following affixes refers to the -o- in "speedometer"?

- a. Prefix
- b. Suffix
- c. Interfix
- d. Circumfix

2. Adding the suffix -ness to a word typically does which of the following?

- a. Changes a verb to a noun
- b. Changes a verb to an adjective
- c. Changes an adjective to a noun
- d. Changes a noun to a verb

3. Which of the following is NOT considered a common adjective suffix?

- a. *-acy*
- b. *-able*
- c. *-ish*
- d. *-less*

4. Which of the following defines the noun suffix -ation?

- a. Act, condition, fact
- b. Action, state, result
- c. Quality, state, result
- d. State, rank, condition

CHAPTER QUIZ ANSWER KEY

1. C: Prefixes are affixes placed in front of words. For example, *heat* means to make hot, while *preheat* means to heat in advance. Suffixes are affixes placed at the ends of words. The *happiness* example above contains the suffix -ness. Circumfixes add parts both before and after words, such as how *light* becomes *enlighten* with the prefix *en-* and the suffix *-en.* Interfixes create compound words via central affixes: *speed* and *meter* become *speedometer* via the interfix *-o-*.

2. C: In English, certain suffixes generally indicate both that a word is a noun, and that the noun represents a state of being or quality. For example, -ness is commonly used to change an adjective into its noun form, as with *happy* and *happiness, kind* and *kindness,* and so on.

3. A: Adjective suffixes:

Suffix	Definition	Examples
-able (-ible)	capable of being	tolerable, edible
-esque	in the style of, like	picturesque, grotesque
-ful	filled with, marked by	thankful, zestful
-ific	make, cause	terrific, beatific
-ish	suggesting, like	churlish, childish
-less	lacking, without	hopeless, countless
-ous	marked by, given to	religious, riotous

4. B: Noun suffixes:

Suffix	Definition	Examples
-acy	state, condition	accuracy, privacy
-ance	act, condition, fact	acceptance, vigilance
-ard	one that does excessively	drunkard, sluggard
-ation	action, state, result	occupation, starvation
-dom	state, rank, condition	serfdom, wisdom
-er (-or)	office, action	teacher, elevator, honor
-ess	feminine	waitress, duchess
-hood	state, condition	manhood, statehood
-ion	action, result, state	union, fusion
-ism	act, manner, doctrine	barbarism, socialism
-ist	worker, follower	monopolist, socialist
-ity (-ty)	state, quality, condition	acidity, civility, twenty
-ment	result, action	refreshment
-ness	quality, state	greatness, tallness
-ship	position	internship, statesmanship
-sion (-tion)	state, result	revision, expedition
-th	act, state, quality	warmth, width
-tude	quality, state, result	magnitude, fortitude

Figurative Language

LITERAL AND FIGURATIVE MEANING

When language is used **literally**, the words mean exactly what they say and nothing more. When language is used **figuratively**, the words mean something beyond their literal meaning. For example, "The weeping willow tree has long, trailing branches and leaves" is a literal description. But "The weeping willow tree looks as if it is bending over and crying" is a figurative description—specifically, a **simile** or stated comparison. Another figurative language form is **metaphor**, or an implied comparison. A good example is the metaphor of a city, state, or city-state as a ship, and its governance as sailing that ship. Ancient Greek lyrical poet Alcaeus is credited with first using this metaphor, and ancient Greek tragedian Aeschylus then used it in *Seven Against Thebes,* and then Plato used it in the *Republic.*

FIGURES OF SPEECH

A **figure of speech** is a verbal expression whose meaning is figurative rather than literal. For example, the phrase "butterflies in the stomach" does not refer to actual butterflies in a person's stomach. It is a metaphor representing the fluttery feelings experienced when a person is nervous or excited—or when one "falls in love," which does not mean physically falling. "Hitting a sales target" does not mean physically hitting a target with arrows as in archery; it is a metaphor for meeting a sales quota. "Climbing the ladder of success" metaphorically likens advancing in one's career to ascending ladder rungs. Similes, such as "light as a feather" (meaning very light, not a feather's actual weight), and hyperbole, like "I'm starving/freezing/roasting," are also figures of speech. Figures of speech are often used and crafted for emphasis, freshness of expression, or clarity.

> **Review Video: Figures of Speech**
> Visit mometrix.com/academy and enter code: 111295

FIGURATIVE LANGUAGE

Figurative language extends past the literal meanings of words. It offers readers new insight into the people, things, events, and subjects covered in a work of literature. Figurative language also enables readers to feel they are sharing the authors' experiences. It can stimulate the reader's senses, make comparisons that readers find intriguing or even startling, and enable readers to view the world in different ways. When looking for figurative language, it is important to consider the context of the sentence or situation. Phrases that appear out of place or make little sense when read literally are likely instances of figurative language. Once figurative language has been recognized, context is also important to determining the type of figurative language being used and its function. For example, when a comparison is being made, a metaphor or simile is likely being used. This means the comparison may emphasize or create irony through the things being compared. Seven specific types of figurative language include: alliteration, onomatopoeia, personification, imagery, similes, metaphors, and hyperbole.

> **Review Video: Figurative Language**
> Visit mometrix.com/academy and enter code: 584902

ALLITERATION AND ONOMATOPOEIA

Alliteration describes a series of words beginning with the same sounds. **Onomatopoeia** uses words imitating the sounds of things they name or describe. For example, in his poem "Come Down, O Maid," Alfred Tennyson writes of "The moan of doves in immemorial elms, / And murmuring of

innumerable bees." The word "moan" sounds like some sounds doves make, "murmuring" represents the sounds of bees buzzing. Onomatopoeia also includes words that are simply meant to represent sounds, such as "meow," "kaboom," and "whoosh."

> **Review Video: <u>Alliterations Are All Around</u>**
> Visit mometrix.com/academy and enter code: 462837

PERSONIFICATION

Another type of figurative language is **personification**. This is describing a non-human thing, like an animal or an object, as if it were human. The general intent of personification is to describe things in a manner that will be comprehensible to readers. When an author states that a tree *groans* in the wind, he or she does not mean that the tree is emitting a low, pained sound from a mouth. Instead, the author means that the tree is making a noise similar to a human groan. Of course, this personification establishes a tone of sadness or suffering. A different tone would be established if the author said that the tree was *swaying* or *dancing*. Alfred Tennyson's poem "The Eagle" uses all of these types of figurative language: "He clasps the crag with crooked hands." Tennyson used alliteration, repeating /k/ and /kr/ sounds. These hard-sounding consonants reinforce the imagery, giving visual and tactile impressions of the eagle.

> **Review Video: <u>Personification</u>**
> Visit mometrix.com/academy and enter code: 260066

SIMILES AND METAPHORS

Similes are stated comparisons using "like" or "as." Similes can be used to stimulate readers' imaginations and appeal to their senses. Because a simile includes *like* or *as*, the device creates more space between the description and the thing being described than a metaphor does. If an author says that *a house was like a shoebox*, then the tone is different than the author saying that the house *was* a shoebox. Authors will choose between a metaphor and a simile depending on their intended tone.

Similes also help compare fictional characters to well-known objects or experiences, so the reader can better relate to them. William Wordsworth's poem about "Daffodils" begins, "I wandered lonely as a cloud." This simile compares his loneliness to that of a cloud. It is also personification, giving a cloud the human quality loneliness. In his novel *Lord Jim* (1900), Joseph Conrad writes in Chapter 33, "I would have given anything for the power to soothe her frail soul, tormenting itself in its invincible ignorance like a small bird beating about the cruel wires of a cage." Conrad uses the word "like" to compare the girl's soul to a small bird. His description of the bird beating at the cage shows the similar helplessness of the girl's soul to gain freedom.

> **Review Video: <u>Similes</u>**
> Visit mometrix.com/academy and enter code: 642949

A **metaphor** is a type of figurative language in which the writer equates something with another thing that is not particularly similar, instead of using *like* or *as*. For instance, *the bird was an arrow arcing through the sky*. In this sentence, the arrow is serving as a metaphor for the bird. The point of a metaphor is to encourage the reader to consider the item being described in a *different way*. Let's continue with this metaphor for a flying bird. You are asked to envision the bird's flight as being similar to the arc of an arrow. So, you imagine the flight to be swift and bending. Metaphors are a way for the author to describe an item *without being direct and obvious*. This literary device is a lyrical and suggestive way of providing information. Note that the reference for a metaphor will not

always be mentioned explicitly by the author. Consider the following description of a forest in winter: *Swaying skeletons reached for the sky and groaned as the wind blew through them.* In this example, the author is using *skeletons* as a metaphor for leafless trees. This metaphor creates a spooky tone while inspiring the reader's imagination.

LITERARY EXAMPLES OF METAPHOR

A **metaphor** is an implied comparison, i.e., it compares something to something else without using "like", "as", or other comparative words. For example, in "The Tyger" (1794), William Blake writes, "Tyger Tyger, burning bright, / In the forests of the night." Blake compares the tiger to a flame not by saying it is like a fire, but by simply describing it as "burning." Henry Wadsworth Longfellow's poem "O Ship of State" (1850) uses an extended metaphor by referring consistently throughout the entire poem to the state, union, or republic as a seagoing vessel, referring to its keel, mast, sail, rope, anchors, and to its braving waves, rocks, gale, tempest, and "false lights on the shore." Within the extended metaphor, Wordsworth uses a specific metaphor: "the anchors of thy hope!"

TED HUGHES' ANIMAL METAPHORS

Ted Hughes frequently used animal metaphors in his poetry. In "The Thought Fox," a model of concise, structured beauty, Hughes characterizes the poet's creative process with succinct, striking imagery of an idea entering his head like a wild fox. Repeating "loneliness" in the first two stanzas emphasizes the poet's lonely work: "Something else is alive / Beside the clock's loneliness." He treats an idea's arrival as separate from himself. Three stanzas detail in vivid images a fox's approach from the outside winter forest at starless midnight—its nose, "Cold, delicately" touching twigs and leaves; "neat" paw prints in snow; "bold" body; brilliant green eyes; and self-contained, focused progress—"Till, with a sudden sharp hot stink of fox," he metaphorically depicts poetic inspiration as the fox's physical entry into "the dark hole of the head." Hughes ends by summarizing his vision of a poet as an interior, passive idea recipient, with the outside world unchanged: "The window is starless still; the clock ticks, / The page is printed."

> **Review Video: Metaphors in Writing**
> Visit mometrix.com/academy and enter code: 133295

HYPERBOLE

Hyperbole is excessive exaggeration used for humor or emphasis rather than for literal meaning. For example, in *To Kill a Mockingbird*, Harper Lee wrote, "People moved slowly then. There was no hurry, for there was nowhere to go, nothing to buy and no money to buy it with, nothing to see outside the boundaries of Maycomb County." This was not literally true; Lee exaggerates the scarcity of these things for emphasis. In "Old Times on the Mississippi," Mark Twain wrote, "I... could have hung my hat on my eyes, they stuck out so far." This is not literal, but makes his description vivid and funny. In his poem "As I Walked Out One Evening", W. H. Auden wrote, "I'll love you, dear, I'll love you / Till China and Africa meet, / And the river jumps over the mountain / And the salmon sing in the street." He used things not literally possible to emphasize the duration of his love.

> **Review Video: Hyperbole and Understatement**
> Visit mometrix.com/academy and enter code: 308470

LITERARY IRONY

In literature, irony demonstrates the opposite of what is said or done. The three types of irony are **verbal irony**, **situational irony**, and **dramatic irony**. Verbal irony uses words opposite to the meaning. Sarcasm may use verbal irony. One common example is describing something that is

111

confusing as "clear as mud." For example, in his 1986 movie *Hannah and Her Sisters,* author, director, and actor Woody Allen says to his character's date, "I had a great evening; it was like the Nuremburg Trials." Notice these employ similes. In situational irony, what happens contrasts with what was expected. O. Henry's short story *The Gift of the Magi* uses situational irony: a husband and wife each sacrifice their most prized possession to buy each other a Christmas present. The irony is that she sells her long hair to buy him a watch fob, while he sells his heirloom pocket-watch to buy her the jeweled combs for her hair she had long wanted; in the end, neither of them can use their gifts. In dramatic irony, narrative informs audiences of more than its characters know. For example, in *Romeo and Juliet,* the audience is made aware that Juliet is only asleep, while Romeo believes her to be dead, which then leads to Romeo's death.

> **Review Video: <u>What is the Definition of Irony?</u>**
> Visit mometrix.com/academy and enter code: 374204

IDIOMS

Idioms create comparisons, and often take the form of similes or metaphors. Idioms are always phrases and are understood to have a meaning that is different from its individual words' literal meaning. For example, "break a leg" is a common idiom that is used to wish someone luck or tell them to perform well. Literally, the phrase "break a leg" means to injure a person's leg, but the phrase takes on a different meaning when used as an idiom. Another example is "call it a day," which means to temporarily stop working on a task, or find a stopping point, rather than literally referring to something as "a day." Many idioms are associated with a region or group. For example, an idiom commonly used in the American South is "'til the cows come home." This phrase is often used to indicate that something will take or may last for a very long time, but not that it will literally last until the cows return to where they reside.

CHAPTER QUIZ

1. Who is credited with first using the metaphor of a city, state, or city-state as a ship?

 a. Theseus
 b. Aeschylus
 c. Alcaeus
 d. Plato

2. How many forms of irony are there?

 a. Two
 b. Three
 c. Four
 d. Five

CHAPTER QUIZ ANSWER KEY

1. C: Another figurative language form is metaphor, or an implied comparison. A good example is the metaphor of a city, state, or city-state as a ship, and its governance as sailing that ship. Ancient Greek lyrical poet Alcaeus is credited with first using this metaphor, followed by ancient Greek tragedian Aeschylus using it in *Seven Against Thebes,* and then Plato using it in the *Republic.*

2. B: In literature, irony demonstrates the opposite of what is said or done. The three types of irony are verbal irony, situational irony, and dramatic irony. Verbal irony uses words opposite to the meaning. Sarcasm may use verbal irony. One common example is describing something that is confusing as "clear as mud." In his 1986 movie *Hannah and Her Sisters,* author, director, and actor Woody Allen says to his character's date, "I had a great evening; it was like the Nuremburg Trials." Notice these employ similes. In situational irony, what happens contrasts with what was expected. O. Henry's short story *The Gift of the Magi* uses situational irony: a husband and wife each sacrifice their most prized possession to buy each other a Christmas present. The irony is that she sells her long hair to buy him a watch fob, while he sells his heirloom pocket-watch to buy her the jeweled combs for her hair she had long wanted; in the end, neither of them can use their gifts. In dramatic irony, narrative informs audiences of more than its characters know. For example, in *Romeo and Juliet,* the audience is made aware that Juliet is only asleep, while Romeo believes her to be dead, which then leads to Romeo's death.

Literary Elements

LITERARY TERMINOLOGY

- In works of prose such as novels, a group of connected sentences covering one main topic is termed a **paragraph**.
- In works of poetry, a group of verses similarly connected is called a **stanza**.
- In drama, when early works used verse, these were also divided into stanzas or **couplets**.
- Drama evolved to use predominantly prose. Overall, whether prose or verse, the conversation in a play is called **dialogue**.
- Large sections of dialogue spoken by one actor are called **soliloquies** or **monologues**.
- Dialogue that informs audiences but is unheard by other characters is called an **aside**.
- Novels and plays share certain common elements, such as:
  - **Characters** - the people in the story.
  - **Plot** - the action of the story.
  - **Climax** - when action or dramatic tension reaches its highest point.
  - **Denouement** - the resolution following the climax.
- Sections dividing novels are called **chapters**, while sections of plays are called **acts**.
- Subsections of plays' acts are called **scenes**. Novel chapters usually do not have subsections. However, some novels do include groups of chapters that form different sections.

LITERARY ANALYSIS

The best literary analysis shows special insight into at least one important aspect of a text. When analyzing literary texts, it can be difficult to find a starting place. Many texts can be analyzed several different ways, often leaving an overwhelming number of options for writers to consider. However, narrowing the focus to a particular element of literature can be helpful when preparing to analyze a text. Symbolism, themes, and motifs are common starting points for literary analysis. These three methods of analysis can lead to a holistic analysis of a text, since they involve elements that are often distributed throughout the text. However, not all texts feature these elements in a way that facilitates a strong analysis, if they are present at all. It is also common to focus on character or plot development for analysis. These elements are compatible with theme, symbolism, and allusion. Setting and imagery, figurative language, and any external contexts can also contribute to analysis or complement one of these other elements. The application of a critical, or literary, theory to a text can also provide a thorough and strong analysis.

SETTING AND TIME FRAME

A literary text has both a setting and time frame. A **setting** is the place in which the story as a whole is set. The **time frame** is the period in which the story is set. This may refer to the historical period the story takes place in or if the story takes place over a single day. Both setting and time frame are relevant to a text's meaning because they help the reader place the story in time and space. An author uses setting and time frame to anchor a text, create a mood, and enhance its meaning. This helps a reader understand why a character acts the way he does, or why certain events in the story are important. The setting impacts the **plot** and character **motivations**, while the time frame helps place the story in **chronological context**.

EXAMPLE

Read the following excerpt from The Adventures of Huckleberry Finn by Mark Twain and analyze the relevance of setting to the text's meaning:

> We said there warn't no home like a raft, after all. Other places do seem so cramped up and smothery, but a raft don't. You feel mighty free and easy and comfortable on a raft.

This excerpt from *The Adventures of Huckleberry Finn* by Mark Twain reveals information about the **setting** of the book. By understanding that the main character, Huckleberry Finn, lives on a raft, the reader can place the story on a river, in this case, the Mississippi River in the South before the Civil War. The information about the setting also gives the reader clues about the **character** of Huck Finn: he clearly values independence and freedom, and he likes the outdoors. The information about the setting in the quote helps the reader to better understand the rest of the text.

THEME

The **theme** of a passage is what the reader learns from the text or the passage. It is the lesson or **moral** contained in the passage. It also is a unifying idea that is used throughout the text; it can take the form of a common setting, idea, symbol, design, or recurring event. A passage can have two or more themes that convey its overall idea. The theme or themes of a passage are often based on **universal themes**. They can frequently be expressed using well-known sayings about life, society, or human nature, such as "Hard work pays off" or "Good triumphs over evil." Themes are not usually stated **explicitly**. The reader must figure them out by carefully reading the passage. Themes are often the reason why passages are written; they give a passage unity and meaning. Themes are created through **plot development**. The events of a story help shape the themes of a passage.

EXAMPLE

Explain why "Take care of what you care about" accurately describes the theme of the following excerpt.

> Luca collected baseball cards, but he wasn't very careful with them. He left them around the house. His dog liked to chew. One day, Luca and his friend Bart were looking at his collection. Then they went outside. When Luca got home, he saw his dog chewing on his cards. They were ruined.

This excerpt tells the story of a boy who is careless with his baseball cards and leaves them lying around. His dog ends up chewing them and ruining them. The lesson is that if you care about something, you need to take care of it. This is the theme, or point, of the story. Some stories have more than one theme, but this is not really true of this excerpt. The reader needs to figure out the theme based on what happens in the story. Sometimes, as in the case of fables, the theme is stated directly in the text. However, this is not usually the case.

> **Review Video: <u>Themes in Literature</u>**
> Visit mometrix.com/academy and enter code: 732074

PLOT AND STORY STRUCTURE

The **plot** includes the events that happen in a story and the order in which they are told to the reader. There are several types of plot structures, as stories can be told in many ways. The most common plot structure is the chronological plot, which presents the events to the reader in the same order they occur for the characters in the story. Chronological plots usually have five main parts, the **exposition**, **rising action**, the **climax**, **falling action**, and the **resolution**. This type of plot structure guides the reader through the story's events as the characters experience them and is the easiest structure to understand and identify. While this is the most common plot structure, many stories are nonlinear, which means the plot does not sequence events in the same order the characters experience them. Such stories might include elements like flashbacks that cause the story to be nonlinear.

> **Review Video: How to Make a Story Map**
> Visit mometrix.com/academy and enter code: 261719

EXPOSITION

The **exposition** is at the beginning of the story and generally takes place before the rising action begins. The purpose of the exposition is to give the reader context for the story, which the author may do by introducing one or more characters, describing the setting or world, or explaining the events leading up to the point where the story begins. The exposition may still include events that contribute to the plot, but the **rising action** and main conflict of the story are not part of the exposition. Some narratives skip the exposition and begin the story with the beginning of the rising action, which causes the reader to learn the context as the story intensifies.

CONFLICT

A **conflict** is a problem to be solved. Literary plots typically include one conflict or more. Characters' attempts to resolve conflicts drive the narrative's forward movement. **Conflict resolution** is often the protagonist's primary occupation. Physical conflicts like exploring, wars, and escapes tend to make plots most suspenseful and exciting. Emotional, mental, or moral conflicts tend to make stories more personally gratifying or rewarding for many audiences. Conflicts can be external or internal. A major type of internal conflict is some inner personal battle, or **man versus self**. Major types of external conflicts include **man versus nature**, **man versus man**, and **man versus society**. Readers can identify conflicts in literary plots by identifying the protagonist and antagonist and asking why they conflict, what events develop the conflict, where the climax occurs, and how they identify with the characters.

Read the following paragraph and discuss the type of conflict present:

> Timothy was shocked out of sleep by the appearance of a bear just outside his tent. After panicking for a moment, he remembered some advice he had read in preparation for this trip: he should make noise so the bear would not be startled. As Timothy started to hum and sing, the bear wandered away.

There are three main types of conflict in literature: **man versus man**, **man versus nature**, and **man versus self**. This paragraph is an example of man versus nature. Timothy is in conflict with the bear. Even though no physical conflict like an attack exists, Timothy is pitted against the bear. Timothy uses his knowledge to "defeat" the bear and keep himself safe. The solution to the conflict is that Timothy makes noise, the bear wanders away, and Timothy is safe.

> **Review Video: Conflict**
> Visit mometrix.com/academy and enter code: 559550
>
> **Review Video: Determining Relationships in a Story**
> Visit mometrix.com/academy and enter code: 929925

RISING ACTION

The **rising action** is the part of the story where conflict **intensifies**. The rising action begins with an event that prompts the main conflict of the story. This may also be called the **inciting incident**. The main conflict generally occurs between the protagonist and an antagonist, but this is not the only type of conflict that may occur in a narrative. After this event, the protagonist works to resolve the main conflict by preparing for an altercation, pursuing a goal, fleeing an antagonist, or doing some other action that will end the conflict. The rising action is composed of several additional events that increase the story's tension. Most often, other developments will occur alongside the growth of the main conflict, such as character development or the development of minor conflicts. The rising action ends with the **climax**, which is the point of highest tension in the story.

CLIMAX

The **climax** is the event in the narrative that marks the height of the story's conflict or tension. The event that takes place at the story's climax will end the rising action and bring about the results of the main conflict. If the conflict was between a good protagonist and an evil antagonist, the climax may be a final battle between the two characters. If the conflict is an adventurer looking for heavily guarded treasure, the climax may be the adventurer's encounter with the final obstacle that protects the treasure. The climax may be made of multiple scenes, but can usually be summarized as one event. Once the conflict and climax are complete, the **falling action** begins.

FALLING ACTION

The **falling action** shows what happens in the story between the climax and the resolution. The falling action often composes a much smaller portion of the story than the rising action does. While the climax includes the end of the main conflict, the falling action may show the results of any minor conflicts in the story. For example, if the protagonist encountered a troll on the way to find some treasure, and the troll demanded the protagonist share the treasure after retrieving it, the falling action would include the protagonist returning to share the treasure with the troll. Similarly, any unexplained major events are usually made clear during the falling action. Once all significant elements of the story are resolved or addressed, the story's resolution will occur. The **resolution** is the end of the story, which shows the final result of the plot's events and shows what life is like for the main characters once they are no longer experiencing the story's conflicts.

RESOLUTION

The way the conflict is **resolved** depends on the type of conflict. The plot of any book starts with the lead up to the conflict, then the conflict itself, and finally the solution, or **resolution**, to the conflict. In **man versus man** conflicts, the conflict is often resolved by two parties coming to some sort of agreement or by one party triumphing over the other party. In **man versus nature** conflicts, the conflict is often resolved by man coming to some realization about some aspect of nature. In **man versus self** conflicts, the conflict is often resolved by the character growing or coming to an understanding about part of himself.

SYNTAX AND WORD CHOICE

Authors use words and **syntax**, or sentence structure, to make their texts unique, convey their own writing style, and sometimes to make a point or emphasis. They know that word choice and syntax contribute to the reader's understanding of the text as well as to the tone and mood of a text.

> **Review Video: What is Syntax?**
> Visit mometrix.com/academy and enter code: 242280

ALLUSION

An allusion is an uncited but recognizable reference to something else. Authors use language to make allusions to places, events, artwork, and other books in order to make their own text richer. For example, an author may allude to a very important text in order to make his own text seem more important. Martin Luther King, Jr. started his "I Have a Dream" speech by saying "Five score years ago..." This is a clear allusion to President Abraham Lincoln's "Gettysburg Address" and served to remind people of the significance of the event. An author may allude to a place to ground his text or make a cultural reference to make readers feel included. There are many reasons that authors make allusions.

> **Review Video: Allusions**
> Visit mometrix.com/academy and enter code: 294065

COMIC RELIEF

Comic relief is the use of comedy by an author to break up a dramatic or tragic scene and infuse it with a bit of **lightheartedness**. In William Shakespeare's *Hamlet*, two gravediggers digging the grave for Ophelia share a joke while they work. The death and burial of Ophelia are tragic moments that directly follow each other. Shakespeare uses an instance of comedy to break up the tragedy and give his audience a bit of a break from the tragic drama. Authors sometimes use comic relief so that their work will be less depressing; other times they use it to create irony or contrast between the darkness of the situation and the lightness of the joke. Often, authors will use comedy to parallel what is happening in the tragic scenes.

> **Review Video: What is Comic Relief?**
> Visit mometrix.com/academy and enter code: 779604

MOOD AND TONE

Mood is a story's atmosphere, or the feelings the reader gets from reading it. The way authors set the mood in writing is comparable to the way filmmakers use music to set the mood in movies. Instead of music, though, writers judiciously select descriptive words to evoke certain **moods**. The mood of a work may convey joy, anger, bitterness, hope, gloom, fear, apprehension, or any other emotion the author wants the reader to feel. In addition to vocabulary choices, authors also use figurative expressions, particular sentence structures, and choices of diction that project and reinforce the moods they want to create. Whereas mood is the reader's emotions evoked by reading what is written, **tone** is the emotions and attitudes of the writer that she or he expresses in the writing. Authors use the same literary techniques to establish tone as they do to establish mood. An author may use a humorous tone, an angry or sad tone, a sentimental or unsentimental tone, or something else entirely.

MOOD AND TONE IN THE GREAT GATSBY

To understand the difference between mood and tone, look at this excerpt from F. Scott Fitzgerald's *The Great Gatsby*. In this passage, Nick Caraway, the novel's narrator, is describing his affordable house, which sits in a neighborhood full of expensive mansions.

> "I lived at West Egg, the—well the less fashionable of the two, though this is a most superficial tag to express the bizarre and not a little sinister contrast between them. My house was at the very tip of the egg, only fifty yard from the Sound, and squeezed between two huge places that rented for twelve or fifteen thousand a season ... My own house was an eyesore, but it was a small eyesore, and it had been overlooked, so I had a view of the water,

a partial view of my neighbor's lawn, and the consoling proximity of millionaires—all for eighty dollars a month."

In this description, the mood created for the reader does not match the tone created through the narrator. The mood in this passage is one of dissatisfaction and inferiority. Nick compares his home to his neighbors', saying he lives in the "less fashionable" neighborhood and that his house is "overlooked," an "eyesore," and "squeezed between two huge" mansions. He also adds that his placement allows him the "consoling proximity of millionaires." A literal reading of these details leads the reader to have negative feelings toward Nick's house and his economic inferiority to his neighbors, creating the mood.

However, Fitzgerald also conveys an opposing attitude, or tone, through Nick's description. Nick calls the distinction between the neighborhoods "superficial," showing a suspicion of the value suggested by the neighborhoods' titles, properties, and residents. Nick also undermines his critique of his own home by calling it "a small eyesore" and claiming it has "been overlooked." However, he follows these statements with a description of his surroundings, claiming that he has "a view of the water" and can see some of his wealthy neighbor's property from his home, and a comparison between the properties' rent. While the mental image created for the reader depicts a small house shoved between looming mansions, the tone suggests that Nick enjoys these qualities about his home, or at least finds it charming. He acknowledges its shortcomings, but includes the benefits of his home's unassuming appearance.

> **Review Video: Style, Tone, and Mood**
> Visit mometrix.com/academy and enter code: 416961

CHARACTER DEVELOPMENT

When depicting characters or figures in a written text, authors generally use actions, dialogue, and descriptions as characterization techniques. Characterization can occur in both fiction and nonfiction and is used to show a character or figure's personality, demeanor, and thoughts. This helps create a more engaging experience for the reader by providing a more concrete picture of a character or figure's tendencies and features. Characterizations also gives authors the opportunity to integrate elements such as dialects, activities, attire, and attitudes into their writing.

To understand the meaning of a story, it is vital to understand the characters as the author describes them. We can look for contradictions in what a character thinks, says, and does. We can notice whether the author's observations about a character differ from what other characters in the story say about that character. A character may be dynamic, meaning they change significantly during the story, or static, meaning they remain the same from beginning to end. Characters may be two-dimensional, not fully developed, or may be well developed with characteristics that stand out vividly. Characters may also symbolize universal properties. Additionally, readers can compare and contrast characters to analyze how each one developed.

A well-known example of character development can be found in Charles Dickens's *Great Expectations*. The novel's main character, Pip, is introduced as a young boy, and he is depicted as innocent, kind, and humble. However, as Pip grows up and is confronted with the social hierarchy of Victorian England, he becomes arrogant and rejects his loved ones in pursuit of his own social advancement. Once he achieves his social goals, he realizes the merits of his former lifestyle, and lives with the wisdom he gained in both environments and life stages. Dickens shows Pip's ever-changing character through his interactions with others and his inner thoughts, which evolve as his personal values and personality shift.

DIALOGUE

Effectively written dialogue serves at least one, but usually several, purposes. It advances the story and moves the plot, develops the characters, sheds light on the work's theme or meaning, and can, often subtly, account for the passage of time not otherwise indicated. It can alter the direction that the plot is taking, typically by introducing some new conflict or changing existing ones. **Dialogue** can establish a work's narrative voice and the characters' voices and set the tone of the story or of particular characters. When fictional characters display enlightenment or realization, dialogue can give readers an understanding of what those characters have discovered and how. Dialogue can illuminate the motivations and wishes of the story's characters. By using consistent thoughts and syntax, dialogue can support character development. Skillfully created, it can also represent real-life speech rhythms in written form. Via conflicts and ensuing action, dialogue also provides drama.

DIALOGUE IN FICTION

In fictional works, effectively written dialogue does more than just break up or interrupt sections of narrative. While **dialogue** may supply exposition for readers, it must nonetheless be believable. Dialogue should be dynamic, not static, and it should not resemble regular prose. Authors should not use dialogue to write clever similes or metaphors, or to inject their own opinions. Nor should they use dialogue at all when narrative would be better. Most importantly, dialogue should not slow the plot movement. Dialogue must seem natural, which means careful construction of phrases rather than actually duplicating natural speech, which does not necessarily translate well to the written word. Finally, all dialogue must be pertinent to the story, rather than just added conversation.

FORESHADOWING

Foreshadowing is a device authors use to give readers **hints** about events that will take place later in a story. Foreshadowing most often takes place through a character's dialogue or actions. Sometimes the character will know what is going to happen and will purposefully allude to future events. For example, consider a protagonist who is about to embark on a journey through the woods. Just before the protagonist begins the trip, another character says, "Be careful, you never know what could be out in those woods!" This alerts the reader that the woods may be dangerous and prompts the reader to expect something to attack the protagonist in the woods. This is an example of foreshadowing through warning. Alternatively, a character may unknowingly foreshadow later events. For example, consider a story where a brother and sister run through their house and knock over a vase and break it. The brother says, "Don't worry, we'll clean it up! Mom will never know!" However, the reader knows that their mother will most likely find out what they have done, so the reader expects the siblings to later get in trouble for running, breaking the vase, and hiding it from their mother.

SYMBOLISM

Symbolism describes an author's use of a **symbol**, an element of the story that **represents** something else. Symbols can impact stories in many ways, including deepening the meaning of a story or its elements, comparing a story to another work, or foreshadowing later events in a story. Symbols can be objects, characters, colors, numbers, or anything else the author establishes as a symbol. Symbols can be clearly established through direct comparison or repetition, but they can also be established subtly or gradually over a large portion of the story. Another form of symbolism is **allusion**, which is when something in a story is used to prompt the reader to think about another work. Many well-known works use **Biblical allusions**, which are allusions to events or details in the Bible that inform a work or an element within it.

POINT OF VIEW

Another element that impacts a text is the author's point of view. The **point of view** of a text is the perspective from which a passage is told. An author will always have a point of view about a story before he or she draws up a plot line. The author will know what events they want to take place, how they want the characters to interact, and how they want the story to resolve. An author will also have an opinion on the topic or series of events which is presented in the story that is based on their prior experience and beliefs.

The two main points of view that authors use, especially in a work of fiction, are first person and third person. If the narrator of the story is also the main character, or *protagonist*, the text is written in first-person point of view. In first person, the author writes from the perspective of *I*. Third-person point of view is probably the most common that authors use in their passages. Using third person, authors refer to each character by using *he* or *she*. In third-person omniscient, the narrator is not a character in the story and tells the story of all of the characters at the same time.

> **Review Video: Point of View**
> Visit mometrix.com/academy and enter code: 383336

FIRST-PERSON NARRATION

First-person narratives let narrators express inner feelings and thoughts, especially when the narrator is the protagonist as Lemuel Gulliver is in Jonathan Swift's *Gulliver's Travels.* The narrator may be a close friend of the protagonist, like Dr. Watson in Sir Arthur Conan Doyle's *Sherlock Holmes.* Or, the narrator can be less involved with the main characters and plot, like Nick Carraway in F. Scott Fitzgerald's *The Great Gatsby.* When a narrator reports others' narratives, she or he is a "**frame narrator**," like the nameless narrator of Joseph Conrad's *Heart of Darkness* or Mr. Lockwood in Emily Brontë's *Wuthering Heights.* **First-person plural** is unusual but can be effective. Isaac Asimov's *I, Robot*, William Faulkner's *A Rose for Emily*, Maxim Gorky's *Twenty-Six Men and a Girl*, and Jeffrey Eugenides' *The Virgin Suicides* all use first-person plural narration. Author Kurt Vonnegut is the first-person narrator in his semi-autobiographical novel *Timequake.* Also unusual, but effective, is a **first-person omniscient** (rather than the more common third-person omniscient) narrator, like Death in Markus Zusak's *The Book Thief* and the ghost in Alice Sebold's *The Lovely Bones.*

SECOND-PERSON NARRATION

While **second-person** address is very commonplace in popular song lyrics, it is the least used form of narrative voice in literary works. Popular serial books of the 1980s like *Fighting Fantasy* or *Choose Your Own Adventure* employed second-person narratives. In some cases, a narrative combines both second-person and first-person voices, using the pronouns *you* and *I*. This can draw readers into the story, and it can also enable the authors to compare directly "your" and "my" feelings, thoughts, and actions. When the narrator is also a character in the story, as in Edgar Allan Poe's short story "The Tell-Tale Heart" or Jay McInerney's novel *Bright Lights, Big City,* the narrative is better defined as first-person despite it also addressing "you."

THIRD-PERSON NARRATION

Narration in the third person is the most prevalent type, as it allows authors the most flexibility. It is so common that readers simply assume without needing to be informed that the narrator is not a character in the story, or involved in its events. **Third-person singular** is used more frequently than **third-person plural**, though some authors have also effectively used plural. However, both singular and plural are most often included in stories according to which characters are being described. The third-person narrator may be either objective or subjective, and either omniscient or limited. **Objective third-person** narration does not include what the characters described are thinking or feeling, while **subjective third-person** narration does. The **third-person omniscient** narrator knows everything about all characters, including their thoughts and emotions, and all related places, times, and events. However, the **third-person limited** narrator may know everything about a particular character, but is limited to that character. In other words, the narrator cannot speak about anything that character does not know.

ALTERNATING-PERSON NARRATION

Although authors more commonly write stories from one point of view, there are also instances wherein they alternate the narrative voice within the same book. For example, they may sometimes use an omniscient third-person narrator and a more intimate first-person narrator at other times. In J. K. Rowling's series of *Harry Potter* novels, she often writes in a third-person limited narrative, but sometimes changes to narration by characters other than the protagonist. George R. R. Martin's series *A Song of Ice and Fire* changes the point of view to coincide with divisions between chapters. The same technique is used by Erin Hunter (a pseudonym for several authors of the *Warriors, Seekers,* and *Survivors* book series). Authors using first-person narrative sometimes switch to third-person to describe significant action scenes, especially those where the narrator was absent or uninvolved, as Barbara Kingsolver does in her novel *The Poisonwood Bible.*

HISTORICAL AND SOCIAL CONTEXT

Fiction that is heavily influenced by a historical or social context cannot be comprehended as the author intended if the reader does not keep this context in mind. Many important elements of the text will be influenced by any context, including symbols, allusions, settings, and plot events. These contexts, as well as the identity of the work's author, can help to inform the reader about the author's concerns and intended meanings. For example, George Orwell published his novel *1984* in the year 1949, soon after the end of World War II. At that time, following the defeat of the Nazis, the Cold War began between the Western Allied nations and the Eastern Soviet Communists. People were therefore concerned about the conflict between the freedoms afforded by Western democracies versus the oppression represented by Communism. Orwell had also previously fought in the Spanish Civil War against a Spanish regime that he and his fellows viewed as oppressive. From this information, readers can infer that Orwell was concerned about oppression by totalitarian governments. This informs *1984*'s story of Winston Smith's rebellion against the oppressive "Big Brother" government, of the fictional dictatorial state of Oceania, and his capture, torture, and ultimate conversion by that government. Some literary theories also seek to use historical and social contexts to reveal deeper meanings and implications in a text.

TEXTUAL EVIDENCE

No literary analysis is complete without textual evidence. Summaries, paraphrases, and quotes are all forms of textual evidence, but direct quotes from the text are the most effective form of evidence. The best textual evidence is relevant, accurate, and clearly supports the writer's claim. This can include pieces of descriptions, dialogue, or exposition that shows the applicability of the analysis to the text. Analysis that is average, or sufficient, shows an understanding of the text; contains supporting textual evidence that is relevant and accurate, if not strong; and shows a specific and clear response. Analysis that partially meets criteria also shows understanding, but the textual evidence is generalized, incomplete, only partly relevant or accurate, or connected only weakly. Inadequate analysis is vague, too general, or incorrect. It may give irrelevant or incomplete textual evidence, or may simply summarize the plot rather than analyzing the work. It is important to incorporate textual evidence from the work being analyzed and any supplemental materials and to provide appropriate attribution for these sources.

CHAPTER QUIZ

1. Which of the following is the least used form of narration used in literature?

    a. First-person
    b. Second-person
    c. Third-person limited
    d. Third-person omniscient

2. Which of the following lists the terms of chronological plots in order from first to last?

    a. Exposition, rising action, climax, falling action, resolution
    b. Rising action, exposition, falling action, climax, resolution
    c. Rising action, exposition, climax, falling action, resolution
    d. Resolution, exposition, climax, falling action, rising action

3. If a writer alludes to another piece of literature, that writer is doing which of the following?

    a. Admiring it
    b. Criticizing it
    c. Defending its conclusions
    d. Referencing it

CHAPTER QUIZ ANSWER KEY

1. B: While second-person address is very commonplace in popular song lyrics, it is the least used form of narrative voice in literary works. Popular serial books of the 1980s like *Fighting Fantasy* or *Choose Your Own Adventure* employed second-person narratives. In some cases, a narrative combines both second-person and first-person voices, using the pronouns *you* and *I*. This can draw readers into the story, and it can also enable the authors to compare directly "your" and "my" feelings, thoughts, and actions. When the narrator is also a character in the story, as in Edgar Allan Poe's short story "The Tell-Tale Heart" or Jay McInerney's novel *Bright Lights, Big City,* the narrative is better defined as first-person despite it also addressing "you."

2. A: The most common plot structure is the chronological plot, which presents the events to the reader in the same order they occur for the characters in the story. Chronological plots usually have five main parts: the exposition, rising action, the climax, falling action, and the resolution. This type of plot structure guides the reader through the story's events as the characters experience them and is the easiest structure to understand and identify.

3. D: An allusion is an uncited but recognizable reference to something else. Authors use language to make allusions to places, events, artwork, and other books in order to make their own text richer. For example, an author may allude to a very important text in order to make his own text seem more important.

Themes and Plots in Literature

THEMES IN LITERATURE

When we read parables, their themes are the lessons they aim to teach. When we read fables, the moral of each story is its theme. When we read fictional works, the authors' perspectives regarding life and human behavior are their themes. Unlike in parables and fables, themes in literary fiction are usually not meant to preach or teach the readers a lesson. Hence, themes in fiction are not as explicit as they are in parables or fables. Instead, they are implicit, and the reader only infers them. By analyzing the fictional characters through thinking about their actions and behavior, understanding the setting of the story, and reflecting on how its plot develops, the reader comes to infer the main theme of the work. When writers succeed, they communicate with their readers such that common ground is established between author and audience. While a reader's individual experience may differ in its details from the author's written story, both may share universal underlying truths which allow author and audience to connect.

DETERMINING THEME

In well-crafted literature, theme, structure, and plot are interdependent and inextricable: each element informs and reflects the others. The structure of a work is how it is organized. The theme is the central idea or meaning found in it. The plot is what happens in the story. Titles can also inform us of a work's theme. For instance, the title of Edgar Allan Poe's "The Tell-Tale Heart" informs readers of the story's theme of guilt before they even read about the repeated heartbeat the protagonist hears immediately before and constantly after committing and hiding a murder. Repetitive patterns of events or behaviors also give clues to themes. The same is true of symbols. For example, in F. Scott Fitzgerald's *The Great Gatsby*, for Jay Gatsby the green light at the end of the dock symbolizes Daisy Buchanan and his own dreams for the future. More generally, it is also understood as a symbol of the American Dream, and narrator Nick Carraway explicitly compares it to early settlers' sight of America rising from the ocean.

THEMATIC DEVELOPMENT
THEME IN THE GREAT GATSBY

In *The Great Gatsby*, F. Scott Fitzgerald portrayed 1920s America as greedy, cynical, and rife with moral decay. Jay Gatsby's lavish weekly parties symbolize the reckless excesses of the Jazz Age. The growth of bootlegging and organized crime in reaction to Prohibition is symbolized by the character of Meyer Wolfsheim and by Gatsby's own ill-gotten wealth. Fitzgerald symbolized social divisions using geography. The "old money" aristocrats like the Buchanans lived on East Egg, while the "new money" bourgeois like Gatsby lived on West Egg. Fitzgerald also used weather, as many authors have, to reinforce narrative and emotional tones in the novel. Just as in *Romeo and Juliet*, where William Shakespeare set the confrontation of Tybalt and Mercutio and its deadly consequences on the hottest summer day under a burning sun, in *The Great Gatsby*, Fitzgerald did the same with Tom Wilson's deadly confrontation with Gatsby. Both works are ostensible love stories carrying socially critical themes about the destructiveness of pointless and misguided behaviors—family feuds in the former, pursuit of money in the latter.

> **Review Video: Thematic Development**
> Visit mometrix.com/academy and enter code: 576507

THEME IN LES MISÉRABLES

In Victor Hugo's novel *Les Misérables*, the overall metamorphosis of protagonist Jean Valjean from a cynical ex-convict into a noble benefactor demonstrates Hugo's theme of the importance of love and compassion for others. Hugo also reflects this in more specific plot events. For example, Valjean's love for Cosette sustains him through many difficult periods and trying events. Hugo illustrates how love and compassion for others beget the same in them: Bishop Myriel's kindness to Valjean eventually inspires him to become honest. Years later, Valjean, as M. Madeleine, has rescued Fauchelevent from under a fallen carriage, Fauchelevent returns the compassionate act by giving Valjean sanctuary in the convent. M. Myriel's kindness also ultimately enables Valjean to rescue Cosette from the Thénardiers. Receiving Valjean's father-like love enables Cosette to fall in love with and marry Marius, and the love between Cosette and Marius enables the couple to forgive Valjean for his past crimes when they are revealed.

THEME IN "THE TELL-TALE HEART"

In one of his shortest stories, "The Tell-Tale Heart," Poe used economy of language to emphasize the murderer-narrator's obsessive focus on bare details like the victim's cataract-milky eye, the sound of a heartbeat, and insistence he is sane. The narrator begins by denying he is crazy, even citing his extreme agitation as proof of sanity. Contradiction is then extended: the narrator loves the old man, yet kills him. His motives are irrational—not greed or revenge, but to relieve the victim of his "evil eye." Because "eye" and "I" are homonyms, readers may infer that eye/I symbolizes the old man's identity, contradicting the killer's delusion that he can separate them. The narrator distances himself from the old man by perceiving his eye as separate, and dismembering his dead body. This backfires when he imagines the victim's heartbeat, which is really his own, just before he kills him and frequently afterward. Guilty and paranoid, he gives himself away. Poe predated Freud in exploring the paradox of killing those we love and the concept of projecting our own processes onto others.

THEME IN THE WORKS OF WILLIAM FAULKNER AND CHARLES DICKENS

William Faulkner contrasts the traditions of the antebellum South with the rapid changes of post-Civil War industrialization in his short story "A Rose for Emily." Living inside the isolated world of her house, Emily Grierson denies the reality of modern progress. Contradictorily, she is both a testament to time-honored history and a mysterious, eccentric, unfathomable burden. Faulkner portrays her with deathlike imagery even in life, comparing her to a drowned woman and referring to her skeleton. Emily symbolizes the Old South; as her social status is degraded, so is the antebellum social order. Like Miss Havisham in Charles Dickens' *Great Expectations,* Emily preserves her bridal bedroom, denying change and time's passage. Emily tries to control death through denial, shown in her necrophilia with her father's corpse and her killing of Homer Barron to stop him from leaving her, then also denying his death. Faulkner uses the motif of dust throughout to represent not only the decay of Emily, her house, and Old Southern traditions, but also how her secrets are obscured from others.

THEME IN MOBY-DICK

The great White Whale in *Moby-Dick* plays various roles to different characters. In Captain Ahab's obsessive, monomaniacal quest to kill it, the whale represents all evil, and Ahab believes it his duty and destiny to rid the world of it. Ishmael attempts through multiple scientific disciplines to understand the whale objectively, but fails—it is hidden underwater and mysterious to humans—reinforcing Melville's theme that humans can never know everything; here the whale represents the unknowable. Melville reverses white's usual connotation of purity in Ishmael's dread of white, associated with crashing waves, polar animals, albinos—all frightening and unnatural. White is often viewed as an absence of color, yet white light is the sum total of all colors in the spectrum. In the same way, white can signify both absence of meaning, and totality of meaning incomprehensible to humans. As a creature of nature, the whale also symbolizes how 19th-century white men's exploitative expansionistic actions were destroying the natural environment.

THEME IN THE OLD MAN AND THE SEA

Because of the old fisherman Santiago's struggle to capture a giant marlin, some people characterize Ernest Hemingway's *The Old Man and the Sea* as telling of man against nature. However, it can more properly be interpreted as telling of man's role as part of nature. Both man and fish are portrayed as brave, proud, and honorable. In Hemingway's world, all creatures, including humans, must either kill or be killed. Santiago reflects, "man can be destroyed but not defeated," following this principle in his life. As heroes are often created through their own deaths, Hemingway seems to believe that while being destroyed is inevitable, destruction enables living beings to transcend it by fighting bravely with honor and dignity. Hemingway echoes Romantic poet John Keats' contention that only immediately before death can we understand beauty as it is about to be destroyed. He also echoes ancient Greek and Roman myths and the Old Testament with the tragic flaw of overweening pride or overreaching. Like Icarus, Prometheus, and Adam and Eve, the old man "went out too far."

UNIVERSAL THEMES

The Old Testament book of Genesis, the Quran, and the Epic of Gilgamesh all contain flood stories. Versions differ somewhat, yet marketed similarities also exist. Genesis describes a worldwide flood, attributing it to God's decision that mankind, his creation, had become incontrovertibly wicked in spirit and must be destroyed for the world to start anew. The Quran describes the flood as regional, caused by Allah after sending Nuh (notice the similarity in name to Noah) as a messenger to his people to cease their evil. The Quran stipulates that Allah only destroys those who deny or ignore messages from his messengers. In the Gilgamesh poems Utnapishtim, like Noah, is instructed to build a ship to survive the flood. Both men also send out birds afterward as tests, using doves and a raven, though with different outcomes. Many historians and archeologists believe a Middle Eastern tidal wave was a real basis for these stories. However, their universal themes remain the same: the flood was seen as God's way of wiping out humans whose behavior had become ungodly.

THEME OF OVERREACHING

A popular theme throughout literature is the human trait of **reaching too far** or **presuming too much**. In Greek mythology, Daedalus constructed wings of feathers and wax that men might fly like birds. He permitted his son Icarus to try them, but cautioned the boy not to fly too close to the sun. The impetuous youth (in what psychologist David Elkind later named adolescence's myth of invincibility) ignored this, flying too close to the sun. The wax melted, the wings disintegrated, and Icarus fell into the sea and perished. In the Old Testament, God warned Adam and Eve not to eat fruit from the tree of knowledge of good and evil. Because they ignored this command, they were banished from Eden's eternal perfection, condemning them to mortality and suffering. The Romans were themselves examples of overreaching in their conquest and assimilation of most of the then-known world and their ultimate demise. In Christopher Marlowe's *Dr. Faustus* and Johann Wolfgang von Goethe's *Faust,* the protagonist sells his soul to the Devil for unlimited knowledge and success, ultimately leading to his own tragic end.

STORY VS. DISCOURSE

In terms of plot, "story" is the characters, places, and events originating in the author's mind, while "discourse" is how the author arranges and sequences events—which may be chronological or not. Story is imaginary; discourse is words on the page. Discourse allows a story to be told in different ways. One element of plot structure is relating events differently from the order in which they occurred. This is easily done with cause-and-effect; for example, in the sentence, "He died following a long illness," we know the illness preceded the death, but the death precedes the illness in words. In Kate Chopin's short story "The Story of an Hour" (1894), she tells some of the events out of chronological order, which has the effect of amplifying the surprise of the ending for the reader. Another element of plot structure is selection. Chopin omits some details, such as Mr. Mallard's trip home; this allows readers to be as surprised at his arrival as Mrs. Mallard is.

PLOT AND MEANING

Novelist E. M. Forster has made the distinction between story as relating a series of events, such as a king dying and then his queen dying, versus plot as establishing motivations for actions and causes for events, such as a king dying and then his queen dying from grief over his death. Thus, plot fulfills the function of helping readers understand cause-and-effect in events and underlying motivations in characters' actions, which in turn helps them understand life. This affects a work's meaning by supporting its ability to explain why things happen, why people do things, and ultimately the meaning of life. Some authors find that while story events convey meaning, they do not tell readers there is any one meaning in life or way of living, but rather are mental experiments with various meanings, enabling readers to explore. Hence stories may not necessarily be constructed to impose one definitive meaning, but rather to find some shape, direction, and meaning within otherwise random events.

CLASSIC ANALYSIS OF PLOT STRUCTURE

In *Poetics,* Aristotle defined plot as "the arrangement of the incidents." He meant not the story, but how it is structured for presentation. In tragedies, Aristotle found results driven by chains of cause and effect preferable to those driven by the protagonist's personality or character. He identified "unity of action" as necessary for a plot's wholeness, meaning its events must be internally connected, not episodic or relying on *deus ex machina* or other external intervention. A plot must have a beginning, middle, and end. Gustav Freytag adapted Aristotle's ideas into his Pyramid (1863). The beginning, today called the exposition, incentive, or inciting moment, emphasizes causes and de-emphasizes effects. Aristotle called the ensuing cause and effect *desis*, or tying up, today called complications which occur during the rising action. These culminate in a crisis or climax, Aristotle's *peripateia.* This occurs at the plot's middle, where cause and effect are both emphasized. The falling action, which Aristotle called the *lusis* or unraveling, is today called the dénouement. The resolution comes at the catastrophe, outcome, or end, when causes are emphasized and effects de-emphasized.

> **Review Video: Plot line Definition**
> Visit mometrix.com/academy and enter code: 944011

ANALYSIS OF PLOT STRUCTURES THROUGH RECURRING PATTERNS

Authors of fiction select characters, places, and events from their imaginations and arrange them to create a story that will affect their readers. One way to analyze plot structure is to compare and contrast different events in a story. For example, in Kate Chopin's "The Story of an Hour," a very simple but key pattern of repetition is the husband's leaving and then returning. Such patterns fulfill the symmetrical aspect that Aristotle said was required of sound plot structure. In James Baldwin's short story, "Sonny's Blues," the narrator is Sonny's brother. In an encounter with one of Sonny's old friends early in the story, the brother initially disregards his communication. In a subsequent flashback, Baldwin informs us that this was the same way he had treated Sonny. In Nathaniel Hawthorne's "Young Goodman Brown," a pattern is created by the protagonist's recurrent efforts not to go farther into the wood. In Herman Melville's "Bartleby the Scrivener" and in William Faulkner's "Barn Burning," patterns are also created by repetition such as Bartleby's repeated refusals and the history of barn-burning episodes, respectively.

LITERARY THEORIES AND CRITICISM AND INTERPRETATION

Literary theory includes ideas that guide readers through the process of interpreting literature. Literary theory, as a subject, encompasses several specific, focused theories that lead readers to interpret or analyze literature through the context of the theory using the subjects and elements it involves. Some commonly used and discussed literary theories include **postcolonial theory, gender and feminist theory, structuralism, new historicism, reader-response theory**, and **sociological criticism**.

- **Postcolonial theory** involves the historical and geographical context of a work and leads readers to consider how colonization informs the plot, characters, setting, and other elements in the work.
- **Gender and feminist theory** invites readers to interpret a text by looking at its treatment of and suggestions about women and a culture's treatment of women. As with most literary theories, this information can be clearly stated or strongly implied in a work, but it may also be gleaned through looking closely at symbols, characters, and plot elements in a work.
- **Structuralism** uses the structure and organization of a work and the foundations of language to examine how and what a text conveys about the human experience and how those findings connect to common human experiences.
- **New historicism** heavily relies on the cultural and historical context of a work, including when it was written, where the author lives or lived, the culture and history of that location, and other works from the same culture. New historical readings seek to examine these details to expose the ideologies of the location and culture that influenced the work.
- **Reader-response theory** uses the individual reader's response to the text and experience while reading the text to examine the meaning of the reader's relationship with the text and what that relationship suggests about the reader or the factors impacting their experience.
- **Sociological criticism** considers the societies that are relevant to a text. The author's society and any reader's society are important to the text, as sociological criticism seeks to uncover what the text implies or reveals about those societies. This method of criticism can also involve studying the presentation of a society within the text and applying it to the author's society or their other writings.

CHAPTER QUIZ

1. David Elkind's term "adolescence's myth of invincibility" is derived from which classical story?
   a. The Epic of Gilgamesh
   b. *Dr. Faustus*
   c. Daedalus and Icarus
   d. *Odyssey*

2. Which of the following is NOT a commonly used and discussed literary theory?
   a. Gender and feminist theory
   b. Sociological criticism
   c. Precolonial theory
   d. New historicism

CHAPTER QUIZ ANSWER KEY

1. C: A popular theme throughout literature is the human trait of reaching too far or presuming too much. In Greek mythology, Daedalus constructed wings from feathers and wax so that men might fly like birds. He permitted his son Icarus to try them, but cautioned the boy not to fly too close to the sun. The impetuous youth (in what psychologist David Elkind later named "adolescence's myth of invincibility") ignored this, flying too close to the sun. The wax melted, the wings disintegrated, and Icarus fell into the sea and perished.

2. C: Literary theory includes ideas that guide readers through the process of interpreting literature. As a subject, literary theory encompasses several specific, focused theories that lead readers to interpret or analyze literature through the context of the theory using the subjects and elements it involves. Some commonly used and discussed literary theories include postcolonial theory, gender and feminist theory, structuralism, new historicism, reader-response theory, and sociological criticism.

Reading Comprehension section.

Reading Comprehension

UNDERSTANDING A PASSAGE

One of the most important skills in reading comprehension is the identification of **topics** and **main ideas**. There is a subtle difference between these two features. The topic is the subject of a text (i.e., what the text is all about). The main idea, on the other hand, is the most important point being made by the author. The topic is usually expressed in a few words at the most while the main idea often needs a full sentence to be completely defined. As an example, a short passage might be written on the topic of penguins, and the main idea could be written as *Penguins are different from other birds in many ways*. In most nonfiction writing, the topic and the main idea will be **stated directly** and often appear in a sentence at the very beginning or end of the text. When being tested on an understanding of the author's topic, you may be able to skim the passage for the general idea by reading only the first sentence of each paragraph. A body paragraph's first sentence is often— but not always—the main **topic sentence** which gives you a summary of the content in the paragraph.

However, there are cases in which the reader must figure out an **unstated** topic or main idea. In these instances, you must read every sentence of the text and try to come up with an overarching idea that is supported by each of those sentences.

Note: The main idea should not be confused with the thesis statement. While the main idea gives a brief, general summary of a text, the thesis statement provides a **specific perspective** on an issue that the author supports with evidence.

> **Review Video: <u>Topics and Main Ideas</u>**
> Visit mometrix.com/academy and enter code: 407801

Supporting details are smaller pieces of evidence that provide backing for the main point. In order to show that a main idea is correct or valid, an author must add details that prove their point. All texts contain details, but they are only classified as supporting details when they serve to reinforce some larger point. Supporting details are most commonly found in informative and persuasive texts. In some cases, they will be clearly indicated with terms like *for example* or *for instance*, or they will be enumerated with terms like *first*, *second*, and *last*. However, you need to be prepared for texts that do not contain those indicators. As a reader, you should consider whether the author's supporting details really back up his or her main point. Details can be factual and correct, yet they may not be **relevant** to the author's point. Conversely, details can be relevant, but be ineffective because they are based on opinion or assertions that cannot be proven.

> **Review Video: <u>Supporting Details</u>**
> Visit mometrix.com/academy and enter code: 396297

An example of a main idea is: *Giraffes live in the Serengeti of Africa*. A supporting detail about giraffes could be: *A giraffe in this region benefits from a long neck by reaching twigs and leaves on tall trees*. The main idea gives the general idea that the text is about giraffes. The supporting detail gives a specific fact about how the giraffes eat.

ORGANIZATION OF THE TEXT

The way a text is organized can help readers understand the author's intent and his or her conclusions. There are various ways to organize a text, and each one has a purpose and use. Usually, authors will organize information logically in a passage so the reader can follow and locate the information within the text. However, since not all passages are written with the same logical structure, you need to be familiar with several different types of passage structure.

Review Video: <u>Organizational Methods to Structure Text</u>
Visit mometrix.com/academy and enter code: 606263

Review Video: <u>Sequence of Events in a Story</u>
Visit mometrix.com/academy and enter code: 807512

CHRONOLOGICAL

When using **chronological** order, the author presents information in the order that it happened. For example, biographies are typically written in chronological order. The subject's birth and childhood are presented first, followed by their adult life, and lastly the events leading up to the person's death.

CAUSE AND EFFECT

One of the most common text structures is **cause and effect**. A **cause** is an act or event that makes something happen, and an **effect** is the thing that happens as a result of the cause. A cause-and-effect relationship is not always explicit, but there are some terms in English that signal causes, such as *since*, *because*, and *due to*. Furthermore, terms that signal effects include *consequently, therefore, this leads to*. As an example, consider the sentence *Because the sky was clear, Ron did not bring an umbrella*. The cause is the clear sky, and the effect is that Ron did not bring an umbrella. However, readers may find that sometimes the cause-and-effect relationship will not be clearly noted. For instance, the sentence *He was late and missed the meeting* does not contain any signaling words, but the sentence still contains a cause (he was late) and an effect (he missed the meeting).

Review Video: <u>Cause and Effect</u>
Visit mometrix.com/academy and enter code: 868099

MULTIPLE EFFECTS

Be aware of the possibility for a single cause to have **multiple effects.** (e.g., *Single cause*: Because you left your homework on the table, your dog engulfed the assignment. *Multiple effects*: As a result, you receive a failing grade, your parents do not allow you to go out with your friends, you miss out on the new movie, and one of your classmates spoils it for you before you have another chance to watch it).

MULTIPLE CAUSES

Also, there is the possibility for a single effect to have **multiple causes.** (e.g., *Single effect*: Alan has a fever. *Multiple causes*: An unexpected cold front came through the area, and Alan forgot to take his multi-vitamin to avoid getting sick.) Additionally, an effect can in turn be the cause of another effect, in what is known as a cause-and-effect chain. (e.g., As a result of her disdain for procrastination, Lynn prepared for her exam. This led to her passing her test with high marks. Hence, her resume was accepted and her application was approved.)

CAUSE AND EFFECT IN PERSUASIVE ESSAYS

Persuasive essays, in which an author tries to make a convincing argument and change the minds of readers, usually include cause-and-effect relationships. However, these relationships should not always be taken at face value. Frequently, an author will assume a cause or take an effect for granted. To read a persuasive essay effectively, readers need to judge the cause-and-effect relationships that the author is presenting. For instance, imagine an author wrote the following: *The* *parking deck has been unprofitable because people would prefer to ride their bikes.* The relationship is clear: the cause is that people prefer to ride their bikes, and the effect is that the parking deck has been unprofitable. However, readers should consider whether this argument is conclusive. Perhaps there are other reasons for the failure of the parking deck: a down economy, excessive fees, etc. Too often, authors present causal relationships as if they are fact rather than opinion. Readers should be on the alert for these dubious claims.

PROBLEM-SOLUTION

Some nonfiction texts are organized to **present a problem** followed by a solution. For this type of text, the problem is often explained before the solution is offered. In some cases, as when the problem is well known, the solution may be introduced briefly at the beginning. Other passages may focus on the solution, and the problem will be referenced only occasionally. Some texts will outline multiple solutions to a problem, leaving readers to choose among them. If the author has an interest or an allegiance to one solution, he or she may fail to mention or describe accurately some of the other solutions. Readers should be careful of the author's agenda when reading a problem-solution text. Only by understanding the author's perspective and interests can one develop a proper judgment of the proposed solution.

COMPARE AND CONTRAST

Many texts follow the **compare-and-contrast** model in which the similarities and differences between two ideas or things are explored. Analysis of the similarities between ideas is called **comparison**. In an ideal comparison, the author places ideas or things in an equivalent structure, i.e., the author presents the ideas in the same way. If an author wants to show the similarities between cricket and baseball, then he or she may do so by summarizing the equipment and rules for each game. Be mindful of the similarities as they appear in the passage and take note of any differences that are mentioned. Often, these small differences will only reinforce the more general similarity.

> **Review Video: Compare and Contrast**
> Visit mometrix.com/academy and enter code: 798319

Thinking critically about ideas and conclusions can seem like a daunting task. One way to ease this task is to understand the basic elements of ideas and writing techniques. Looking at the ways different ideas relate to each other can be a good way for readers to begin their analysis. For instance, sometimes authors will write about two ideas that are in opposition to each other. Or, one author will provide his or her ideas on a topic, and another author may respond in opposition. The analysis of these opposing ideas is known as **contrast**. Contrast is often marred by the author's obvious partiality to one of the ideas. A discerning reader will be put off by an author who does not engage in a fair fight. In an analysis of opposing ideas, both ideas should be presented in clear and reasonable terms. If the author does prefer a side, you need to read carefully to determine the areas where the author shows or avoids this preference. In an analysis of opposing ideas, you should proceed through the passage by marking the major differences point by point with an eye that is looking for an explanation of each side's view. For instance, in an analysis of capitalism and communism, there is an importance in outlining each side's view on labor, markets, prices, personal responsibility, etc. Additionally, as you read through the passages, you should note whether the opposing views present each side in a similar manner.

SEQUENCE

Readers must be able to identify a text's **sequence**, or the order in which things happen. Often, when the sequence is very important to the author, the text is indicated with signal words like *first*, *then*, *next*, and *last*. However, a sequence can be merely implied and must be noted by the reader. Consider the sentence *He walked through the garden and gave water and fertilizer to the plants.* Clearly, the man did not walk through the garden before he collected water and fertilizer for the plants. So, the implied sequence is that he first collected water, then he collected fertilizer, next he walked through the garden, and last he gave water or fertilizer as necessary to the plants. Texts do not always proceed in an orderly sequence from first to last. Sometimes they begin at the end and start over at the beginning. As a reader, you can enhance your understanding of the passage by taking brief notes to clarify the sequence.

MAKING CONNECTIONS TO ENHANCE COMPREHENSION

Reading involves thinking. For good comprehension, readers make **text-to-self**, **text-to-text**, and **text-to-world connections**. Making connections helps readers understand text better and predict what might occur next based on what they already know, such as how characters in the story feel or what happened in another text. Text-to-self connections with the reader's life and experiences make literature more personally relevant and meaningful to readers. Readers can make connections before, during, and after reading—including whenever the text reminds them of something similar they have encountered in life or other texts. The genre, setting, characters, plot elements, literary structure and devices, and themes an author uses allow a reader to make connections to other works of literature or to people and events in their own lives. Venn diagrams and other graphic organizers help visualize connections. Readers can also make double-entry notes: key content, ideas, events, words, and quotations on one side, and the connections with these on the other.

SUMMARIZING LITERATURE TO SUPPORT COMPREHENSION

When reading literature, especially demanding works, **summarizing** helps readers identify important information and organize it in their minds. They can also identify themes, problems, and solutions, and can sequence the story. Readers can summarize before, during, and after they read. They should use their own words, as they do when describing a personal event or giving directions. Previewing a text's organization before reading by examining the book cover, table of contents, and illustrations also aids summarizing. Making notes of key words and ideas in a graphic organizer while reading can benefit readers in the same way. Graphic organizers are another useful method; readers skim the text to determine main ideas and then narrow the list with the aid of the organizer. Unimportant details should be omitted in summaries. Summaries can be organized using description, problem-solution, comparison-contrast, sequence, main ideas, or cause-and-effect.

> **Review Video: Summarizing Text**
> Visit mometrix.com/academy and enter code: 172903

PARAPHRASING

Paraphrasing is another method that the reader can use to aid in comprehension. When paraphrasing, one puts what they have read into their own words by rephrasing what the author has written, or one "translates" all of what the author shared into their own words by including as many details as they can.

CHAPTER QUIZ

1. All of the following are used for good comprehension, EXCEPT:

    a. Text-to-self connections.
    b. Text-to-others connections.
    c. Text-to-text connections.
    d. Text-to-world connections.

2. All of the following are terms in English that signal causes, EXCEPT:

    a. Because.
    b. Due to.
    c. Since.
    d. Therefore.

CHAPTER QUIZ ANSWER KEY

1. B: Reading involves thinking. For good comprehension, readers make text-to-self, text-to-text, and text-to-world connections. Making connections helps readers understand text better and predict what might occur next based on what they already know, such as how characters in the story feel or what happened in another text. Text-to-self connections with the reader's life and experiences make literature more personally relevant and meaningful to readers. Readers can make connections before, during, and after reading—including whenever the text reminds them of something similar they have encountered in life or other texts. The genre, setting, characters, plot elements, themes, and literary structure and devices an author uses allow a reader to make connections to other works of literature or to people and events in their own lives. Venn diagrams and other graphic organizers help visualize connections. Readers can also make double-entry notes: key content, ideas, events, words, and quotations on one side, and the connections with these on the other.

2. D: One of the most common text structures is cause and effect. A cause is an act or event that makes something happen, and an effect is the thing that happens as a result of the cause. A cause-and-effect relationship is not always explicit, but there are some terms in English that signal causes, such as *since*, *because*, and *due to*. Furthermore, terms that signal effects include *consequently*, *therefore*, and *this leads to*. As an example, consider the sentence, "Because the sky was clear, Ron did not bring an umbrella." The cause is the clear sky, and the effect is that Ron did not bring an umbrella. However, readers may find that sometimes the cause-and-effect relationship will not be clearly noted. For instance, the sentence, "He was late and missed the meeting," does not contain any signaling words, but the sentence still contains a cause ("he was late") and an effect ("he missed the meeting").

Making Predictions and Inferences

MAKING PREDICTIONS

When we read literature, **making predictions** about what will happen in the writing reinforces our purpose for reading and prepares us mentally. A **prediction** is a guess about what will happen next. Readers constantly make predictions based on what they have read and what they already know. We can make predictions before we begin reading and during our reading. Consider the following sentence: *Staring at the computer screen in shock, Kim blindly reached over for the brimming glass of water on the shelf to her side.* The sentence suggests that Kim is distracted, and that she is not looking at the glass that she is going to pick up. So, a reader might predict that Kim is going to knock over the glass. Of course, not every prediction will be accurate: perhaps Kim will pick the glass up cleanly. Nevertheless, the author has certainly created the expectation that the water might be spilled.

As we read on, we can test the accuracy of our predictions, revise them in light of additional reading, and confirm or refute our predictions. Predictions are always subject to revision as the reader acquires more information. A reader can make predictions by observing the title and illustrations; noting the structure, characters, and subject; drawing on existing knowledge relative to the subject; and asking "why" and "who" questions. Connecting reading to what we already know enables us to learn new information and construct meaning. For example, before third-graders read a book about Johnny Appleseed, they may start a KWL chart—a list of what they *Know*, what they *Want* to know or learn, and what they have *Learned* after reading. Activating existing background knowledge and thinking about the text before reading improves comprehension.

> **Review Video: Predictive Reading**
> Visit mometrix.com/academy and enter code: 437248

Test-taking tip: To respond to questions requiring future predictions, your answers should be based on evidence of past or present behavior and events.

EVALUATING PREDICTIONS

When making predictions, readers should be able to explain how they developed their prediction. One way readers can defend their thought process is by citing textual evidence. Textual evidence to evaluate reader predictions about literature includes specific synopses of the work, paraphrases of the work or parts of it, and direct quotations from the work. These references to the text must support the prediction by indicating, clearly or unclearly, what will happen later in the story. A text may provide these indications through literary devices such as foreshadowing. Foreshadowing is anything in a text that gives the reader a hint about what is to come by emphasizing the likelihood of an event or development. Foreshadowing can occur through descriptions, exposition, and dialogue. Foreshadowing in dialogue usually occurs when a character gives a warning or expresses a strong feeling that a certain event will occur. Foreshadowing can also occur through irony. However, unlike other forms of foreshadowing, the events that seem the most likely are the opposite of what actually happens. Instances of foreshadowing and irony can be summarized, paraphrased, or quoted to defend a reader's prediction.

> **Review Video: Textual Evidence for Predictions**
> Visit mometrix.com/academy and enter code: 261070

DRAWING CONCLUSIONS FROM INFERENCES

Inferences about literary text are logical conclusions that readers make based on their observations and previous knowledge. An inference is based on both what is found in a passage or a story and what is known from personal experience. For instance, a story may say that a character is frightened and can hear howling in the distance. Based on both what is in the text and personal knowledge, it is a logical conclusion that the character is frightened because he hears the sound of wolves. A good inference is supported by the information in a passage.

IMPLICIT AND EXPLICIT INFORMATION

By inferring, readers construct meanings from text that are personally relevant. By combining their own schemas or concepts and their background information pertinent to the text with what they read, readers interpret it according to both what the author has conveyed and their own unique perspectives. Inferences are different from **explicit information**, which is clearly stated in a passage. Authors do not always explicitly spell out every meaning in what they write; many meanings are implicit. Through inference, readers can comprehend implied meanings in the text, and also derive personal significance from it, making the text meaningful and memorable to them. Inference is a natural process in everyday life. When readers infer, they can draw conclusions about what the author is saying, predict what may reasonably follow, amend these predictions as they continue to read, interpret the import of themes, and analyze the characters' feelings and motivations through their actions.

EXAMPLE OF DRAWING CONCLUSIONS FROM INFERENCES

Read the excerpt and decide why Jana finally relaxed.

> Jana loved her job, but the work was very demanding. She had trouble relaxing. She called a friend, but she still thought about work. She ordered a pizza, but eating it did not help. Then, her kitten jumped on her lap and began to purr. Jana leaned back and began to hum a little tune. She felt better.

You can draw the conclusion that Jana relaxed because her kitten jumped on her lap. The kitten purred, and Jana leaned back and hummed a tune. Then she felt better. The excerpt does not explicitly say that this is the reason why she was able to relax. The text leaves the matter unclear, but the reader can infer or make a "best guess" that this is the reason she is relaxing. This is a logical conclusion based on the information in the passage. It is the best conclusion a reader can make based on the information he or she has read. Inferences are based on the information in a passage, but they are not directly stated in the passage.

Test-taking tip: While being tested on your ability to make correct inferences, you must look for **contextual clues**. An answer can be true, but not the best or most correct answer. The contextual clues will help you find the answer that is the **best answer** out of the given choices. Be careful in your reading to understand the context in which a phrase is stated. When asked for the implied meaning of a statement made in the passage, you should immediately locate the statement and read the **context** in which the statement was made. Also, look for an answer choice that has a similar phrase to the statement in question.

> **Review Video: Inference**
> Visit mometrix.com/academy and enter code: 379203
>
> **Review Video: How to Support a Conclusion**
> Visit mometrix.com/academy and enter code: 281653

CHAPTER QUIZ

1. Which of the following describes logical conclusions that readers make based on their observations and previous knowledge?

    a. Imperatives
    b. Interrogatives
    c. Inferences
    d. Predictions

CHAPTER QUIZ ANSWER KEY

1. C: Inferences about literary text are logical conclusions that readers make based on their observations and previous knowledge. An inference is based on both what is found in a passage or a story and what is known from personal experience. For instance, a story may say that a character is frightened and can hear howling in the distance. Based on both what is in the text and personal knowledge, it is a logical conclusion that the character is frightened because they hear the sound of wolves. A good inference is supported by the information in a passage.

Interactions with Texts

PURPOSES FOR WRITING

In order to be an effective reader, one must pay attention to the author's **position** and **purpose**. Even those texts that seem objective and impartial, like textbooks, have a position and bias. Readers need to take these positions into account when considering the author's message. When an author uses emotional language or clearly favors one side of an argument, his or her position is clear. However, the author's position may be evident not only in what he or she writes, but also in what he or she doesn't write. In a normal setting, a reader would want to review some other texts on the same topic in order to develop a view of the author's position. If this was not possible, then you would want to at least acquire some background about the author. However, since you are in the middle of an exam and the only source of information is the text, you should look for language and argumentation that seems to indicate a particular stance on the subject.

> **Review Video: Author's Position**
> Visit mometrix.com/academy and enter code: 827954

Usually, identifying the author's **purpose** is easier than identifying his or her position. In most cases, the author has no interest in hiding his or her purpose. A text that is meant to entertain, for instance, should be written to please the reader. Most narratives, or stories, are written to entertain, though they may also inform or persuade. Informative texts are easy to identify, while the most difficult purpose of a text to identify is persuasion because the author has an interest in making this purpose hard to detect. When a reader discovers that the author is trying to persuade, he or she should be skeptical of the argument. For this reason, persuasive texts often try to establish an entertaining tone and hope to amuse the reader into agreement. On the other hand, an informative tone may be implemented to create an appearance of authority and objectivity.

An author's purpose is evident often in the organization of the text (e.g., section headings in bold font points to an informative text). However, you may not have such organization available to you in your exam. Instead, if the author makes his or her main idea clear from the beginning, then the likely purpose of the text is to inform. If the author begins by making a claim and provides various arguments to support that claim, then the purpose is probably to persuade. If the author tells a story or wants to gain the reader's attention more than to push a particular point or deliver information, then his or her purpose is most likely to entertain. As a reader, you must judge authors on how well they accomplish their purpose. In other words, you need to consider the type of passage (e.g., technical, persuasive, etc.) that the author has written and if the author has followed the requirements of the passage type.

MAKING LOGICAL CONCLUSIONS ABOUT A PASSAGE

A reader should always be drawing conclusions from the text. Sometimes conclusions are **implied** from written information, and other times the information is **stated directly** within the passage. One should always aim to draw conclusions from information stated within a passage, rather than to draw them from mere implications. At times an author may provide some information and then describe a counterargument. Readers should be alert for direct statements that are subsequently rejected or weakened by the author. Furthermore, you should always read through the entire passage before drawing conclusions. Many readers are trained to expect the author's conclusions at either the beginning or the end of the passage, but many texts do not adhere to this format.

Drawing conclusions from information implied within a passage requires confidence on the part of the reader. **Implications** are things that the author does not state directly, but readers can assume based on what the author does say. Consider the following passage: *I stepped outside and opened my umbrella. By the time I got to work, the cuffs of my pants were soaked.* The author never states that it is raining, but this fact is clearly implied. Conclusions based on implication must be well supported by the text. In order to draw a solid conclusion, readers should have **multiple pieces of evidence**. If readers have only one piece, they must be assured that there is no other possible explanation than their conclusion. A good reader will be able to draw many conclusions from information implied by the text, which will be a great help on the exam.

DRAWING CONCLUSIONS

A common type of inference that a reader has to make is **drawing a conclusion**. The reader makes this conclusion based on the information provided within a text. Certain facts are included to help a reader come to a specific conclusion. For example, a story may open with a man trudging through the snow on a cold winter day, dragging a sled behind him. The reader can logically **infer** from the setting of the story that the man is wearing heavy winter clothes in order to stay warm. Information is implied based on the setting of a story, which is why **setting** is an important element of the text. If the same man in the example was trudging down a beach on a hot summer day, dragging a surf board behind him, the reader would assume that the man is not wearing heavy clothes. The reader makes inferences based on their own experiences and the information presented to them in the story.

Test-taking tip: When asked to identify a conclusion that may be drawn, look for critical "hedge" phrases, such as *likely*, *may*, *can*, and *will often*, among many others. When you are being tested on this knowledge, remember the question that writers insert into these hedge phrases to cover every possibility. Often an answer will be wrong simply because there is no room for exception. Extreme positive or negative answers (such as always or never) are usually not correct. When answering these questions, the reader **should not** use any outside knowledge that is not gathered directly or reasonably inferred from the passage. Correct answers can be derived straight from the passage.

EXAMPLE

Read the following sentence from *Little Women* by Louisa May Alcott and draw a conclusion based upon the information presented:

> *You know the reason Mother proposed not having any presents this Christmas was because it is going to be a hard winter for everyone; and she thinks we ought not to spend money for pleasure, when our men are suffering so in the army.*

Based on the information in the sentence, the reader can conclude, or **infer**, that the men are away at war while the women are still at home. The pronoun *our* gives a clue to the reader that the character is speaking about men she knows. In addition, the reader can assume that the character is speaking to a brother or sister, since the term "Mother" is used by the character while speaking to another person. The reader can also come to the conclusion that the characters celebrate Christmas, since it is mentioned in the **context** of the sentence. In the sentence, the mother is presented as an unselfish character who is opinionated and thinks about the wellbeing of other people.

COMPARING TWO STORIES

When presented with two different stories, there will be **similarities** and **differences** between the two. A reader needs to make a list, or other graphic organizer, of the points presented in each story. Once the reader has written down the main point and supporting points for each story, the two sets of ideas can be compared. The reader can then present each idea and show how it is the same or different in the other story. This is called **comparing and contrasting ideas**.

The reader can compare ideas by stating, for example: "In Story 1, the author believes that humankind will one day land on Mars, whereas in Story 2, the author believes that Mars is too far away for humans to ever step foot on." Note that the two viewpoints are different in each story that the reader is comparing. A reader may state that: "Both stories discussed the likelihood of humankind landing on Mars." This statement shows how the viewpoint presented in both stories is based on the same topic, rather than how each viewpoint is different. The reader will complete a comparison of two stories with a conclusion.

> **Review Video: Comparing Two Stories**
> Visit mometrix.com/academy and enter code: 833765

OUTLINING A PASSAGE

As an aid to drawing conclusions, **outlining** the information contained in the passage should be a familiar skill to readers. An effective outline will reveal the structure of the passage and will lead to solid conclusions. An effective outline will have a title that refers to the basic subject of the text, though the title does not need to restate the main idea. In most outlines, the main idea will be the first major section. Each major idea in the passage will be established as the head of a category. For instance, the most common outline format calls for the main ideas of the passage to be indicated with Roman numerals. In an effective outline of this kind, each of the main ideas will be represented by a Roman numeral and none of the Roman numerals will designate minor details or secondary ideas. Moreover, all supporting ideas and details should be placed in the appropriate place on the outline. An outline does not need to include every detail listed in the text, but it should feature all of those that are central to the argument or message. Each of these details should be listed under the corresponding main idea.

> **Review Video: Outlining**
> Visit mometrix.com/academy and enter code: 584445

USING GRAPHIC ORGANIZERS

Ideas from a text can also be organized using **graphic organizers**. A graphic organizer is a way to simplify information and take key points from the text. A graphic organizer such as a timeline may have an event listed for a corresponding date on the timeline, while an outline may have an event listed under a key point that occurs in the text. Each reader needs to create the type of graphic organizer that works the best for him or her in terms of being able to recall information from a story. Examples include a spider-map, which takes a main idea from the story and places it in a bubble with supporting points branching off the main idea. An outline is useful for diagramming the main and supporting points of the entire story, and a Venn diagram compares and contrasts characteristics of two or more ideas.

> **Review Video: Graphic Organizers**
> Visit mometrix.com/academy and enter code: 665513

SUMMARIZING

A helpful tool is the ability to **summarize** the information that you have read in a paragraph or passage format. This process is similar to creating an effective outline. First, a summary should accurately define the main idea of the passage, though the summary does not need to explain this main idea in exhaustive detail. The summary should continue by laying out the most important supporting details or arguments from the passage. All of the significant supporting details should be included, and none of the details included should be irrelevant or insignificant. Also, the summary should accurately report all of these details. Too often, the desire for brevity in a summary leads to the sacrifice of clarity or accuracy. Summaries are often difficult to read because they omit all of the graceful language, digressions, and asides that distinguish great writing. However, an effective summary should communicate the same overall message as the original text.

EVALUATING A PASSAGE

It is important to understand the logical conclusion of the ideas presented in an informational text. **Identifying a logical conclusion** can help you determine whether you agree with the writer or not. Coming to this conclusion is much like making an inference: the approach requires you to combine the information given by the text with what you already know and make a logical conclusion. If the author intended for the reader to draw a certain conclusion, then you can expect the author's argumentation and detail to be leading in that direction.

One way to approach the task of drawing conclusions is to make brief **notes** of all the points made by the author. When the notes are arranged on paper, they may clarify the logical conclusion. Another way to approach conclusions is to consider whether the reasoning of the author raises any pertinent questions. Sometimes you will be able to draw several conclusions from a passage. On occasion these will be conclusions that were never imagined by the author. Therefore, be aware that these conclusions must be **supported directly by the text**.

EVALUATION OF SUMMARIES

A summary of a literary passage is a condensation in the reader's own words of the passage's main points. Several guidelines can be used in evaluating a summary. The summary should be complete yet concise. It should be accurate, balanced, fair, neutral, and objective, excluding the reader's own opinions or reactions. It should reflect in similar proportion how much each point summarized was covered in the original passage. Summary writers should include tags of attribution, like "Macaulay argues that" to reference the original author whose ideas are represented in the summary. Summary writers should not overuse quotations; they should only quote central concepts or phrases they cannot precisely convey in words other than those of the original author. Another aspect of evaluating a summary is considering whether it can stand alone as a coherent, unified composition. In addition, evaluation of a summary should include whether its writer has cited the original source of the passage they have summarized so that readers can find it.

CHAPTER QUIZ

1. Which of the following is most important when drawing conclusions from a text?

  a. The conclusions make sense to others.
  b. The conclusions are supported directly by the text.
  c. The conclusions agree with previous convictions.
  d. The conclusions align with the author's purpose for writing the text.

2. All of the following are true about summaries, EXCEPT:

  a. They should focus on the main point of the text rather than proportional to how much each point was covered in the passage.
  b. They should be accurate, balanced, fair, neutral, and objective.
  c. They should be complete and concise.
  d. They should only quote central concepts or phrases that cannot be precisely conveyed in words other than those of the original author.

CHAPTER QUIZ ANSWER KEY

1. B: It is important to understand the logical conclusion of the ideas presented in an informational text. Identifying a logical conclusion can help readers determine whether they agree with the writer or not. Coming to this conclusion is much like making an inference: the approach requires readers to combine the information given by the text with what they already know and make a logical conclusion. If the author intended for the reader to draw a certain conclusion, then readers can expect the author's argumentation and detail to be leading in that direction. Sometimes a reader will be able to draw several conclusions from a passage. On occasion these will be conclusions that were never imagined by the author. Therefore, be aware that these conclusions must be supported directly by the text.

2. A: A summary of a literary passage is a condensation in the reader's own words of the passage's main points. Several guidelines can be used in evaluating a summary. The summary should be complete yet concise. It should be accurate, balanced, fair, neutral, and objective, excluding the reader's own opinions or reactions. It should reflect in similar proportion how much each point summarized was covered in the original passage. Summary writers should include tags of attribution, like "Macaulay argues that" to reference the original author whose ideas are represented in the summary. Summary writers should not overuse quotations, but only quote central concepts or phrases they cannot precisely convey in words other than those of the original author. Another aspect of evaluating a summary is considering whether it can stand alone as a coherent, unified composition. In addition, evaluation of a summary should include whether its writer has cited the original source of the passage they have summarized so that readers can find it.

Quantitative Reasoning

Numbers

CLASSIFICATIONS OF NUMBERS

Numbers are the basic building blocks of mathematics. Specific features of numbers are identified by the following terms:

Integer – any positive or negative whole number, including zero. Integers do not include fractions $\left(\frac{1}{3}\right)$, decimals (0.56), or mixed numbers $\left(7\frac{3}{4}\right)$.

Integer do not include fractions decimals, or mixed numbers

Prime number – any whole number greater than 1 that has only two factors, itself and 1; that is, a number that can be divided evenly only by 1 and itself. *?*

Composite number – any whole number greater than 1 that has more than two different factors; in other words, any whole number that is not a prime number. For example: The composite number 8 has the factors of 1, 2, 4, and 8. *has multiple divisers*

Even number – any integer that can be divided by 2 without leaving a remainder. For example: 2, 4, 6, 8, and so on.

Odd number – any integer that cannot be divided evenly by 2. For example: 3, 5, 7, 9, and so on.

Decimal number – any number that uses a decimal point to show the part of the number that is less than one. Example: 1.234.

Decimal point – a symbol used to separate the ones place from the tenths place in decimals or dollars from cents in currency.

Decimal place – the position of a number to the right of the decimal point. In the decimal 0.123, the 1 is in the first place to the right of the decimal point, indicating tenths; the 2 is in the second place, indicating hundredths; and the 3 is in the third place, indicating thousandths.

The **decimal**, or base 10, system is a number system that uses ten different digits (0, 1, 2, 3, 4, 5, 6, 7, 8, 9). An example of a number system that uses something other than ten digits is the **binary**, or base 2, number system, used by computers, which uses only the numbers 0 and 1. It is thought that the decimal system originated because people had only their 10 fingers for counting.

Rational numbers include all integers, decimals, and fractions. Any terminating or repeating decimal number is a rational number.

Irrational numbers cannot be written as fractions or decimals because the number of decimal places is infinite and there is no recurring pattern of digits within the number. For example, pi (π) begins with 3.141592 and continues without terminating or repeating, so pi is an irrational number.

145

Real numbers are the set of all rational and irrational numbers.

I know this

Review Video: Classification of Numbers
Visit mometrix.com/academy and enter code: 461071
Review Video: Prime and Composite Numbers
Visit mometrix.com/academy and enter code: 565581

THE NUMBER LINE

A number line is a graph to see the distance between numbers. Basically, this graph shows the relationship between numbers. So a number line may have a point for zero and may show negative numbers on the left side of the line. Any positive numbers are placed on the right side of the line. For example, consider the points labeled on the following number line:

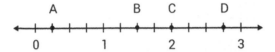

We can use the dashed lines on the number line to identify each point. Each dashed line between two whole numbers is $\frac{1}{4}$. The line halfway between two numbers is $\frac{1}{2}$.

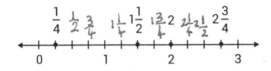

Review Video: The Number Line
Visit mometrix.com/academy and enter code: 816439

NUMBERS IN WORD FORM AND PLACE VALUE

When writing numbers out in word form or translating word form to numbers, it is essential to understand how a place value system works. In the decimal or base-10 system, each digit of a number represents how many of the corresponding place value—a specific factor of 10—are contained in the number being represented. To make reading numbers easier, every three digits to the left of the decimal place is preceded by a comma. The following table demonstrates some of the place values:

Power of 10	10^3	10^2	10^1	10^0	10^{-1}	10^{-2}	10^{-3}
Value	1,000	100	10	1	0.1	0.01	0.001
Place	thousands	hundreds	tens	ones	tenths	hundredths	thousandths

For example, consider the number 4,546.09, which can be separated into each place value like this:

> 4: thousands
> 5: hundreds
> 4: tens
> 6: ones
> 0: tenths
> 9: hundredths

This number in word form would be *four thousand five hundred forty-six and nine hundredths*.

Review Video: Place Value
Visit mometrix.com/academy and enter code: 205433

ABSOLUTE VALUE

A precursor to working with negative numbers is understanding what **absolute values** are. A number's absolute value is simply the distance away from zero a number is on the number line. The absolute value of a number is always positive and is written $|x|$. For example, the absolute value of 3, written as $|3|$, is 3 because the distance between 0 and 3 on a number line is three units. Likewise, the absolute value of –3, written as $|-3|$, is 3 because the distance between 0 and –3 on a number line is three units. So $|3| = |-3|$.

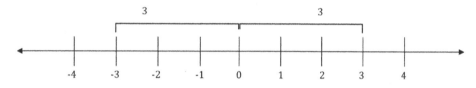

Review Video: Absolute Value
Visit mometrix.com/academy and enter code: 314669

PRACTICE

P1. Write the place value of each digit in 14,059.826

[handwritten: 1: ten thousand / 4: thousand / 0: hundred / 5: tens / 9: ones / 8: tenth / 2: hundredth / 6: thousand]

P2. Write out each of the following in words:

  (a) 29   *[handwritten: twenty-nine]*
  (b) 478   *[handwritten: four hundred and seventy-eight]*
  (c) 98,542   *[handwritten: ninety-eight thousand, five hundred and fourty-two]*
  (d) 0.06   *[handwritten: sixth hundreths]*
  (e) 13.113   *[handwritten: Thirteen and One hundred and thirteen thousand]*

P3. Write each of the following in numbers:

  (a) nine thousand four hundred thirty-five   *[handwritten: 9,435]*
  (b) three hundred two thousand eight hundred seventy-six   *[handwritten: 302,876]*
  (c) nine hundred one thousandths   *[handwritten: 0.901]*
  (d) nineteen thousandths   *[handwritten: .019]*
  (e) seven thousand one hundred forty-two and eighty-five hundredths   *[handwritten: 700,142.85 / 7,142.85]*

Practice Solutions

P1. The place value for each digit would be as follows:

Digit	Place Value
1	ten-thousands
4	thousands
0	hundreds
5	tens
9	ones
8	tenths
2	hundredths
6	thousandths

P2. Each written out in words would be:

(a) twenty-nine
(b) four hundred seventy-eight
(c) ninety-eight thousand five hundred forty-two
(d) six hundredths
(e) thirteen and one hundred thirteen thousandths

P3. Each in numeric form would be:

(a) 9,435
(b) 302876
(c) 0.901
(d) 0.019
(e) 7,142.85

— know
— Donot now
— kinda

Operations

OPERATIONS

An **operation** is simply a mathematical process that takes some value(s) as input(s) and produces an output. Elementary operations are often written in the following form: *value operation value*. For instance, in the expression $1 + 2$ the values are 1 and 2 and the operation is addition. Performing the operation gives the output of 3. In this way we can say that $1 + 2$ and 3 are equal, or $1 + 2 = 3$.

ADDITION

Addition increases the value of one quantity by the value of another quantity (both called **addends**). Example: $2 + 4 = 6$ or $8 + 9 = 17$. The result is called the **sum**. With addition, the order does not matter, $4 + 2 = 2 + 4$.

resut = sum

When adding signed numbers, if the signs are the same simply add the absolute values of the addends and apply the original sign to the sum. For example, $(+4) + (+8) = +12$ and $(-4) + (-8) = -12$. When the original signs are different, take the absolute values of the addends and subtract the smaller value from the larger value, then apply the original sign of the larger value to the difference. Example: $(+4) + (-8) = -4$ and $(-4) + (+8) = +4$.

SUBTRACTION

Subtraction is the opposite operation to addition; it decreases the value of one quantity (the **minuend**) by the value of another quantity (the **subtrahend**). For example, $6 - 4 = 2$ or $17 - 8 = 9$. The result is called the **difference**. Note that with subtraction, the order does matter, $6 - 4 \neq 4 - 6$.

result = differenc

For subtracting signed numbers, change the sign of the subtrahend and then follow the same rules used for addition. Example: $(+4) - (+8) = (+4) + (-8) = -4$

MULTIPLICATION

Multiplication can be thought of as repeated addition. One number (the **multiplier**) indicates how many times to add the other number (the **multiplicand**) to itself. Example: $3 \times 2 = 2 + 2 + 2 = 6$. With multiplication, the order does not matter, $2 \times 3 = 3 \times 2$ or $3 + 3 = 2 + 2 + 2$, either way the result (the **product**) is the same.

If the signs are the same, the product is positive when multiplying signed numbers. Example: $(+4) \times (+8) = +32$ and $(-4) \times (-8) = +32$. If the signs are opposite, the product is negative. Example: $(+4) \times (-8) = -32$ and $(-4) \times (+8) = -32$. When more than two factors are multiplied together, the sign of the product is determined by how many negative factors are present. If there are an odd number of negative factors then the product is negative, whereas an even number of negative factors indicates a positive product. Example: $(+4) \times (-8) \times (-2) = +64$ and $(-4) \times (-8) \times (-2) = -64$.

result = produt   *I didn't know that.*

DIVISION

Division is the opposite operation to multiplication; one number (the **divisor**) tells us how many parts to divide the other number (the **dividend**) into. The result of division is called the **quotient**. Example: $20 \div 4 = 5$. If 20 is split into 4 equal parts, each part is 5. With division, the order of the numbers does matter, $20 \div 4 \neq 4 \div 20$.

resut = quotient

The rules for dividing signed numbers are similar to multiplying signed numbers. If the dividend and divisor have the same sign, the quotient is positive. If the dividend and divisor have opposite signs, the quotient is negative. Example: $(-4) \div (+8) = -0.5$.

PARENTHESES

Parentheses are used to designate which operations should be done first when there are multiple operations. Example: $4 - (2 + 1) = 1$; the parentheses tell us that we must add 2 and 1, and then subtract the sum from 4, rather than subtracting 2 from 4 and then adding 1 (this would give us an answer of 3).

EXPONENTS

An **exponent** is a superscript number placed next to another number at the top right. It indicates how many times the base number is to be multiplied by itself. Exponents provide a shorthand way to write what would be a longer mathematical expression, Example: $2^4 = 2 \times 2 \times 2 \times 2$. A number with an exponent of 2 is said to be "squared," while a number with an exponent of 3 is said to be "cubed." The value of a number raised to an exponent is called its power. So 8^4 is read as "8 to the 4th power," or "8 raised to the power of 4."

The properties of exponents are as follows:

Property	Description
$a^1 = a$	Any number to the power of 1 is equal to itself
$1^n = 1$	The number 1 raised to any power is equal to 1
$a^0 = 1$	Any number raised to the power of 0 is equal to 1
$a^n \times a^m = a^{n+m}$	Add exponents to multiply powers of the same base number
$a^n \div a^m = a^{n-m}$	Subtract exponents to divide powers of the same base number
$(a^n)^m = a^{n \times m}$	When a power is raised to a power, the exponents are multiplied
$(a \times b)^n = a^n \times b^n$ $(a \div b)^n = a^n \div b^n$	Multiplication and division operations inside parentheses can be raised to a power. This is the same as each term being raised to that power.
$a^{-n} = \dfrac{1}{a^n}$	A negative exponent is the same as the reciprocal of a positive exponent

Note that exponents do not have to be integers. Fractional or decimal exponents follow all the rules above as well. Example: $5^{\frac{1}{4}} \times 5^{\frac{3}{4}} = 5^{\frac{1}{4} + \frac{3}{4}} = 5^1 = 5$.

Roots

A **root**, such as a square root, is another way of writing a fractional exponent. Instead of using a superscript, roots use the radical symbol ($\sqrt{}$) to indicate the operation. A radical will have a number underneath the bar, and may sometimes have a number in the upper left: $\sqrt[n]{a}$, read as "the nth root of a." The relationship between radical notation and exponent notation can be described by this equation:

$$\sqrt[n]{a} = a^{\frac{1}{n}}$$

[handwritten: explain more]

The two special cases of $n = 2$ and $n = 3$ are called square roots and cube roots. If there is no number to the upper left, the radical is understood to be a square root ($n = 2$). Nearly all of the roots you encounter will be square roots. A square root is the same as a number raised to the one-half power. When we say that a is the square root of b ($a = \sqrt{b}$), we mean that a multiplied by itself equals b: ($a \times a = b$).

[handwritten: no # = square root]

[handwritten: $\sqrt{a} = a^{\frac{1}{2}}$]

A **perfect square** is a number that has an integer for its square root. There are 10 perfect squares from 1 to 100: 1, 4, 9, 16, 25, 36, 49, 64, 81, 100 (the squares of integers 1 through 10).

[handwritten: Didn't know thier were 10]

Order of Operations

The **order of operations** is a set of rules that dictates the order in which we must perform each operation in an expression so that we will evaluate it accurately. If we have an expression that includes multiple different operations, the order of operations tells us which operations to do first. The most common mnemonic for the order of operations is **PEMDAS**, or "Please Excuse My Dear Aunt Sally." PEMDAS stands for parentheses, exponents, multiplication, division, addition, and subtraction. It is important to understand that multiplication and division have equal precedence, as do addition and subtraction, so those pairs of operations are simply worked from left to right in order.

[handwritten: Prefom mo from Left + right inequation]

For example, evaluating the expression $5 + 20 \div 4 \times (2 + 3)^2 - 6$ using the correct order of operations would be done like this:

[handwritten: $4 \times 25 - 6$]

[handwritten: $5 + 20 \div 4 \times 25 - 6$; $5 + 5 \times 25 - 6$; $5 + 125 - 6$; $130 - 6 = 124$]

- **P:** Perform the operations inside the parentheses: $(2 + 3) = 5$
- **E:** Simplify the exponents: $(5)^2 = 5 \times 5 = 25$
  - The expression now looks like this: $5 + 20 \div 4 \times 25 - 6$
- **MD:** Perform multiplication and division from left to right: $20 \div 4 = 5$; then $5 \times 25 = 125$
  - The expression now looks like this: $5 + 125 - 6$
- **AS:** Perform addition and subtraction from left to right: $5 + 125 = 130$; then $130 - 6 = 124$

SUBTRACTION WITH REGROUPING

A great way to make use of some of the features built into the decimal system would be regrouping when attempting longform subtraction operations. When subtracting within a place value, sometimes the minuend is smaller than the subtrahend, **regrouping** enables you to 'borrow' a unit from a place value to the left in order to get a positive difference. For example, consider subtracting 189 from 525 with regrouping.

> **Review Video: Subtracting Large Numbers**
> Visit mometrix.com/academy and enter code: 603350

First, set up the subtraction problem in vertical form:

$$
\begin{array}{r}
525 \\
- \ \ 189 \\
\hline
336
\end{array}
$$

Notice that the numbers in the ones and tens columns of 525 are smaller than the numbers in the ones and tens columns of 189. This means you will need to use regrouping to perform subtraction:

$$
\begin{array}{ccc}
5 & 2 & 5 \\
- \quad 1 & 8 & 9 \\
\hline
\end{array}
$$

To subtract 9 from 5 in the ones column you will need to borrow from the 2 in the tens columns:

$$
\begin{array}{ccc}
5 & 1 & 15 \\
- \quad 1 & 8 & 9 \\
\hline
 & & 6 \\
\end{array}
$$

Next, to subtract 8 from 1 in the tens column you will need to borrow from the 5 in the hundreds column:

$$
\begin{array}{ccc}
4 & 11 & 15 \\
- \quad 1 & 8 & 9 \\
\hline
 & 3 & 6 \\
\end{array}
$$

Last, subtract the 1 from the 4 in the hundreds column:

$$
\begin{array}{ccc}
4 & 11 & 15 \\
- \quad 1 & 8 & 9 \\
\hline
3 & 3 & 6 \\
\end{array}
$$

WORD PROBLEMS AND MATHEMATICAL SYMBOLS

When working on word problems, you must be able to translate verbal expressions or "math words" into math symbols. This chart contains several "math words" and their appropriate symbols:

Phrase	Symbol
equal, is, was, will be, has, costs, gets to, is the same as, becomes	=
times, of, multiplied by, product of, twice, doubles, halves, triples	×
divided by, per, ratio of/to, out of	÷
plus, added to, sum, combined, and, more than, totals of	+
subtracted from, less than, decreased by, minus, difference between	−
what, how much, original value, how many, a number, a variable	x, n, etc.

EXAMPLES OF TRANSLATED MATHEMATICAL PHRASES

- The phrase four more than twice a number can be written algebraically as $2x + 4$.
- The phrase half a number decreased by six can be written algebraically as $\frac{1}{2}x - 6$.
- The phrase the sum of a number and the product of five and that number can be written algebraically as $x + 5x$.
- You may see a test question that says, "Olivia is constructing a bookcase from seven boards. Two of them are for vertical supports and five are for shelves. The height of the bookcase is twice the width of the bookcase. If the seven boards total 36 feet in length, what will be the height of Olivia's bookcase?" You would need to make a sketch and then create the equation to determine the width of the shelves. The height can be represented as double the width. (If x represents the width of the shelves in feet, then the height of the bookcase is $2x$. Since the seven boards total 36 feet, $2x + 2x + x + x + x + x + x = 36$ or $9x = 36$; $x = 4$. The height is twice the width, or 8 feet.)

$2x + 2x$

PRACTICE

P1. Demonstrate how to subtract 477 from 620 using regrouping.

P2. Simplify the following expressions with exponents:

(a) $37^0 = 1$
(b) $1^{30} = 1$
(c) $2^3 \times 2^4 \times 2^x$ 2^{7+x}
(d) $(3^x)^3$
(e) $(12 \div 3)^2 = 16$ 4^2

Practice Solutions

P1. First, set up the subtraction problem in vertical form:

```
    6  2  0
 -  4  7  7
```

To subtract 7 from 0 in the ones column you will need to borrow from the 2 in the tens column:

```
    6  1  10
 -  4  7  7
          3
```

Next, to subtract 7 from the 1 that's still in the tens column you will need to borrow from the 6 in the hundreds column:

```
    5  11  10
 -  4  7   7
       4   3
```

Lastly, subtract 4 from the 5 remaining in the hundreds column:

```
    5  11  10
 -  4  7   7
    1  4   3
```

153

P2. Using the properties of exponents and the proper order of operations:

    (a) Any number raised to the power of 0 is equal to 1: $37^0 = 1$
    (b) The number 1 raised to any power is equal to 1: $1^{30} = 1$
    (c) Add exponents to multiply powers of the same base: $2^3 \times 2^4 \times 2^x = 2^{(3+4+x)} = 2^{(7+x)}$
    (d) When a power is raised to a power, the exponents are multiplied: $(3^x)^3 = 3^{3x}$
    (e) Perform the operation inside the parentheses first: $(12 \div 3)^2 = 4^2 = 16$

Factoring

FACTORS AND GREATEST COMMON FACTOR

Factors are numbers that are multiplied together to obtain a **product**. For example, in the equation $2 \times 3 = 6$, the numbers 2 and 3 are factors. A **prime number** has only two factors (1 and itself), but other numbers can have many factors.

A **common factor** is a number that divides exactly into two or more other numbers. For example, the factors of 12 are 1, 2, 3, 4, 6, and 12, while the factors of 15 are 1, 3, 5, and 15. The common factors of 12 and 15 are 1 and 3.

A **prime factor** is also a prime number. Therefore, the prime factors of 12 are 2 and 3. For 15, the prime factors are 3 and 5.

The **greatest common factor (GCF)** is the largest number that is a factor of two or more numbers. For example, the factors of 15 are 1, 3, 5, and 15; the factors of 35 are 1, 5, 7, and 35. Therefore, the greatest common factor of 15 and 35 is 5.

> **Review Video: Factors**
> Visit mometrix.com/academy and enter code: 920086
>
> **Review Video: Prime Numbers and Factorization**
> Visit mometrix.com/academy and enter code: 760669
>
> **Review Video: Greatest Common Factor and Least Common Multiple**
> Visit mometrix.com/academy and enter code: 838699

MULTIPLES AND LEAST COMMON MULTIPLE

Often listed out in multiplication tables, **multiples** are integer increments of a given factor. In other words, dividing a multiple by the factor will result in an integer. For example, the multiples of 7 include: $1 \times 7 = 7, 2 \times 7 = 14, 3 \times 7 = 21, 4 \times 7 = 28, 5 \times 7 = 35$. Dividing 7, 14, 21, 28, or 35 by 7 will result in the integers 1, 2, 3, 4, and 5, respectively.

The least common multiple (**LCM**) is the smallest number that is a multiple of two or more numbers. For example, the multiples of 3 include 3, 6, 9, 12, 15, etc.; the multiples of 5 include 5, 10, 15, 20, etc. Therefore, the least common multiple of 3 and 5 is 15.

> **Review Video: Multiples**
> Visit mometrix.com/academy and enter code: 626738

Rational Numbers

FRACTIONS

A **fraction** is a number that is expressed as one integer written above another integer, with a dividing line between them $\left(\frac{x}{y}\right)$. It represents the **quotient** of the two numbers "x divided by y." It can also be thought of as x out of y equal parts.

The top number of a fraction is called the **numerator**, and it represents the number of parts under consideration. The 1 in $\frac{1}{4}$ means that 1 part out of the whole is being considered in the calculation. The bottom number of a fraction is called the **denominator**, and it represents the total number of equal parts. The 4 in $\frac{1}{4}$ means that the whole consists of 4 equal parts. A fraction cannot have a denominator of zero; this is referred to as "*undefined.*"

Fractions can be manipulated, without changing the value of the fraction, by multiplying or dividing (but not adding or subtracting) both the numerator and denominator by the same number. If you divide both numbers by a common factor, you are **reducing** or simplifying the fraction. Two fractions that have the same value but are expressed differently are known as **equivalent fractions**. For example, $\frac{2}{10}, \frac{3}{15}, \frac{4}{20}$, and $\frac{5}{25}$ are all equivalent fractions. They can also all be reduced or simplified to $\frac{1}{5}$.

When two fractions are manipulated so that they have the same denominator, this is known as finding a **common denominator**. The number chosen to be that common denominator should be the least common multiple of the two original denominators. Example: $\frac{3}{4}$ and $\frac{5}{6}$; the least common multiple of 4 and 6 is 12. Manipulating to achieve the common denominator: $\frac{3}{4} = \frac{9}{12}; \frac{5}{6} = \frac{10}{12}$.

PROPER FRACTIONS AND MIXED NUMBERS

A fraction whose denominator is greater than its numerator is known as a **proper fraction**, while a fraction whose numerator is greater than its denominator is known as an **improper fraction**. Proper fractions have values *less than one* and improper fractions have values *greater than one*.

A **mixed number** is a number that contains both an integer and a fraction. Any improper fraction can be rewritten as a mixed number. Example: $\frac{8}{3} = \frac{6}{3} + \frac{2}{3} = 2 + \frac{2}{3} = 2\frac{2}{3}$. Similarly, any mixed number can be rewritten as an improper fraction. Example: $1\frac{3}{5} = 1 + \frac{3}{5} = \frac{5}{5} + \frac{3}{5} = \frac{8}{5}$.

Review Video: Improper Fractions and Mixed Numbers
Visit mometrix.com/academy and enter code: 211077

Review Video: Overview of Fractions
Visit mometrix.com/academy and enter code: 262335

156

ADDING AND SUBTRACTING FRACTIONS

If two fractions have a common denominator, they can be added or subtracted simply by adding or subtracting the two numerators and retaining the same denominator. If the two fractions do not already have the same denominator, one or both of them must be manipulated to achieve a common denominator before they can be added or subtracted. Example: $\frac{1}{2} + \frac{1}{4} = \frac{2}{4} + \frac{1}{4} = \frac{3}{4}$.

> **Review Video: Adding and Subtracting Fractions**
> Visit mometrix.com/academy and enter code: 378080

MULTIPLYING FRACTIONS

Two fractions can be multiplied by multiplying the two numerators to find the new numerator and the two denominators to find the new denominator. Example: $\frac{1}{3} \times \frac{2}{3} = \frac{1 \times 2}{3 \times 3} = \frac{2}{9}$.

DIVIDING FRACTIONS

Two fractions can be divided by flipping the numerator and denominator of the second fraction and then proceeding as though it were a multiplication problem. Example: $\frac{2}{3} \div \frac{3}{4} = \frac{2}{3} \times \frac{4}{3} = \frac{8}{9}$.

> **Review Video: Multiplying and Dividing Fractions**
> Visit mometrix.com/academy and enter code: 473632

MULTIPLYING A MIXED NUMBER BY A WHOLE NUMBER OR A DECIMAL

When multiplying a mixed number by something, it is usually best to convert it to an improper fraction first. Additionally, if the multiplicand is a decimal, it is most often simplest to convert it to a fraction. For instance, to multiply $4\frac{3}{8}$ by 3.5, begin by rewriting each quantity as a whole number plus a proper fraction. Remember, a mixed number is a fraction added to a whole number and a decimal is a representation of the sum of fractions, specifically tenths, hundredths, thousandths, and so on:

$$4\frac{3}{8} \times 3.5 = \left(4 + \frac{3}{8}\right) \times \left(3 + \frac{1}{2}\right)$$

Next, the quantities being added need to be expressed with the same denominator. This is achieved by multiplying and dividing the whole number by the denominator of the fraction. Recall that a whole number is equivalent to that number divided by 1:

$$= \left(\frac{4}{1} \times \frac{8}{8} + \frac{3}{8}\right) \times \left(\frac{3}{1} \times \frac{2}{2} + \frac{1}{2}\right)$$

When multiplying fractions, remember to multiply the numerators and denominators separately:

$$= \left(\frac{4 \times 8}{1 \times 8} + \frac{3}{8}\right) \times \left(\frac{3 \times 2}{1 \times 2} + \frac{1}{2}\right)$$

$$= \left(\frac{32}{8} + \frac{3}{8}\right) \times \left(\frac{6}{2} + \frac{1}{2}\right)$$

Now that the fractions have the same denominators, they can be added:

$$= \frac{35}{8} \times \frac{7}{2}$$

Finally, perform the last multiplication and then simplify:

$$= \frac{35 \times 7}{8 \times 2} = \frac{245}{16} = \frac{240}{16} + \frac{5}{16} = 15\frac{5}{16}$$

DECIMALS

Decimals are one way to represent parts of a whole. Using the place value system, each digit to the right of a decimal point denotes the number of units of a corresponding *negative* power of ten. For example, consider the decimal 0.24. We can use a model to represent the decimal. Since a dime is worth one-tenth of a dollar and a penny is worth one-hundredth of a dollar, one possible model to represent this fraction is to have 2 dimes representing the 2 in the tenths place and 4 pennies representing the 4 in the hundredths place:

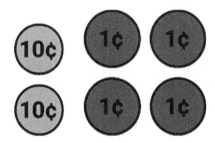

To write the decimal as a fraction, put the decimal in the numerator with 1 in the denominator. Multiply the numerator and denominator by tens until there are no more decimal places. Then simplify the fraction to lowest terms. For example, converting 0.24 to a fraction:

$$0.24 = \frac{0.24}{1} = \frac{0.24 \times 100}{1 \times 100} = \frac{24}{100} = \frac{6}{25}$$

Review Video: Decimals
Visit mometrix.com/academy and enter code: 837268

OPERATIONS WITH DECIMALS

ADDING AND SUBTRACTING DECIMALS

When adding and subtracting decimals, the decimal points must always be aligned. Adding decimals is just like adding regular whole numbers. Example: $4.5 + 2.0 = 6.5$.

If the problem-solver does not properly align the decimal points, an incorrect answer of 4.7 may result. An easy way to add decimals is to align all of the decimal points in a vertical column visually. This will allow you to see exactly where the decimal should be placed in the final answer. Begin adding from right to left. Add each column in turn, making sure to carry the number to the left if a column adds up to more than 9. The same rules apply to the subtraction of decimals.

Review Video: Adding and Subtracting Decimals
Visit mometrix.com/academy and enter code: 381101

MULTIPLYING DECIMALS

A simple multiplication problem has two components: a **multiplicand** and a **multiplier**. When multiplying decimals, work as though the numbers were whole rather than decimals. Once the final product is calculated, count the number of places to the right of the decimal in both the multiplicand and the multiplier. Then, count that number of places from the right of the product and place the decimal in that position.

For example, 12.3 × 2.56 has a total of three places to the right of the respective decimals. Multiply 123 × 256 to get 31,488. Now, beginning on the right, count three places to the left and insert the decimal. The final product will be 31.488.

Review Video: How to Multiply Decimals
Visit mometrix.com/academy and enter code: 731574

DIVIDING DECIMALS

Every division problem has a **divisor** and a **dividend**. The dividend is the number that is being divided. In the problem 14 ÷ 7, 14 is the dividend and 7 is the divisor. In a division problem with decimals, the divisor must be converted into a whole number. Begin by moving the decimal in the divisor to the right until a whole number is created. Next, move the decimal in the dividend the same number of spaces to the right. For example, 4.9 into 24.5 would become 49 into 245. The decimal was moved one space to the right to create a whole number in the divisor, and then the same was done for the dividend. Once the whole numbers are created, the problem is carried out normally: 245 ÷ 49 = 5.

Review Video: How to Divide Decimals
Visit mometrix.com/academy and enter code: 560690

Review Video: Dividing Decimals by Whole Numbers
Visit mometrix.com/academy and enter code: 535669

PERCENTAGES

Percentages can be thought of as fractions that are based on a whole of 100; that is, one whole is equal to 100%. The word **percent** means "per hundred." Percentage problems are often presented in three main ways:

- Find what percentage of some number another number is.
  - Example: What percentage of 40 is 8?
- Find what number is some percentage of a given number.
  - Example: What number is 20% of 40?
- Find what number another number is a given percentage of.
  - Example: What number is 8 20% of?

There are three components in each of these cases: a **whole** (W), a **part** (P), and a **percentage** (%). These are related by the equation: $P = W \times \%$. This can easily be rearranged into other forms that may suit different questions better: $\% = \frac{P}{W}$ and $W = \frac{P}{\%}$. Percentage problems are often also word problems. As such, a large part of solving them is figuring out which quantities are what. For example, consider the following word problem:

In a school cafeteria, 7 students choose pizza, 9 choose hamburgers, and 4 choose tacos. What percentage of student choose tacos?

To find the whole, you must first add all of the parts: 7 + 9 + 4 = 20. The percentage can then be found by dividing the part by the whole $\left(\% = \frac{P}{W}\right)$: $\frac{4}{20} = \frac{20}{100} = 20\%$.

Review Video: Computation with Percentages
Visit mometrix.com/academy and enter code: 693099

CONVERTING BETWEEN PERCENTAGES, FRACTIONS, AND DECIMALS

Converting decimals to percentages and percentages to decimals is as simple as moving the decimal point. To *convert from a decimal to a percentage*, move the decimal point **two places to the right**. To *convert from a percentage to a decimal*, move it **two places to the left**. It may be helpful to remember that the percentage number will always be larger than the equivalent decimal number. Example:

$$0.23 = 23\% \quad 5.34 = 534\% \quad 0.007 = 0.7\%$$
$$700\% = 7.00 \quad 86\% = 0.86 \quad 0.15\% = 0.0015$$

To convert a fraction to a decimal, simply divide the numerator by the denominator in the fraction. To convert a decimal to a fraction, put the decimal in the numerator with 1 in the denominator. Multiply the numerator and denominator by tens until there are no more decimal places. Then simplify the fraction to lowest terms. For example, converting 0.24 to a fraction:

$$0.24 = \frac{0.24}{1} = \frac{0.24 \times 100}{1 \times 100} = \frac{24}{100} = \frac{6}{25}$$

Fractions can be converted to a percentage by finding equivalent fractions with a denominator of 100. Example:

$$\frac{7}{10} = \frac{70}{100} = 70\% \quad \frac{1}{4} = \frac{25}{100} = 25\%$$

To convert a percentage to a fraction, divide the percentage number by 100 and reduce the fraction to its simplest possible terms. Example:

$$60\% = \frac{60}{100} = \frac{3}{5} \quad 96\% = \frac{96}{100} = \frac{24}{25}$$

> **Review Video: <u>Converting Fractions to Percentages and Decimals</u>**
> Visit mometrix.com/academy and enter code: 306233
>
> **Review Video: <u>Converting Percentages to Decimals and Fractions</u>**
> Visit mometrix.com/academy and enter code: 287297
>
> **Review Video: <u>Converting Decimals to Fractions and Percentages</u>**
> Visit mometrix.com/academy and enter code: 986765
>
> **Review Video: <u>Converting Decimals, Improper Fractions, and Mixed Numbers</u>**
> Visit mometrix.com/academy and enter code: 696924

RATIONAL NUMBERS

The term **rational** means that the number can be expressed as a ratio or fraction. That is, a number, r, is rational if and only if it can be represented by a fraction $\frac{a}{b}$ where a and b are integers and b does not equal 0. The set of rational numbers includes integers and decimals. If there is no finite

way to represent a value with a fraction of integers, then the number is **irrational**. Common examples of irrational numbers include: $\sqrt{5}$, $\left(1 + \sqrt{2}\right)$, and π.

> **Review Video: <u>Rational and Irrational Numbers</u>**
> Visit mometrix.com/academy and enter code: 280645

Momemtrix

PRACTICE

P1. What is 30% of 120?

P2. What is 150% of 20?

P3. What is 14.5% of 96?

P4. Simplify the following expressions:

(a) $\frac{2}{5} \div \frac{4}{7}$

(b) $\frac{7}{8} - \frac{8}{16}$

(c) $\frac{1}{2} + \left(3\left(\frac{3}{4}\right) - 2\right) + 4$

(d) $0.22 + 0.5 - (5.5 + 3.3 \div 3)$

(e) $\frac{3}{2} + (4(0.5) - 0.75) + 2$

P5. Convert the following to a fraction and to a decimal: **(a)** 15%; **(b)** 24.36%

P6. Convert the following to a decimal and to a percentage. **(a)** $\frac{4}{5}$; **(b)** $3\frac{2}{5}$

P7. A woman's age is thirteen more than half of 60. How old is the woman?

P8. A patient was given pain medicine at a dosage of 0.22 grams. The patient's dosage was then increased to 0.80 grams. By how much was the patient's dosage increased?

P9. At a hotel, $\frac{3}{4}$ of the 100 rooms are occupied today. Yesterday, $\frac{4}{5}$ of the 100 rooms were occupied. On which day were more of the rooms occupied and by how much more?

P10. At a school, 40% of the teachers teach English. If 20 teachers teach English, how many teachers work at the school?

P11. A patient was given blood pressure medicine at a dosage of 2 grams. The patient's dosage was then decreased to 0.45 grams. By how much was the patient's dosage decreased?

P12. Two weeks ago, $\frac{2}{3}$ of the 60 customers at a skate shop were male. Last week, $\frac{3}{6}$ of the 80 customers were male. During which week were there more male customers?

P13. Jane ate lunch at a local restaurant. She ordered a $4.99 appetizer, a $12.50 entrée, and a $1.25 soda. If she wants to tip her server 20%, how much money will she spend in all?

P14. According to a survey, about 82% of engineers were highly satisfied with their job. If 145 engineers were surveyed, how many reported that they were highly satisfied?

P15. A patient was given 40 mg of a certain medicine. Later, the patient's dosage was increased to 45 mg. What was the percent increase in his medication?

P16. Order the following rational numbers from least to greatest: $0.55, 17\%, \sqrt{25}, \frac{64}{4}, \frac{25}{50}, 3$.

P17. Order the following rational numbers from greatest to least: $0.3, 27\%, \sqrt{100}, \frac{72}{9}, \frac{1}{9}, 4.5$

162

Mometrix

P18. Perform the following multiplication. Write each answer as a mixed number.

(a) $\left(1\frac{11}{16}\right) \times 4$

(b) $\left(12\frac{1}{3}\right) \times 1.1$

(c) $3.71 \times \left(6\frac{1}{5}\right)$

P19. Suppose you are making doughnuts and you want to triple the recipe you have. If the following list is the original amounts for the ingredients, what would be the amounts for the tripled recipe?

$1\frac{3}{4}$	cup	Flour	$1\frac{1}{2}$	Tbsp	Butter
$1\frac{1}{4}$	tsp	Baking powder	2	large	Eggs
$\frac{3}{4}$	tsp	Salt	$\frac{3}{4}$	tsp	Vanilla extract
$\frac{3}{8}$	cup	Sugar	$\frac{3}{8}$	cup	Sour cream

PRACTICE SOLUTIONS

P1. The word *of* indicates multiplication, so 30% of 120 is found by multiplying 120 by 30%. Change 30% to a decimal, then multiply: $120 \times 0.3 = 36$

P2. The word *of* indicates multiplication, so 150% of 20 is found by multiplying 20 by 150%. Change 150% to a decimal, then multiply: $20 \times 1.5 = 30$

P3. Change 14.5% to a decimal before multiplying. $0.145 \times 96 = 13.92$.

P4. Follow the order of operations and utilize properties of fractions to solve each:

(a) Rewrite the problem as a multiplication problem: $\frac{2}{5} \times \frac{7}{4} = \frac{2\times7}{5\times4} = \frac{14}{20}$. Make sure the fraction is reduced to lowest terms. Both 14 and 20 can be divided by 2.

$$\frac{14}{20} = \frac{14 \div 2}{20 \div 2} = \frac{7}{10}$$

(b) The denominators of $\frac{7}{8}$ and $\frac{8}{16}$ are 8 and 16, respectively. The lowest common denominator of 8 and 16 is 16 because 16 is the least common multiple of 8 and 16. Convert the first fraction to its equivalent with the newly found common denominator of 16: $\frac{7\times2}{8\times2} = \frac{14}{16}$. Now that the fractions have the same denominator, you can subtract them.

$$\frac{14}{16} - \frac{8}{16} = \frac{6}{16} = \frac{3}{8}$$

163

(c) When simplifying expressions, first perform operations within groups. Within the set of parentheses are multiplication and subtraction operations. Perform the multiplication first to get $\frac{1}{2} + \left(\frac{9}{4} - 2\right) + 4$. Then, subtract two to obtain $\frac{1}{2} + \frac{1}{4} + 4$. Finally, perform addition from left to right:

$$\frac{1}{2} + \frac{1}{4} + 4 = \frac{2}{4} + \frac{1}{4} + \frac{16}{4} = \frac{19}{4} = 4\frac{3}{4}$$

(d) First, evaluate the terms in the parentheses $(5.5 + 3.3 \div 3)$ using order of operations. $3.3 \div 3 = 1.1$, and $5.5 + 1.1 = 6.6$. Next, rewrite the problem: $0.22 + 0.5 - 6.6$. Finally, add and subtract from left to right: $0.22 + 0.5 = 0.72$; $0.72 - 6.6 = -5.88$. The answer is -5.88.

(e) First, simplify within the parentheses, then change the fraction to a decimal and perform addition from left to right:

$$\frac{3}{2} + (2 - 0.75) + 2 =$$
$$\frac{3}{2} + 1.25 + 2 =$$
$$1.5 + 1.25 + 2 = 4.75$$

P5. (a) 15% can be written as $\frac{15}{100}$. Both 15 and 100 can be divided by 5: $\frac{15 \div 5}{100 \div 5} = \frac{3}{20}$

When converting from a percentage to a decimal, drop the percent sign and move the decimal point two places to the left: $15\% = 0.15$

(b) 24.36% written as a fraction is $\frac{24.36}{100}$, or $\frac{2436}{10,000}$, which reduces to $\frac{609}{2500}$. 24.36% written as a decimal is 0.2436. Recall that dividing by 100 moves the decimal two places to the left.

P6. (a) Recall that in the decimal system the first decimal place is one tenth: $\frac{4 \times 2}{5 \times 2} = \frac{8}{10} = 0.8$

Percent means "per hundred." $\frac{4 \times 20}{5 \times 20} = \frac{80}{100} = 80\%$

(b) The mixed number $3\frac{2}{5}$ has a whole number and a fractional part. The fractional part $\frac{2}{5}$ can be written as a decimal by dividing 5 into 2, which gives 0.4. Adding the whole to the part gives 3.4.

To find the equivalent percentage, multiply the decimal by 100. $3.4(100) = 340\%$. Notice that this percentage is greater than 100%. This makes sense because the original mixed number $3\frac{2}{5}$ is greater than 1.

P7. "More than" indicates addition, and "of" indicates multiplication. The expression can be written as $\frac{1}{2}(60) + 13$. So, the woman's age is equal to $\frac{1}{2}(60) + 13 = 30 + 13 = 43$. The woman is 43 years old.

P8. The first step is to determine what operation (addition, subtraction, multiplication, or division) the problem requires. Notice the keywords and phrases "by how much" and "increased."

"Increased" means that you go from a smaller amount to a larger amount. This change can be found by subtracting the smaller amount from the larger amount: 0.80 grams– 0.22 grams = 0.58 grams.

Remember to line up the decimal when subtracting:

$$
\begin{array}{r}
0.80 \\
-\ \ 0.22 \\
\hline
0.58
\end{array}
$$

P9. First, find the number of rooms occupied each day. To do so, multiply the fraction of rooms occupied by the number of rooms available:

$$\text{Number occupied} = \text{Fraction occupied} \times \text{Total number}$$

$$\text{Number of rooms occupied today} = \frac{3}{4} \times 100 = 75$$

$$\text{Number of rooms occupied yesterday} = \frac{4}{5} \times 100 = 80$$

The difference in the number of rooms occupied is: $80 - 75 = 5$ rooms

P10. To answer this problem, first think about the number of teachers that work at the school. Will it be more or less than the number of teachers who work in a specific department such as English? More teachers work at the school, so the number you find to answer this question will be greater than 20.

40% of the teachers are English teachers. "Of" indicates multiplication, and words like "is" and "are" indicate equivalence. Translating the problem into a mathematical sentence gives $40\% \times t = 20$, where t represents the total number of teachers. Solving for t gives $t = \frac{20}{40\%} = \frac{20}{0.40} = 50$. Fifty teachers work at the school.

P11. The decrease is represented by the difference between the two amounts:

$$2 \text{ grams} - 0.45 \text{ grams} = 1.55 \text{ grams.}$$

Remember to line up the decimal point before subtracting.

$$
\begin{array}{r}
2.00 \\
-\ \ 0.45 \\
\hline
1.55
\end{array}
$$

P12. First, you need to find the number of male customers that were in the skate shop each week. You are given this amount in terms of fractions. To find the actual number of male customers, multiply the fraction of male customers by the number of customers in the store.

$$\text{Actual number of male customers} = \text{fraction of male customers} \times \text{total customers}$$

$$\text{Number of male customers two weeks ago} = \frac{2}{3} \times 60 = \frac{120}{3} = 40$$

$$\text{Number of male customers last week} = \frac{3}{6} \times 80 = \frac{1}{2} \times 80 = \frac{80}{2} = 40$$

The number of male customers was the same both weeks.

P13. To find total amount, first find the sum of the items she ordered from the menu and then add 20% of this sum to the total.

$$\$4.99 + \$12.50 + \$1.25 = \$18.74$$

$$\$18.74 \times 20\% = (0.20)(\$18.74) = \$3.748 \approx \$3.75$$

$$\text{Total} = \$18.74 + \$3.75 = \$22.49$$

P14. 82% of 145 is 0.82 × 145 = 118.9. Because you can't have 0.9 of a person, we must round up to say that 119 engineers reported that they were highly satisfied with their jobs.

P15. To find the percent increase, first compare the original and increased amounts. The original amount was 40 mg, and the increased amount is 45 mg, so the dosage of medication was increased by 5 mg (45– 40 = 5). Note, however, that the question asks not by how much the dosage increased but by what percentage it increased.

$$\text{Percent increase} = \frac{\text{new amount} - \text{original amount}}{\text{original amount}} \times 100\%$$

$$= \frac{45 \text{ mg} - 40 \text{ mg}}{40 \text{ mg}} \times 100\% = \frac{5}{40} \times 100\% = 0.125 \times 100\% = 12.5\%$$

P16. Recall that the term rational simply means that the number can be expressed as a ratio or fraction. Notice that each of the numbers in the problem can be written as a decimal or integer:

$$17\% = 0.17$$

$$\sqrt{25} = 5$$

$$\frac{64}{4} = 16$$

$$\frac{25}{50} = \frac{1}{2} = 0.5$$

So, the answer is 17%, $\frac{25}{50}$, 0.55, 3, $\sqrt{25}$, $\frac{64}{4}$.

P17. Converting all the numbers to integers and decimals makes it easier to compare the values:

$$27\% = 0.27$$

$$\sqrt{100} = 10$$

$$\frac{72}{9} = 8$$

$$\frac{1}{9} \approx 0.11$$

So, the answer is $\sqrt{100}$, $\frac{72}{9}$, 4.5, 0.3, 27%, $\frac{1}{9}$.

Review Video: <u>Ordering Rational Numbers</u>
Visit mometrix.com/academy and enter code: 419578

P18. For each, convert improper fractions, adjust to a common denominator, perform the operations, and then simplify:

(a) Sometimes, you can skip converting the denominator and just distribute the multiplication.

$$\left(1\frac{11}{16}\right) \times 4 = \left(1 + \frac{11}{16}\right) \times 4$$

$$= 1 \times 4 + \frac{11}{16} \times 4$$

$$= 4 + \frac{11}{16} \times \frac{4}{1}$$

$$= 4 + \frac{44}{16} = 4 + \frac{11}{4} = 4 + 2\frac{3}{4} = 6\frac{3}{4}$$

(b)

$$\left(12\frac{1}{3}\right) \times 1.1 = \left(12 + \frac{1}{3}\right) \times \left(1 + \frac{1}{10}\right)$$

$$= \left(\frac{12}{1} \times \frac{3}{3} + \frac{1}{3}\right) \times \left(\frac{10}{10} + \frac{1}{10}\right)$$

$$= \left(\frac{36}{3} + \frac{1}{3}\right) \times \frac{11}{10}$$

$$= \frac{37}{3} \times \frac{11}{10}$$

$$= \frac{407}{30} = \frac{390}{30} + \frac{17}{30} = 13\frac{17}{30}$$

(c)

$$3.71 \times \left(6\frac{1}{5}\right) = \left(3 + \frac{71}{100}\right) \times \left(6 + \frac{1}{5}\right)$$

$$= \left(\frac{300}{100} + \frac{71}{100}\right) \times \left(\frac{6}{1} \times \frac{5}{5} + \frac{1}{5}\right)$$

$$= \frac{371}{100} \times \left(\frac{30}{5} + \frac{1}{5}\right)$$

$$= \frac{371}{100} \times \frac{31}{5}$$

$$= \frac{11501}{500} = \frac{11500}{500} + \frac{1}{500} = 23\frac{1}{500}$$

P19. Fortunately, some of the amounts are duplicated, so we do not need to convert every amount.

$$1\frac{3}{4} \times 3 = (1 \times 3) + \left(\frac{3}{4} \times 3\right)$$
$$= 3 + \frac{9}{4}$$
$$= 3 + 2\frac{1}{4}$$
$$= 5\frac{1}{4}$$

$$1\frac{1}{4} \times 3 = (1 \times 3) + \left(\frac{1}{4} \times 3\right)$$
$$= 3 + \frac{3}{4}$$
$$= 3\frac{3}{4}$$

$$\frac{3}{4} \times 3 = \frac{3}{4} \times 3$$
$$= \frac{9}{4}$$
$$= 2\frac{1}{4}$$

$$\frac{3}{8} \times 3 = \frac{3}{8} \times 3$$
$$= \frac{9}{8}$$
$$= 1\frac{1}{8}$$

$$1\frac{1}{2} \times 3 = 1 \times 3 + \frac{1}{2} \times 3$$
$$= 3 + \frac{3}{2}$$
$$= 3 + 1\frac{1}{2}$$
$$= 4\frac{1}{2}$$

$$2 \times 3 = 6$$

So, the result for the triple recipe is:

$5\frac{1}{4}$	cup	Flour	$4\frac{1}{2}$	Tbsp	Butter
$3\frac{3}{4}$	tsp	Baking powder	6	large	Eggs
$2\frac{1}{4}$	tsp	Salt	$2\frac{1}{4}$	tsp	Vanilla extract
$1\frac{1}{8}$	cup	Sugar	$1\frac{1}{8}$	cup	Sour cream

Proportions and Ratios

PROPORTIONS

A proportion is a relationship between two quantities that dictates how one changes when the other changes. A **direct proportion** describes a relationship in which a quantity increases by a set amount for every increase in the other quantity, or decreases by that same amount for every decrease in the other quantity. Example: Assuming a constant driving speed, the time required for a car trip increases as the distance of the trip increases. The distance to be traveled and the time required to travel are directly proportional.

An **inverse proportion** is a relationship in which an increase in one quantity is accompanied by a decrease in the other, or vice versa. Example: the time required for a car trip decreases as the speed increases and increases as the speed decreases, so the time required is inversely proportional to the speed of the car.

> **Review Video: Proportions**
> Visit mometrix.com/academy and enter code: 505355

RATIOS

A **ratio** is a comparison of two quantities in a particular order. Example: If there are 14 computers in a lab, and the class has 20 students, there is a student to computer ratio of 20 to 14, commonly written as 20: 14. Ratios are normally reduced to their smallest whole number representation, so 20: 14 would be reduced to 10: 7 by dividing both sides by 2.

> **Review Video: Ratios**
> Visit mometrix.com/academy and enter code: 996914

CONSTANT OF PROPORTIONALITY

When two quantities have a proportional relationship, there exists a **constant of proportionality** between the quantities. The product of this constant and one of the quantities is equal to the other quantity. For example, if one lemon costs $0.25, two lemons cost $0.50, and three lemons cost $0.75, there is a proportional relationship between the total cost of lemons and the number of lemons purchased. The constant of proportionality is the **unit price**, namely $0.25/lemon. Notice that the total price of lemons, t, can be found by multiplying the unit price of lemons, p, and the number of lemons, n: $t = pn$.

WORK/UNIT RATE

Unit rate expresses a quantity of one thing in terms of one unit of another. For example, if you travel 30 miles every two hours, a unit rate expresses this comparison in terms of one hour: in one hour you travel 15 miles, so your unit rate is 15 miles per hour. Other examples are how much one ounce of food costs (price per ounce) or figuring out how much one egg costs out of the dozen (price per 1 egg, instead of price per 12 eggs). The denominator of a unit rate is always 1. Unit rates are used to compare different situations to solve problems. For example, to make sure you get the best deal when deciding which kind of soda to buy, you can find the unit rate of each. If soda #1 costs $1.50 for a 1-liter bottle, and soda #2 costs $2.75 for a 2-liter bottle, it would be a better deal to buy soda #2, because its unit rate is only $1.375 per 1-liter, which is cheaper than soda #1. Unit rates can also help determine the length of time a given event will take. For example, if you can paint 2 rooms in 4.5 hours, you can determine how long it will take you to paint 5 rooms by solving for the unit rate per room and then multiplying that by 5.

SLOPE

On a graph with two points, (x_1, y_1) and (x_2, y_2), the **slope** is found with the formula $m = \frac{y_2 - y_1}{x_2 - x_1}$; where $x_1 \neq x_2$ and m stands for slope. If the value of the slope is **positive**, the line has an *upward direction* from left to right. If the value of the slope is **negative**, the line has a *downward direction* from left to right. Consider the following example:

A new book goes on sale in bookstores and online stores. In the first month, 5,000 copies of the book are sold. Over time, the book continues to grow in popularity. The data for the number of copies sold is in the table below.

# of Months on Sale	1	2	3	4	5
# of Copies Sold (In Thousands)	5	10	15	20	25

So, the number of copies that are sold and the time that the book is on sale is a proportional relationship. In this example, an equation can be used to show the data: $y = 5x$, where x is the number of months that the book is on sale. Also, y is the number of copies sold. So, the slope of the corresponding line is $\frac{\text{rise}}{\text{run}} = \frac{5}{1} = 5$.

FINDING AN UNKNOWN IN EQUIVALENT EXPRESSIONS

It is often necessary to apply information given about a rate or proportion to a new scenario. For example, if you know that Jedha can run a marathon (26.2 miles) in 3 hours, how long would it take her to run 10 miles at the same pace? Start by setting up equivalent expressions:

$$\frac{26.2 \text{ mi}}{3 \text{ hr}} = \frac{10 \text{ mi}}{x \text{ hr}}$$

Now, cross multiply and solve for x:

$$26.2x = 30$$
$$x = \frac{30}{26.2} = \frac{15}{13.1}$$
$$x \approx 1.15 \text{ hrs } or \text{ 1 hr 9 min}$$

So, at this pace, Jedha could run 10 miles in about 1.15 hours or about 1 hour and 9 minutes.

PRACTICE

P1. Solve the following for x.

(a) $\frac{45}{12} = \frac{15}{x}$

(b) $\frac{0.50}{2} = \frac{1.50}{x}$

(c) $\frac{40}{8} = \frac{x}{24}$

P2. At a school, for every 20 female students there are 15 male students. This same student ratio happens to exist at another school. If there are 100 female students at the second school, how many male students are there?

P3. In a hospital emergency room, there are 4 nurses for every 12 patients. What is the ratio of nurses to patients? If the nurse-to-patient ratio remains constant, how many nurses must be present to care for 24 patients?

P4. In a bank, the banker-to-customer ratio is $1 : 2$. If seven bankers are on duty, how many customers are currently in the bank?

P5. Janice made $40 during the first 5 hours she spent babysitting. She will continue to earn money at this rate until she finishes babysitting in 3 more hours. Find how much money Janice earns per hour and the total she earned babysitting.

P6. The McDonalds are taking a family road trip, driving 300 miles to their cabin. It took them 2 hours to drive the first 120 miles. They will drive at the same speed all the way to their cabin. Find the speed at which the McDonalds are driving and how much longer it will take them to get to their cabin.

P7. It takes Andy 10 minutes to read 6 pages of his book. He has already read 150 pages in his book that is 210 pages long. Find how long it takes Andy to read 1 page and also find how long it will take him to finish his book if he continues to read at the same speed.

PRACTICE SOLUTIONS

P1. Cross multiply, then solve for x:

(a)

$$45x = 12 \times 15$$
$$45x = 180$$
$$x = \frac{180}{45} = 4$$

(b)

$$0.5x = 1.5 \times 2$$
$$0.5x = 3$$
$$x = \frac{3}{0.5} = 6$$

(c)

$$8x = 40 \times 24$$
$$8x = 960$$
$$x = \frac{960}{8} = 120$$

P2. One way to find the number of male students is to set up and solve a proportion.

$$\frac{\text{number of female students}}{\text{number of male students}} = \frac{20}{15} = \frac{100}{\text{number of male students}}$$

Represent the unknown number of male students as the variable x: $\frac{20}{15} = \frac{100}{x}$

Cross multiply and then solve for x:

$$20x = 15 \times 100$$
$$x = \frac{1500}{20}$$
$$x = 75$$

P3. The ratio of nurses to patients can be written as 4 to 12, 4: 12, or $\frac{4}{12}$. Because four and twelve have a common factor of four, the ratio should be reduced to 1: 3, which means that there is one nurse present for every three patients. If this ratio remains constant, there must be eight nurses present to care for 24 patients.

P4. Use proportional reasoning or set up a proportion to solve. Because there are twice as many customers as bankers, there must be fourteen customers when seven bankers are on duty. Setting up and solving a proportion gives the same result:

$$\frac{\text{number of bankers}}{\text{number of customers}} = \frac{1}{2} = \frac{7}{\text{number of customers}}$$

Represent the unknown number of customers as the variable x: $\frac{1}{2} = \frac{7}{x}$.

To solve for x, cross multiply: $1 \times x = 7 \times 2$, so $x = 14$.

P5. Janice earns \$8 per hour. This can be found by taking her initial amount earned, \$40, and dividing it by the number of hours worked, 5. Since $\frac{40}{5} = 8$, Janice makes \$8 in one hour. This can also be found by finding the unit rate, money earned per hour: $\frac{40}{5} = \frac{x}{1}$. Since cross multiplying yields $5x = 40$, and division by 5 shows that $x = 8$, Janice earns \$8 per hour.

Janice will earn \$64 babysitting in her 8 total hours (adding the first 5 hours to the remaining 3 gives the 8-hour total). Since Janice earns \$8 per hour and she worked 8 hours, $\frac{\$8}{\text{hr}} \times 8 \text{ hrs} = \$64$. This can also be found by setting up a proportion comparing money earned to babysitting hours. Since she earns \$40 for 5 hours and since the rate is constant, she will earn a proportional amount in 8 hours: $\frac{40}{5} = \frac{x}{8}$. Cross multiplying will yield $5x = 320$, and division by 5 shows that $x = 64$.

P6. The McDonalds are driving 60 miles per hour. This can be found by setting up a proportion to find the unit rate, the number of miles they drive per one hour: $\frac{120}{2} = \frac{x}{1}$. Cross multiplying yields $2x = 120$ and division by 2 shows that $x = 60$.

Since the McDonalds will drive this same speed for the remaining miles, it will take them another 3 hours to get to their cabin. This can be found by first finding how many miles the McDonalds have left to drive, which is $300 - 120 = 180$. The McDonalds are driving at 60 miles per hour, so a proportion can be set up to determine how many hours it will take them to drive 180 miles: $\frac{180}{x} = \frac{60}{1}$. Cross multiplying yields $60x = 180$, and division by 60 shows that $x = 3$. This can also be found by using the formula $D = r \times t$ (or distance = rate × time), where $180 = 60 \times t$, and division by 60 shows that $t = 3$.

P7. It takes Andy 10 minutes to read 6 pages, $\frac{10}{6} = 1\frac{2}{3}$ minutes, which is 1 minute and 40 seconds.

Next, determine how many pages Andy has left to read, $210 - 150 = 60$. Since it is now known that it takes him $1\frac{2}{3}$ minutes to read each page, that rate must be multiplied by however many pages he has left to read (60) to find the time he'll need: $60 \times 1\frac{2}{3} = 100$, so it will take him 100 minutes, or 1 hour and 40 minutes, to read the rest of his book.

Expressions

TERMS AND COEFFICIENTS

Mathematical expressions consist of a combination of one or more values arranged in terms that are added together. As such, an expression could be just a single number, including zero. A **variable term** is the product of a real number, also called a **coefficient**, and one or more variables, each of which may be raised to an exponent. Expressions may also include numbers without a variable, called **constants** or **constant terms**. The expression $6s^2$, for example, is a single term where the coefficient is the real number 6 and the variable term is s^2. Note that if a term is written as simply a variable to some exponent, like t^2, then the coefficient is 1, because $t^2 = 1t^2$.

LINEAR EXPRESSIONS

A **single variable linear expression** is the sum of a single variable term, where the variable has no exponent, and a constant, which may be zero. For instance, the expression $2w + 7$ has $2w$ as the variable term and 7 as the constant term. It is important to realize that terms are separated by addition or subtraction. Since an expression is a sum of terms, expressions such as $5x - 3$ can be written as $5x + (-3)$ to emphasize that the constant term is negative. A real-world example of a single variable linear expression is the perimeter of a square, four times the side length, often expressed: $4s$.

In general, a **linear expression** is the sum of any number of variable terms so long as none of the variables have an exponent. For example, $3m + 8n - \frac{1}{4}p + 5.5q - 1$ is a linear expression, but $3y^3$ is not. In the same way, the expression for the perimeter of a general triangle, the sum of the side lengths $(a + b + c)$ is considered to be linear, but the expression for the area of a square, the side length squared (s^2) is not.

Equations

LINEAR EQUATIONS

Equations that can be written as $ax + b = 0$, where $a \neq 0$, are referred to as **one variable linear equations**. A solution to such an equation is called a **root**. In the case where we have the equation $5x + 10 = 0$, if we solve for x we get a solution of $x = -2$. In other words, the root of the equation is –2. This is found by first subtracting 10 from both sides, which gives $5x = -10$. Next, simply divide both sides by the coefficient of the variable, in this case 5, to get $x = -2$. This can be checked by plugging –2 back into the original equation $(5)(-2) + 10 = -10 + 10 = 0$.

The **solution set** is the set of all solutions of an equation. In our example, the solution set would simply be –2. If there were more solutions (there usually are in multivariable equations) then they would also be included in the solution set. When an equation has no true solutions, it is referred to as an **empty set**. Equations with identical solution sets are **equivalent equations**. An **identity** is a term whose value or determinant is equal to 1.

Linear equations can be written many ways. Below is a list of some forms linear equations can take:

- **Standard Form**: $Ax + By = C$; the slope is $\frac{-A}{B}$ and the y-intercept is $\frac{C}{B}$
- **Slope Intercept Form**: $y = mx + b$, where m is the slope and b is the y-intercept
- **Point-Slope Form**: $y - y_1 = m(x - x_1)$, where m is the slope and (x_1, y_1) is a point on the line
- **Two-Point Form**: $\frac{y - y_1}{x - x_1} = \frac{y_2 - y_1}{x_2 - x_1}$, where (x_1, y_1) and (x_2, y_2) are two points on the given line
- **Intercept Form**: $\frac{x}{x_1} + \frac{y}{y_1} = 1$, where $(x_1, 0)$ is the point at which a line intersects the x-axis, and $(0, y_1)$ is the point at which the same line intersects the y-axis

> **Review Video: Slope-Intercept and Point-Slope Forms**
> Visit mometrix.com/academy and enter code: 113216
>
> **Review Video: Linear Equations Basics**
> Visit mometrix.com/academy and enter code: 793005

SOLVING ONE-VARIABLE LINEAR EQUATIONS

Multiply all terms by the lowest common denominator to eliminate any fractions. Look for addition or subtraction to undo so you can isolate the variable on one side of the equal sign. Divide both sides by the coefficient of the variable. When you have a value for the variable, substitute this value into the original equation to make sure you have a true equation. Consider the following example:

Kim's savings are represented by the table below. Represent her savings, using an equation.

X (Months)	Y (Total Savings)
2	$1,300
5	$2,050
9	$3,050
11	$3,550
16	$4,800

The table shows a function with a constant rate of change, or slope, of 250. Given the points on the table, the slopes can be calculated as $\frac{(2{,}050-1300)}{(5-2)}$, $\frac{(3{,}050-2{,}050)}{(9-5)}$, $\frac{(3{,}550-3{,}050)}{(11-9)}$, and $\frac{(4{,}800-3{,}550)}{(16-11)}$, each of which equals 250. Thus, the table shows a constant rate of change, indicating a linear function. The slope-intercept form of a linear equation is written as $y = mx + b$, where m represents the slope and b represents the y-intercept. Substituting the slope into this form gives $y = 250x + b$. Substituting corresponding x- and y-values from any point into this equation will give the y-intercept, or b. Using the point, $(2, 1{,}300)$, gives $1{,}300 = 250(2) + b$, which simplifies as $b = 800$. Thus, her savings may be represented by the equation, $y = 250x + 800$.

RULES FOR MANIPULATING EQUATIONS
LIKE TERMS

Like terms are terms in an equation that have the same variable, regardless of whether or not they also have the same coefficient. This includes terms that *lack* a variable; all constants (i.e., numbers without variables) are considered like terms. If the equation involves terms with a variable raised to different powers, the like terms are those that have the variable raised to the same power.

For example, consider the equation $x^2 + 3x + 2 = 2x^2 + x - 7 + 2x$. In this equation, 2 and –7 are like terms; they are both constants. $3x$, x, and $2x$ are like terms, they all include the variable x raised to the first power. x^2 and $2x^2$ are like terms, they both include the variable x, raised to the second power. $2x$ and $2x^2$ are not like terms; although they both involve the variable x, the variable is not raised to the same power in both terms. The fact that they have the same coefficient, 2, is not relevant.

> **Review Video: Rules for Manipulating Equations**
> Visit mometrix.com/academy and enter code: 838871

CARRYING OUT THE SAME OPERATION ON BOTH SIDES OF AN EQUATION

When solving an equation, the general procedure is to carry out a series of operations on both sides of an equation, choosing operations that will tend to simplify the equation when doing so. The reason why the same operation must be carried out on both sides of the equation is because that leaves the meaning of the equation unchanged, and yields a result that is equivalent to the original equation. This would not be the case if we carried out an operation on one side of an equation and not the other. Consider what an equation means: it is a statement that two values or expressions are equal. If we carry out the same operation on both sides of the equation—add 3 to both sides, for example—then the two sides of the equation are changed in the same way, and so remain equal. If we do that to only one side of the equation—add 3 to one side but not the other—then that wouldn't be true; if we change one side of the equation but not the other then the two sides are no longer equal.

ADVANTAGE OF COMBINING LIKE TERMS

Combining like terms refers to adding or subtracting like terms—terms with the same variable—and therefore reducing sets of like terms to a single term. The main advantage of doing this is that it simplifies the equation. Often, combining like terms can be done as the first step in solving an equation, though it can also be done later, such as after distributing terms in a product.

For example, consider the equation $2(x + 3) + 3(2 + x + 3) = -4$. The 2 and the 3 in the second set of parentheses are like terms, and we can combine them, yielding $2(x + 3) + 3(x + 5) = -4$.

Now we can carry out the multiplications implied by the parentheses, distributing the outer 2 and 3 accordingly: $2x + 6 + 3x + 15 = -4$. The $2x$ and the $3x$ are like terms, and we can add them together: $5x + 6 + 15 = -4$. Now, the constants 6, 15, and –4 are also like terms, and we can combine them as well: subtracting 6 and 15 from both sides of the equation, we get $5x = -4 - 6 - 15$, or $5x = -25$, which simplifies further to $x = -5$.

> **Review Video: <u>Solving Equations by Combining Like Terms</u>**
> Visit mometrix.com/academy and enter code: 668506

CANCELING TERMS ON OPPOSITE SIDES OF AN EQUATION

Two terms on opposite sides of an equation can be canceled if and only if they *exactly* match each other. They must have the same variable raised to the same power and the same coefficient. For example, in the equation $3x + 2x^2 + 6 = 2x^2 - 6$, $2x^2$ appears on both sides of the equation and can be canceled, leaving $3x + 6 = -6$. The 6 on each side of the equation *cannot* be canceled, because it is added on one side of the equation and subtracted on the other. While they cannot be canceled, however, the 6 and –6 are like terms and can be combined, yielding $3x = -12$, which simplifies further to $x = -4$.

It's also important to note that the terms to be canceled must be independent terms and cannot be part of a larger term. For example, consider the equation $2(x + 6) = 3(x + 4) + 1$. We cannot cancel the x's, because even though they match each other they are part of the larger terms $2(x + 6)$ and $3(x + 4)$. We must first distribute the 2 and 3, yielding $2x + 12 = 3x + 12 + 1$. Now we see that the terms with the x's do not match, but the 12s do, and can be canceled, leaving $2x = 3x + 1$, which simplifies to $x = -1$.

PROCESS FOR MANIPULATING EQUATIONS

ISOLATING VARIABLES

To **isolate a variable** means to manipulate the equation so that the variable appears by itself on one side of the equation, and does not appear at all on the other side. Generally, an equation or inequality is considered to be solved once the variable is isolated and the other side of the equation or inequality is simplified as much as possible. In the case of a two-variable equation or inequality, only one variable needs to be isolated; it will not usually be possible to simultaneously isolate both variables.

For a linear equation—an equation in which the variable only appears raised to the first power—isolating a variable can be done by first moving all the terms with the variable to one side of the equation and all other terms to the other side. (*Moving* a term really means adding the inverse of the term to both sides; when a term is *moved* to the other side of the equation its sign is flipped.) Then combine like terms on each side. Finally, divide both sides by the coefficient of the variable, if applicable. The steps need not necessarily be done in this order, but this order will always work.

> **Review Video: <u>Solving One-Step Equations</u>**
> Visit mometrix.com/academy and enter code: 777004

EQUATIONS WITH MORE THAN ONE SOLUTION

Some types of non-linear equations, such as equations involving squares of variables, may have more than one solution. For example, the equation $x^2 = 4$ has two solutions: 2 and –2. Equations with absolute values can also have multiple solutions: $|x| = 1$ has the solutions $x = 1$ and $x = -1$.

It is also possible for a linear equation to have more than one solution, but only if the equation is true regardless of the value of the variable. In this case, the equation is considered to have infinitely many solutions, because any possible value of the variable is a solution. We know a linear equation has infinitely many solutions if when we combine like terms the variables cancel, leaving a true statement. For example, consider the equation $2(3x + 5) = x + 5(x + 2)$. Distributing, we get $6x + 10 = x + 5x + 10$; combining like terms gives $6x + 10 = 6x + 10$, and the $6x$-terms cancel to leave $10 = 10$. This is clearly true, so the original equation is true for any value of x. We could also have canceled the 10s leaving $0 = 0$, but again this is clearly true—in general if both sides of the equation match exactly, it has infinitely many solutions.

EQUATIONS WITH NO SOLUTION

Some types of non-linear equations, such as equations involving squares of variables, may have no solution. For example, the equation $x^2 = -2$ has no solutions in the real numbers, because the square of any real number must be positive. Similarly, $|x| = -1$ has no solution, because the absolute value of a number is always positive.

It is also possible for an equation to have no solution even if does not involve any powers greater than one, absolute values, or other special functions. For example, the equation $2(x + 3) + x = 3x$ has no solution. We can see that if we try to solve it: first we distribute, leaving $2x + 6 + x = 3x$. But now if we try to combine all the terms with the variable, we find that they cancel: we have $3x$ on the left and $3x$ on the right, canceling to leave us with $6 = 0$. This is clearly false. In general, whenever the variable terms in an equation cancel leaving different constants on both sides, it means that the equation has no solution. (If we are left with the *same* constant on both sides, the equation has infinitely many solutions instead.)

FEATURES OF EQUATIONS THAT REQUIRE SPECIAL TREATMENT
LINEAR EQUATIONS

A linear equation is an equation in which variables only appear by themselves: not multiplied together, not with exponents other than one, and not inside absolute value signs or any other functions. For example, the equation $x + 1 - 3x = 5 - x$ is a linear equation; while x appears multiple times, it never appears with an exponent other than one, or inside any function. The two-variable equation $2x - 3y = 5 + 2x$ is also a linear equation. In contrast, the equation $x^2 - 5 = 3x$ is *not* a linear equation, because it involves the term x^2. $\sqrt{x} = 5$ is not a linear equation, because it involves a square root. $(x - 1)^2 = 4$ is not a linear equation because even though there's no exponent on the x directly, it appears as part of an expression that is squared. The two-variable equation $x + xy - y = 5$ is not a linear equation because it includes the term xy, where two variables are multiplied together.

Linear equations can always be solved (or shown to have no solution) by combining like terms and performing simple operations on both sides of the equation. Some non-linear equations can be solved by similar methods, but others may require more advanced methods of solution, if they can be solved analytically at all.

SOLVING EQUATIONS INVOLVING ROOTS

In an equation involving roots, the first step is to isolate the term with the root, if possible, and then raise both sides of the equation to the appropriate power to eliminate it. Consider an example equation, $2\sqrt{x + 1} - 1 = 3$. In this case, begin by adding 1 to both sides, yielding $2\sqrt{x + 1} = 4$, and then dividing both sides by 2, yielding $\sqrt{x + 1} = 2$. Now square both sides, yielding $x + 1 = 4$. Finally, subtracting 1 from both sides yields $x = 3$.

Squaring both sides of an equation may, however, yield a spurious solution—a solution to the squared equation that is *not* a solution of the original equation. It's therefore necessary to plug the solution back into the original equation to make sure it works. In this case, it does: $2\sqrt{3+1} - 1 = 2\sqrt{4} - 1 = 2(2) - 1 = 4 - 1 = 3$.

The same procedure applies for other roots as well. For example, given the equation $3 + \sqrt[3]{2x} = 5$, we can first subtract 3 from both sides, yielding $\sqrt[3]{2x} = 2$ and isolating the root. Raising both sides to the third power yields $2x = 2^3$; i.e., $2x = 8$. We can now divide both sides by 2 to get $x = 4$.

> **Review Video: Solving Equations Involving Roots**
> Visit mometrix.com/academy and enter code: 297670

SOLVING EQUATIONS WITH EXPONENTS

To solve an equation involving an exponent, the first step is to isolate the variable with the exponent. We can then take the appropriate root of both sides to eliminate the exponent. For instance, for the equation $2x^3 + 17 = 5x^3 - 7$, we can subtract $5x^3$ from both sides to get $-3x^3 + 17 = -7$, and then subtract 17 from both sides to get $-3x^3 = -24$. Finally, we can divide both sides by –3 to get $x^3 = 8$. Finally, we can take the cube root of both sides to get $x = \sqrt[3]{8} = 2$.

One important but often overlooked point is that equations with an exponent greater than 1 may have more than one answer. The solution to $x^2 = 9$ isn't simply $x = 3$; it's $x = \pm 3$ (that is, $x = 3$ or $x = -3$). For a slightly more complicated example, consider the equation $(x - 1)^2 - 1 = 3$. Adding 1 to both sides yields $(x - 1)^2 = 4$; taking the square root of both sides yields $x - 1 = 2$. We can then add 1 to both sides to get $x = 3$. However, there's a second solution. We also have the possibility that $x - 1 = -2$, in which case $x = -1$. Both $x = 3$ and $x = -1$ are valid solutions, as can be verified by substituting them both into the original equation.

> **Review Video: Solving Equations with Exponents**
> Visit mometrix.com/academy and enter code: 514557

SOLVING EQUATIONS WITH ABSOLUTE VALUES

When solving an equation with an absolute value, the first step is to isolate the absolute value term. We then consider two possibilities: when the expression inside the absolute value is positive or when it is negative. In the former case, the expression in the absolute value equals the expression on the other side of the equation; in the latter, it equals the additive inverse of that expression—the expression times negative one. We consider each case separately and finally check for spurious solutions.

For instance, consider solving $|2x - 1| + x = 5$ for x. We can first isolate the absolute value by moving the x to the other side: $|2x - 1| = -x + 5$. Now, we have two possibilities. First, that $2x - 1$ is positive, and hence $2x - 1 = -x + 5$. Rearranging and combining like terms yields $3x = 6$, and hence $x = 2$. The other possibility is that $2x - 1$ is negative, and hence $2x - 1 = -(-x + 5) = x - 5$. In this case, rearranging and combining like terms yields $x = -4$. Substituting $x = 2$ and $x = -4$ back into the original equation, we see that they are both valid solutions.

Note that the absolute value of a sum or difference applies to the sum or difference as a whole, not to the individual terms; in general, $|2x - 1|$ is not equal to $|2x + 1|$ or to $|2x| - 1$.

SPURIOUS SOLUTIONS

A **spurious solution** may arise when we square both sides of an equation as a step in solving it or under certain other operations on the equation. It is a solution to the squared or otherwise modified equation that is *not* a solution of the original equation. To identify a spurious solution, it's useful when you solve an equation involving roots or absolute values to plug the solution back into the original equation to make sure it's valid.

CHOOSING WHICH VARIABLE TO ISOLATE IN TWO-VARIABLE EQUATIONS

Similar to methods for a one-variable equation, solving a two-variable equation involves isolating a variable: manipulating the equation so that a variable appears by itself on one side of the equation, and not at all on the other side. However, in a two-variable equation, you will usually only be able to isolate one of the variables; the other variable may appear on the other side along with constant terms, or with exponents or other functions.

Often one variable will be much more easily isolated than the other, and therefore that's the variable you should choose. If one variable appears with various exponents, and the other is only raised to the first power, the latter variable is the one to isolate: given the equation $a^2 + 2b = a^3 + b + 3$, the b only appears to the first power, whereas a appears squared and cubed, so b is the variable that can be solved for: combining like terms and isolating the b on the left side of the equation, we get $b = a^3 - a^2 + 3$. If both variables are equally easy to isolate, then it's best to isolate the independent variable, if one is defined; if the two variables are x and y, the convention is that y is the independent variable.

PRACTICE

P1. Seeing the equation $2x + 4 = 4x + 7$, a student divides the first terms on each side by 2, yielding $x + 4 = 2x + 7$, and then combines like terms to get $x = -3$. However, this is incorrect, as can be seen by substituting –3 into the original equation. Explain what is wrong with the student's reasoning.

P2. Describe the steps necessary to solve the equation $2x + 1 - x = 4 + 3x + 7$.

P3. Describe the steps necessary to solve the equation $2(x + 5) = 7(4 - x)$.

P4. Find all real solutions to the equation $1 - \sqrt{x} = 2$.

P5. Find all real solutions to the equation $|x + 1| = 2x + 5$.

P6. Solve for x: $-x + 2\sqrt{x + 5} + 1 = 3$.

P7. Ray earns $10 an hour at his job. Write an equation for his earnings as a function of time spent working. Determine how long Ray has to work in order to earn $360.

P8. Simplify the following: $3x + 2 + 2y = 5y - 7 + |2x - 1|$

PRACTICE SOLUTIONS

P1. As stated, it's easy to verify that the student's solution is incorrect: $2(-3) + 4 = -2$ and $4(-3) + 7 = -5$; clearly $-2 \neq -5$. The mistake was in the first step, which illustrates a common type of error in solving equations. The student tried to simplify the two variable terms by dividing them by 2. However, it's not valid to multiply or divide only one term on each side of an equation by a number; when multiplying or dividing, the operation must be applied to *every* term in the equation. So, dividing by 2 would yield not $x + 4 = 2x + 7$, but $x + 2 = 2x + \frac{7}{2}$. While this is now valid, that fraction is inconvenient to work with, so this may not be the best first step in solving the equation. Rather, it may have been better to first combine like terms. Subtracting $4x$ from both sides yields $-2x + 4 = 7$; subtracting 4 from both sides yields $-2x = 3$; *now* we can divide both sides by –2 to get $x = -\frac{3}{2}$.

P2. Our ultimate goal is to isolate the variable, x. To that end we first move all the terms containing x to the left side of the equation, and all the constant terms to the right side. Note that when we move a term to the other side of the equation its sign changes. We are therefore now left with $2x - x - 3x = 4 + 7 - 1$.

Next, we combine the like terms on each side of the equation, adding and subtracting the terms as appropriate. This leaves us with $-2x = 10$.

At this point, we're almost done; all that remains is to divide both sides by -2 to leave the x by itself. We now have our solution, $x = -5$. We can verify that this is a correct solution by substituting it back into the original equation.

P3. Generally, in equations that have a sum or difference of terms multiplied by another value or expression, the first step is to multiply those terms, distributing as necessary: $2(x + 5) = 2(x) + 2(5) = 2x + 10$, and $7(4 - x) = 7(4) - 7(x) = 28 - 7x$. So, the equation becomes $2x + 10 = 28 - 7x$. We can now add $7x$ to both sides to eliminate the variable from the right-hand side: $9x + 10 = 28$. Similarly, we can subtract 10 from both sides to move all the constants to the right: $9x = 18$. Finally, we can divide both sides by 9, yielding the final answer, $x = 2$.

P4. It's not hard to isolate the root: subtract one from both sides, yielding $-\sqrt{x} = 1$. Finally, multiply both sides by –1, yielding $\sqrt{x} = -1$. Squaring both sides of the equation yields $x = 1$. However, if we plug this back into the original equation, we get $1 - \sqrt{1} = 2$, which is false. Therefore $x = 1$ is a spurious solution, and the equation has no real solutions.

P5. This equation has two possibilities: $x + 1 = 2x + 5$, which simplifies to $x = -4$; or $x + 1 = -(2x + 5) = -2x - 5$, which simplifies to $x = -2$. However, if we try substituting both values back into the original equation, we see that only $x = -2$ yields a true statement. $x = -4$ is a spurious solution; $x = -2$ is the only valid solution to the equation.

P6. Start by isolating the term with the root. We can do that by moving the $-x$ and the 1 to the other side, yielding $2\sqrt{x + 5} = 3 + x - 1$, or $2\sqrt{x + 5} = x + 2$. Dividing both sides of the equation by 2 would give us a fractional term that could be messy to deal with, so we won't do that for now. Instead, we square both sides of the equation; note that on the left-hand side the 2 is outside the square root sign, so we have to square it. As a result, we get $4(x + 5) = (x + 2)^2$. Expanding both sides gives us $4x + 20 = x^2 + 4x + 4$. In this case, we see that we have $4x$ on both sides, so we can cancel the $4x$ (which is what allows us to solve this equation despite the different powers of x). We now have $20 = x^2 + 4$, or $x^2 = 16$. Since the variable is raised to an even power, we need to take the positive and negative roots, so $x = \pm 4$: that is, $x = 4$ or $x = -4$. Substituting both values into the original equation, we see that $x = 4$ satisfies the equation but $x = -4$ does not; hence $x = -4$ is a spurious solution, and the only solution to the equation is $x = 4$.

P7. The number of dollars that Ray earns is dependent on the number of hours he works, so earnings will be represented by the dependent variable y and hours worked will be represented by the independent variable x. He earns 10 dollars per hour worked, so his earnings can be calculated as $y = 10x$. To calculate the number of hours Ray must work in order to earn \$360, plug in 360 for y and solve for x:

$$360 = 10x$$
$$x = \frac{360}{10} = 36$$

P8. To simplify this equation, we must isolate one of its variables on one side of the equation. In this case, the x appears under an absolute value sign, which makes it difficult to isolate. The y, on the other hand, only appears without an exponent—the equation is linear in y. We will therefore choose to isolate the y. The first step, then, is to move all the terms with y to the left side of the equation, which we can do by subtracting $5y$ from both sides:

$$3x + 2 - 3y = -7 + |2x - 1|$$

We can then move all the terms that do *not* include y to the right side of the equation, by subtracting $3x$ and 2 from both sides of the equation:

$$-3y = -3x - 9 + |2x - 1|$$

Finally, we can isolate the y by dividing both sides by –3.

$$y = x + 3 - \frac{1}{3}|2x - 1|$$

This is as far as we can simplify the equation; we cannot combine the terms inside and outside the absolute value sign. We can therefore consider the equation to be solved.

Inequalities

WORKING WITH INEQUALITIES

Commonly in algebra and other upper-level fields of math you find yourself working with mathematical expressions that do not equal each other. The statement comparing such expressions with symbols such as < (less than) or > (greater than) is called an *inequality*. An example of an inequality is $7x > 5$. To solve for x, simply divide both sides by 7 and the solution is shown to be $x > \frac{5}{7}$. Graphs of the solution set of inequalities are represented on a number line. Open circles are used to show that an expression approaches a number but is never quite equal to that number.

> **Review Video: Solving Multi-Step Inequalities**
> Visit mometrix.com/academy and enter code: 347842
>
> **Review Video: Solving Inequalities Using All 4 Basic Operations**
> Visit mometrix.com/academy and enter code: 401111

Conditional inequalities are those with certain values for the variable that will make the condition true and other values for the variable where the condition will be false. **Absolute inequalities** can have any real number as the value for the variable to make the condition true, while there is no real number value for the variable that will make the condition false. Solving inequalities is done by following the same rules for solving equations with the exception that when multiplying or dividing by a negative number the direction of the inequality sign must be flipped or reversed. **Double inequalities** are situations where two inequality statements apply to the same variable expression. Example: $-c < ax + b < c$.

> **Review Video: Conditional and Absolute Inequalities**
> Visit mometrix.com/academy and enter code: 980164

DETERMINING SOLUTIONS TO INEQUALITIES

To determine whether a coordinate is a solution of an inequality, you can substitute the values of the coordinate into the inequality, simplify, and check whether the resulting statement holds true. For instance, to determine whether $(-2,4)$ is a solution of the inequality $y \geq -2x + 3$, substitute the values into the inequality, $4 \geq -2(-2) + 3$. Simplify the right side of the inequality and the result is $4 \geq 7$, which is a false statement. Therefore, the coordinate is not a solution of the inequality. You can also use this method to determine which part of the graph of an inequality is shaded. The graph of $y \geq -2x + 3$ includes the solid line $y = -2x + 3$ and, since it excludes the point $(-2,4)$ to the left of the line, it is shaded to the right of the line.

> **Review Video: Graphing Linear Inequalities**
> Visit mometrix.com/academy and enter code: 439421

FLIPPING INEQUALITY SIGNS

When given an inequality, we can always turn the entire inequality around, swapping the two sides of the inequality and changing the inequality sign. For instance, $x + 2 > 2x - 3$ is equivalent to $2x - 3 < x + 2$. Aside from that, normally the inequality does not change if we carry out the same operation on both sides of the inequality. There is, however, one principal exception: if we *multiply* or *divide* both sides of the inequality by a *negative number*, the inequality is flipped. For example, if we take the inequality $-2x < 6$ and divide both sides by –2, the inequality flips and we are left with

$x > -3$. This *only* applies to multiplication and division, and only with negative numbers. Multiplying or dividing both sides by a positive number, or adding or subtracting any number regardless of sign, does not flip the inequality. Another special case that flips the inequality sign is when reciprocals are used. For instance, $3 > 2$ but the relation of the reciprocals is $\frac{1}{2} < \frac{1}{3}$.

COMPOUND INEQUALITIES

A **compound inequality** is an equality that consists of two inequalities combined with *and* or *or*. The two components of a proper compound inequality must be of opposite type: that is, one must be greater than (or greater than or equal to), the other less than (or less than or equal to). For instance, "$x + 1 < 2$ or $x + 1 > 3$" is a compound inequality, as is "$2x \geq 4$ and $2x \leq 6$." An *and* inequality can be written more compactly by having one inequality on each side of the common part: "$2x \geq 1$ and $2x \leq 6$," can also be written as $1 \leq 2x \leq 6$.

In order for the compound inequality to be meaningful, the two parts of an *and* inequality must overlap; otherwise, no numbers satisfy the inequality. On the other hand, if the two parts of an *or* inequality overlap, then *all* numbers satisfy the inequality and as such the inequality is usually not meaningful.

Solving a compound inequality requires solving each part separately. For example, given the compound inequality "$x + 1 < 2$ or $x + 1 > 3$," the first inequality, $x + 1 < 2$, reduces to $x < 1$, and the second part, $x + 1 > 3$, reduces to $x > 2$, so the whole compound inequality can be written as "$x < 1$ or $x > 2$." Similarly, $1 \leq 2x \leq 6$ can be solved by dividing each term by 2, yielding $\frac{1}{2} \leq x \leq 3$.

> **Review Video: Compound Inequalities**
> Visit mometrix.com/academy and enter code: 786318

SOLVING INEQUALITIES INVOLVING ABSOLUTE VALUES

To solve an inequality involving an absolute value, first isolate the term with the absolute value. Then proceed to treat the two cases separately as with an absolute value equation, but flipping the inequality in the case where the expression in the absolute value is negative (since that essentially involves multiplying both sides by –1.) The two cases are then combined into a compound inequality; if the absolute value is on the greater side of the inequality, then it is an *or* compound inequality, if on the lesser side, then it's an *and*.

Consider the inequality $2 + |x - 1| \geq 3$. We can isolate the absolute value term by subtracting 2 from both sides: $|x - 1| \geq 1$. Now, we're left with the two cases $x - 1 \geq 1$ or $x - 1 \leq -1$: note that in the latter, negative case, the inequality is flipped. $x - 1 \geq 1$ reduces to $x \geq 2$, and $x - 1 \leq -1$ reduces to $x \leq 0$. Since in the inequality $|x - 1| \geq 1$ the absolute value is on the greater side, the two cases combine into an *or* compound inequality, so the final, solved inequality is "$x \leq 0$ or $x \geq 2$."

> **Review Video: Solving Absolute Value Inequalities**
> Visit mometrix.com/academy and enter code: 997008

SOLVING INEQUALITIES INVOLVING SQUARE ROOTS

Solving an inequality with a square root involves two parts. First, we solve the inequality as if it were an equation, isolating the square root and then squaring both sides of the equation. Second, we restrict the solution to the set of values of x for which the value inside the square root sign is non-negative.

For example, in the inequality, $\sqrt{x-2}+1 < 5$, we can isolate the square root by subtracting 1 from both sides, yielding $\sqrt{x-2} < 4$. Squaring both sides of the inequality yields $x-2 < 16$, so $x < 18$. Since we can't take the square root of a negative number, we also require the part inside the square root to be non-negative. In this case, that means $x-2 \geq 0$. Adding 2 to both sides of the inequality yields $x \geq 2$. Our final answer is a compound inequality combining the two simple inequalities: $x \geq 2$ and $x < 18$, or $2 \leq x < 18$.

Note that we only get a compound inequality if the two simple inequalities are in opposite directions; otherwise, we take the one that is more restrictive.

The same technique can be used for other even roots, such as fourth roots. It is *not*, however, used for cube roots or other odd roots—negative numbers *do* have cube roots, so the condition that the quantity inside the root sign cannot be negative does not apply.

> **Review Video: Solving Inequalities Involving Square Roots**
> Visit mometrix.com/academy and enter code: 800288

SPECIAL CIRCUMSTANCES

Sometimes an inequality involving an absolute value or an even exponent is true for all values of x, and we don't need to do any further work to solve it. This is true if the inequality, once the absolute value or exponent term is isolated, says that term is greater than a negative number (or greater than or equal to zero). Since an absolute value or a number raised to an even exponent is *always* non-negative, this inequality is always true.

GRAPHICAL SOLUTIONS TO EQUATIONS AND INEQUALITIES

When equations are shown graphically, they are usually shown on a **Cartesian coordinate plane**. The Cartesian coordinate plane consists of two number lines placed perpendicular to each other and intersecting at the zero point, also known as the origin. The horizontal number line is known as the x-axis, with positive values to the right of the origin, and negative values to the left of the origin. The vertical number line is known as the y-axis, with positive values above the origin, and negative values below the origin. Any point on the plane can be identified by an ordered pair in the form (x, y), called coordinates. The x-value of the coordinate is called the abscissa, and the y-value of the coordinate is called the ordinate. The two number lines divide the plane into **four quadrants**: I, II, III, and IV.

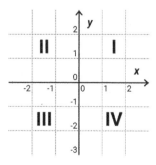

Note that in quadrant I $x > 0$ and $y > 0$, in quadrant II $x < 0$ and $y > 0$, in quadrant III $x < 0$ and $y < 0$, and in quadrant IV $x > 0$ and $y < 0$.

Recall that if the value of the slope of a line is positive, the line slopes upward from left to right. If the value of the slope is negative, the line slopes downward from left to right. If the y-coordinates are the same for two points on a line, the slope is 0 and the line is a **horizontal line**. If the x-

coordinates are the same for two points on a line, there is no slope and the line is a **vertical line**. Two or more lines that have equivalent slopes are **parallel lines**. **Perpendicular lines** have slopes that are negative reciprocals of each other, such as $\frac{a}{b}$ and $\frac{-b}{a}$.

> **Review Video: Cartesian Coordinate Plane and Graphing**
> Visit mometrix.com/academy and enter code: 115173

GRAPHING SIMPLE INEQUALITIES

To graph a simple inequality, we first mark on the number line the value that signifies the end point of the inequality. If the inequality is strict (involves a less than or greater than), we use a hollow circle; if it is not strict (less than or equal to or greater than or equal to), we use a solid circle. We then fill in the part of the number line that satisfies the inequality: to the left of the marked point for less than (or less than or equal to), to the right for greater than (or greater than or equal to).

For example, we would graph the inequality $x < 5$ by putting a hollow circle at 5 and filling in the part of the line to the left:

GRAPHING COMPOUND INEQUALITIES

To graph a compound inequality, we fill in both parts of the inequality for an *or* inequality, or the overlap between them for an *and* inequality. More specifically, we start by plotting the endpoints of each inequality on the number line. For an *or* inequality, we then fill in the appropriate side of the line for each inequality. Typically, the two component inequalities do not overlap, which means the shaded part is *outside* the two points. For an *and* inequality, we instead fill in the part of the line that meets both inequalities.

For the inequality "$x \le -3$ or $x > 4$," we first put a solid circle at –3 and a hollow circle at 4. We then fill the parts of the line *outside* these circles:

GRAPHING INEQUALITIES INCLUDING ABSOLUTE VALUES

An inequality with an absolute value can be converted to a compound inequality. To graph the inequality, first convert it to a compound inequality, and then graph that normally. If the absolute value is on the greater side of the inequality, we end up with an *or* inequality; we plot the endpoints of the inequality on the number line and fill in the part of the line *outside* those points. If the absolute value is on the smaller side of the inequality, we end up with an *and* inequality; we plot the endpoints of the inequality on the number line and fill in the part of the line *between* those points.

For example, the inequality $|x + 1| \ge 4$ can be rewritten as $x \ge 3$ or $x \le -5$. We place solid circles at the points 3 and –5 and fill in the part of the line *outside* them:

GRAPHING EQUATIONS IN TWO VARIABLES

One way of graphing an equation in two variables is to plot enough points to get an idea for its shape and then draw the appropriate curve through those points. A point can be plotted by substituting in a value for one variable and solving for the other. If the equation is linear, we only need two points and can then draw a straight line between them.

For example, consider the equation $y = 2x - 1$. This is a linear equation—both variables only appear raised to the first power—so we only need two points. When $x = 0$, $y = 2(0) - 1 = -1$. When $x = 2$, $y = 2(2) - 1 = 3$. We can therefore choose the points $(0, -1)$ and $(2, 3)$, and draw a line between them:

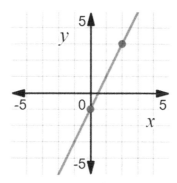

GRAPHING INEQUALITIES IN TWO VARIABLES

To graph an inequality in two variables, we first graph the border of the inequality. This means graphing the equation that we get if we replace the inequality sign with an equals sign. If the inequality is strict ($>$ or $<$), we graph the border with a dashed or dotted line; if it is not strict ($\geq$ or $\leq$), we use a solid line. We can then test any point not on the border to see if it satisfies the inequality. If it does, we shade in that side of the border; if not, we shade in the other side. As an example, consider $y > 2x + 2$. To graph this inequality, we first graph the border, $y = 2x + 2$. Since it is a strict inequality, we use a dashed line. Then, we choose a test point. This can be any point not on the border; in this case, we will choose the origin, $(0,0)$. (This makes the calculation easy and is generally a good choice unless the border passes through the origin.) Putting this into the original inequality, we get $0 > 2(0) + 2$, i.e., $0 > 2$. This is *not* true, so we shade in the side of the border that does *not* include the point $(0,0)$:

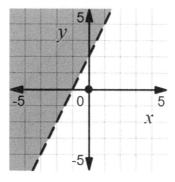

GRAPHING COMPOUND INEQUALITIES IN TWO VARIABLES

One way to graph a compound inequality in two variables is to first graph each of the component inequalities. For an *and* inequality, we then shade in only the parts where the two graphs overlap; for an *or* inequality, we shade in any region that pertains to either of the individual inequalities.

Consider the graph of "$y \geq x - 1$ and $y \leq -x$":

We first shade in the individual inequalities:

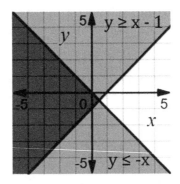

Now, since the compound inequality has an *and*, we only leave shaded the overlap—the part that pertains to *both* inequalities:

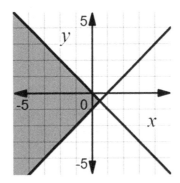

If instead the inequality had been "$y \geq x - 1$ or $y \leq -x$," our final graph would involve the *total* shaded area:

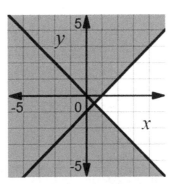

> **Review Video: Graphing Solutions to Inequalities**
> Visit mometrix.com/academy and enter code: 391281

PRACTICE

P1. Analyze the following inequalities:

(a) $2 - |x + 1| < 3$

(b) $2(x - 1)^2 + 7 \leq 1$

P2. Graph the following on a number line:

    (a) $x \geq 3$

    (b) $-2 \leq x \leq 6$

    (c) $|x| < 2$

PRACTICE SOLUTIONS

P1. (a) Subtracting 2 from both sides yields $-|x + 1| < 1$; multiplying by -1 and flipping the inequality, since we're multiplying by a negative number, yields $|x + 1| > -1$. But since the absolute value cannot be negative, it's *always* greater than -1, so this inequality is true for all values of x.

(b) Subtracting 7 from both sides yields $2(x - 1)^2 \leq -6$; dividing by 2 yields $(x - 1)^2 \leq -3$. But $(x - 1)^2$ must be nonnegative, and hence cannot be less than or equal to -3; this inequality has no solution.

P2. (a) We would graph the inequality $x \geq 3$ by putting a solid circle at 3 and filling in the part of the line to the right:

(b) The inequality $-2 \leq x \leq 6$ is equivalent to "$x \geq -2$ and $x \leq 6$." To plot this compound inequality, we first put solid circles at -2 and 6, and then fill in the part of the line *between* these circles:

(c) The inequality $|x| < 2$ can be rewritten as "$x > -2$ and $x < 2$." We place hollow circles at the points -2 and 2 and fill in the part of the line between them:

Systems of Equations

SOLVING SYSTEMS OF EQUATIONS

A **system of equations** is a set of simultaneous equations that all use the same variables. A solution to a system of equations must be true for each equation in the system. **Consistent systems** are those with at least one solution. **Inconsistent systems** are systems of equations that have no solution.

> **Review Video: Solving Systems and Linear Equations**
> Visit mometrix.com/academy and enter code: 746745

SUBSTITUTION

To solve a system of linear equations by **substitution**, start with the easier equation and solve for one of the variables. Express this variable in terms of the other variable. Substitute this expression in the other equation and solve for the other variable. The solution should be expressed in the form (x, y). Substitute the values into both of the original equations to check your answer. Consider the following system of equations:

$$x + 6y = 15$$
$$3x - 12y = 18$$

Solving the first equation for x: $x = 15 - 6y$

Substitute this value in place of x in the second equation, and solve for y:

$$3(15 - 6y) - 12y = 18$$
$$45 - 18y - 12y = 18$$
$$30y = 27$$
$$y = \frac{27}{30} = \frac{9}{10} = 0.9$$

Plug this value for y back into the first equation to solve for x:

$$x = 15 - 6(0.9) = 15 - 5.4 = 9.6$$

Check both equations if you have time:

$$9.6 + 6(0.9) = 15 \qquad 3(9.6) - 12(0.9) = 18$$
$$9.6 + 5.4 = 15 \qquad 28.8 - 10.8 = 18$$
$$15 = 15 \qquad 18 = 18$$

Therefore, the solution is (9.6, 0.9).

> **Review Video: The Substitution Method**
> Visit mometrix.com/academy and enter code: 565151

ELIMINATION

To solve a system of equations using **elimination**, begin by rewriting both equations in standard form $Ax + By = C$. Check to see if the coefficients of one pair of like variables add to zero. If not, multiply one or both of the equations by a non-zero number to make one set of like variables add to

190

zero. Add the two equations to solve for one of the variables. Substitute this value into one of the original equations to solve for the other variable. Check your work by substituting into the other equation. Now, let's look at solving the following system using the elimination method:

$$5x + 6y = 4$$
$$x + 2y = 4$$

If we multiply the second equation by -3, we can eliminate the y-terms:

$$5x + 6y = 4$$
$$-3x - 6y = -12$$

Add the equations together and solve for x:

$$2x = -8$$
$$x = \frac{-8}{2} = -4$$

Plug the value for x back in to either of the original equations and solve for y:

$$-4 + 2y = 4$$
$$y = \frac{4+4}{2} = 4$$

Check both equations if you have time:

$$5(-4) + 6(4) = 4 \qquad -4 + 2(4) = 4$$
$$-20 + 24 = 4 \qquad -4 + 8 = 4$$
$$4 = 4 \qquad 4 = 4$$

Therefore, the solution is $(-4, 4)$.

Review Video: <u>The Elimination Method</u>
Visit mometrix.com/academy and enter code: 449121

GRAPHICALLY

To solve a system of linear equations **graphically**, plot both equations on the same graph. The solution of the equations is the point where both lines cross. If the lines do not cross (are parallel), then there is **no solution**.

For example, consider the following system of equations:

$$y = 2x + 7$$
$$y = -x + 1$$

Since these equations are given in slope-intercept form, they are easy to graph; the y-intercepts of the lines are $(0,7)$ and $(0,1)$. The respective slopes are 2 and -1, thus the graphs look like this:

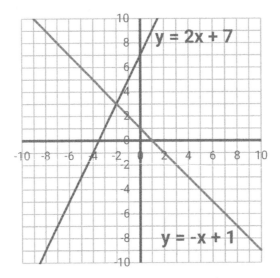

The two lines intersect at the point $(-2,3)$, thus this is the solution to the system of equations.

Solving a system graphically is generally only practical if both coordinates of the solution are integers; otherwise the intersection will lie between gridlines on the graph and the coordinates will be difficult or impossible to determine exactly. It also helps if, as in this example, the equations are in slope-intercept form or some other form that makes them easy to graph. Otherwise, another method of solution (by substitution or elimination) is likely to be more useful.

> **Review Video: Solving Systems by Graphing**
> Visit mometrix.com/academy and enter code: 634812

SOLVING SYSTEMS OF EQUATIONS USING THE TRACE FEATURE

Using the trace feature on a calculator requires that you rewrite each equation, isolating the y-variable on one side of the equal sign. Enter both equations in the graphing calculator and plot the graphs simultaneously. Use the trace cursor to find where the two lines cross. Use the zoom feature if necessary to obtain more accurate results. Always check your answer by substituting into the original equations. The trace method is likely to be less accurate than other methods due to the resolution of graphing calculators but is a useful tool to provide an approximate answer.

CALCULATIONS USING POINTS

Sometimes you need to perform calculations using only points on a graph as input data. Using points, you can determine what the **midpoint** and **distance** are. If you know the equation for a line, you can calculate the distance between the line and the point.

To find the **midpoint** of two points (x_1, y_1) and (x_2, y_2), average the x-coordinates to get the x-coordinate of the midpoint, and average the y-coordinates to get the y-coordinate of the midpoint. The formula is: $\left(\frac{x_1+x_2}{2}, \frac{y_1+y_2}{2}\right)$.

The **distance** between two points is the same as the length of the hypotenuse of a right triangle with the two given points as endpoints, and the two sides of the right triangle parallel to the x-axis and y-axis, respectively. The length of the segment parallel to the x-axis is the difference between the x-coordinates of the two points. The length of the segment parallel to the y-axis is the difference between the y-coordinates of the two points. Use the Pythagorean theorem $a^2 + b^2 = c^2$ or $c = \sqrt{a^2 + b^2}$ to find the distance. The formula is $d = \sqrt{(x_2 - x_1)^2 + (y_2 - y_1)^2}$.

When a line is in the format $Ax + By + C = 0$, where A, B, and C are coefficients, you can use a point (x_1, y_1) not on the line and apply the formula $d = \frac{|Ax_1 + By_1 + C|}{\sqrt{A^2 + B^2}}$ to find the distance between the line and the point (x_1, y_1).

> **Review Video: <u>Calculations Using Points on a Graph</u>**
> Visit mometrix.com/academy and enter code: 883228

PRACTICE

P1. Solve the following systems of equations:

(a) $\quad 3x + 4y = 9$
$\quad\quad -12x + 7y = 10$

(b) $-3x + 2y = -1$
$\quad\quad 4x - 5y = 6$

P2. Find the distance and midpoint between points (2,4) and (8,6).

PRACTICE SOLUTIONS

P1. (a) If we multiply the first equation by 4, we can eliminate the x-terms:

$$12x + 16y = 36$$
$$-12x + 7y = 10$$

Add the equations together and solve for y:

$$23y = 46$$
$$y = 2$$

Plug the value for y back in to either of the original equations and solve for x:

$$3x + 4(2) = 9$$
$$x = \frac{9 - 8}{3} = \frac{1}{3}$$

The solution is $\left(\frac{1}{3}, 2\right)$

(b) Solving the first equation for y:

$$-3x + 2y = -1$$
$$2y = 3x - 1$$
$$y = \frac{3x - 1}{2}$$

Substitute this expression in place of y in the second equation, and solve for x:

$$4x - 5\left(\frac{3x-1}{2}\right) = 6$$

$$4x - \frac{15x}{2} + \frac{5}{2} = 6$$

$$8x - 15x + 5 = 12$$

$$-7x = 7$$

$$x = -1$$

Plug the value for x back in to either of the original equations and solve for y:

$$-3(-1) + 2y = -1$$

$$3 + 2y = -1$$

$$2y = -4$$

$$y = -2$$

The solution is $(-1, -2)$.

P2. Use the formulas for distance and midpoint:

$$\text{Distance} = \sqrt{(x_2 - x_1)^2 + (y_2 - y_1)^2}$$
$$= \sqrt{(8-2)^2 + (6-4)^2}$$
$$= \sqrt{(6)^2 + (2)^2}$$
$$= \sqrt{36 + 4}$$
$$= \sqrt{40} \text{ or } 2\sqrt{10}$$

$$\text{Midpoint} = \left(\frac{x_1 + x_2}{2}, \frac{y_1 + y_2}{2}\right)$$
$$= \left(\frac{2+8}{2}, \frac{4+6}{2}\right)$$
$$= \left(\frac{10}{2}, \frac{10}{2}\right)$$
$$= (5,5)$$

Polynomial Algebra

MONOMIALS AND POLYNOMIALS

A **monomial** is a single constant, variable, or product of constants and variables, such as 7, x, $2x$, or x^3y. There will never be addition or subtraction symbols in a monomial. Like monomials have like variables, but they may have different coefficients. **Polynomials** are algebraic expressions that use addition and subtraction to combine two or more monomials. Two terms make a **binomial**, three terms make a **trinomial**, etc. The **degree of a monomial** is the sum of the exponents of the variables. The **degree of a polynomial** is the highest degree of any individual term.

> **Review Video: Polynomials**
> Visit mometrix.com/academy and enter code: 305005

SIMPLIFYING POLYNOMIALS

Simplifying polynomials requires combining like terms. The like terms in a polynomial expression are those that have the same variable raised to the same power. It is often helpful to connect the like terms with arrows or lines in order to separate them from the other monomials. Once you have determined the like terms, you can rearrange the polynomial by placing them together. Remember to include the sign that is in front of each term. Once the like terms are placed together, you can apply each operation and simplify. When adding and subtracting polynomials, only add and subtract the **coefficient**, or the number part; the variable and exponent stay the same.

> **Review Video: Adding and Subtracting Polynomials**
> Visit mometrix.com/academy and enter code: 124088

THE FOIL METHOD

In general, multiplying polynomials is done by multiplying each term in one polynomial by each term in the other and adding the results. In the specific case for multiplying binomials, there is a useful acronym, FOIL, that can help you make sure to cover each combination of terms. The **FOIL method** for $(Ax + By)(Cx + Dy)$ would be:

F Multiply the *first* terms of each binomial $(\overset{first}{Ax} + By)(\overset{first}{Cx} + Dy)$ ACx^2

O Multiply the *outer* terms $(\overset{outer}{Ax} + By)(Cx + \overset{outer}{Dy})$ $ADxy$

I Multiply the *inner* terms $(Ax + \overset{inner}{By})(\overset{inner}{Cx} + Dy)$ $BCxy$

L Multiply the *last* terms of each binomial $(Ax + \overset{last}{By})(Cx + \overset{last}{Dy})$ BDy^2

Then, add up the result of each and combine like terms: $ACx^2 + (AD + BC)xy + BDy^2$.

For example, using the FOIL method on binomials $(x + 2)$ and $(x - 3)$:

First: $(\boxed{x} + 2)(\boxed{x} + (-3)) \rightarrow (x)(x) = x^2$
Outer: $(\boxed{x} + 2)(x + \boxed{(-3)}) \rightarrow (x)(-3) = -3x$
Inner: $(x + \boxed{2})(\boxed{x} + (-3)) \rightarrow (2)(x) = 2x$
Last: $(x + \boxed{2})(x + \boxed{(-3)}) \rightarrow (2)(-3) = -6$

This results in: $(x^2) + (-3x) + (2x) + (-6)$

Combine like terms: $x^2 + (-3 + 2)x + (-6) = x^2 - x - 6$

> **Review Video: Multiplying Terms Using the FOIL Method**
> Visit mometrix.com/academy and enter code: 854792

DIVIDING POLYNOMIALS

Use long division to divide a polynomial by either a monomial or another polynomial of equal or lesser degree.

When **dividing by a monomial**, divide each term of the polynomial by the monomial.

When **dividing by a polynomial**, begin by arranging the terms of each polynomial in order of one variable. You may arrange in ascending or descending order, but be consistent with both polynomials. To get the first term of the quotient, divide the first term of the dividend by the first term of the divisor. Multiply the first term of the quotient by the entire divisor and subtract that product from the dividend. Repeat for the second and successive terms until you either get a remainder of zero or a remainder whose degree is less than the degree of the divisor. If the quotient has a remainder, write the answer as a mixed expression in the form:

$$\text{quotient} + \frac{\text{remainder}}{\text{divisor}}$$

For example, we can evaluate the following expression in the same way as long division:

$$\frac{x^3 - 3x^2 - 2x + 5}{x - 5}$$

$$
\begin{array}{r}
x^2 + 2x + 8 \\
x - 5 \overline{)\, x^3 - 3x^2 - 2x + 5} \\
-(x^3 - 5x^2) \\
\hline
2x^2 - 2x \\
-(2x^2 - 10x) \\
\hline
8x + 5 \\
-(8x - 40) \\
\hline
45
\end{array}
$$

$$\frac{x^3 - 3x^2 - 2x + 5}{x - 5} = x^2 + 2x + 8 + \frac{45}{x - 5}$$

When **factoring** a polynomial, first check for a common monomial factor, that is, look to see if each coefficient has a common factor or if each term has an x in it. If the factor is a trinomial but not a perfect trinomial square, look for a factorable form, such as one of these:

$$x^2 + (a + b)x + ab = (x + a)(x + b)$$
$$(ac)x^2 + (ad + bc)x + bd = (ax + b)(cx + d)$$

For factors with four terms, look for groups to factor. Once you have found the factors, write the original polynomial as the product of all the factors. Make sure all of the polynomial factors are prime. Monomial factors may be *prime* or *composite*. Check your work by multiplying the factors to make sure you get the original polynomial.

Below are patterns of some special products to remember to help make factoring easier:

- Perfect trinomial squares: $x^2 + 2xy + y^2 = (x + y)^2$ or $x^2 - 2xy + y^2 = (x - y)^2$
- Difference between two squares: $x^2 - y^2 = (x + y)(x - y)$
- Sum of two cubes: $x^3 + y^3 = (x + y)(x^2 - xy + y^2)$
  - Note: the second factor is *not* the same as a perfect trinomial square, so do not try to factor it further.
- Difference between two cubes: $x^3 - y^3 = (x - y)(x^2 + xy + y^2)$
  - Again, the second factor is *not* the same as a perfect trinomial square.
- Perfect cubes: $x^3 + 3x^2y + 3xy^2 + y^3 = (x + y)^3$ and $x^3 - 3x^2y + 3xy^2 - y^3 = (x - y)^3$

RATIONAL EXPRESSIONS

Rational expressions are fractions with polynomials in both the numerator and the denominator; the value of the polynomial in the denominator cannot be equal to zero. Be sure to keep track of values that make the denominator of the original expression zero as the final result inherits the same restrictions. For example, a denominator of $x - 3$ indicates that the expression is not defined when $x = 3$ and, as such, regardless of any operations done to the expression, it remains undefined there.

To **add or subtract** rational expressions, first find the common denominator, then rewrite each fraction as an equivalent fraction with the common denominator. Finally, add or subtract the numerators to get the numerator of the answer, and keep the common denominator as the denominator of the answer.

When **multiplying** rational expressions, factor each polynomial and cancel like factors (a factor which appears in both the numerator and the denominator). Then, multiply all remaining factors in the numerator to get the numerator of the product, and multiply the remaining factors in the denominator to get the denominator of the product. Remember: cancel entire factors, not individual terms.

To **divide** rational expressions, take the reciprocal of the divisor (the rational expression you are dividing by) and multiply by the dividend.

> **Review Video: Rational Expressions**
> Visit mometrix.com/academy and enter code: 415183

SIMPLIFYING RATIONAL EXPRESSIONS

To simplify a rational expression, factor the numerator and denominator completely. Factors that are the same and appear in the numerator and denominator have a ratio of 1. For example, look at the following expression:

$$\frac{x - 1}{1 - x^2}$$

The denominator, $(1 - x^2)$, is a difference of squares. It can be factored as $(1 - x)(1 + x)$. The factor $1 - x$ and the numerator $x - 1$ are opposites and have a ratio of –1. Rewrite the numerator as $-1(1 - x)$. So, the rational expression can be simplified as follows:

$$\frac{x - 1}{1 - x^2} = \frac{-1(1 - x)}{(1 - x)(1 + x)} = \frac{-1}{1 + x}$$

Note that since the original expression is only defined for $x \neq \{-1, 1\}$, the simplified expression has the same restrictions.

Review Video: <u>Reducing Rational Expressions</u>
Visit mometrix.com/academy and enter code: 788868

PRACTICE

P1. Expand the following polynomials:

   (a) $(x + 3)(x - 7)(2x)$

   (b) $(x + 2)^2(x - 2)^2$

   (c) $(x^2 + 5x + 5)(3x - 1)$

P2. Evaluate the following rational expressions:

   (a) $\dfrac{x^3 - 2x^2 - 5x + 6}{3x + 6}$

   (b) $\dfrac{x^2 + 4x + 4}{4 - x^2}$

PRACTICE SOLUTIONS

P1. (a) Apply the FOIL method and the distributive property of multiplication:

$$\begin{aligned}
(x + 3)(x - 7)(2x) &= (x^2 - 7x + 3x - 21)(2x) \\
&= (x^2 - 4x - 21)(2x) \\
&= 2x^3 - 8x^2 - 42x
\end{aligned}$$

(b) Note the difference of squares form:

$$\begin{aligned}
(x + 2)^2(x - 2)^2 &= (x + 2)(x + 2)(x - 2)(x - 2) \\
&= [(x + 2)(x - 2)][(x + 2)(x - 2)] \\
&= (x^2 - 4)(x^2 - 4) \\
&= x^4 - 8x^2 + 16
\end{aligned}$$

(c) Multiply each pair of monomials and combine like terms:

$$\begin{aligned}
(x^2 + 5x + 5)(3x - 1) &= 3x^3 + 15x^2 + 15x - x^2 - 5x - 5 \\
&= 3x^3 + 14x^2 + 10x - 5
\end{aligned}$$

P2. (a) Rather than trying to factor the third-degree polynomial, we can use long division:

$$\frac{x^3 - 2x^2 - 5x + 6}{3x + 6} = \frac{x^3 - 2x^2 - 5x + 6}{3(x + 2)}$$

$$
\begin{array}{r}
x^2 \quad - 4x \quad + 3 \\
x + 2 \,\overline{)\, x^3 \quad - 2x^2 \quad - 5x \quad + 6} \\
\underline{x^3 \quad + 2x^2} \\
- 4x^2 \quad - 5x \\
\underline{- 4x^2 \quad - 8x} \\
3x \quad + 6 \\
\underline{3x \quad + 6} \\
0
\end{array}
$$

$$\frac{x^3 - 2x^2 - 5x + 6}{3(x + 2)} = \frac{x^2 - 4x + 3}{3}$$

Note that since the original expression is only defined for $x \neq \{-2\}$, the simplified expression has the same restrictions.

(b) The denominator, $(4 - x^2)$, is a difference of squares. It can be factored as $(2 - x)(2 + x)$. The numerator, $(x^2 + 4x + 4)$, is a perfect square. It can be factored as $(x + 2)(x + 2)$. So, the rational expression can be simplified as follows:

$$\frac{x^2 + 4x + 4}{4 - x^2} = \frac{(x + 2)(x + 2)}{(2 - x)(2 + x)} = \frac{(x + 2)}{(2 - x)}$$

Note that since the original expression is only defined for $x \neq \{-2, 2\}$, the simplified expression has the same restrictions.

Quadratics

SOLVING QUADRATIC EQUATIONS

Quadratic equations are a special set of trinomials of the form $y = ax^2 + bx + c$ that occur commonly in math and real-world applications. The **roots** of a quadratic equation are the solutions that satisfy the equation when $y = 0$; in other words, where the graph touches the x-axis. There are several ways to determine these solutions including using the quadratic formula, factoring, completing the square, and graphing the function.

> **Review Video: Quadratic Equations Overview**
> Visit mometrix.com/academy and enter code: 476276
>
> **Review Video: Solutions of a Quadratic Equation on a Graph**
> Visit mometrix.com/academy and enter code: 328231

QUADRATIC FORMULA

The **quadratic formula** is used to solve quadratic equations when other methods are more difficult. To use the quadratic formula to solve a quadratic equation, begin by rewriting the equation in standard form $ax^2 + bx + c = 0$, where a, b, and c are coefficients. Once you have identified the values of the coefficients, substitute those values into the quadratic formula

$$x = \frac{-b \pm \sqrt{b^2 - 4ac}}{2a}$$

Evaluate the equation and simplify the expression. Again, check each root by substituting into the original equation. In the quadratic formula, the portion of the formula under the radical ($b^2 - 4ac$) is called the **discriminant**. If the discriminant is zero, there is only one root: $-\frac{b}{2a}$. If the discriminant is positive, there are two different real roots. If the discriminant is negative, there are no real roots; you will instead find complex roots. Often these solutions don't make sense in context and are ignored.

> **Review Video: Using the Quadratic Formula**
> Visit mometrix.com/academy and enter code: 163102

FACTORING

To solve a quadratic equation by factoring, begin by rewriting the equation in standard form, $x^2 + bx + c = 0$. Remember that the goal of factoring is to find numbers f and g such that $(x + f)(x + g) = x^2 + (f + g)x + fg$, in other words $(f + g) = b$ and $fg = c$. This can be a really useful method when b and c are integers. Determine the factors of c and look for pairs that could sum to b.

For example, consider finding the roots of $x^2 + 6x - 16 = 0$. The factors of -16 include, -4 and 4, -8 and 2, -2 and 8, -1 and 16, and 1 and -16. The factors that sum to 6 are -2 and 8. Write these factors as the product of two binomials, $0 = (x - 2)(x + 8)$. Finally, since these binomials multiply together to equal zero, set them each equal to zero and solve each for x. This results in $x - 2 = 0$, which simplifies to $x = 2$ and $x + 8 = 0$, which simplifies to $x = -8$. Therefore, the roots of the equation are 2 and -8.

> **Review Video: Factoring Quadratic Equations**
> Visit mometrix.com/academy and enter code: 336566

COMPLETING THE SQUARE

One way to find the roots of a quadratic equation is to find a way to manipulate it such that it follows the form of a perfect square $(x^2 + 2px + p^2)$ by adding and subtracting a constant. This process is called **completing the square**. In other words, if you are given a quadratic that is not a perfect square, $x^2 + bx + c = 0$, you can find a constant d that could be added in to make it a perfect square:

$$x^2 + bx + c + (d - d) = 0; \ \{\text{Let } b = 2p \text{ and } c + d = p^2\}$$

then:

$$x^2 + 2px + p^2 - d = 0 \text{ and } d = \frac{b^2}{4} - c$$

Once you have completed the square you can find the roots of the resulting equation:

$$x^2 + 2px + p^2 - d = 0$$
$$(x + p)^2 = d$$
$$x + p = \pm\sqrt{d}$$
$$x = -p \pm \sqrt{d}$$

It is worth noting that substituting the original expressions into this solution gives the same result as the quadratic formula where $a = 1$:

$$x = -p \pm \sqrt{d} = -\frac{b}{2} \pm \sqrt{\frac{b^2}{4} - c} = -\frac{b}{2} \pm \frac{\sqrt{b^2 - 4c}}{2} = \frac{-b \pm \sqrt{b^2 - 4c}}{2}$$

Completing the square can be seen as arranging block representations of each of the terms to be as close to a square as possible and then filling in the gaps. For example, consider the quadratic expression $x^2 + 6x + 2$:

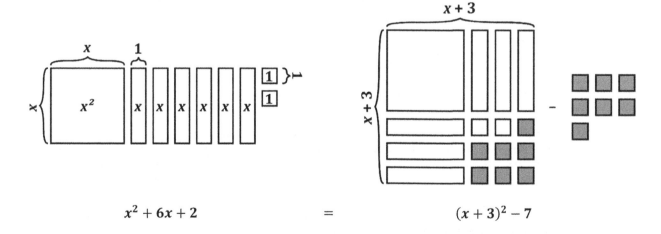

$$x^2 + 6x + 2 \qquad\qquad = \qquad\qquad (x + 3)^2 - 7$$

> **Review Video: Completing the Square**
> Visit mometrix.com/academy and enter code: 982479

USING GIVEN ROOTS TO FIND QUADRATIC EQUATION

One way to find the roots of a quadratic equation is to factor the equation and use the **zero product property**, setting each factor of the equation equal to zero to find the corresponding root. We can use this technique in reverse to find an equation given its roots. Each root corresponds to a linear equation which in turn corresponds to a factor of the quadratic equation.

For example, we can find a quadratic equation whose roots are $x = 2$ and $x = -1$. The root $x = 2$ corresponds to the equation $x - 2 = 0$, and the root $x = -1$ corresponds to the equation $x + 1 = 0$.

These two equations correspond to the factors $(x - 2)$ and $(x + 1)$, from which we can derive the equation $(x - 2)(x + 1) = 0$, or $x^2 - x - 2 = 0$.

Any integer multiple of this entire equation will also yield the same roots, as the integer will simply cancel out when the equation is factored. For example, $2x^2 - 2x - 4 = 0$ factors as $2(x - 2)(x + 1) = 0$.

SOLVING A SYSTEM OF EQUATIONS CONSISTING OF A LINEAR EQUATION AND A QUADRATIC EQUATION

ALGEBRAICALLY

Generally, the simplest way to solve a system of equations consisting of a linear equation and a quadratic equation algebraically is through the method of substitution. One possible strategy is to solve the linear equation for y and then substitute that expression into the quadratic equation. After expansion and combining like terms, this will result in a new quadratic equation for x, which, like all quadratic equations, may have zero, one, or two solutions. Plugging each solution for x back into one of the original equations will then produce the corresponding value of y.

For example, consider the following system of equations:

$$x + y = 1$$
$$y = (x + 3)^2 - 2$$

We can solve the linear equation for y to yield $y = -x + 1$. Substituting this expression into the quadratic equation produces $-x + 1 = (x + 3)^2 - 2$. We can simplify this equation:

$$-x + 1 = (x + 3)^2 - 2$$
$$-x + 1 = x^2 + 6x + 9 - 2$$
$$-x + 1 = x^2 + 6x + 7$$
$$0 = x^2 + 7x + 6$$

This quadratic equation can be factored as $(x + 1)(x + 6) = 0$. It therefore has two solutions: $x_1 = -1$ and $x_2 = -6$. Plugging each of these back into the original linear equation yields $y_1 = -x_1 + 1 = -(-1) + 1 = 2$ and $y_2 = -x_2 + 1 = -(-6) + 1 = 7$. Thus, this system of equations has two solutions, $(-1,2)$ and $(-6,7)$.

It may help to check your work by putting each x- and y-value back into the original equations and verifying that they do provide a solution.

GRAPHICALLY

To solve a system of equations consisting of a linear equation and a quadratic equation graphically, plot both equations on the same graph. The linear equation will, of course, produce a straight line, while the quadratic equation will produce a parabola. These two graphs will intersect at zero, one, or two points; each point of intersection is a solution of the system.

For example, consider the following system of equations:

$$y = -2x + 2$$
$$y = -2x^2 + 4x + 2$$

The linear equation describes a line with a y-intercept of $(0,2)$ and a slope of -2.

To graph the quadratic equation, we can first find the vertex of the parabola: the x-coordinate of the vertex is $h = -\frac{b}{2a} = -\frac{4}{2(-2)} = 1$, and the y-coordinate is $k = -2(1)^2 + 4(1) + 2 = 4$. Thus, the vertex lies at $(1,4)$. To get a feel for the rest of the parabola, we can plug in a few more values of x to find more points; by putting in $x = 2$ and $x = 3$ in the quadratic equation, we find that the points $(2,2)$ and $(3,-4)$ lie on the parabola; by symmetry, so must $(0,2)$ and $(-1,-4)$. We can now plot both equations:

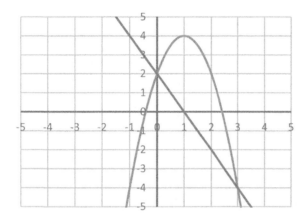

These two curves intersect at the points $(0,2)$ and $(3,-4)$, thus these are the solutions of the equation.

> **Review Video: Solving a System of Equations Consisting of a Linear Equation and Quadratic Equations**
> Visit mometrix.com/academy and enter code: 194870
>
> **Review Video: Parabolas**
> Visit mometrix.com/academy and enter code: 129187
>
> **Review Video: Vertex of a Parabola**
> Visit mometrix.com/academy and enter code: 272300

PRACTICE

P1. Find the roots of $y = 2x^2 + 8x + 4$.

P2. Find a quadratic equation with roots $x = 4$ and $x = -6$.

PRACTICE SOLUTIONS

P1. First, substitute 0 in for y in the quadratic equation: $0 = 2x^2 + 8x + 4$.

Next, try to factor the quadratic equation. Since $a \neq 1$, list the factors of ac, or 8:

$$(1,8), (-1,-8), (2,4), (-2,-4)$$

Look for the factors of ac that add up to b, or 8. Since none do, the equation cannot be factored with whole numbers. Substitute the values of a, b, and c into the quadratic formula, $x = \frac{-b \pm \sqrt{b^2 - 4ac}}{2a}$:

$$x = \frac{-8 \pm \sqrt{8^2 - 4(2)(4)}}{2(2)}$$

Use the order of operations to simplify:

$$x = \frac{-8 \pm \sqrt{64 - 32}}{4}$$
$$x = \frac{-8 \pm \sqrt{32}}{4}$$

Reduce and simplify:

$$x = \frac{-8 \pm \sqrt{(16)(2)}}{4}$$
$$x = \frac{-8 \pm 4\sqrt{2}}{4}$$
$$x = -2 \pm \sqrt{2}$$
$$x = \left(-2 + \sqrt{2}\right) \text{ and } \left(-2 - \sqrt{2}\right)$$

P2. The root $x = 4$ corresponds to the equation $x - 4 = 0$, and the root $x = -6$ corresponds to the equation $x + 6 = 0$. These two equations correspond to the factors $(x - 4)$ and $(x + 6)$, from which we can derive the equation $(x - 4)(x + 6) = 0$, or $x^2 + 2x - 24 = 0$.

Basic Functions

FUNCTION AND RELATION

When expressing functional relationships, the **variables** x and y are typically used. These values are often written as the **coordinates** (x, y). The x-value is the independent variable and the y-value is the dependent variable. A **relation** is a set of data in which there is not a unique y-value for each x-value in the dataset. This means that there can be two of the same x-values assigned to different y-values. A relation is simply a relationship between the x- and y-values in each coordinate but does not apply to the relationship between the values of x and y in the data set. A **function** is a relation where one quantity depends on the other. For example, the amount of money that you make depends on the number of hours that you work. In a function, each x-value in the data set has one unique y-value because the y-value depends on the x-value.

FUNCTIONS

A function has exactly one value of **output variable** (dependent variable) for each value of the **input variable** (independent variable). The set of all values for the input variable (here assumed to be x) is the domain of the function, and the set of all corresponding values of the output variable (here assumed to be y) is the range of the function. When looking at a graph of an equation, the easiest way to determine if the equation is a function or not is to conduct the vertical line test. If a vertical line drawn through any value of x crosses the graph in more than one place, the equation is not a function.

DETERMINING A FUNCTION

You can determine whether an equation is a **function** by substituting different values into the equation for x. You can display and organize these numbers in a data table. A **data table** contains the values for x and y, which you can also list as coordinates. In order for a function to exist, the table cannot contain any repeating x-values that correspond with different y-values. If each x-coordinate has a unique y-coordinate, the table contains a function. However, there can be repeating y-values that correspond with different x-values. An example of this is when the function contains an exponent. Example: if $x^2 = y$, $2^2 = 4$, and $(-2)^2 = 4$.

> **Review Video: Definition of a Function**
> Visit mometrix.com/academy and enter code: 784611

FINDING THE DOMAIN AND RANGE OF A FUNCTION

The **domain** of a function $f(x)$ is the set of all input values for which the function is defined. The **range** of a function $f(x)$ is the set of all possible output values of the function—that is, of every possible value of $f(x)$, for any value of x in the function's domain. For a function expressed in a table, every input-output pair is given explicitly. To find the domain, we just list all the x-values and to find the range, we just list all the values of $f(x)$. Consider the following example:

x	−1	4	2	1	0	3	8	6
$f(x)$	3	0	3	−1	−1	2	4	6

In this case, the domain would be $\{-1, 4, 2, 1, 0, 3, 8, 6\}$ or, putting them in ascending order, $\{-1, 0, 1, 2, 3, 4, 6, 8\}$. (Putting the values in ascending order isn't strictly necessary, but generally makes the set easier to read.) The range would be $\{3, 0, 3, -1, -1, 2, 4, 6\}$. Note that some of these values appear more than once. This is entirely permissible for a function; while each value of x must be matched to a unique value of $f(x)$, the converse is not true. We don't need to list each value more than once, so eliminating duplicates, the range is $\{3, 0, -1, 2, 4, 6\}$, or, putting them in ascending order, $\{-1, 0, 2, 3, 4, 6\}$.

Note that by definition of a function, no input value can be matched to more than one output value. It is good to double-check to make sure that the data given follows this and is therefore actually a function.

WRITING A FUNCTION RULE USING A TABLE

If given a set of data, place the corresponding x- and y-values into a table and analyze the relationship between them. Consider what you can do to each x-value to obtain the corresponding y-value. Try adding or subtracting different numbers to and from x and then try multiplying or dividing different numbers to and from x. If none of these **operations** give you the y-value, try combining the operations. Once you find a rule that works for one pair, make sure to try it with each additional set of ordered pairs in the table. If the same operation or combination of operations satisfies each set of coordinates, then the table contains a function. The rule is then used to write the equation of the function in "$y = f(x)$" form.

DIRECT AND INVERSE VARIATIONS OF VARIABLES

Variables that vary directly are those that either both increase at the same rate or both decrease at the same rate. For example, in the functions $y = kx$ or $y = kx^n$, where k and n are positive, the value of y increases as the value of x increases and decreases as the value of x decreases.

Variables that vary inversely are those where one increases while the other decreases. For example, in the functions $y = \frac{k}{x}$ or $y = \frac{k}{x^n}$ where k and n are positive, the value of y increases as the value of x decreases and decreases as the value of x increases.

In both cases, k is the constant of variation.

PROPERTIES OF FUNCTIONS

There are many different ways to classify functions based on their structure or behavior. Important features of functions include:

- **End behavior**: the behavior of the function at extreme values ($f(x)$ as $x \to \pm\infty$)
- **y-intercept**: the value of the function at $f(0)$
- **Roots**: the values of x where the function equals zero ($f(x) = 0$)
- **Extrema**: minimum or maximum values of the function or where the function changes direction ($f(x) \geq k$ or $f(x) \leq k$)

CLASSIFICATION OF FUNCTIONS

An **invertible function** is defined as a function, $f(x)$, for which there is another function, $f^{-1}(x)$, such that $f^{-1}(f(x)) = x$. For example, if $f(x) = 3x - 2$ the inverse function, $f^{-1}(x)$, can be found:

$$x = 3\left(f^{-1}(x)\right) - 2$$
$$\frac{x+2}{3} = f^{-1}(x)$$

$$f^{-1}(f(x)) = \frac{3x - 2 + 2}{3}$$
$$= \frac{3x}{3}$$
$$= x$$

Note that $f^{-1}(x)$ is a valid function over all values of x.

In a **one-to-one function**, each value of x has exactly one value for y on the coordinate plane (this is the definition of a function) and each value of y has exactly one value for x. While the vertical line test will determine if a graph is that of a function, the horizontal line test will determine if a function is a one-to-one function. If a horizontal line drawn at any value of y intersects the graph in more than one place, the graph is not that of a one-to-one function. Do not make the mistake of using the horizontal line test exclusively in determining if a graph is that of a one-to-one function. A one-to-one function must pass both the vertical line test and the horizontal line test. As such, one-to-one functions are invertible functions.

A **many-to-one function** is a function whereby the relation is a function, but the inverse of the function is not a function. In other words, each element in the domain is mapped to one and only one element in the range. However, one or more elements in the range may be mapped to the same element in the domain. A graph of a many-to-one function would pass the vertical line test, but not the horizontal line test. This is why many-to-one functions are not invertible.

A **monotone function** is a function whose graph either constantly increases or constantly decreases. Examples include the functions $f(x) = x$, $f(x) = -x$, or $f(x) = x^3$.

An **even function** has a graph that is symmetric with respect to the y-axis and satisfies the equation $f(x) = f(-x)$. Examples include the functions $f(x) = x^2$ and $f(x) = ax^n$, where a is any real number and n is a positive even integer.

An **odd function** has a graph that is symmetric with respect to the origin and satisfies the equation $f(x) = -f(-x)$. Examples include the functions $f(x) = x^3$ and $f(x) = ax^n$, where a is any real number and n is a positive odd integer.

> **Review Video: <u>Even and Odd Functions</u>**
> Visit mometrix.com/academy and enter code: 278985

Constant functions are given by the equation $f(x) = b$, where b is a real number. There is no independent variable present in the equation, so the function has a constant value for all x. The graph of a constant function is a horizontal line of slope 0 that is positioned b units from the x-axis. If b is positive, the line is above the x-axis; if b is negative, the line is below the x-axis.

Identity functions are identified by the equation $f(x) = x$, where every value of the function is equal to its corresponding value of x. The only zero is the point (0,0). The graph is a line with a slope of 1.

In **linear functions**, the value of the function changes in direct proportion to x. The rate of change, represented by the slope on its graph, is constant throughout. The standard form of a linear equation is $ax + cy = d$, where a, c, and d are real numbers. As a function, this equation is commonly in the form $y = mx + b$ or $f(x) = mx + b$ where $m = -\frac{a}{c}$ and $b = \frac{d}{c}$. This is known as the slope-intercept form, because the coefficients give the slope of the graphed function (m) and its y-intercept (b). Solve the equation $mx + b = 0$ for x to get $x = -\frac{b}{m}$, which is the only zero of the function. The domain and range are both the set of all real numbers.

Algebraic functions are those that exclusively use polynomials and roots. These would include polynomial functions, rational functions, square root functions, and all combinations of these functions, such as polynomials as the radicand. These combinations may be joined by addition, subtraction, multiplication, or division, but may not include variables as exponents.

ABSOLUTE VALUE FUNCTIONS

An **absolute value function** is in the format $f(x) = |ax + b|$. Like other functions, the domain is the set of all real numbers. However, because absolute value indicates positive numbers, the range is limited to positive real numbers. To find the zero of an absolute value function, set the portion inside the absolute value sign equal to zero and solve for x. An absolute value function is also known as a piecewise function because it must be solved in pieces—one for if the value inside the absolute value sign is positive, and one for if the value is negative. The function can be expressed as:

$$f(x) = \begin{cases} ax + b \text{ if } ax + b \geq 0 \\ -(ax + b) \text{ if } ax + b < 0 \end{cases}$$

This will allow for an accurate statement of the range. The graph of an example absolute value function, $f(x) = |2x - 1|$, is below:

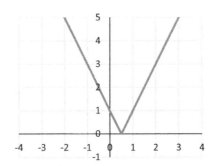

PIECEWISE FUNCTIONS

A **piecewise function** is a function that has different definitions on two or more different intervals. The following, for instance, is one example of a piecewise-defined function:

$$f(x) = \begin{cases} x^2, & x < 0 \\ x, & 0 \leq x \leq 2 \\ (x-2)^2, & x > 2 \end{cases}$$

To graph this function, you would simply graph each part separately in the appropriate domain. The final graph would look like this:

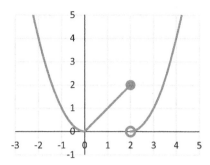

Note the filled and hollow dots at the discontinuity at $x = 2$. This is important to show which side of the graph that point corresponds to. Because $f(x) = x$ on the closed interval $0 \le x \le 2$, $f(2) = 2$. The point $(2, 2)$ is therefore marked with a filled circle, and the point $(2, 0)$, which is the endpoint of the rightmost $(x - 2)^2$ part of the graph but *not actually part of the function*, is marked with a hollow dot to indicate this.

> **Review Video: <u>Piecewise Functions</u>**
> Visit mometrix.com/academy and enter code: 707921

QUADRATIC FUNCTIONS

A **quadratic function** is a function in the form $y = ax^2 + bx + c$, where a does not equal 0. While a linear function forms a line, a quadratic function forms a **parabola**, which is a u-shaped figure that either opens upward or downward. A parabola that opens upward is said to be a **positive quadratic function,** and a parabola that opens downward is said to be a **negative quadratic function**. The shape of a parabola can differ, depending on the values of a, b, and c. All parabolas contain a **vertex**, which is the highest possible point, the **maximum**, or the lowest possible point, the **minimum**. This is the point where the graph begins moving in the opposite direction. A quadratic function can have zero, one, or two solutions, and therefore zero, one, or two x-intercepts. Recall that the x-intercepts are referred to as the zeros, or roots, of a function. A quadratic function will have only one y-intercept. Understanding the basic components of a quadratic function can give you an idea of the shape of its graph.

Example graph of a positive quadratic function, $x^2 + 2x - 3$:

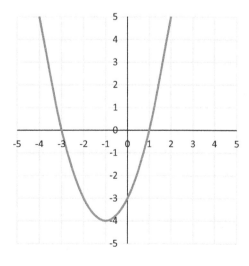

POLYNOMIAL FUNCTIONS

A **polynomial function** is a function with multiple terms and multiple powers of x, such as:

$$f(x) = a_n x^n + a_{n-1} x^{n-1} + a_{n-2} x^{n-2} + \cdots + a_1 x + a_0$$

where n is a non-negative integer that is the highest exponent in the polynomial and $a_n \neq 0$. The domain of a polynomial function is the set of all real numbers. If the greatest exponent in the polynomial is even, the polynomial is said to be of even degree and the range is the set of real numbers that satisfy the function. If the greatest exponent in the polynomial is odd, the polynomial is said to be odd and the range, like the domain, is the set of all real numbers.

RATIONAL FUNCTIONS

A **rational function** is a function that can be constructed as a ratio of two polynomial expressions: $f(x) = \frac{p(x)}{q(x)}$, where $p(x)$ and $q(x)$ are both polynomial expressions and $q(x) \neq 0$. The domain is the set of all real numbers, except any values for which $q(x) = 0$. The range is the set of real numbers that satisfies the function when the domain is applied. When you graph a rational function, you will have vertical asymptotes wherever $q(x) = 0$. If the polynomial in the numerator is of lesser degree than the polynomial in the denominator, the x-axis will also be a horizontal asymptote. If the numerator and denominator have equal degrees, there will be a horizontal asymptote not on the x-axis. If the degree of the numerator is exactly one greater than the degree of the denominator, the graph will have an oblique, or diagonal, asymptote. The asymptote will be along the line $y = \frac{p_n}{q_{n-1}} x + \frac{p_{n-1}}{q_{n-1}}$, where p_n and q_{n-1} are the coefficients of the highest degree terms in their respective polynomials.

SQUARE ROOT FUNCTIONS

A **square root function** is a function that contains a radical and is in the format $f(x) = \sqrt{ax + b}$. The domain is the set of all real numbers that yields a positive radicand or a radicand equal to zero. Because square root values are assumed to be positive unless otherwise identified, the range is all real numbers from zero to infinity. To find the zero of a square root function, set the radicand equal to zero and solve for x. The graph of a square root function is always to the right of the zero and always above the x-axis.

Example graph of a square root function, $f(x) = \sqrt{2x + 1}$:

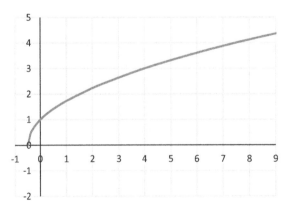

PRACTICE

P1. Martin needs a 20% medicine solution. The pharmacy has a 5% solution and a 30% solution. He needs 50 mL of the solution. If the pharmacist must mix the two solutions, how many milliliters of 5% solution and 30% solution should be used?

P2. Describe two different strategies for solving the following problem:

Kevin can mow the yard in 4 hours. Mandy can mow the same yard in 5 hours. If they work together, how long will it take them to mow the yard?

P3. A car, traveling at 65 miles per hour, leaves Flagstaff and heads east on I-40. Another car, traveling at 75 miles per hour, leaves Flagstaff 2 hours later, from the same starting point and also heads east on I-40. Determine how many hours it will take the second car to catch the first car by:

(a) Using a table.

(b) Using algebra.

PRACTICE SOLUTIONS

P1. To solve this problem, a table may be created to represent the variables, percentages, and total amount of solution. Such a table is shown below:

	mL solution	% medicine	Total mL medicine
5% solution	x	0.05	$0.05x$
30% solution	y	0.30	$0.30y$
Mixture	$x + y = 50$	0.20	$(0.20)(50) = 10$

The variable x may be rewritten as $50 - y$, so the equation $0.05(50 - y) + 0.30y = 10$ may be written and solved for y. Doing so gives $y = 30$. So, 30 mL of 30% solution are needed. Solving the equation $x = 50 - y$ for x shows that 20 mL of 5% solution are needed.

P2. Two possible strategies both involve the use of rational equations to solve. The first strategy involves representing the fractional part of the yard mowed by each person in one hour and setting this sum equal to the ratio of 1 to the total time needed. The appropriate equation is $\frac{1}{4} + \frac{1}{5} = \frac{1}{t}$, which simplifies as $\frac{9}{20} = \frac{1}{t}$, and finally as $t = \frac{20}{9}$. So, the time it will take them to mow the yard, when working together, is a little more than 2.2 hours.

A second strategy involves representing the time needed for each person as two fractions and setting the sum equal to 1 (representing 1 yard). The appropriate equation is $\frac{t}{4} + \frac{t}{5} = 1$, which simplifies as $\frac{9t}{20} = 1$, and finally as $t = \frac{20}{9}$. This strategy also shows the total time to be a little more than 2.2 hours.

P3. (a) One strategy might involve creating a table of values for the number of hours and distances for each car. The table may be examined to find the same distance traveled and the corresponding number of hours taken. Such a table is shown below:

Car A		Car B	
x (hours)	y (distance)	x (hours)	y (distance)
0	0	0	
1	65	1	
2	130	2	0
3	195	3	75
4	260	4	150
5	325	5	225
6	390	6	300
7	455	7	375
8	520	8	450
9	585	9	525
10	650	10	600
11	715	11	675
12	780	12	750
13	845	13	825
14	910	14	900
15	975	15	975

The table shows that after 15 hours, the distance traveled is the same. Thus, the second car catches up with the first car after a distance of 975 miles and 15 hours.

(b) A second strategy might involve setting up and solving an algebraic equation. This situation may be modeled as $65x = 75(x - 2)$. This equation sets the distances traveled by each car equal to one another. Solving for x gives $x = 15$. Thus, once again, the second car will catch up with the first car after 15 hours.

Sequences

SEQUENCES

A **sequence** is an ordered set of numbers that continues in a defined pattern. The function that defines a sequence has a domain composed of the set of positive integers. Each member of the sequence is an element, or individual term. Each element is identified by the notation a_n, where a is the term of the sequence, and n is the integer identifying which term in the sequence a is.

There are two different ways to represent a sequence that contains the element a_n. The first is the simple notation $\{a_n\}$. The second is the expanded notation of a sequence: $a_1, a_2, a_3, \dots a_n, \dots$. Notice that the expanded form does not end with the nth term. There is no indication that the nth term is the last term in the sequence, only that the nth term is an element of the sequence.

ARITHMETIC SEQUENCES

An **arithmetic sequence**, or arithmetic progression, is a special kind of sequence in which a specific quantity, called the common difference, is added to each term to make the next term. The common difference may be positive or negative. The general form of an arithmetic sequence containing n terms is $a_1, a_1 + d, a_1 + 2d, \dots, a_1 + (n-1)d$, where d is the common difference. The general formula for any term of an arithmetic sequence is $a_n = a_1 + (n-1)d$, where a_n is the term you are looking for and d is the common difference. To find the sum of the first n terms of an arithmetic sequence, use the formula $s_n = \frac{n}{2}(a_1 + a_n)$.

> **Review Video: Arithmetic Sequence**
> Visit mometrix.com/academy and enter code: 676885

MONOTONIC SEQUENCES

A **monotonic sequence** is a sequence that is either nonincreasing or nondecreasing. A **nonincreasing** sequence is one whose terms either get progressively smaller in value or remain the same. Such a sequence is always bounded above, that is, all elements of the sequence must be less than some real number. A **nondecreasing** sequence is one whose terms either get progressively larger in value or remain the same. Such a sequence is always bounded below, that is, all elements of the sequence must be greater than some real number.

RECURSIVE SEQUENCES

When one element of a sequence is defined in terms of a previous element or elements of the sequence, the sequence is a **recursive sequence**. For example, given the recursive definition $a_1 = 1$; $a_2 = 1$; $a_n = a_{n-1} + a_{n-2}$ for all $n > 2$, you get the sequence $1,1,2,3,5,8,\dots$. This is known as the Fibonacci sequence: a continuing sequence of numbers in which each number (after a_2) is the sum of the two previous numbers. The Fibonacci sequence can be defined as starting with either 1,1 or 0,1. Both definitions are considered correct in mathematics. Make sure you know which definition you are working with when dealing with Fibonacci numbers.

Sometimes in a recursive sequence, the terms can be found using a general formula that does not involve the previous terms of the sequence. Such a formula is called a **closed-form** expression for a recursive definition—an alternate formula that will generate the same sequence of numbers. However, not all sequences based on recursive definitions will have a closed-form expression. Some sequences will require the use of the recursive definition.

THE GOLDEN RATIO AND THE FIBONACCI SEQUENCE

The golden ratio is approximately 1.6180339887 and is often represented by the Greek letter phi, Φ. The exact value of Φ is $\frac{(1+\sqrt{5})}{2}$ and it is one of the solutions to $x - \frac{1}{x} = 1$. The golden ratio can be found using the Fibonacci sequence, since the ratio of a term to the previous term approaches Φ as the sequence approaches infinity:

n	a_n	a_{n-1}	$\frac{a_n}{a_{n-1}}$
3	2	1	2
4	3	2	1.5
5	5	3	$1.\overline{6}$
6	8	5	1.6
7	13	8	1.625
8	21	13	$1.\overline{615384}$
9	34	21	$1.\overline{619047}$
⋮	⋮	⋮	⋮
20	6,765	4,181	1.618033963 ...

GEOMETRIC SEQUENCES

A geometric sequence is a sequence in which each term is multiplied by a constant number (called the common ratio) to get the next term. Essentially, it's the same concept as an arithmetic sequence, but with multiplication instead of addition.

Consider the following example of a geometric sequence: Andy opens a savings account with $10. During each subsequent week, he plans to double the amount from the previous week.

Sequence: $10, 20, 40, 80, 160, ...$

Function: $a_n = 10 \times 2^{n-1}$

This is a geometric sequence with a common ratio of 2. All geometric sequences represent exponential functions. The nth term in any geometric sequence is $a_n = a_1 \times r^{n-1}$, where a_n represents the value of the nth term, a_1 is the initial term, r is the common ratio, and n is the number of terms. Thus, substituting the initial value of 10 and common ratio of 2 gives the function $a_n = 10 \times 2^{n-1}$.

> **Review Video: Geometric Sequences**
> Visit mometrix.com/academy and enter code: 140779

LIMIT OF A SEQUENCE

Some sequences will have a **limit**—a value the sequence approaches, or sometimes even reaches, but never passes. A sequence with a limit is called a **convergent** sequence because all the values of the sequence seemingly converge at that point. Sequences that do not converge at a particular limit are **divergent** sequences. The easiest way to determine whether a sequence converges or diverges is to find the limit of the sequence. If the limit is a real number, the sequence is convergent. If the limit is infinity, the sequence is divergent.

Remember the following rules for finding limits:

- $\lim\limits_{n\to\infty} k = k$, for all real numbers k

- $\lim\limits_{n\to\infty} \dfrac{1}{n} = 0$

- $\lim\limits_{n\to\infty} n = \infty$

- $\lim\limits_{n\to\infty} \dfrac{k}{n^p} = 0$, for all real numbers k and positive rational numbers p

- The limit of the sum of two sequences is equal to the sum of the limits of the two sequences: $\lim\limits_{n\to\infty} (a_n + b_n) = \lim\limits_{n\to\infty} a_n + \lim\limits_{n\to\infty} b_n$

- The limit of the difference between two sequences is equal to the difference between the limits of the two sequences: $\lim\limits_{n\to\infty} (a_n - b_n) = \lim\limits_{n\to\infty} a_n - \lim\limits_{n\to\infty} b_n$

- The limit of the product of two sequences is equal to the product of the limits of the two sequences: $\lim\limits_{n\to\infty} (a_n \times b_n) = \lim\limits_{n\to\infty} a_n \times \lim\limits_{n\to\infty} b_n$

- The limit of the quotient of two sequences is equal to the quotient of the limits of the two sequences, with some exceptions: $\lim\limits_{n\to\infty} \left(\dfrac{a_n}{b_n}\right) = \dfrac{\lim\limits_{n\to\infty} a_n}{\lim\limits_{n\to\infty} b_n}$. In the quotient formula, it is important that $b_n \neq 0$ and that $\lim\limits_{n\to\infty} b_n \neq 0$.

- The limit of a sequence multiplied by a scalar is equal to the scalar multiplied by the limit of the sequence: $\lim\limits_{n\to\infty} ka_n = k \lim\limits_{n\to\infty} a_n$, where k is any real number

> **Review Video: Limit of a Sequence**
> Visit mometrix.com/academy and enter code: 847732

INFINITE SERIES

Both arithmetic and geometric sequences have formulas to find the sum of the first n terms in the sequence, assuming you know what the first term is. The sum of all the terms in a sequence is called a series. An **infinite series** is an infinite sum. In other words, it is what you get by adding up all the terms in an infinite sequence: $\sum_{n=1}^{\infty} a_n = a_1 + a_2 + a_3 + \cdots + a_n + \cdots$. This notation can be shortened to $\sum_{n=1}^{\infty} a_n$ or $\sum a_n$.

While we can't add up an infinite list of numbers one at a time, we can still determine the infinite sum. As we add the terms in a series, we can imagine an infinite sequence of partial sums, where the first partial sum is the first element of the series, the second partial sum is the sum of the first two elements of the series, and the nth partial sum is the sum of the first n elements of the series.

Every infinite sequence of partial sums (infinite series) either converges or diverges. As with the test for convergence in a sequence, finding the limit of the sequence of partial sums will indicate whether it is a converging series or a diverging series. If there exists a real number S such that $\lim\limits_{n\to\infty} S_n = S$, where S_n is the sequence of partial sums, then the series converges. If the limit equals infinity, then the series diverges. If $\lim\limits_{n \to \infty} S_n = S$ and S is a real number, then S is also the convergence value of the series.

To find the sum as n approaches infinity for the sum of two convergent series, find the sum as n approaches infinity for each individual series and add the results.

$$\sum_{n=1}^{\infty}(a_n + b_n) = \sum_{n=1}^{\infty} a_n + \sum_{n=1}^{\infty} b_n$$

The same idea works for subtraction.

$$\sum_{n=1}^{\infty}(a_n - b_n) = \sum_{n=1}^{\infty} a_n - \sum_{n=1}^{\infty} b_n$$

To find the sum as n approaches infinity for the product of a constant (also called a scalar) and a convergent series, find the sum as n approaches infinity for the series and multiply the result by the scalar.

$$\sum_{n=1}^{\infty} k a_n = k \sum_{n=1}^{\infty} a_n$$

Review Video: <u>Infinite Series</u>
Visit mometrix.com/academy and enter code: 271404

The **n^{th} term test for divergence** means taking the limit of a sequence a_n as n goes to infinity $\left(\lim\limits_{n \to \infty} a_n\right)$ and checking whether the limit is zero. If the limit is not zero, then the series $\sum a_n$ is a diverging series. This test only works to prove divergence, however. If the limit is zero, the test is inconclusive, meaning the series could be either convergent or divergent.

Review Video: <u>Nth Term Test for Divergence</u>
Visit mometrix.com/academy and enter code: 346400

PRACTICE

P1. Suppose Rachel has \$4,500 in her account in month 1. With each passing month, her account is one-half of what it was during the previous month. What would be a formula for the value of her account in any future month?

P2. Determine whether the following geometric sequences converge or diverge:

(a) $a_n = 500(3^{n-1})$; where $n = 1,2,3,\dots$

(b) $a_n = 5(1^{n-1})$; where $n = 1,2,3,\dots$

(c) $a_n = 50(-1)^{n-1}$; where $n = 1,2,3,\dots$

(d) $a_n = 5{,}000 \left(\frac{1}{5}\right)^{n-1}$; where $n = 1,2,3,\dots$

P3. Determine a recursive expression for the following sequences:

(a) $3, 7, 19, 55, 163, \ldots$

(b) $8, 6, 5, 4.5, 4.25, \ldots$

PRACTICE SOLUTIONS

P1. The sequence 4,500, 2,250, 1,125, 562.50, 281.25, ... is geometric, since there is a common ratio of $\frac{1}{2}$. Thus, this sequence represents an exponential function, like all geometric sequences. Recall that the general form of a geometric sequence is $a_n = a_1 \times r^{n-1}$, and substituting the initial value of 4,500 and common ratio of $\frac{1}{2}$ gives $a_n = 4,500 \times \left(\frac{1}{2}\right)^{n-1}$.

P2. (a) $\lim\limits_{n\to\infty} a_n \to 500(3^{\infty-1}) \to 500(\infty) \to \infty$. This sequence diverges.

(b) $\lim\limits_{n\to\infty} a_n \to 5(1^{\infty-1}) \to 5(1) \to 5$. This sequence converges.

(c) $\lim\limits_{n\to\infty} a_n \to 50(-1)^{\infty-1} \to 50(-1)^{\infty} \to undefined$. Since –1 raised to an integer power is either –1 or +1, this sequence oscillates between 50 and –50, and does not converge. Any sequence that does not converge is divergent, so this sequence diverges.

(d) $\lim\limits_{n\to\infty} a_n \to 5,000 \left(\frac{1}{5}\right)^{\infty-1} \to 5,000(0) \to 0$. This sequence converges.

P3. (a) Use a table to determine the pattern:

n	1	2	3	4	5
a_n	3	7	19	55	163
$d_n = a_n - a_{n-1}$	–	4	12	36	108
$r_n = \dfrac{d_n}{d_{n-1}}$	–	–	3	3	3

Since the difference between successive terms is increasing at a uniform rate, we can use that to guess at a sequence: $a_n = 3a_{n-1} + d$. Substitute the first terms to find d:

$$7 = 3(3) + d$$
$$-2 = d$$

Thus, the recursive form would be $a_n = 3a_{n-1} - 2$.

(b) Use a table to determine the pattern:

n	1	2	3	4	5
a_n	8	6	5	4.5	4.25
$d_n = a_n - a_{n-1}$	–	2	1	0.5	0.25
$r_n = \dfrac{d_n}{d_{n-1}}$	–	–	$\dfrac{1}{2}$	$\dfrac{1}{2}$	$\dfrac{1}{2}$

Since the difference between successive terms is increasing at a uniform rate, we can use that to guess at a sequence: $a_n = \frac{a_{n-1}}{2} + d$. Substitute the first terms to find d:

$$6 = \frac{8}{2} + d$$
$$2 = d$$

Thus, the recursive form would be $a_n = \frac{a_{n-1}}{2} + 2$.

Lines and Planes

POINTS AND LINES

A **point** is a fixed location in space, has no size or dimensions, and is commonly represented by a dot. A **line** is a set of points that extends infinitely in two opposite directions. It has length, but no width or depth. A line can be defined by any two distinct points that it contains. A **line segment** is a portion of a line that has definite endpoints. A **ray** is a portion of a line that extends from a single point on that line in one direction along the line. It has a definite beginning, but no ending.

Point   Line   Segment   Ray

INTERACTIONS BETWEEN LINES

Intersecting lines are lines that have exactly one point in common. **Concurrent lines** are multiple lines that intersect at a single point. **Perpendicular lines** are lines that intersect at right angles. They are represented by the symbol ⊥. The shortest distance from a line to a point not on the line is a perpendicular segment from the point to the line. **Parallel lines** are lines in the same plane that have no points in common and never meet. It is possible for lines to be in different planes, have no points in common, and never meet, but they are not parallel because they are in different planes.

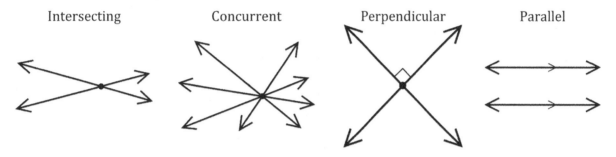

Intersecting   Concurrent   Perpendicular   Parallel

Review Video: Parallel and Perpendicular Lines
Visit mometrix.com/academy and enter code: 815923

A **transversal** is a line that intersects at least two other lines, which may or may not be parallel to one another. A transversal that intersects parallel lines is a common occurrence in geometry. A **bisector** is a line or line segment that divides another line segment into two equal lengths. A **perpendicular bisector** of a line segment is composed of points that are equidistant from the endpoints of the segment it is dividing.

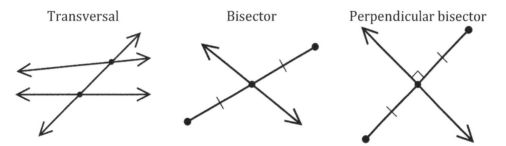

Transversal   Bisector   Perpendicular bisector

The **projection of a point on a line** is the point at which a perpendicular line drawn from the given point to the given line intersects the line. This is also the shortest distance from the given point to the line. The **projection of a segment on a line** is a segment whose endpoints are the points formed when perpendicular lines are drawn from the endpoints of the given segment to the given line. This is similar to the length a diagonal line appears to be when viewed from above.

Projection of a point on a line   Projection of a segment on a line

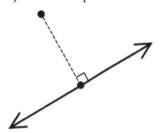
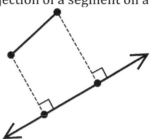

PLANES

A **plane** is a two-dimensional flat surface defined by three non-collinear points. A plane extends an infinite distance in all directions in those two dimensions. It contains an infinite number of points, parallel lines and segments, intersecting lines and segments, as well as parallel or intersecting rays. A plane will never contain a three-dimensional figure or skew lines, which are lines that don't intersect and are not parallel. Two given planes are either parallel or they intersect at a line. A plane may intersect a circular conic surface to form **conic sections**, such as a parabola, hyperbola, circle or ellipse.

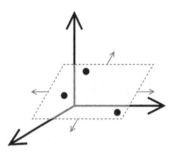

Review Video: Lines and Planes
Visit mometrix.com/academy and enter code: 554267

Angles

ANGLES AND VERTICES

An **angle** is formed when two lines or line segments meet at a common point. It may be a common starting point for a pair of segments or rays, or it may be the intersection of lines. Angles are represented by the symbol ∠.

The **vertex** is the point at which two segments or rays meet to form an angle. If the angle is formed by intersecting rays, lines, and/or line segments, the vertex is the point at which four angles are formed. The pairs of angles opposite one another are called vertical angles, and their measures are equal.

- An **acute** angle is an angle with a degree measure less than 90°.
- A **right** angle is an angle with a degree measure of exactly 90°.
- An **obtuse** angle is an angle with a degree measure greater than 90° but less than 180°.
- A **straight angle** is an angle with a degree measure of exactly 180°. This is also a semicircle.
- A **reflex angle** is an angle with a degree measure greater than 180° but less than 360°.

A **full angle** is an angle with a degree measure of exactly 360°. This is also a circle.

> **Review Video: Angles**
> Visit mometrix.com/academy and enter code: 264624

RELATIONSHIPS BETWEEN ANGLES

Two angles whose sum is exactly 90° are said to be **complementary**. The two angles may or may not be adjacent. In a right triangle, the two acute angles are complementary.

Two angles whose sum is exactly 180° are said to be **supplementary**. The two angles may or may not be adjacent. Two intersecting lines always form two pairs of supplementary angles. Adjacent supplementary angles will always form a straight line.

Two angles that have the same vertex and share a side are said to be **adjacent**. Vertical angles are not adjacent because they share a vertex but no common side.

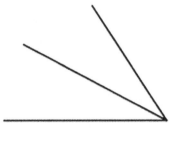

Adjacent
Share vertex and side

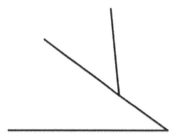

Not adjacent
Share part of a side, but not vertex

When two parallel lines are cut by a transversal, the angles that are between the two parallel lines are **interior angles**. In the diagram below, angles 3, 4, 5, and 6 are interior angles.

When two parallel lines are cut by a transversal, the angles that are outside the parallel lines are **exterior angles**. In the diagram below, angles 1, 2, 7, and 8 are exterior angles.

When two parallel lines are cut by a transversal, the angles that are in the same position relative to the transversal and a parallel line are **corresponding angles**. The diagram below has four pairs of corresponding angles: angles 1 and 5, angles 2 and 6, angles 3 and 7, and angles 4 and 8. Corresponding angles formed by parallel lines are congruent.

When two parallel lines are cut by a transversal, the two interior angles that are on opposite sides of the transversal are called **alternate interior angles**. In the diagram below, there are two pairs of alternate interior angles: angles 3 and 6, and angles 4 and 5. Alternate interior angles formed by parallel lines are congruent.

When two parallel lines are cut by a transversal, the two exterior angles that are on opposite sides of the transversal are called **alternate exterior angles**.

In the diagram below, there are two pairs of alternate exterior angles: angles 1 and 8, and angles 2 and 7. Alternate exterior angles formed by parallel lines are congruent.

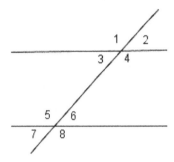

When two lines intersect, four angles are formed. The non-adjacent angles at this vertex are called vertical angles. Vertical angles are congruent. In the diagram, $\angle ABD \cong \angle CBE$ and $\angle ABC \cong \angle DBE$. The other pairs of angles, ($\angle ABC, \angle CBE$) and ($\angle ABD, \angle DBE$), are supplementary, meaning the pairs sum to 180°.

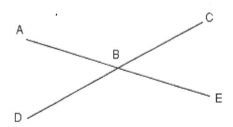

PRACTICE

P1. Find the measure of angles ∠a, ∠b, and ∠c based on the figure with two parallel lines, two perpendicular lines and one transversal:

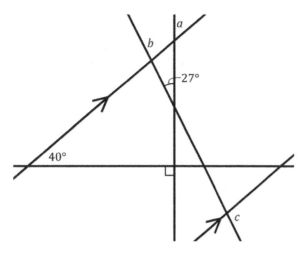

PRACTICE SOLUTIONS

P1. (a) The vertical angle paired with ∠a is part of a right triangle with the 40° angle. Thus the measure can be found:

$$90° = 40° + a$$
$$a = 50°$$

(b) The triangle formed by the supplementary angle to ∠b is part of a triangle with the vertical angle paired with ∠a and the given angle of 27°. Since ∠a = 50°:

$$180° = (180° - b) + 50° + 27°$$
$$103° = 180° - b$$
$$-77° = -b$$
$$77° = b$$

(c) As they are part of a transversal crossing parallel lines, angles ∠b and ∠c are supplementary. Thus ∠c = 103°.

Transformations

ROTATION

A **rotation** is a transformation that turns a figure around a point called the **center of rotation**, which can lie anywhere in the plane. If a line is drawn from a point on a figure to the center of rotation, and another line is drawn from the center to the rotated image of that point, the angle between the two lines is the **angle of rotation**. The vertex of the angle of rotation is the center of rotation.

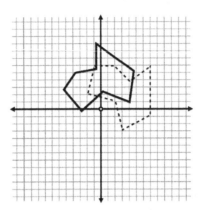

TRANSLATION AND DILATION

A **translation** is a transformation which slides a figure from one position in the plane to another position in the plane. The original figure and the translated figure have the same size, shape, and orientation. A **dilation** is a transformation which proportionally stretches or shrinks a figure by a **scale factor**. The dilated image is the same shape and orientation as the original image but a different size. A polygon and its dilated image are similar.

Translation

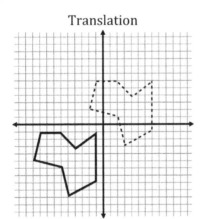

Dilation

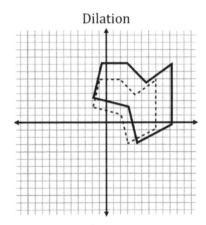

A **reflection of a figure over a line** (a "flip") creates a congruent image that is the same distance from the line as the original figure but on the opposite side. The **line of reflection** is the perpendicular bisector of any line segment drawn from a point on the original figure to its reflected image (unless the point and its reflected image happen to be the same point, which happens when a figure is reflected over one of its own sides). A **reflection of a figure over a point** (an inversion) in two dimensions is the same as the rotation of the figure 180° about that point. The image of the figure is congruent to the original figure. The **point of reflection** is the midpoint of a line segment which connects a point in the figure to its image (unless the point and its reflected image happen to be the same point, which happens when a figure is reflected in one of its own points).

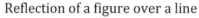

Reflection of a figure over a line

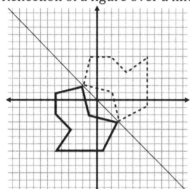

Reflection of a figure over a point

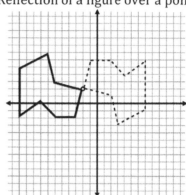

Review Video: Reflection
Visit mometrix.com/academy and enter code: 955068

PRACTICE

P1. Use the coordinate plane to reflect the figure below across the *y*-axis.

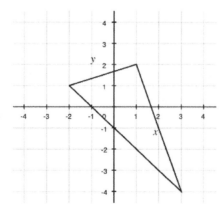

P2. Use the coordinate plane to enlarge the figure below by a factor of 2.

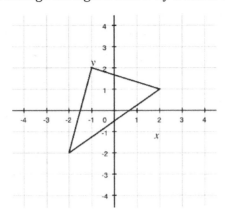

PRACTICE SOLUTIONS

P1. To reflect the image across the y-axis, replace each x-coordinate of the points that are the vertex of the triangle, x, with its negative, $-x$.

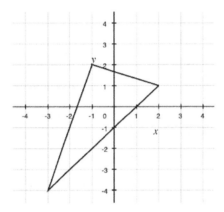

P2. An enlargement can be found by multiplying each coordinate of the coordinate pairs located at the triangle's vertices by 2. The original coordinates were $(-1, 2), (2, 1), (-2, -2)$, so the new coordinates are $(-2, 4), (4, 2), (-4, -4)$:

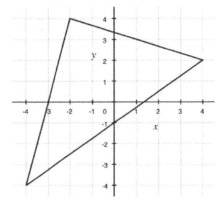

Two-Dimensional Shapes

POLYGONS

A **polygon** is a closed, two-dimensional figure with three or more straight line segments called **sides**. The point at which two sides of a polygon intersect is called the **vertex**. In a polygon, the number of sides is always equal to the number of vertices. A polygon with all sides congruent and all angles equal is called a **regular polygon**. Common polygons are:

Triangle = 3 sides
Quadrilateral = 4 sides
Pentagon = 5 sides
Hexagon = 6 sides
Heptagon = 7 sides
Octagon = 8 sides
Nonagon = 9 sides
Decagon = 10 sides
Dodecagon = 12 sides

More generally, an n-gon is a polygon that has n angles and n sides.

> **Review Video: Intro to Polygons**
> Visit mometrix.com/academy and enter code: 271869
>
> **Review Video: Sum of Interior Angles**
> Visit mometrix.com/academy and enter code: 984991

The sum of the interior angles of an n-sided polygon is $(n - 2) \times 180°$. For example, in a triangle $n = 3$. So the sum of the interior angles is $(3 - 2) \times 180° = 180°$. In a quadrilateral, $n = 4$, and the sum of the angles is $(4 - 2) \times 180° = 360°$.

> **Review Video: Sum of Interior Angles**
> Visit mometrix.com/academy and enter code: 984991

APOTHEM AND RADIUS

A line segment from the center of a polygon that is perpendicular to a side of the polygon is called the **apothem**. A line segment from the center of a polygon to a vertex of the polygon is called a **radius**. In a regular polygon, the apothem can be used to find the area of the polygon using the formula $A = \frac{1}{2}ap$, where a is the apothem, and p is the perimeter.

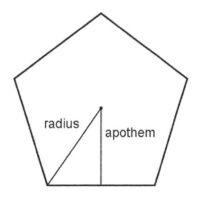

A **diagonal** is a line segment that joins two non-adjacent vertices of a polygon. The number of diagonals a polygon has can be found by using the formula:

$$\text{number of diagonals} = \frac{n(n-3)}{2}$$

Note that n is the number of sides in the polygon. This formula works for all polygons, not just regular polygons.

CONVEX AND CONCAVE POLYGONS

A **convex polygon** is a polygon whose diagonals all lie within the interior of the polygon. A **concave polygon** is a polygon with a least one diagonal that is outside the polygon. In the diagram below, quadrilateral $ABCD$ is concave because diagonal $\overline{AC}$ lies outside the polygon and quadrilateral $EFGH$ is convex because both diagonals lie inside the polygon.

Concave
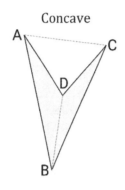

Convex
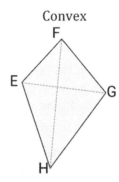

CONGRUENCE AND SIMILARITY

Congruent figures are geometric figures that have the same size and shape. All corresponding angles are equal, and all corresponding sides are equal. Congruence is indicated by the symbol $\cong$.

Congruent polygons

Similar figures are geometric figures that have the same shape, but do not necessarily have the same size. All corresponding angles are equal, and all corresponding sides are proportional, but they do not have to be equal. It is indicated by the symbol ~.

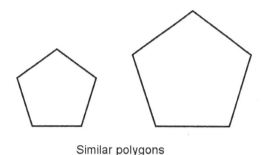

Similar polygons

Note that all congruent figures are also similar, but not all similar figures are congruent.

Review Video: <u>What is a Congruent Shape?</u>
Visit mometrix.com/academy and enter code: 492281

LINE OF SYMMETRY

A line that divides a figure or object into congruent parts is called a **line of symmetry**. An object may have no lines of symmetry, one line of symmetry, or multiple (i.e., more than one) lines of symmetry.

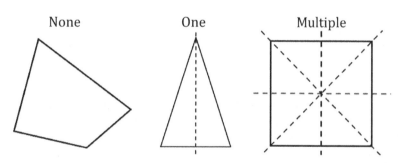

Review Video: <u>Symmetry</u>
Visit mometrix.com/academy and enter code: 528106

TRIANGLES

A triangle is a three-sided figure with the sum of its interior angles being 180°. The **perimeter of any triangle** is found by summing the three side lengths; $P = a + b + c$. For an equilateral triangle, this is the same as $P = 3a$, where a is any side length, since all three sides are the same length.

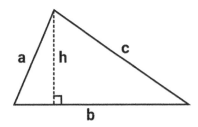

> **Review Video:** <u>Proof that a Triangle is 180 Degrees</u>
> Visit mometrix.com/academy and enter code: 687591
>
> **Review Video:** <u>Area and Perimeter of a Triangle</u>
> Visit mometrix.com/academy and enter code: 853779

The **area of any triangle** can be found by taking half the product of one side length referred to as the base, often given the variable b and the perpendicular distance from that side to the opposite vertex called the altitude or height and given the variable h. In equation form that is $A = \frac{1}{2}bh$. Another formula that works for any triangle is $A = \sqrt{s(s-a)(s-b)(s-c)}$, where s is the semiperimeter: $\frac{a+b+c}{2}$, and a, b, and c are the lengths of the three sides. Special cases include isosceles triangles, $A = \frac{1}{2}b\sqrt{a^2 - \frac{b^2}{4}}$, where b is the unique side and a is the length of one of the two congruent sides, and equilateral triangles, $A = \frac{\sqrt{3}}{4}a^2$, where a is the length of a side.

> **Review Video:** <u>Area of Any Triangle</u>
> Visit mometrix.com/academy and enter code: 138510

PARTS OF A TRIANGLE

An **altitude** of a triangle is a line segment drawn from one vertex perpendicular to the opposite side. In the diagram that follows, $\overline{BE}$, $\overline{AD}$, and $\overline{CF}$ are altitudes. The length of an altitude is also called the height of the triangle. The three altitudes in a triangle are always concurrent. The point of concurrency of the altitudes of a triangle, O, is called the **orthocenter**. Note that in an obtuse triangle, the orthocenter will be outside the triangle, and in a right triangle, the orthocenter is the vertex of the right angle.

A **median** of a triangle is a line segment drawn from one vertex to the midpoint of the opposite side. In the diagram that follows, $\overline{BH}$, $\overline{AG}$, and $\overline{CI}$ are medians. This is not the same as the altitude, except the altitude to the base of an isosceles triangle and all three altitudes of an equilateral triangle. The point of concurrency of the medians of a triangle, T, is called the **centroid**. This is the same point as the orthocenter only in an equilateral triangle. Unlike the orthocenter, the centroid is always inside the triangle. The centroid can also be considered the exact center of the triangle. Any shape triangle can be perfectly balanced on a tip placed at the centroid. The centroid is also the point that is two-thirds the distance from the vertex to the opposite side.

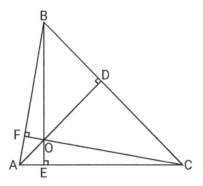 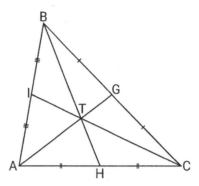

QUADRILATERALS

A **quadrilateral** is a closed two-dimensional geometric figure that has four straight sides. The sum of the interior angles of any quadrilateral is 360°.

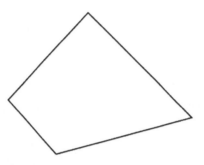

KITE

A **kite** is a quadrilateral with two pairs of adjacent sides that are congruent. A result of this is perpendicular diagonals. A kite can be concave or convex and has one line of symmetry.

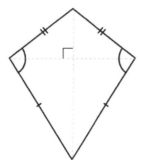 

TRAPEZOID

Trapezoid: A trapezoid is defined as a quadrilateral that has at least one pair of parallel sides. There are no rules for the second pair of sides. So, there are no rules for the diagonals and no lines of symmetry for a trapezoid.

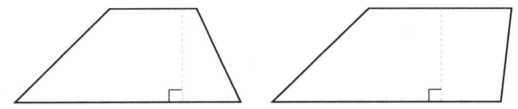

The **area of a trapezoid** is found by the formula $A = \frac{1}{2}h(b_1 + b_2)$, where h is the height (segment joining and perpendicular to the parallel bases), and b_1 and b_2 are the two parallel sides (bases). Do not use one of the other two sides as the height unless that side is also perpendicular to the parallel bases.

The **perimeter of a trapezoid** is found by the formula $P = a + b_1 + c + b_2$, where a, b_1, c, and b_2 are the four sides of the trapezoid.

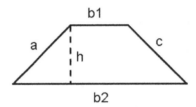

> **Review Video: <u>Area and Perimeter of a Trapezoid</u>**
> Visit mometrix.com/academy and enter code: 587523

Isosceles trapezoid: A trapezoid with equal base angles. This gives rise to other properties including: the two nonparallel sides have the same length, the two non-base angles are also equal, and there is one line of symmetry through the midpoints of the parallel sides.

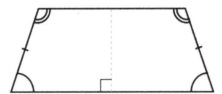

PARALLELOGRAM

A **parallelogram** is a quadrilateral that has two pairs of opposite parallel sides. As such it is a special type of trapezoid. The sides that are parallel are also congruent. The opposite interior angles are always congruent, and the consecutive interior angles are supplementary. The diagonals of a parallelogram divide each other. Each diagonal divides the parallelogram into two congruent triangles. A parallelogram has no line of symmetry, but does have 180-degree rotational symmetry about the midpoint.

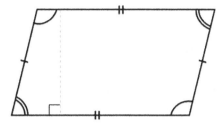

The **area of a parallelogram** is found by the formula $A = bh$, where b is the length of the base, and h is the height. Note that the base and height correspond to the length and width in a rectangle, so this formula would apply to rectangles as well. Do not confuse the height of a parallelogram with the length of the second side. The two are only the same measure in the case of a rectangle.

The **perimeter of a parallelogram** is found by the formula $P = 2a + 2b$ or $P = 2(a + b)$, where a and b are the lengths of the two sides.

> **Review Video: How to Find the Area and Perimeter of a Parallelogram**
> Visit mometrix.com/academy and enter code: 718313

RECTANGLE

A **rectangle** is a quadrilateral with four right angles. All rectangles are parallelograms and trapezoids, but not all parallelograms or trapezoids are rectangles. The diagonals of a rectangle are congruent. Rectangles have two lines of symmetry (through each pair of opposing midpoints) and 180-degree rotational symmetry about the midpoint.

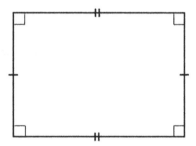

The **area of a rectangle** is found by the formula $A = lw$, where A is the area of the rectangle, l is the length (usually considered to be the longer side) and w is the width (usually considered to be the shorter side). The numbers for l and w are interchangeable.

The **perimeter of a rectangle** is found by the formula $P = 2l + 2w$ or $P = 2(l + w)$, where l is the length, and w is the width. It may be easier to add the length and width first and then double the result, as in the second formula.

RHOMBUS

A **rhombus** is a quadrilateral with four congruent sides. All rhombuses are parallelograms and kites; thus, they inherit all the properties of both types of quadrilaterals. The diagonals of a rhombus are perpendicular to each other. Rhombi have two lines of symmetry (along each of the diagonals) and 180° rotational symmetry. The **area of a rhombus** is half the product of the diagonals: $A = \frac{d_1 d_2}{2}$ and the perimeter of a rhombus is: $P = 2\sqrt{(d_1)^2 + (d_2)^2}$.

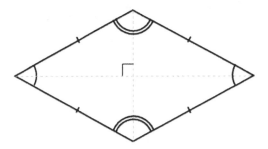

SQUARE

A **square** is a quadrilateral with four right angles and four congruent sides. Squares satisfy the criteria of all other types of quadrilaterals. The diagonals of a square are congruent and perpendicular to each other. Squares have four lines of symmetry (through each pair of opposing midpoints and along each of the diagonals) as well as 90° rotational symmetry about the midpoint.

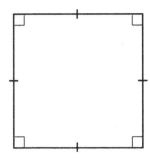

The **area of a square** is found by using the formula $A = s^2$, where s is the length of one side. The **perimeter of a square** is found by using the formula $P = 4s$, where s is the length of one side. Because all four sides are equal in a square, it is faster to multiply the length of one side by 4 than to add the same number four times. You could use the formulas for rectangles and get the same answer.

HIERARCHY OF QUADRILATERALS

The hierarchy of quadrilaterals is as follows:

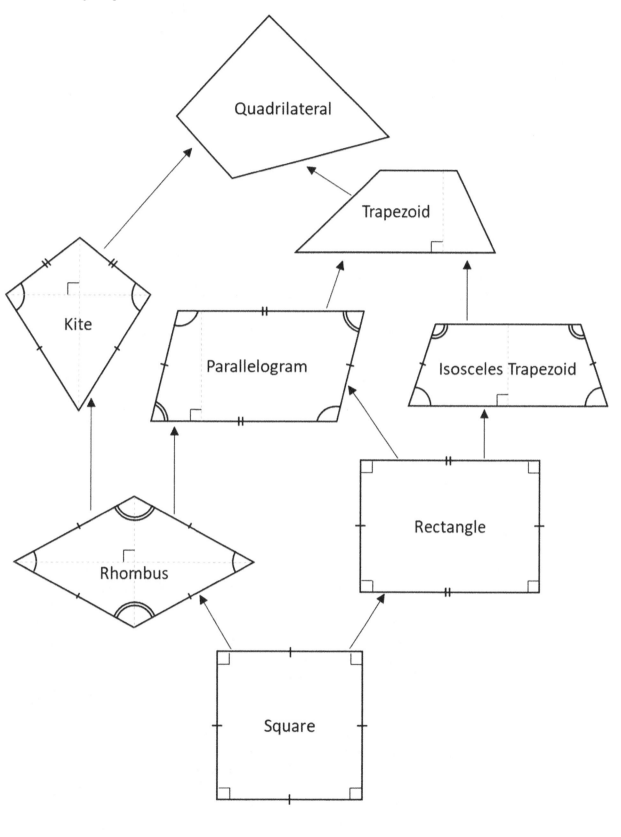

CIRCLES

The **center** of a circle is the single point from which every point on the circle is **equidistant**. The **radius** is a line segment that joins the center of the circle and any one point on the circle. All radii of a circle are equal. Circles that have the same center but not the same length of radii are **concentric**. The **diameter** is a line segment that passes through the center of the circle and has both endpoints on the circle. The length of the diameter is exactly twice the length of the radius. Point O in the diagram below is the center of the circle, segments $\overline{OX}$, $\overline{OY}$, and $\overline{OZ}$ are radii; and segment $\overline{XZ}$ is a diameter.

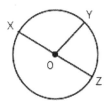

Review Video: Points of a Circle
Visit mometrix.com/academy and enter code: 420746

Review Video: The Diameter, Radius, and Circumference of Circles
Visit mometrix.com/academy and enter code: 448988

The **area of a circle** is found by the formula $A = \pi r^2$, where r is the length of the radius. If the diameter of the circle is given, remember to divide it in half to get the length of the radius before proceeding.

The **circumference** of a circle is found by the formula $C = 2\pi r$, where r is the radius. Again, remember to convert the diameter if you are given that measure rather than the radius.

Review Video: Area and Circumference of a Circle
Visit mometrix.com/academy and enter code: 243015

INSCRIBED AND CIRCUMSCRIBED FIGURES

These terms can both be used to describe a given arrangement of figures, depending on perspective. If each of the vertices of figure A lie on figure B, then it can be said that figure A is **inscribed** in figure B, but it can also be said that figure B is **circumscribed** about figure A. The following table and examples help to illustrate the concept. Note that the figures cannot both be circles, as they would be completely overlapping and neither would be inscribed or circumscribed.

Given	Description	Equivalent Description	Figures
Each of the sides of a pentagon is tangent to a circle	The circle is inscribed in the pentagon	The pentagon is circumscribed about the circle	
Each of the vertices of a pentagon lie on a circle	The pentagon is inscribed in the circle	The circle is circumscribed about the pentagon	

PRACTICE

P1. Find the area and perimeter of the following quadrilaterals:

(a) A square with side length 2.5 cm.

(b) A parallelogram with height 3 m, base 4 m, and other side 6 m.

(c) A rhombus with diagonals 15 in and 20 in.

P2. Calculate the area of a triangle with side lengths of 7 ft, 8 ft, and 9 ft.

P3. Square $ABCD$ is inscribed in a circle with radius 20 m. What is the area of the part of the circle outside of the square?

PRACTICE SOLUTIONS

P1. (a) $A = s^2 = (2.5 \text{ cm})^2 = 6.25 \text{ cm}^2; P = 4s = 4 \times 2.5 \text{ cm} = 10 \text{ cm}$

(b) $A = bh = (3 \text{ m})(4 \text{ m}) = 12 \text{ m}^2; P = 2a + 2b = 2 \times 6 \text{ m} + 2 \times 4 \text{ m} = 20 \text{ m}$

(c) $A = \frac{d_1 d_2}{2} = \frac{(15 \text{ in})(20 \text{ in})}{2} = 150 \text{ in}^2;$
$$P = 2\sqrt{(d_1)^2 + (d_2)^2} = 2\sqrt{(15 \text{ in})^2 + (20 \text{ in})^2} = 2\sqrt{625 \text{ in}^2} = 50 \text{ in}$$

P2. Given only side lengths, we can use the semi perimeter to the find the area based on the formula, $A = \sqrt{s(s-a)(s-b)(s-c)}$, where s is the semiperimeter, $\frac{a+b+c}{2} = \frac{7+8+9}{2} = 12$ ft:

$$A = \sqrt{12(12-7)(12-8)(12-9)}$$
$$= \sqrt{(12)(5)(4)(3)}$$
$$= 12\sqrt{5} \text{ ft}^2$$

P3. Begin by drawing a diagram of the situation, where we want to find the shaded area:

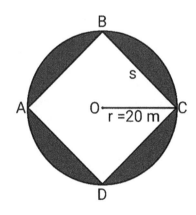

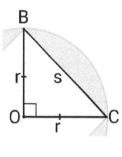

The area of the square is s^2, so the area we want to find is: $\pi r^2 - s^2$. Since the inscribed figure is a square, the triangle BCO is a 45-45-90 right triangle. Now we can find $s^2 = r^2 + r^2 = 2r^2$. So the shaded area is:

$$A = \pi r^2 - s^2$$
$$= \pi r^2 - 2r^2$$
$$= (\pi - 2)r^2$$
$$= (\pi - 2) \times 400$$
$$\approx 456.6 \text{ m}^2$$

Three-Dimensional Shapes

SOLIDS

The **surface area of a solid object** is the area of all sides or exterior surfaces. For objects such as prisms and pyramids, a further distinction is made between base surface area (B) and lateral surface area (LA). For a prism, the total surface area (SA) is $SA = LA + 2B$. For a pyramid or cone, the total surface area is $SA = LA + B$.

The **surface area of a sphere** can be found by the formula $A = 4\pi r^2$, where r is the radius. The volume is given by the formula $V = \frac{4}{3}\pi r^3$, where r is the radius. Both quantities are generally given in terms of π.

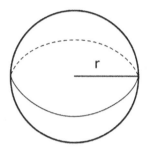

> **Review Video: <u>Volume and Surface Area of a Sphere</u>**
> Visit mometrix.com/academy and enter code: 786928

The **volume of any prism** is found by the formula $V = Bh$, where B is the area of the base, and h is the height (perpendicular distance between the bases). The surface area of any prism is the sum of the areas of both bases and all sides. It can be calculated as $SA = 2B + Ph$, where P is the perimeter of the base.

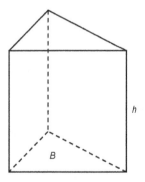

> **Review Video: <u>Volume and Surface Area of a Prism</u>**
> Visit mometrix.com/academy and enter code: 420158

For a **rectangular prism**, the volume can be found by the formula $V = lwh$, where V is the volume, l is the length, w is the width, and h is the height. The surface area can be calculated as $SA = 2lw + 2hl + 2wh$ or $SA = 2(lw + hl + wh)$.

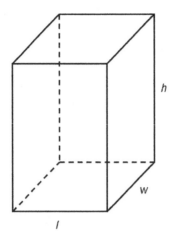

Review Video: <u>Volume and Surface Area of a Rectangular Prism</u>
Visit mometrix.com/academy and enter code: 282814

The **volume of a cube** can be found by the formula $V = s^3$, where s is the length of a side. The surface area of a cube is calculated as $SA = 6s^2$, where SA is the total surface area and s is the length of a side. These formulas are the same as the ones used for the volume and surface area of a rectangular prism, but simplified since all three quantities (length, width, and height) are the same.

Review Video: <u>Volume and Surface Area of a Cube</u>
Visit mometrix.com/academy and enter code: 664455

The **volume of a cylinder** can be calculated by the formula $V = \pi r^2 h$, where r is the radius, and h is the height. The surface area of a cylinder can be found by the formula $SA = 2\pi r^2 + 2\pi rh$. The first term is the base area multiplied by two, and the second term is the perimeter of the base multiplied by the height.

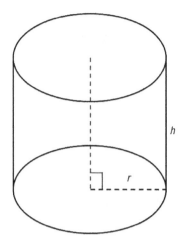

The **volume of a pyramid** is found by the formula $V = \frac{1}{3}Bh$, where B is the area of the base, and h is the height (perpendicular distance from the vertex to the base). Notice this formula is the same as $\frac{1}{3}$ times the volume of a prism. Like a prism, the base of a pyramid can be any shape.

Finding the **surface area of a pyramid** is not as simple as the other shapes we've looked at thus far. If the pyramid is a right pyramid, meaning the base is a regular polygon and the vertex is directly over the center of that polygon, the surface area can be calculated as $SA = B + \frac{1}{2}Ph_s$, where P is the perimeter of the base, and h_s is the slant height (distance from the vertex to the midpoint of one side of the base). If the pyramid is irregular, the area of each triangle side must be calculated individually and then summed, along with the base.

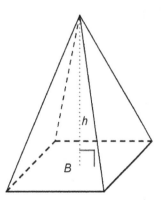

241

The **volume of a cone** is found by the formula $V = \frac{1}{3}\pi r^2 h$, where r is the radius, and h is the height. Notice this is the same as $\frac{1}{3}$ times the volume of a cylinder. The surface area can be calculated as $SA = \pi r^2 + \pi rs$, where s is the slant height. The slant height can be calculated using the Pythagorean theorem to be $\sqrt{r^2 + h^2}$, so the surface area formula can also be written as $SA = \pi r^2 + \pi r\sqrt{r^2 + h^2}$.

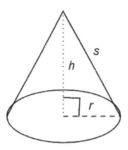

| Review Video: **Volume and Surface Area of a Right Circular Cone** |
| Visit mometrix.com/academy and enter code: 573574 |

PRACTICE

P1. Find the surface area and volume of the following solids:

(a) A cylinder with radius 5 m and height 0.5 m.

(b) A trapezoidal prism with base area of 254 mm², base perimeter 74 mm, and height 10 mm.

(c) A half sphere (radius 5 yds) on the base of an inverted cone with the same radius and a height of 7 yds.

PRACTICE SOLUTIONS

P1. (a) $SA = 2\pi r^2 + 2\pi rh = 2\pi(5\text{ m})^2 + 2\pi(5\text{ m})(0.5\text{ m}) = 55\pi\text{ m}^2 \approx 172.79\text{ m}^2$;
$V = \pi r^2 h = \pi(5\text{ m})^2(0.5\text{ m}) = 12.5\pi\text{ m}^3 \approx 39.27\text{ m}^3$

(b) $SA = 2B + Ph = 2(254\text{ mm}^2) + (74\text{ mm})(10\text{ mm}) = 1{,}248\text{ mm}^2$;
$V = Bh = (254\text{ mm}^2)(10\text{ mm}) = 2{,}540\text{ mm}^3$

(c) We can find s, the slant height using the Pythagorean theorem, and since this solid is made of parts of simple solids, we can combine the formulas to find surface area and volume:

$$s = \sqrt{r^2 + h^2} = \sqrt{(5\text{ yd})^2 + (7\text{ yd})^2} = \sqrt{74}\text{ yd}$$

$$SA_{Total} = \frac{(SA_{sphere})}{2} + SA_{cone} - SA_{base}$$
$$= \frac{4\pi r^2}{2} + (\pi rs + \pi r^2) - \pi r^2$$
$$= 2\pi(5\text{ yd})^2 + \pi(5\text{ yd})(\sqrt{74}\text{ yd})$$
$$= 5\pi(10 + \sqrt{74})\text{ yd}^2$$
$$\approx 292.20\text{ yd}^2$$

$$V_{Total} = \frac{(V_{sphere})}{2} + V_{cone}$$
$$= \frac{\frac{4}{3}\pi r^3}{2} + \frac{1}{3}\pi r^2 h$$
$$= \frac{2}{3}\pi(5\text{ yd})^3 + \frac{1}{3}\pi(5\text{ yd})^2(7\text{ yd})$$
$$= \frac{5^2 \times \pi}{3}(10 + 7)\text{ yd}^3$$
$$\approx 445.06\text{ yd}^3$$

Triangle Classification and Properties

CLASSIFICATIONS OF TRIANGLES

A **scalene triangle** is a triangle with no congruent sides. A scalene triangle will also have three angles of different measures. The angle with the largest measure is opposite the longest side, and the angle with the smallest measure is opposite the shortest side. An **acute triangle** is a triangle whose three angles are all less than 90°. If two of the angles are equal, the acute triangle is also an **isosceles triangle**. An isosceles triangle will also have two congruent angles opposite the two congruent sides. If the three angles are all equal, the acute triangle is also an **equilateral triangle**. An equilateral triangle will also have three congruent angles, each 60°. All equilateral triangles are also acute triangles. An **obtuse triangle** is a triangle with exactly one angle greater than 90°. The other two angles may or may not be equal. If the two remaining angles are equal, the obtuse triangle is also an isosceles triangle. A **right triangle** is a triangle with exactly one angle equal to 90°. All right triangles follow the Pythagorean theorem. A right triangle can never be acute or obtuse.

The table below illustrates how each descriptor places a different restriction on the triangle:

Angles \ Sides	Acute: All angles < 90°	Obtuse: One angle > 90°	Right: One angle = 90°
Scalene: No equal side lengths	$90° > \angle a > \angle b > \angle c$ $x > y > z$	$\angle a > 90° > \angle b > \angle c$ $x > y > z$	$90° = \angle a > \angle b > \angle c$ $x > y > z$
Isosceles: Two equal side lengths	$90° > \angle a, \angle b,$ or $\angle c$ $\angle b = \angle c, \quad y = z$	$\angle a > 90° > \angle b = \angle c$ $x > y = z$	$\angle a = 90°$ $\angle b = \angle c = 45°$ $x > y = z$
Equilateral: Three equal side lengths	$60° = \angle a = \angle b = \angle c$ $x = y = z$		

SIMILARITY AND CONGRUENCE RULES

Similar triangles are triangles whose corresponding angles are equal and whose corresponding sides are proportional. Represented by AAA. Similar triangles whose corresponding sides are congruent are also congruent triangles.

Triangles can be shown to be **congruent** in 5 ways:

- **SSS**: Three sides of one triangle are congruent to the three corresponding sides of the second triangle.
- **SAS**: Two sides and the included angle (the angle formed by those two sides) of one triangle are congruent to the corresponding two sides and included angle of the second triangle.
- **ASA**: Two angles and the included side (the side that joins the two angles) of one triangle are congruent to the corresponding two angles and included side of the second triangle.

- **AAS**: Two angles and a non-included side of one triangle are congruent to the corresponding two angles and non-included side of the second triangle.
- **HL**: The hypotenuse and leg of one right triangle are congruent to the corresponding hypotenuse and leg of the second right triangle.

> **Review Video: Similar Triangles**
> Visit mometrix.com/academy and enter code: 398538

GENERAL RULES FOR TRIANGLES

The **triangle inequality theorem** states that the sum of the measures of any two sides of a triangle is always greater than the measure of the third side. If the sum of the measures of two sides were equal to the third side, a triangle would be impossible because the two sides would lie flat across the third side and there would be no vertex. If the sum of the measures of two of the sides was less than the third side, a closed figure would be impossible because the two shortest sides would never meet. In other words, for a triangle with sides lengths A, B, and C: $A + B > C$, $B + C > A$, and $A + C > B$.

The sum of the measures of the interior angles of a triangle is always 180°. Therefore, a triangle can never have more than one angle greater than or equal to 90°.

In any triangle, the angles opposite congruent sides are congruent, and the sides opposite congruent angles are congruent. The largest angle is always opposite the longest side, and the smallest angle is always opposite the shortest side.

The line segment that joins the midpoints of any two sides of a triangle is always parallel to the third side and exactly half the length of the third side.

> **Review Video: General Rules (Triangle Inequality Theorem)**
> Visit mometrix.com/academy and enter code: 166488

PRACTICE

P1. Given the following pairs of triangles, determine whether they are similar, congruent, or neither (note that the figures are not drawn to scale):

(a).

(b).

(c).

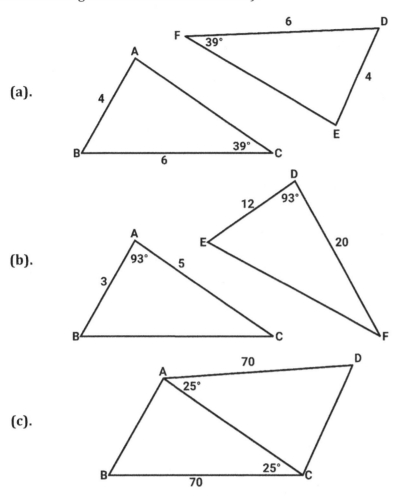

PRACTICE SOLUTIONS

P1. (a). Neither: We are given that two sides lengths and an angle are equal, however, the angle given is not between the given side lengths. That means there are two possible triangles that could satisfy the given measurements. Thus, we cannot be certain of congruence:

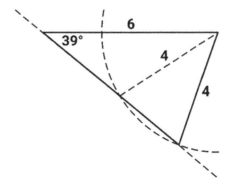

247

(b) Similar: Since we are given a side-angle-side of each triangle and the side lengths given are scaled evenly $\left(\frac{3}{5} \times \frac{4}{4} = \frac{12}{20}\right)$ and the angles are equal. Thus, $\Delta ABC \sim \Delta DEF$. If the side lengths were equal, then they would be congruent.

(c) Congruent: Even though we aren't given a measurement for the shared side of the figure, since it is shared it is equal. So, this is a case of SAS. Thus, $\Delta ABC \cong \Delta CDA$.

Introductory Trigonometry

PYTHAGOREAN THEOREM

The side of a triangle opposite the right angle is called the **hypotenuse**. The other two sides are called the legs. The Pythagorean theorem states a relationship among the legs and hypotenuse of a right triangle: $(a^2 + b^2 = c^2)$, where a and b are the lengths of the legs of a right triangle, and c is the length of the hypotenuse. Note that this formula will only work with right triangles.

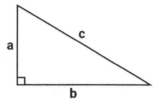

Review Video: Pythagorean Theorem
Visit mometrix.com/academy and enter code: 906576

TRIGONOMETRIC FORMULAS

In the diagram below, angle C is the right angle, and side c is the hypotenuse. Side a is the side opposite to angle A and side b is the side opposite to angle B. Using ratios of side lengths as a means to calculate the sine, cosine, and tangent of an acute angle only works for right triangles.

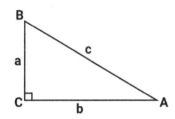

$$\sin A = \frac{\text{opposite side}}{\text{hypotenuse}} = \frac{a}{c} \qquad \csc A = \frac{1}{\sin A} = \frac{\text{hypotenuse}}{\text{opposite side}} = \frac{c}{a}$$

$$\cos A = \frac{\text{adjacent side}}{\text{hypotenuse}} = \frac{b}{c} \qquad \sec A = \frac{1}{\cos A} = \frac{\text{hypotenuse}}{\text{adjacent side}} = \frac{c}{b}$$

$$\tan A = \frac{\text{opposite side}}{\text{adjacent side}} = \frac{a}{b} \qquad \cot A = \frac{1}{\tan A} = \frac{\text{adjacent side}}{\text{opposite side}} = \frac{b}{a}$$

LAWS OF SINES AND COSINES

The **law of sines** states that $\frac{\sin A}{a} = \frac{\sin B}{b} = \frac{\sin C}{c}$, where A, B, and C are the angles of a triangle, and a, b, and c are the sides opposite their respective angles. This formula will work with all triangles, not just right triangles.

The **law of cosines** is given by the formula $c^2 = a^2 + b^2 - 2ab(\cos C)$, where a, b, and c are the sides of a triangle, and C is the angle opposite side c. This is a generalized form of the Pythagorean theorem that can be used on any triangle.

Review Video: Law of Sines
Visit mometrix.com/academy and enter code: 206844

Review Video: Law of Cosines
Visit mometrix.com/academy and enter code: 158911

PRACTICE

P1. Calculate the following values based on triangle MNO:

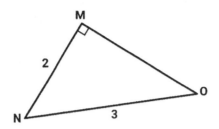

(a) length of $\overline{MO}$

(b) $\sin(\angle NOM)$

(c) area of the triangle, if the units of the measurements are in miles

PRACTICE SOLUTIONS

P1. (a) Since triangle MNO is a right triangle, we can use the simple form of Pythagoras theorem to find the missing side length:

$$\left(\overline{MO}\right)^2 + 2^2 = 3^2$$
$$\left(\overline{MO}\right)^2 = 9 - 4$$
$$\overline{MO} = \sqrt{5}$$

(b) Recall that sine of an angle in a right triangle is the ratio of the opposite side to the hypotenuse. So, $\sin(\angle NOM) = \frac{2}{3}$

(c) Since triangle MNO is a right triangle, we can use either of the legs as the height and the other as the base in the simple formula for the area of a triangle:

$$A = \frac{bh}{2}$$
$$= \frac{(2 \text{ mi})\left(\sqrt{5} \text{ mi}\right)}{2}$$
$$= \sqrt{5} \text{ mi}^2$$

Probability

PROBABILITY

Probability is the likelihood of a certain outcome occurring for a given event. An **event** is any situation that produces a result. It could be something as simple as flipping a coin or as complex as launching a rocket. Determining the probability of an outcome for an event can be equally simple or complex. As such, there are specific terms used in the study of probability that need to be understood:

- **Compound event**—an event that involves two or more independent events (rolling a pair of dice and taking the sum)
- **Desired outcome** (or success)—an outcome that meets a particular set of criteria (a roll of 1 or 2 if we are looking for numbers less than 3)
- **Independent events**—two or more events whose outcomes do not affect one another (two coins tossed at the same time)
- **Dependent events**—two or more events whose outcomes affect one another (two cards drawn consecutively from the same deck)
- **Certain outcome**—probability of outcome is 100% or 1
- **Impossible outcome**—probability of outcome is 0% or 0
- **Mutually exclusive outcomes**—two or more outcomes whose criteria cannot all be satisfied in a single event (a coin coming up heads and tails on the same toss)
- **Random variable**—refers to all possible outcomes of a single event which may be discrete or continuous.

> **Review Video: Intro to Probability**
> Visit mometrix.com/academy and enter code: 212374

THEORETICAL AND EXPERIMENTAL PROBABILITY

Theoretical probability can usually be determined without actually performing the event. The likelihood of an outcome occurring, or the probability of an outcome occurring, is given by the formula:

$$P(A) = \frac{\text{Number of acceptable outcomes}}{\text{Number of possible outcomes}}$$

Note that $P(A)$ is the probability of an outcome A occurring, and each outcome is just as likely to occur as any other outcome. If each outcome has the same probability of occurring as every other possible outcome, the outcomes are said to be equally likely to occur. The total number of acceptable outcomes must be less than or equal to the total number of possible outcomes. If the two are equal, then the outcome is certain to occur and the probability is 1. If the number of acceptable outcomes is zero, then the outcome is impossible and the probability is 0. For example, if there are 20 marbles in a bag and 5 are red, then the theoretical probability of randomly selecting a red marble is 5 out of 20, $\left(\frac{5}{20} = \frac{1}{4}, 0.25, \text{ or } 25\%\right)$.

If the theoretical probability is unknown or too complicated to calculate, it can be estimated by an experimental probability. **Experimental probability**, also called empirical probability, is an estimate of the likelihood of a certain outcome based on repeated experiments or collected data. In other words, while theoretical probability is based on what *should* happen, experimental probability is based on what *has* happened. Experimental probability is calculated in the same way as theoretical probability, except that actual outcomes are used instead of possible outcomes. The more experiments performed or datapoints gathered, the better the estimate should be.

Theoretical and experimental probability do not always line up with one another. Theoretical probability says that out of 20 coin-tosses, 10 should be heads. However, if we were actually to toss 20 coins, we might record just 5 heads. This doesn't mean that our theoretical probability is incorrect; it just means that this particular experiment had results that were different from what was predicted. A practical application of empirical probability is the insurance industry. There are no set functions that define lifespan, health, or safety. Insurance companies look at factors from hundreds of thousands of individuals to find patterns that they then use to set the formulas for insurance premiums.

> **Review Video: Empirical Probability**
> Visit mometrix.com/academy and enter code: 513468

OBJECTIVE AND SUBJECTIVE PROBABILITY

Objective probability is based on mathematical formulas and documented evidence. Examples of objective probability include raffles or lottery drawings where there is a pre-determined number of possible outcomes and a predetermined number of outcomes that correspond to an event. Other cases of objective probability include probabilities of rolling dice, flipping coins, or drawing cards. Most gambling games are based on objective probability.

In contrast, **subjective probability** is based on personal or professional feelings and judgments. Often, there is a lot of guesswork following extensive research. Areas where subjective probability is applicable include sales trends and business expenses. Attractions set admission prices based on subjective probabilities of attendance based on varying admission rates in an effort to maximize their profit.

SAMPLE SPACE

The total set of all possible results of a test or experiment is called a **sample space**, or sometimes a universal sample space. The sample space, represented by one of the variables S, Ω, or U (for universal sample space) has individual elements called outcomes. Other terms for outcome that may be used interchangeably include elementary outcome, simple event, or sample point. The number of outcomes in a given sample space could be infinite or finite, and some tests may yield multiple unique sample sets. For example, tests conducted by drawing playing cards from a standard deck would have one sample space of the card values, another sample space of the card suits, and a third sample space of suit-denomination combinations. For most tests, the sample spaces considered will be finite.

An **event**, represented by the variable E, is a portion of a sample space. It may be one outcome or a group of outcomes from the same sample space. If an event occurs, then the test or experiment will generate an outcome that satisfies the requirement of that event. For example, given a standard deck of 52 playing cards as the sample space, and defining the event as the collection of face cards, then the event will occur if the card drawn is a J, Q, or K. If any other card is drawn, the event is said to have not occurred.

For every sample space, each possible outcome has a specific likelihood, or probability, that it will occur. The probability measure, also called the **distribution**, is a function that assigns a real number probability, from zero to one, to each outcome. For a probability measure to be accurate, every outcome must have a real number probability measure that is greater than or equal to zero and less than or equal to one. Also, the probability measure of the sample space must equal one, and the probability measure of the union of multiple outcomes must equal the sum of the individual probability measures.

Probabilities of events are expressed as real numbers from zero to one. They give a numerical value to the chance that a particular event will occur. The probability of an event occurring is the sum of the probabilities of the individual elements of that event. For example, in a standard deck of 52 playing cards as the sample space and the collection of face cards as the event, the probability of drawing a specific face card is $\frac{1}{52} = 0.019$, but the probability of drawing any one of the twelve face cards is $12(0.019) = 0.228$. Note that rounding of numbers can generate different results. If you multiplied 12 by the fraction $\frac{1}{52}$ before converting to a decimal, you would get the answer $\frac{12}{52} = 0.231$.

TREE DIAGRAM

For a simple sample space, possible outcomes may be determined by using a **tree diagram** or an organized chart. In either case, you can easily draw or list out the possible outcomes. For example, to determine all the possible ways three objects can be ordered, you can draw a tree diagram:

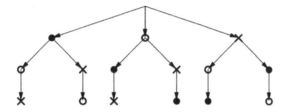

Review Video: <u>Tree Diagrams</u>
Visit mometrix.com/academy and enter code: 829158

You can also make a chart to list all the possibilities:

First object	Second object	Third object
●	X	O
●	O	X
O	●	X
O	X	●
X	●	O
X	O	●

Either way, you can easily see there are six possible ways the three objects can be ordered.

If two events have no outcomes in common, they are said to be **mutually exclusive**. For example, in a standard deck of 52 playing cards, the event of all card suits is mutually exclusive to the event of all card values. If two events have no bearing on each other so that one event occurring has no influence on the probability of another event occurring, the two events are said to be independent. For example, rolling a standard six-sided die multiple times does not change that probability that a particular number will be rolled from one roll to the next. If the outcome of one event does affect the probability of the second event, the two events are said to be dependent. For example, if cards are drawn from a deck, the probability of drawing an ace after an ace has been drawn is different than the probability of drawing an ace if no ace (or no other card, for that matter) has been drawn.

In probability, the **odds in favor of an event** are the number of times the event will occur compared to the number of times the event will not occur. To calculate the odds in favor of an event, use the formula $\frac{P(A)}{1-P(A)}$, where $P(A)$ is the probability that the event will occur. Many times, odds in favor is given as a ratio in the form $\frac{a}{b}$ or $a:b$, where a is the probability of the event occurring and b is the complement of the event, the probability of the event not occurring. If the odds in favor are given as 2:5, that means that you can expect the event to occur two times for every 5 times that it does not occur. In other words, the probability that the event will occur is $\frac{2}{2+5} = \frac{2}{7}$.

In probability, the **odds against an event** are the number of times the event will not occur compared to the number of times the event will occur. To calculate the odds against an event, use the formula $\frac{1-P(A)}{P(A)}$, where $P(A)$ is the probability that the event will occur. Many times, odds against is given as a ratio in the form $\frac{b}{a}$ or $b:a$, where b is the probability the event will not occur (the complement of the event) and a is the probability the event will occur. If the odds against an event are given as 3:1, that means that you can expect the event to not occur 3 times for every one time it does occur. In other words, 3 out of every 4 trials will fail.

PERMUTATIONS AND COMBINATIONS

When trying to calculate the probability of an event using the $\frac{\text{desired outcomes}}{\text{total outcomes}}$ formula, you may frequently find that there are too many outcomes to individually count them. **Permutation** and **combination formulas** offer a shortcut to counting outcomes. A permutation is an arrangement of a specific number of a set of objects in a specific order. The number of **permutations** of r items given a set of n items can be calculated as $_nP_r = \frac{n!}{(n-r)!}$. Combinations are similar to permutations, except there are no restrictions regarding the order of the elements. While ABC is considered a different permutation than BCA, ABC and BCA are considered the same combination. The number of **combinations** of r items given a set of n items can be calculated as $_nC_r = \frac{n!}{r!(n-r)!}$ or $_nC_r = \frac{_nP_r}{r!}$.

Suppose you want to calculate how many different 5-card hands can be drawn from a deck of 52 cards. This is a combination since the order of the cards in a hand does not matter. There are 52 cards available, and 5 to be selected. Thus, the number of different hands is $_{52}C_5 = \frac{52!}{5! \times 47!} = 2{,}598{,}960$.

> **Review Video: Probability - Permutation and Combination**
> Visit mometrix.com/academy and enter code: 907664

UNION AND INTERSECTION OF TWO SETS OF OUTCOMES

If A and B are each a set of elements or outcomes from an experiment, then the **union** (symbol ∪) of the two sets is the set of elements found in set A or set B. For example, if $A = \{2, 3, 4\}$ and $B = \{3, 4, 5\}$, $A \cup B = \{2, 3, 4, 5\}$. Note that the outcomes 3 and 4 appear only once in the union. For statistical events, the union is equivalent to "or"; $P(A \cup B)$ is the same thing as $P(A \text{ or } B)$. The **intersection** (symbol ∩) of two sets is the set of outcomes common to both sets. For the above sets

A and B, $A \cap B = \{3, 4\}$. For statistical events, the intersection is equivalent to "and"; $P(A \cap B)$ is the same thing as $P(A \text{ and } B)$. It is important to note that union and intersection operations commute. That is:

$$A \cup B = B \cup A \text{ and } A \cap B = B \cap A$$

COMPLEMENT OF AN EVENT

Sometimes it may be easier to calculate the possibility of something not happening, or the **complement of an event**. Represented by the symbol $\bar{A}$, the complement of A is the probability that event A does not happen. When you know the probability of event A occurring, you can use the formula $P(\bar{A}) = 1 - P(A)$, where $P(\bar{A})$ is the probability of event A not occurring, and $P(A)$ is the probability of event A occurring.

ADDITION RULE

The **addition rule** for probability is used for finding the probability of a compound event. Use the formula $P(A \cup B) = P(A) + P(B) - P(A \cap B)$, where $P(A \cap B)$ is the probability of both events occurring to find the probability of a compound event. The probability of both events occurring at the same time must be subtracted to eliminate any overlap in the first two probabilities.

CONDITIONAL PROBABILITY

Given two events A and B, the **conditional probability** $P(A|B)$ is the probability that event A will occur, given that event B has occurred. The conditional probability cannot be calculated simply from $P(A)$ and $P(B)$; these probabilities alone do not give sufficient information to determine the conditional probability. It can, however, be determined if you are also given the probability of the intersection of events A and B, $P(A \cap B)$, the probability that events A and B both occur.

Specifically, $P(A|B) = \frac{P(A \cap B)}{P(B)}$. For instance, suppose you have a jar containing two red marbles and two blue marbles, and you draw two marbles at random. Consider event A being the event that the first marble drawn is red, and event B being the event that the second marble drawn is blue. If we want to find the probability that B occurs given that A occurred, $P(B|A)$, then we can compute it using the fact that $P(A)$ is $\frac{1}{2}$, and $P(A \cap B)$ is $\frac{1}{3}$. (The latter may not be obvious, but may be determined by finding the product of $\frac{1}{2}$ and $\frac{2}{3}$). Therefore $P(B|A) = \frac{P(A \cap B)}{P(A)} = \frac{1/3}{1/2} = \frac{2}{3}$.

CONDITIONAL PROBABILITY IN EVERYDAY SITUATIONS

Conditional probability often arises in everyday situations in, for example, estimating the risk or benefit of certain activities. The conditional probability of having a heart attack given that you exercise daily may be smaller than the overall probability of having a heart attack. The conditional probability of having lung cancer given that you are a smoker is larger than the overall probability of having lung cancer. Note that changing the order of the conditional probability changes the meaning: the conditional probability of having lung cancer given that you are a smoker is a very different thing from the probability of being a smoker given that you have lung cancer. In an extreme case, suppose that a certain rare disease is caused only by eating a certain food, but even then, it is unlikely. Then the conditional probability of having that disease given that you eat the dangerous food is nonzero but low, but the conditional probability of having eaten that food given that you have the disease is 100%!

INDEPENDENCE

The conditional probability $P(A|B)$ is the probability that event A will occur given that event B occurs. If the two events are independent, we do not expect that whether or not event B occurs should have any effect on whether or not event A occurs. In other words, we expect $P(A|B) = P(A)$.

This can be proven using the usual equations for conditional probability and the joint probability of independent events. The conditional probability $P(A|B) = \frac{P(A \cap B)}{P(B)}$. If A and B are independent, then $P(A \cap B) = P(A)P(B)$. So $P(A|B) = \frac{P(A)P(B)}{P(B)} = P(A)$. By similar reasoning, if A and B are independent then $P(B|A) = P(B)$.

TWO-WAY FREQUENCY TABLES

If we have a two-way frequency table, it is generally a straightforward matter to read off the probabilities of any two events A and B, as well as the joint probability of both events occurring, $P(A \cap B)$. We can then find the conditional probability $P(A|B)$ by calculating $P(A|B) = \frac{P(A \cap B)}{P(B)}$. We could also check whether or not events are independent by verifying whether $P(A)P(B) = P(A \cap B)$.

For example, a certain store's recent T-shirt sales:

	Small	Medium	Large	Total
Blue	25	40	35	100
White	27	25	22	74
Black	8	23	15	46
Total	60	88	72	220

Suppose we want to find the conditional probability that a customer buys a black shirt (event A), given that the shirt he buys is size small (event B). From the table, the probability $P(B)$ that a customer buys a small shirt is $\frac{60}{220} = \frac{3}{11}$. The probability $P(A \cap B)$ that he buys a small, black shirt is $\frac{8}{220} = \frac{2}{55}$. The conditional probability $P(A|B)$ that he buys a black shirt, given that he buys a small shirt, is therefore $P(A|B) = \frac{2/55}{3/11} = \frac{2}{15}$.

Similarly, if we want to check whether the event a customer buys a blue shirt, A, is independent of the event that a customer buys a medium shirt, B. From the table, $P(A) = \frac{100}{220} = \frac{5}{11}$ and $P(B) = \frac{88}{220} = \frac{4}{10}$. Also, $P(A \cap B) = \frac{40}{220} = \frac{2}{11}$. Since $\left(\frac{5}{11}\right)\left(\frac{4}{10}\right) = \frac{20}{110} = \frac{2}{11}$, $P(A)P(B) = P(A \cap B)$ and these two events are indeed independent.

MULTIPLICATION RULE

The **multiplication rule** can be used to find the probability of two independent events occurring using the formula $P(A \cap B) = P(A) \times P(B)$, where $P(A \cap B)$ is the probability of two independent events occurring, $P(A)$ is the probability of the first event occurring, and $P(B)$ is the probability of the second event occurring.

The multiplication rule can also be used to find the probability of two dependent events occurring using the formula $P(A \cap B) = P(A) \times P(B|A)$, where $P(A \cap B)$ is the probability of two dependent events occurring and $P(B|A)$ is the probability of the second event occurring after the first event has already occurred.

Use a **combination of the multiplication** rule and the rule of complements to find the probability that at least one outcome of the element will occur. This is given by the general formula $P(\text{at least one event occurring}) = 1 - P(\text{no outcomes occurring})$. For example, to find the probability that at least one even number will show when a pair of dice is rolled, find the probability that two odd numbers will be rolled (no even numbers) and subtract from one. You can always use a tree diagram or make a chart to list the possible outcomes when the sample space is small, such as in the dice-rolling example, but in most cases it will be much faster to use the multiplication and complement formulas.

> **Review Video: Multiplication Rule**
> Visit mometrix.com/academy and enter code: 782598

EXPECTED VALUE

Expected value is a method of determining the expected outcome in a random situation. It is a sum of the weighted probabilities of the possible outcomes. Multiply the probability of an event occurring by the weight assigned to that probability (such as the amount of money won or lost). A practical application of the expected value is to determine whether a game of chance is really fair. If the sum of the weighted probabilities is equal to zero, the game is generally considered fair because the player has a fair chance to at least break even. If the expected value is less than zero, then players are expected to lose more than they win. For example, a lottery drawing might allow the player to choose any three-digit number, 000–999. The probability of choosing the winning number is 1:1000. If it costs \$1 to play, and a winning number receives \$500, the expected value is $\left(-\$1 \times \frac{999}{1,000}\right) + \left(\$499 \times \frac{1}{1,000}\right) = -\$0.50$. You can expect to lose on average 50 cents for every dollar you spend.

> **Review Video: Expected Value**
> Visit mometrix.com/academy and enter code: 643554

EXPECTED VALUE AND SIMULATORS

A die roll simulator will show the results of n rolls of a die. The result of each die roll may be recorded. For example, suppose a die is rolled 100 times. All results may be recorded. The numbers of 1s, 2s, 3s, 4s, 5s, and 6s, may be counted. The experimental probability of rolling each number will equal the ratio of the frequency of the rolled number to the total number of rolls. As the number of rolls increases, or approaches infinity, the experimental probability will approach the theoretical probability of $\frac{1}{6}$. Thus, the expected value for the roll of a die is shown to be $\left(1 \times \frac{1}{6}\right) + \left(2 \times \frac{1}{6}\right) + \left(3 \times \frac{1}{6}\right) + \left(4 \times \frac{1}{6}\right) + \left(5 \times \frac{1}{6}\right) + \left(6 \times \frac{1}{6}\right)$, or 3.5.

PRACTICE

P1. Determine the theoretical probability of the following events:

    (a) Rolling an even number on a regular 6-sided die.

    (b) Not getting a red ball when selecting one from a bag of 3 red balls, 4 black balls, and 2 green balls.

    (c) Rolling a standard die and then selecting a card from a standard deck that is less than the value rolled.

P2. There is a game of chance involving a standard deck of cards that has been shuffled and then laid on a table. The player wins $10 if they can turn over 2 cards of matching color (black or red), $50 for 2 cards with matching value (A-K), and $100 for 2 cards with both matching color and value. What is the expected value of playing this game?

P3. Today, there were two food options for lunch at a local college cafeteria. Given the following survey data, what is the probability that a junior selected at random from the sample had a sandwich?

	Freshman	Sophomore	Junior	Senior
Salad	15	12	27	36
Sandwich	24	40	43	35
Nothing	42	23	23	30

PRACTICE SOLUTIONS

P1. (a). The values on the faces of a regular die are 1, 2, 3, 4, 5, and 6. Since three of these are even numbers (2, 4, 6), The probability of rolling an even number is $\frac{3}{6} = \frac{1}{2} = 0.5 = 50\%$.

    (b) The bag contains a total of 9 balls, 6 of which are not red, so the probability of selecting one non-red ball would be $\frac{6}{9} = \frac{2}{3} \cong 0.667 \cong 66.7\%$.

    (c) In this scenario, we need to determine how many cards could satisfy the condition for each possible value of the die roll. If a one is rolled, there is no way to achieve the desired outcome, since no cards in a standard deck are less than 1. If a two is rolled, then any of the four aces would achieve the desired result. If a three is rolled, then either an ace or a two would satisfy the condition, and so on. Note that any value on the die is equally likely to occur, meaning that the probability of each roll is $\frac{1}{6}$. Putting all this in a table can help:

Roll	Cards < Roll	Probability of Card	Probability of Event
1	-	$\frac{0}{52} = 0$	$\frac{1}{6} \times 0 = 0$
2	1	$\frac{4}{52} = \frac{1}{13}$	$\frac{1}{6} \times \frac{1}{13} = \frac{1}{78}$
3	1,2	$\frac{8}{52} = \frac{2}{13}$	$\frac{1}{6} \times \frac{2}{13} = \frac{2}{78}$
4	1,2,3	$\frac{12}{52} = \frac{3}{13}$	$\frac{1}{6} \times \frac{3}{13} = \frac{3}{78}$
5	1,2,3,4	$\frac{16}{52} = \frac{4}{13}$	$\frac{1}{6} \times \frac{4}{13} = \frac{4}{78}$
6	1,2,3,4,5	$\frac{20}{52} = \frac{5}{13}$	$\frac{1}{6} \times \frac{5}{13} = \frac{5}{78}$

Assuming that each value of the die is equally likely, then the probability of selecting a card less than the value of the die is the sum of the probabilities of each way to achieve the desired outcome: $\frac{0+1+2+3+4+5}{78} = \frac{15}{78} = \frac{5}{26} \cong 0.192 \cong 19.2\%$.

P2. First, determine the probability of each way of winning. In each case, the first card simply determines which of the remaining 51 cards in the deck correspond to a win. For the color of the cards to match, there are 25 cards remaining in the deck that match the color of the first, but one of the 25 also matches the value, so only 24 are left in this category. For the value of the cards to match, there are 3 cards remaining in the deck that match the value of the first, but one of the three also matches the color, so only 2 are left in this category. There is only one card in the deck that will match both the color and value. Finally, there are 24 cards left that don't match at all.

Now we can find the expected value of playing the game, where we multiply the value of each event by the probability it will occur and sum over all of them:

$$\$10 \times \frac{24}{51} = \$4.71$$

$$\$50 \times \frac{2}{51} = \$1.96$$

$$\$100 \times \frac{1}{51} = \$1.96$$

$$\$0 \times \frac{24}{51} = \$0$$

$$\$4.71 + \$1.96 + \$1.96 = \$8.63$$

This game therefore has an expected value of $8.63 each time you play, which means if the cost to play is less than $8.63 then you would, on average, *gain* money. However, if the cost to play is more than $8.63, then you would, on average, *lose* money.

P3. With two-way tables it is often most helpful to start by totaling the rows and columns:

	Freshman	Sophomore	Junior	Senior	Total
Salad	15	12	27	36	90
Sandwich	24	40	43	35	142
Nothing	42	23	23	30	118
Total	81	75	93	101	350

Since the question is focused on juniors, we can focus on that column. There was a total of 93 juniors surveyed and 43 of them had a sandwich for lunch. Thus, the probability that a junior selected at random had a sandwich would be $\frac{43}{93} \cong 0.462 \cong 46.2\%$.

Statistics

STATISTICS

Statistics is the branch of mathematics that deals with collecting, recording, interpreting, illustrating, and analyzing large amounts of **data**. The following terms are often used in the discussion of data and **statistics**:

- **Data** – the collective name for pieces of information (singular is datum)
- **Quantitative data** – measurements (such as length, mass, and speed) that provide information about quantities in numbers
- **Qualitative data** – information (such as colors, scents, tastes, and shapes) that cannot be measured using numbers
- **Discrete data** – information that can be expressed only by a specific value, such as whole or half numbers. (e.g., since people can be counted only in whole numbers, a population count would be discrete data.)
- **Continuous data** – information (such as time and temperature) that can be expressed by any value within a given range
- **Primary data** – information that has been collected directly from a survey, investigation, or experiment, such as a questionnaire or the recording of daily temperatures. (Primary data that has not yet been organized or analyzed is called **raw data**.)
- **Secondary data** – information that has been collected, sorted, and processed by the researcher
- **Ordinal data** – information that can be placed in numerical order, such as age or weight
- **Nominal data** – information that *cannot* be placed in numerical order, such as names or places

DATA COLLECTION

POPULATION

In statistics, the **population** is the entire collection of people, plants, etc., that data can be collected from. For example, a study to determine how well students in local schools perform on a standardized test would have a population of all the students enrolled in those schools, although a study may include just a small sample of students from each school. A **parameter** is a numerical value that gives information about the population, such as the mean, median, mode, or standard deviation. Remember that the symbol for the mean of a population is μ and the symbol for the standard deviation of a population is σ.

SAMPLE

A **sample** is a portion of the entire population. Whereas a parameter helped describe the population, a **statistic** is a numerical value that gives information about the sample, such as mean, median, mode, or standard deviation. Keep in mind that the symbols for mean and standard deviation are different when they are referring to a sample rather than the entire population. For a sample, the symbol for mean is $\bar{x}$ and the symbol for standard deviation is s. The mean and standard deviation of a sample may or may not be identical to that of the entire population due to a sample only being a subset of the population. However, if the sample is random and large enough, statistically significant values can be attained. Samples are generally used when the population is too large to justify including every element or when acquiring data for the entire population is impossible.

INFERENTIAL STATISTICS

Inferential statistics is the branch of statistics that uses samples to make predictions about an entire population. This type of statistic is often seen in political polls, where a sample of the population is questioned about a particular topic or politician to gain an understanding of the attitudes of the entire population of the country. Often, exit polls are conducted on election days using this method. Inferential statistics can have a large margin of error if you do not have a valid sample.

SAMPLING DISTRIBUTION

Statistical values calculated from various samples of the same size make up the **sampling distribution**. For example, if several samples of identical size are randomly selected from a large population and then the mean of each sample is calculated, the distribution of values of the means would be a sampling distribution.

The **sampling distribution of the mean** is the distribution of the sample mean, $\bar{x}$, derived from random samples of a given size. It has three important characteristics. First, the mean of the sampling distribution of the mean is equal to the mean of the population that was sampled. Second, assuming the standard deviation is non-zero, the standard deviation of the sampling distribution of the mean equals the standard deviation of the sampled population divided by the square root of the sample size. This is sometimes called the standard error. Finally, as the sample size gets larger, the sampling distribution of the mean gets closer to a normal distribution via the central limit theorem.

SURVEY STUDY

A **survey study** is a method of gathering information from a small group in an attempt to gain enough information to make accurate general assumptions about the population. Once a survey study is completed, the results are then put into a summary report.

Survey studies are generally in the format of surveys, interviews, or questionnaires as part of an effort to find opinions of a particular group or to find facts about a group.

It is important to note that the findings from a survey study are only as accurate as the sample chosen from the population.

CORRELATIONAL STUDIES

Correlational studies seek to determine how much one variable is affected by changes in a second variable. For example, correlational studies may look for a relationship between the amount of time a student spends studying for a test and the grade that student earned on the test or between student scores on college admissions tests and student grades in college.

It is important to note that correlational studies cannot show a cause and effect, but rather can show only that two variables are or are not potentially correlated.

EXPERIMENTAL STUDIES

Experimental studies take correlational studies one step farther, in that they attempt to prove or disprove a cause-and-effect relationship. These studies are performed by conducting a series of experiments to test the hypothesis. For a study to be scientifically accurate, it must have both an experimental group that receives the specified treatment and a control group that does not get the treatment. This is the type of study pharmaceutical companies do as part of drug trials for new medications. Experimental studies are only valid when the proper scientific method has been followed. In other words, the experiment must be well-planned and executed without bias in the testing process, all subjects must be selected at random, and the process of determining which subject is in which of the two groups must also be completely random.

OBSERVATIONAL STUDIES

Observational studies are the opposite of experimental studies. In observational studies, the tester cannot change or in any way control all of the variables in the test. For example, a study to determine which gender does better in math classes in school is strictly observational. You cannot change a person's gender, and you cannot change the subject being studied. The big downfall of observational studies is that you have no way of proving a cause-and-effect relationship because you cannot control outside influences. Events outside of school can influence a student's performance in school, and observational studies cannot take that into consideration.

RANDOM SAMPLES

For most studies, a **random sample** is necessary to produce valid results. Random samples should not have any particular influence to cause sampled subjects to behave one way or another. The goal is for the random sample to be a **representative sample**, or a sample whose characteristics give an accurate picture of the characteristics of the entire population. To accomplish this, you must make sure you have a proper **sample size**, or an appropriate number of elements in the sample.

BIASES

In statistical studies, biases must be avoided. **Bias** is an error that causes the study to favor one set of results over another. For example, if a survey to determine how the country views the president's job performance only speaks to registered voters in the president's party, the results will be skewed because a disproportionately large number of responders would tend to show approval, while a disproportionately large number of people in the opposite party would tend to express disapproval. **Extraneous variables** are, as the name implies, outside influences that can affect the outcome of a study. They are not always avoidable but could trigger bias in the result.

PRACTICE

P1. Determine if the following statements are TRUE or FALSE:

(a) Just because a sample is random, does not guarantee that it is representative.

(b) Qualitative data cannot be statistically analyzed, since the data is non-numeric.

(c) Sample statistics are a useful tool to estimate population parameters.

PRACTICE SOLUTIONS

P1. (a). TRUE: A good representative sample will also be a random sample, but sampling 10 random people from a city of 4 million will not be a representative sample.

(b) FALSE: Even though qualitative data is often non-numeric, there are special methods designed to specifically tally and analyze qualitative data.

(c) TRUE: The entire field of statistics is built upon this, since it is almost always beyond the scope of researchers to survey or collect data on an entire population.

Statistical Analysis

MEASURES OF CENTRAL TENDENCY

A **measure of central tendency** is a statistical value that gives a reasonable estimate for the center of a group of data. There are several different ways of describing the measure of central tendency. Each one has a unique way it is calculated, and each one gives a slightly different perspective on the data set. Whenever you give a measure of central tendency, always make sure the units are the same. If the data has different units, such as hours, minutes, and seconds, convert all the data to the same unit, and use the same unit in the measure of central tendency. If no units are given in the data, do not give units for the measure of central tendency.

MEAN

The **statistical mean** of a group of data is the same as the arithmetic average of that group. To find the mean of a set of data, first convert each value to the same units, if necessary. Then find the sum of all the values, and count the total number of data values, making sure you take into consideration each individual value. If a value appears more than once, count it more than once. Divide the sum of the values by the total number of values and apply the units, if any. Note that the mean does not have to be one of the data values in the set, and may not divide evenly.

$$\text{mean} = \frac{\text{sum of the data values}}{\text{quantity of data values}}$$

For instance, the mean of the data set {88, 72, 61, 90, 97, 68, 88, 79, 86, 93, 97, 71, 80, 84, 89} would be the sum of the fifteen numbers divided by 15:

$$\frac{88 + 72 + 61 + 90 + 97 + 68 + 88 + 79 + 86 + 93 + 97 + 71 + 80 + 84 + 88}{15} = \frac{1242}{15}$$
$$= 82.8$$

While the mean is relatively easy to calculate and averages are understood by most people, the mean can be very misleading if it is used as the sole measure of central tendency. If the data set has outliers (data values that are unusually high or unusually low compared to the rest of the data values), the mean can be very distorted, especially if the data set has a small number of values. If unusually high values are countered with unusually low values, the mean is not affected as much. For example, if five of twenty students in a class get a 100 on a test, but the other 15 students have an average of 60 on the same test, the class average would appear as 70. Whenever the mean is skewed by outliers, it is always a good idea to include the median as an alternate measure of central tendency.

A **weighted mean**, or weighted average, is a mean that uses "weighted" values. The formula is weighted mean $= \frac{w_1 x_1 + w_2 x_2 + w_3 x_3 \dots + w_n x_n}{w_1 + w_2 + w_3 + \dots + w_n}$. Weighted values, such as $w_1, w_2, w_3, \dots w_n$ are assigned to each member of the set $x_1, x_2, x_3, \dots x_n$. When calculating the weighted mean, make sure a weight value for each member of the set is used.

> **Review Video: All About Averages**
> Visit mometrix.com/academy and enter code: 176521

MEDIAN

The **statistical median** is the value in the middle of the set of data. To find the median, list all data values in order from smallest to largest or from largest to smallest. Any value that is repeated in the set must be listed the number of times it appears. If there are an odd number of data values, the median is the value in the middle of the list. If there is an even number of data values, the median is the arithmetic mean of the two middle values.

For example, the median of the data set {88, 72, 61, 90, 97, 68, 88, 79, 86, 93, 97, 71, 80, 84, 88} is 86 since the ordered set is {61, 68, 71, 72, 79, 80, 84, **86**, 88, 88, 88, 90, 93, 97, 97}.

The big disadvantage of using the median as a measure of central tendency is that is relies solely on a value's relative size as compared to the other values in the set. When the individual values in a set of data are evenly dispersed, the median can be an accurate tool. However, if there is a group of rather large values or a group of rather small values that are not offset by a different group of values, the information that can be inferred from the median may not be accurate because the distribution of values is skewed.

MODE

The **statistical mode** is the data value that occurs the greatest number of times in the data set. It is possible to have exactly one mode, more than one mode, or no mode. To find the mode of a set of data, arrange the data like you do to find the median (all values in order, listing all multiples of data values). Count the number of times each value appears in the data set. If all values appear an equal number of times, there is no mode. If one value appears more than any other value, that value is the mode. If two or more values appear the same number of times, but there are other values that appear fewer times and no values that appear more times, all of those values are the modes.

For example, the mode of the data set {**88**, 72, 61, 90, 97, 68, **88**, 79, 86, 93, 97, 71, 80, 84, **88**} is 88.

The main disadvantage of the mode is that the values of the other data in the set have no bearing on the mode. The mode may be the largest value, the smallest value, or a value anywhere in between in the set. The mode only tells which value or values, if any, occurred the greatest number of times. It does not give any suggestions about the remaining values in the set.

> **Review Video: Mean, Median, and Mode**
> Visit mometrix.com/academy and enter code: 286207

DISPERSION

A **measure of dispersion** is a single value that helps to "interpret" the measure of central tendency by providing more information about how the data values in the set are distributed about the measure of central tendency. The measure of dispersion helps to eliminate or reduce the disadvantages of using the mean, median, or mode as a single measure of central tendency, and give a more accurate picture of the dataset as a whole. To have a measure of dispersion, you must know or calculate the range, standard deviation, or variance of the data set.

RANGE

The **range** of a set of data is the difference between the greatest and lowest values of the data in the set. To calculate the range, you must first make sure the units for all data values are the same, and then identify the greatest and lowest values. If there are multiple data values that are equal for the highest or lowest, just use one of the values in the formula. Write the answer with the same units as the data values you used to do the calculations.

> **Review Video: Statistical Range**
> Visit mometrix.com/academy and enter code: 778541

SAMPLE STANDARD DEVIATION

Standard deviation is a measure of dispersion that compares all the data values in the set to the mean of the set to give a more accurate picture. To find the **standard deviation of a sample**, use the formula

$$s = \sqrt{\frac{\sum_{i=1}^{n}(x_i - \bar{x})^2}{n-1}}$$

Note that s is the standard deviation of a sample, x_i represents the individual values in the data set, $\bar{x}$ is the mean of the data values in the set, and n is the number of data values in the set. The higher the value of the standard deviation is, the greater the variance of the data values from the mean. The units associated with the standard deviation are the same as the units of the data values.

> **Review Video: Standard Deviation**
> Visit mometrix.com/academy and enter code: 419469

SAMPLE VARIANCE

The **variance of a sample** is the square of the sample standard deviation (denoted s^2). While the mean of a set of data gives the average of the set and gives information about where a specific data value lies in relation to the average, the variance of the sample gives information about the degree to which the data values are spread out and tells you how close an individual value is to the average compared to the other values. The units associated with variance are the same as the units of the data values squared.

PERCENTILE

Percentiles and quartiles are other methods of describing data within a set. **Percentiles** tell what percentage of the data in the set fall below a specific point. For example, achievement test scores are often given in percentiles. A score at the 80th percentile is one which is equal to or higher than 80 percent of the scores in the set. In other words, 80 percent of the scores were lower than that score.

Quartiles are percentile groups that make up quarter sections of the data set. The first quartile is the 25th percentile. The second quartile is the 50th percentile; this is also the median of the dataset. The third quartile is the 75th percentile.

SKEWNESS

Skewness is a way to describe the symmetry or asymmetry of the distribution of values in a dataset. If the distribution of values is symmetrical, there is no skew. In general the closer the mean of a data set is to the median of the data set, the less skew there is. Generally, if the mean is to the right of the median, the data set is *positively skewed*, or right-skewed, and if the mean is to the left of the median, the data set is *negatively skewed*, or left-skewed. However, this rule of thumb is not infallible. When the data values are graphed on a curve, a set with no skew will be a perfect bell curve.

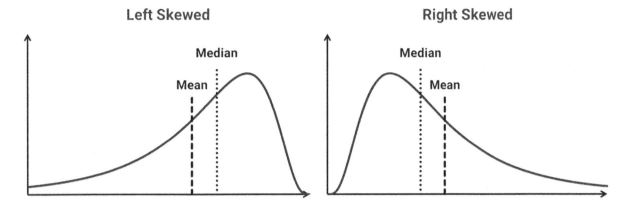

To estimate skew, use the formula:

$$\text{skew} = \frac{\sqrt{n(n-1)}}{n-2}\left(\frac{\frac{1}{n}\sum_{i=1}^{n}(x_i - \bar{x})^3}{\left(\frac{1}{n}\sum_{i=1}^{n}(x_i - \bar{x})^2\right)^{\frac{3}{2}}}\right)$$

Note that n is the datapoints in the set, x_i is the ith value in the set, and $\bar{x}$ is the mean of the set.

> **Review Video: Skew**
> Visit mometrix.com/academy and enter code: 661486

UNIMODAL VS. BIMODAL

If a distribution has a single peak, it would be considered **unimodal**. If it has two discernible peaks it would be considered **bimodal**. Bimodal distributions may be an indication that the set of data being considered is actually the combination of two sets of data with significant differences. A **uniform distribution** is a distribution in which there is *no distinct peak or variation* in the data. No values or ranges are particularly more common than any other values or ranges.

OUTLIER

An outlier is an extremely high or extremely low value in the data set. It may be the result of measurement error, in which case, the outlier is not a valid member of the data set. However, it may also be a valid member of the distribution. Unless a measurement error is identified, the experimenter cannot know for certain if an outlier is or is not a member of the distribution. There are arbitrary methods that can be employed to designate an extreme value as an outlier. One method designates an outlier (or possible outlier) to be any value less than $Q_1 - 1.5(IQR)$ or any value greater than $Q_3 + 1.5(IQR)$.

DATA ANALYSIS
SIMPLE REGRESSION

In statistics, **simple regression** is using an equation to represent a relation between independent and dependent variables. The independent variable is also referred to as the explanatory variable or the predictor and is generally represented by the variable x in the equation. The dependent variable, usually represented by the variable y, is also referred to as the response variable. The equation may be any type of function – linear, quadratic, exponential, etc. The best way to handle this task is to use the regression feature of your graphing calculator. This will easily give you the curve of best fit and provide you with the coefficients and other information you need to derive an equation.

LINE OF BEST FIT

In a scatter plot, the **line of best fit** is the line that best shows the trends of the data. The line of best fit is given by the equation $\hat{y} = ax + b$, where a and b are the regression coefficients. The regression coefficient a is also the slope of the line of best fit, and b is also the y-coordinate of the point at which the line of best fit crosses the y-axis. Not every point on the scatter plot will be on the line of best fit. The differences between the y-values of the points in the scatter plot and the corresponding y-values according to the equation of the line of best fit are the residuals. The line of best fit is also called the least-squares regression line because it is also the line that has the lowest sum of the squares of the residuals.

CORRELATION COEFFICIENT

The **correlation coefficient** is the numerical value that indicates how strong the relationship is between the two variables of a linear regression equation. A correlation coefficient of –1 is a perfect negative correlation. A correlation coefficient of +1 is a perfect positive correlation. Correlation coefficients close to –1 or +1 are very strong correlations. A correlation coefficient equal to zero indicates there is no correlation between the two variables. This test is a good indicator of whether or not the equation for the line of best fit is accurate. The formula for the correlation coefficient is

$$r = \frac{\sum_{i=1}^{n}(x_i - \bar{x})(y_i - \bar{y})}{\sqrt{\sum_{i=1}^{n}(x_i - \bar{x})^2}\sqrt{\sum_{i=1}^{n}(y_i - \bar{y})^2}}$$

where r is the correlation coefficient, n is the number of data values in the set, (x_i, y_i) is a point in the set, and $\bar{x}$ and $\bar{y}$ are the means.

Z-SCORE

A **z-score** is an indication of how many standard deviations a given value falls from the sample mean. To calculate a z-score, use the formula:

$$\frac{x - \bar{x}}{\sigma}$$

In this formula x is the data value, $\bar{x}$ is the mean of the sample data, and σ is the standard deviation of the population. If the z-score is positive, the data value lies above the mean. If the z-score is negative, the data value falls below the mean. These scores are useful in interpreting data such as standardized test scores, where every piece of data in the set has been counted, rather than just a small random sample. In cases where standard deviations are calculated from a random sample of the set, the z-scores will not be as accurate.

CENTRAL LIMIT THEOREM

According to the **central limit theorem**, regardless of what the original distribution of a sample is, the distribution of the means tends to get closer and closer to a normal distribution as the sample size gets larger and larger (this is necessary because the sample is becoming more all-encompassing of the elements of the population). As the sample size gets larger, the distribution of the sample mean will approach a normal distribution with a mean of the population mean and a variance of the population variance divided by the sample size.

PRACTICE

P1. Suppose the class average on a final exam is 87, with a standard deviation of 2 points. Find the z-score of a student that got an 82.

P2. Given the following graph, determine the range of patient ages:

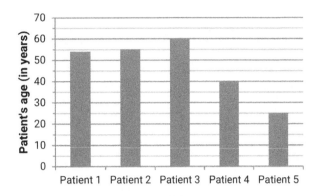

P3. Calculate the sample variance for the dataset $\{10, 13, 12, 5, 8, 18\}$

PRACTICE SOLUTIONS

P1. Using the formula for z-score: $z = \frac{82-87}{2} = -2.5$

P2. Patient 1 is 54 years old; Patient 2 is 55 years old; Patient 3 is 60 years old; Patient 4 is 40 years old; and Patient 5 is 25 years old. The range of patient ages is the age of the oldest patient minus the age of the youngest patient. In other words, $60 - 25 = 35$. The range of ages is 35 years.

P3. To find the variance, first find the mean:

$$\frac{10 + 13 + 12 + 5 + 8 + 18}{6} = \frac{66}{6} = 11$$

Now, apply the formula for sample variance:

$$\begin{aligned}
s^2 &= \frac{\sum_{i=1}^{n}(x_i - \bar{x})^2}{n-1} = \frac{\sum_{i=1}^{6}(x_i - 11)^2}{6-1} \\
&= \frac{(10-11)^2 + (13-11)^2 + (12-11)^2 + (5-11)^2 + (8-11)^2 + (18-11)^2}{5} \\
&= \frac{(-1)^2 + 2^2 + 1^2 + (-6)^2 + (-3)^2 + 7^2}{5} \\
&= \frac{1 + 4 + 1 + 36 + 9 + 49}{5} \\
&= \frac{100}{5} = 20
\end{aligned}$$

Displaying Information

FREQUENCY TABLES

Frequency tables show how frequently each unique value appears in a set. A **relative frequency table** is one that shows the proportions of each unique value compared to the entire set. Relative frequencies are given as percentages; however, the total percent for a relative frequency table will not necessarily equal 100 percent due to rounding. An example of a frequency table with relative frequencies is below.

Favorite Color	Frequency	Relative Frequency
Blue	4	13%
Red	7	22%
Green	3	9%
Purple	6	19%
Cyan	12	38%

> **Review Video: Data Interpretation of Graphs**
> Visit mometrix.com/academy and enter code: 200439

CIRCLE GRAPHS

Circle graphs, also known as *pie charts*, provide a visual depiction of the relationship of each type of data compared to the whole set of data. The circle graph is divided into sections by drawing radii to create central angles whose percentage of the circle is equal to the individual data's percentage of the whole set. Each 1% of data is equal to 3.6° in the circle graph. Therefore, data represented by a 90° section of the circle graph makes up 25% of the whole. When complete, a circle graph often looks like a pie cut into uneven wedges. The pie chart below shows the data from the frequency table referenced earlier where people were asked their favorite color.

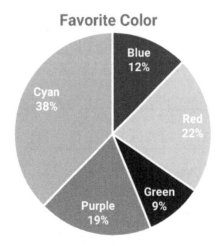

PICTOGRAPHS

A **pictograph** is a graph, generally in the horizontal orientation, that uses pictures or symbols to represent the data. Each pictograph must have a key that defines the picture or symbol and gives the quantity each picture or symbol represents. Pictures or symbols on a pictograph are not always shown as whole elements. In this case, the fraction of the picture or symbol shown represents the same fraction of the quantity a whole picture or symbol stands for. For example, a row with $3\frac{1}{2}$ ears

270

of corn, where each ear of corn represents 100 stalks of corn in a field, would equal $3\frac{1}{2} \times 100 = 350$ stalks of corn in the field.

LINE GRAPHS

Line graphs have one or more lines of varying styles (solid or broken) to show the different values for a set of data. The individual data are represented as ordered pairs, much like on a Cartesian plane. In this case, the x- and y-axes are defined in terms of their units, such as dollars or time. The individual plotted points are joined by line segments to show whether the value of the data is increasing (line sloping upward), decreasing (line sloping downward), or staying the same (horizontal line). Multiple sets of data can be graphed on the same line graph to give an easy visual comparison. An example of this would be graphing achievement test scores for different groups of students over the same time period to see which group had the greatest increase or decrease in performance from year to year (as shown below).

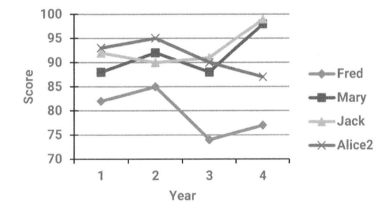

LINE PLOTS

A **line plot**, also known as a *dot plot*, has plotted points that are not connected by line segments. In this graph, the horizontal axis lists the different possible values for the data, and the vertical axis lists the number of times the individual value occurs. A single dot is graphed for each value to show the number of times it occurs. This graph is more closely related to a bar graph than a line graph. Do not connect the dots in a line plot or it will misrepresent the data.

STEM AND LEAF PLOTS

A **stem and leaf plot** is useful for depicting groups of data that fall into a range of values. Each piece of data is separated into two parts: the first, or left, part is called the stem; the second, or right, part is called the leaf. Each stem is listed in a column from smallest to largest. Each leaf that has the common stem is listed in that stem's row from smallest to largest. For example, in a set of two-digit numbers, the digit in the tens place is the stem, and the digit in the ones place is the leaf. With a stem and leaf plot, you can easily see which subset of numbers (10s, 20s, 30s, etc.) is the largest. This information is also readily available by looking at a histogram, but a stem and leaf plot also allows you to look closer and see exactly which values fall in that range. Using a sample set of test scores (82, 88, 92, 93, 85, 90, 92, 95, 74, 88, 90, 91, 78, 87, 98, 99), we can assemble a stem and leaf plot like the one below.

Test Scores

7	4	8						
8	2	5	7	8	8			
9	0	0	1	2	2	3	5	8	9

> **Review Video: Stem and Leaf Plots**
> Visit mometrix.com/academy and enter code: 302339

BAR GRAPHS

A **bar graph** is one of the few graphs that can be drawn correctly in two different configurations – both horizontally and vertically. A bar graph is similar to a line plot in the way the data is organized on the graph. Both axes must have their categories defined for the graph to be useful. Rather than placing a single dot to mark the point of the data's value, a bar, or thick line, is drawn from zero to the exact value of the data, whether it is a number, percentage, or other numerical value. Longer bar lengths correspond to greater data values. To read a bar graph, read the labels for the axes to find the units being reported. Then, look where the bars end in relation to the scale given on the corresponding axis and determine the associated value.

The bar chart below represents the responses from our favorite-color survey.

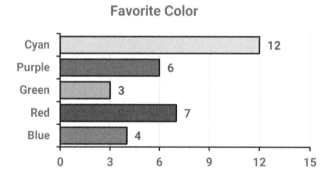

HISTOGRAMS

At first glance, a **histogram** looks like a vertical bar graph. The difference is that a bar graph has a separate bar for each piece of data and a histogram has one continuous bar for each *range* of data. For example, a histogram may have one bar for the range 0–9, one bar for 10–19, etc. While a bar graph has numerical values on one axis, a histogram has numerical values on both axes. Each range is of equal size, and they are ordered left to right from lowest to highest. The height of each column on a histogram represents the number of data values within that range. Like a stem and leaf plot, a histogram makes it easy to glance at the graph and quickly determine which range has the greatest quantity of values. A simple example of a histogram is below.

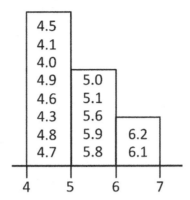

BIVARIATE DATA

Bivariate data is simply data from two different variables. (The prefix *bi-* means *two.*) In a *scatter plot*, each value in the set of data is plotted on a grid similar to a Cartesian plane, where each axis represents one of the two variables. By looking at the pattern formed by the points on the grid, you can often determine whether or not there is a relationship between the two variables, and what that relationship is, if it exists. The variables may be directly proportionate, inversely proportionate, or show no proportion at all. It may also be possible to determine if the data is linear, and if so, to find an equation to relate the two variables. The following scatter plot shows the relationship between preference for brand "A" and the age of the consumers surveyed.

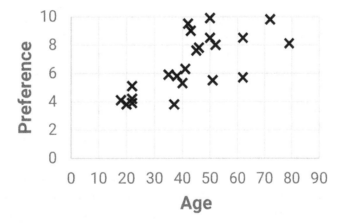

SCATTER PLOTS

Scatter plots are also useful in determining the type of function represented by the data and finding the simple regression. Linear scatter plots may be positive or negative. Nonlinear scatter plots are generally exponential or quadratic. Below are some common types of scatter plots:

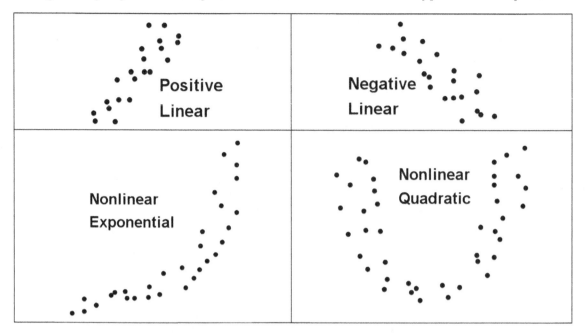

5-NUMBER SUMMARY

The **5-number summary** of a set of data gives a very informative picture of the set. The five numbers in the summary include the minimum value, maximum value, and the three quartiles. This information gives the reader the range and median of the set, as well as an indication of how the data is spread about the median.

BOX AND WHISKER PLOTS

A **box-and-whiskers plot** is a graphical representation of the 5-number summary. To draw a box-and-whiskers plot, plot the points of the 5-number summary on a number line. Draw a box whose ends are through the points for the first and third quartiles. Draw a vertical line in the box through the median to divide the box in half. Draw a line segment from the first quartile point to the minimum value, and from the third quartile point to the maximum value.

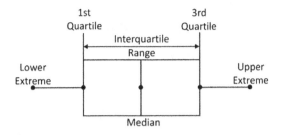

68-95-99.7 RULE

The **68–95–99.7 rule** describes how a normal distribution of data should appear when compared to the mean. This is also a description of a normal bell curve. According to this rule, 68 percent of the data values in a normally distributed set should fall within one standard deviation of the mean (34 percent above and 34 percent below the mean), 95 percent of the data values should fall within two standard deviations of the mean (47.5 percent above and 47.5 percent below the mean), and 99.7 percent of the data values should fall within three standard deviations of the mean, again, equally distributed on either side of the mean. This means that only 0.3 percent of all data values should fall more than three standard deviations from the mean. On the graph below, the normal curve is centered on the y-axis. The x-axis labels are how many standard deviations away from the center you are. Therefore, it is easy to see how the 68-95-99.7 rule can apply.

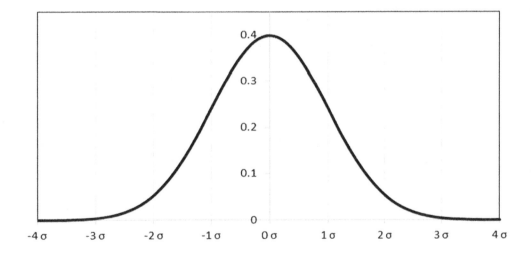

GRE Practice Test #1

Section 1: Analytical Writing

Time – 30 minutes

ANALYZE AN ISSUE

You will have a choice between two Issue topics. Each topic will appear as a brief quotation that states or implies an issue of general interest. Read each topic carefully; then decide on which topic you could write a more effective and well-reasoned response. You will have 45 minutes to plan and compose a response that presents your perspective on the topic you select. A response on any other topic will receive a zero. You are free to accept, reject, or qualify the claim made in the topic you selected, as long as the ideas you present are clearly relevant to the topic. Support your views with reasons and examples drawn from such areas as your reading, experience, observations, or academic studies.

GRE readers, who are college and university faculty, will read your response and evaluate its overall quality, based on how well you do the following:

- consider the complexities and implications of the issue
- organize, develop, and express your ideas on the issue
- support your ideas with relevant reasons and examples
- control the elements of standard written English

You may want to take a few minutes to think about the issue and to plan a response before you begin writing. Because the space for writing your response is limited, use the next page to plan your response. Be sure to develop your ideas fully and organize them coherently, but leave time to reread what you have written and make any revisions that you think are necessary.

> All government, indeed every human benefit and enjoyment, every virtue, and every prudent act, is founded on compromise and barter.

Write a short essay discussing whether you agree or disagree with this statement. Your essay should include the degree to which you agree or disagree as well as your reasoning for taking this position. In addition, you must include specific examples of the elements discussed in the statement and explain how these examples impact your position.

Section 2: Analytical Writing

Time – 30 minutes

ANALYZE AN ARGUMENT

You will have 30 minutes to plan and write a critique of an argument presented in the form of a short passage. A critique of any other argument will receive a score of zero. Analyze the line of reasoning in the argument. Be sure to consider what, if any, questionable assumptions underlie the thinking and, if evidence is cited, how well it supports the conclusion. You can also discuss what sort of evidence would strengthen or refute the argument, what changes in the argument would make it more logically sound, and what additional information might help you better evaluate its conclusion. *Note that you are NOT being asked to present your views on the subject.*

GRE readers, who are college and university faculty, will read your critique and evaluate its overall quality, based on how well you

- identify and analyze important features of the argument
- organize, develop, and express your critique of the argument
- support your critique with relevant reasons and examples
- control the elements of standard written English

Before you begin writing, you may want to take a few minutes to evaluate the argument and plan a response. Because the space for writing your response is limited, use the next page to plan your response. Be sure to develop your ideas fully and organize them coherently, but leave time to reread what you have written and make any revisions that you think are necessary.

> Last year the city of East Lake decided to reallocate limited police resources by no longer responding to burglar alarms in commercial buildings. Since that change took effect, the number of break-ins in commercial buildings in East Lake has increased by 10 percent. In neighboring West Lake, the police continued to respond to burglar alarms in commercial buildings. There, the number of break-ins in commercial buildings declined in the last year by five percent. Therefore, if citizens want to reduce commercial break-ins in the region, they should pressure the East Lake Police Chief and local officials to restore the practice of police response to burglar alarms in commercial buildings.

Write a short essay describing the argument's explicit and implicit assumptions. In your essay, explain whether the argument depends on any of these assumptions. In addition, evaluate the reasonableness of the assumptions as well as the likely consequences for the argument if the assumptions prove false.

Section 3: Verbal Reasoning

Time – 35 Minutes

20 Questions

Directions – Questions 1-10: Each passage in this group is followed by questions based on its content. After reading a passage, choose the best answer to each question. Answer all the questions following a passage on the basis of what is stated or *implied* in that passage.

Questions 1 to 3 are based on this passage.

It might be surprising to discover that Europe's first republic pre-dated the turn of the 11th century, long before Europe would see the rise of another such system. Around 870 AD, settlers from Norway began arriving in Iceland, and they eventually established a government system that gave all free men on the island a voice in legislative and judicial affairs. In approximately 930 AD, the leaders of Iceland created the Althing, considered the oldest parliament in the world. This system, and Iceland's identity as a republic, remained in place until 1262, when the decision of the Althing agreed to the Old Covenant and placed Iceland under the authority of the king of Norway. Iceland would not become a self-governing republic again until 1944, when the people of Iceland voted to end their political relationship with the kingdom of Denmark.

1. The passage indicates which of the following about the development of republics in Europe?

    a. Monarchy was a far more common system of government for most of Europe's history.
    b. The republic in Iceland ultimately was unable to withstand subjugation by another nation.
    c. It would be many years before another republic would develop in Europe.
    d. The republic that developed in Iceland lacked the stability it needed to survive.
    e. The modern republics in Europe have far more sophistication than Iceland's early republic.

2. The author of the passage fails to explain which of the following pieces of information that would complete the material within the passage? Consider each of the three choices separately, and select all that apply.

    a. When Iceland converted to Christianity and thus infused Christian ideas into their political system.
    b. Why the first settlers to Iceland left Norway to seek out a new home.
    c. When Iceland came to be part of the kingdom of Denmark.

3. The mention of the Althing in relation to the Old Covenant suggests which of the following? Consider each of the three choices separately, and select all that apply.

    a. There was a later covenant that followed the Old Covenant.
    b. The free men of Iceland had a voice in deciding on the Old Covenant.
    c. The people of Iceland resisted the union with Norway but ultimately agreed to it.

Questions 4 and 5 are based on this passage.

Iceland's Althing represented an important development in making the people of a nation an active part of the system that governed them. The meeting of the Althing brought together the main leaders of communities across the island; these local

278

leaders all gathered to discuss and determine legal issues. The Althing also welcomed the free men of Iceland to present their claims, disputes, and the like. Althing attendees met at Lögberg, meaning "Law Rock," and the Lögsögumaður, or Lawspeaker, would oversee the event. The first activity was for the Lawspeaker to read a list of all applicable laws. The Lawspeaker would also offer necessary moderation in the case of disputes and provide an overriding sense of order. Also part of the Althing was the Lögretta, a legislative organization that supported the Lawspeaker by determining laws and settling legal disagreements.

4. The passage provides information about the Lawspeaker and his role at the Althing. Using the information in the passage as a guide, which of the following modern political roles is most similar to that of the Icelandic Lawspeaker?

a. President
b. Secretary of State
c. President of the Senate
d. Speaker of the House
e. Lieutenant Governor

5. Based on the information provided in the passage, which of the following best summarizes the purpose of the Althing within Iceland's political system?

a. To determine the laws of Iceland and to provide the free men with a role in their government.
b. To provide a stable system of government for the free men of Iceland.
c. To develop leaders within the communities and to make them as self-governing as possible.
d. To unite the citizenry of Iceland against the invasion of foreign powers.
e. To develop an island-wide legislative system that was consistent in application.

Questions 6 to 8 are based on this passage.

Food science authorities have, in recent years, begun recommending that those persons who prepare their own whole grains begin by soaking the grains. Most grains contain phytic acid, which can prevent proper mineral absorption. For instance, phytic acid can block the body's ability to absorb iron from foods and thus raise the potential over time for anemia. Soaking the grains for several hours, however, reduces the level of phytic acid within them and makes the grains–such as rice, wheat, and quinoa–easier to digest. In fact, persons who struggle with digesting gluten, a common ingredient within grains like wheat, find that they are considerably more tolerant once the phytic acid has been reduced or removed. The soaking process is as simple as adding warm water to the grains for as long as twelve hours in advance of preparing them and then allowing the grains to sit in the water for a while.

6. **Which of the following best describes the problem with phytic acid in grains?**

    a. Phytic acid binds with the naturally occurring minerals in food and creates toxicity during cooking.

    b. Phytic acid is a natural ingredient within most foods, but it increases in whole grains and makes them difficult to digest.

    c. Phytic acid has a tendency to attach itself to gluten and thus make grains indigestible for persons with a gluten intolerance.

    d. Phytic acid attacks the body's digestive system and raises the potential for health problems.

    e. Phytic acid prevents the body from absorbing essential minerals that occur naturally in food.

7. **The author of the passage indicates that soaking grains provides which of the following benefits? Consider each of the three choices separately, and select all that apply.**

    a. Soaking grains reduces the amount of phytic acid within them.

    b. Soaking grains removes the gluten and makes the grains digestible.

    c. Soaking grains improves the body's ability to digest them.

8. **Based on the information provided within the passage, which of the following statements best defines the term food science?**

    a. The science of food preparation and the way that the chemical content of food alters during cooking.

    b. The study of the chemical ingredients within food and the properties of those chemical ingredients.

    c. The complex chemical ingredients that are found within grains and the way these chemicals affect the body.

    d. The study of domestic food preparation and the differences between cooking food at home and the commercial preparation of food.

    e. An emerging field that utilizes modern technology to study ancient grains and how the body utilizes them.

Questions 9 and 10 are based on this passage.

The mystery of the Roanoke Colony never has been solved to any satisfaction, although a number of theories have arisen over the years. Some historians have suggested that the Roanoke colonists simply attempted to return to England but died in the effort. Cannibalism by area tribes and attacks by the Spanish have also been proposed as explanations for the disappearance of the colonists, but neither theory holds much weight among historical experts who argue conflicting evidence. Two other theories, however, remain popular as potential solutions. One historian has put forth the idea that the Roanoke colonists relocated away from the original settlement and eventually were killed by the powerful Chief Powhatan; the chief is said to have claimed responsibility for their deaths, because the colonists allied themselves with a tribe that did not support the powerful chief. Alternatively, other historians have located evidence to suggest that the people of Roanoke took shelter with area tribes and eventually became part of them. A number of Native American groups along the Mid-Atlantic claim European descent and share common features generally recognized as European.

9. Considering the information in the passage, which of the following could explain why historical experts reject the theory of the Spanish attacking Roanoke Colony?

  a. Archeologists have not located any evidence of ammunition in the area around Roanoke Colony and have concluded that no guns were fired at the colonists.

  b. Historical documents indicate that at the time the Roanoke colonists disappeared, the Spanish government had not yet discovered where the English had settled in the New World.

  c. The English settlements in the New World had continued to anger the Spanish government, and led to ongoing tension between the two nations.

  d. There is historical evidence that the Spanish government was working closely with Chief Powhatan to develop a treaty with the English.

  e. The large number of Native American tribes around Roanoke Colony makes it more likely that cannibals attacked the settlers before the Spanish could.

10. Which of the following statements best summarizes the main point of the passage?

  a. Most likely the colonists of Roanoke ultimately joined a friendly tribe in the area and intermarried with them, thereby producing offspring that carried European features.

  b. Due to the lack of solid evidence regarding the events of Roanoke Colony, historians are in complete disagreement about why the Roanoke colonists disappeared.

  c. The best explanation for what happened to the Roanoke colonists is most likely a combination of available theories, with some of them being killed and some of them joining other tribes.

  d. There is a range of theories about what happened to the settlers at Roanoke Colony, but not enough evidence exists to explain the colony's disappearance with any certainty.

  e. Historical evidence that survives indicates that the settlers at Roanoke Colony were caught in the metaphorical crossfire of warring Native American tribes and died as a result.

Directions - Questions 11-16: For each blank select one entry from the corresponding column of choices. Fill all blanks in the way that best completes the text.

---

11. He believed that in order to (i) _____ the problem fully, he would need to understand all of its (ii) _____.

Blank (i)
a. solve
b. address
c. comprehend

Blank (ii)
d. thoughts
e. nuances
f. intricacies

12. The rumors were (i) _____ and she welcomed the opportunity to (ii) _____ them.

Blank (i)
a. fabricated
b. pertinent
c. appealing

Blank (ii)
d. refute
e. enjoy
f. demystify

13. The disarray was _____; the office had to be closed for the day so all the furniture could be placed where it belonged, papers could be re-filed and a general cleaning done.

a. inconsequential
b. contemptible
c. severe
d. intermittent
e. trifling

14. He told the kids not to be so (i) _____ when he was gone. He was afraid they would (ii) _____ the babysitter.

Blank (i)
a. truculent
b. boisterous
c. egotistical

Blank (ii)
d. appease
e. endear
f. overwhelm

15. Although (i) _____ by the young Prince Hal in Shakespeare's two *Henry IV* plays, the jovial character Falstaff fails to put away his youthful antics alongside the (ii)_____ prince and faces the consequences: in *Henry V*, the newly crowned king is forced to (iii) _____ his former friend.

Blank (i)
a. preferred
b. cherished
c. disgusted

Blank (ii)
d. maturing
e. impatient
f. tiresome

Blank (iii)
g. reform
h. renounce
i. restore

16. Tradition always has dictated that the (i) _____ King Richard III was responsible for the murder of his nephews, King Edward V, and Prince Richard, Duke of York. In her book *The Daughter of Time*, however, writer Josephine Tey (ii) _____ an alternative. She claimed instead that the real murderer was King Richard III's successor King Henry VII, and that the new king essentially rewrote history in his favor and (iii) _____ pinned the crime on his predecessor.

Blank (i)
a. popularly malevolent
b. utterly detestable
c. consistently suspicious

Blank (ii)
d. demanded
e. propounded
f. enlightened

Blank (iii)
g. eagerly
h. intentionally
i. retrospectively

Directions – Questions 17-20: Select the *two* answer choices that, when used to complete the sentence, fit the meaning of the sentence as a whole *and* produce completed sentences that are alike in meaning.

17. Because the student had failed to take the prerequisite literature course, he found himself completely unable to determine the _____ within the poetry.

- a. counterfeit
- b. nuance
- c. resonance
- d. presumption
- e. subtlety
- f. pariah

18. To manage their growing debt and live within a budget, the couple decided to cut back and reduce any spending that was _____ to the support of basic needs.

- a. superfluous
- b. indispensable
- c. unequivocal
- d. indifferent
- e. paramount
- f. irrelevant

19. Although vehicle manufacturer had advertised that the car featured _____ storage space in the trunk, the new owners quickly discovered that very little actually fit there.

- a. ostentatious
- b. inadvertent
- c. capacious
- d. commodious
- e. palatable
- f. analogous

20. Having upheld her for years as the _____ of beauty, he was shocked to discover how much she had changed when he saw her at the high school reunion.

- a. conjecture
- b. exemplar
- c. precedent
- d. archetype
- e. malefactor
- f. dilettante

Section 4: Verbal Reasoning

Time – 35 Minutes

20 Questions

Directions – Questions 1-10: Each passage in this group is followed by questions based on its content. After reading a passage, choose the best answer to each question. Answer all the questions following a passage on the basis of what is stated or *implied* in that passage.

Questions 1 through 5 are based on this passage.

The divide between the Christian churches of the East and those of the West went beyond a mere theological break and had broad social, political, and cultural effects. The event known as the Great Schism occurred in 1054, although some historians argue that it had been building for many years before this date and the final straw proved to be the addition of two words–*et filioque*–to the Nicene Creed. The expression was added to the Creed in the Western churches, and under the authority of the pope, but it was widely rebuked by the Eastern churches as lacking theological foundation. Additionally, the Roman Catholic Church in the West demanded that the Eastern Orthodox Church acknowledge the superior authority of Rome and the pope's infallibility. The Eastern leaders refused, and the schism was in effect.

It might seem that theological disputes have their place only in the church, but it is essential to consider the wide influence of the Christian church in medieval Europe. The church was the center of life and governed most aspects of it. Kings and emperors turned to the church for guidance. They ruled with the support of the church, and the church had only to remove that support to create a foundational weakness in the ruler's power. In the West, the pope was recognized as the infallible head of the church. The pope operated essentially as the mouthpiece of God for those under the authority of the Roman Catholic Church. The Eastern Orthodox Church, which operated under a recognizably fallible patriarch and a more regional system of bishops, rejected this outright. In breaking communion with the West, the East also broke the sense of accountability that each church had traditionally held toward the other. Broken communion also meant less cultural influence upon one another. Thus, the East and the West developed largely in isolation, and the divide between them spanned far more than geography and continues even to the modern day.

1. Based on the information in the passage, why did the church in the East object to the inclusion of the expression *et filioque*?

    a. The expression, which is in Latin, did not reflect the liturgical language of the Eastern Orthodox Church.

    b. The request from the pope for the title of supreme head of the church offended the Eastern Church and led them to reject the expression within the creed.

    c. The church in the East was concerned that the church in the West was updating an ancient creed with the theological understanding of the day.

    d. The church in the East believed that the expression altered the acknowledged understanding of scripture and thus was not acceptable.

    e. The addition of *et filioque* to the Nicene Creed was simply the last in a long line of differences between the Eastern and Western churches and represented the final break.

2. Taking the information from the passage into account, why did the church in the East object to the pope in Rome being named supreme head of the Christian church? Consider each of the three choices separately, and select all that apply.

    a. The patriarch of the church in the East believed that he should hold the title of supreme head of the church.

    b. Naming the pope as supreme head of the church would consolidate the Eastern churches under Western authority and undermine their own traditions.

    c. The church in the East could not agree to acknowledge the pope as infallible.

3. Which of the following statements describes the role of the Christian church in medieval Europe? Consider each of the three choices separately, and select all that apply.

    a. The Christian church offered citizens moral guidance for everyday life.

    b. The Christian church provided moral direction to leaders and influenced their decision.

    c. The Christian church was responsible for governing the people through its leaders.

4. Based on the information in the passage, why might the church in the East object to acknowledging the infallibility of the pope in Rome?

    a. The theological teachings of the church in the East claimed that no man could be infallible, thus nullifying the pope's own claim to infallibility.

    b. As supreme head of the church, the pope would have the right to name and appoint all bishops to the churches in the East.

    c. The relationship between the two churches provided accountability, but the pope's claim of infallibility would remove any need for accountability between East and West.

    d. Based on the pope's claim of infallibility, the patriarch in the East felt obligated to excommunicate the pope in Rome and thus break off all communion between the churches.

    e. The widening theological divide between the two churches meant that the East defined infallibility differently than the West, and the two could not agree on the correct definition.

5. Which of the following best summarizes the main point of the passage?

a. The Great Schism that occurred in 1054 had wide-ranging effects that were not limited to theological differences between East and West.

b. The Great Schism resulted after decades of conflict between the Eastern and Western churches and can still be felt today in theological differences between the churches.

c. The Great Schism isolated the East from the West and led to vast cultural differences between the two parts of Europe.

d. The Great Schism resulted in significant differences between the churches of the East and West but was probably inevitable given the distinctions already in place at the time.

e. The Great Schism had such an impact on the differences between the churches of the East and the West that leaders of each church have continued to excommunicate one another.

Questions 6 through 8 are based on this passage.

The question of global warming is one that cannot be answered easily, even by the scientists who devote their careers to studying global climate change. On one hand, these scientists have little doubt that the earth has experienced a warming trend over the last few decades. On the other hand, scientists do not agree entirely about whether or not this warming trend resulted from human activity, or particularly from greenhouse gas emissions. Some scientists have suggested that the increased warming is due to a natural cycle of climate change that will eventually end and reverse to a cooling phase. (In fact, these "mini ice ages" are not unknown in history; Europe recorded unusually low temperatures between the 13th century and the 16th century, thus explaining why so many paintings of monarchs such as Elizabeth I present her heavily clothed and even gloved.) Other scientists have raised questions about whether or not human greenhouse gas emissions could be enough to raise the entire temperature of the earth. These doubts aside, the consensus among scientific journals supports the theory of global warming from greenhouse gas emissions.

6. Based on the information in the passage, why do some scientists question the accuracy of human greenhouse gas emissions as the cause of global warming? Consider each of the three choices separately, and select all that apply.

a. Scientists are unsure if humans can create enough greenhouse gas emissions to have an effect on worldwide climate.

b. Scientists believe that it is more likely the earth is experiencing a normal period of warming to be followed by a period of cooling.

c. Scientists believe that the causes of climate change are too complex to be limited to human activity.

7. Which of the following statements describes the purpose of the parenthetical comment about the "mini ice age"? Consider each of the three choices separately, and select all that apply.

a. The "mini ice age" explains why painted subjects in Elizabethan England were so often portrayed in heavy clothing and gloves.

b. The "mini ice age" conflicts with the evidence in scientific journals that widely supports the theory of greenhouse gas emissions.

c. The "mini ice age" represents a time when the earth experienced a normal climate cycle that altered global temperatures.

8. Which of the following best summarizes the meaning in the final sentence of the passage in the context of the entire passage?

a. Although scientific journals strongly support the theory of greenhouse gas emissions, an increasing number of scientists are beginning to doubt this idea.

b. Scientific journals refuse to acknowledge the questions that many scientists have about the cause of global warming.

c. Regardless of the questions that scientists have about the cause of global warming, the official line with scientific authorities supports the theory of greenhouse gas emissions.

d. The authors of scientific journals believe that there is enough evidence to support the theory of greenhouse gas emissions and a lack of evidence to support alternative theories.

e. The theory of greenhouse gas emissions has significant implications for political policy, so scientific journals feel obligated to acknowledge the theory as the official position.

Questions 9 and 10 are based on this passage.

If the Great Schism between East and West was not enough, the Western church experienced its own schism between 1378 and 1417. Unlike the earlier schism, though, this Western Schism resulted from political disputes among the factions within the church. Prior to the divide, the pope had moved from Rome to Avignon, France, during a period of crisis. Pope Gregory IX relocated to Rome in 1376, but he died soon thereafter. The Roman people demanded a Roman pope, but no qualified candidates could be found. As a result, the choice fell on a man from Naples, who ultimately became Pope Urban VI. He proved to be a disaster, and the now-sorry cardinals left Rome for Avignon again. There they elected the rival Pope Clement VII. Now the cardinals had elected two separate popes, and Rome and Avignon spent nearly three decades warring with each other, and the nations across Europe took sides as well. Order returned with the election of Pope Martin V in 1417, although Avignon continued a feeble resistance until 1429.

9. Based on the information in the passage, which of the following distinguishes the cause of the Western Schism from the cause of the Great Schism? Consider each of the three choices separately, and select all that apply.

a. Social and political upheaval leading to a lack of continuity in church decisions.

b. Internal conflict and political disagreements among the leaders of the church.

c. Inability of church leadership to make astute decisions about appointees to the role of pope.

10. Which of the following statements best explains the implication in the final sentence of the passage?

a. Pope Martin V provided the stability that was needed for the pope to regain authority in Europe.

b. Although historians claim that the Western Schism ended in 1417, they fail to acknowledge the disputes that continued in Avignon until 1429.

c. Pope Martin V's appointment was approved by all factions, because the new pope had links both to Rome and to Avignon.

d. The confusion over papal appointments threw Europe into a state of confusion and led to other political disputes among nations.

e. The appointment of Pope Martin V was widely accepted, but a claimant to the papacy continued in Avignon for a few more years.

Directions – Questions 11-16: For each blank select one entry from the corresponding column of choices. Fill all blanks in the way that best completes the text.

11. He was modest in his (i) _____ and did not (ii) _____ a promotion to higher levels of responsibility at work.

Blank (i)
a. dreams
b. habits
c. ambition

Blank (ii)
d. necessitate
e. pursue
f. refuse

12. History did not feel (i) _____ to her. Seeking a more (ii) _____ major she decided to study economics.

Blank (i)
a. esoteric
b. relevant
c. important

Blank (ii)
d. topical
e. sycophantic
f. trivial

13. She considered herself to be _____ and liked to predict events before they occurred.

a. precocious
b. prescient
c. predated
d. prefatory
e. preferential

14. Elijah noticed that the crowd had (i) _____ and it was possible once again to walk around the museum (ii) _____.

Blank (i)
a. startled
b. dispersed
c. intensified

Blank (ii)
d. with ease
e. convincingly
f. on foot

15. In the same novel, Josephine Tey suggested that the truth about events in history becomes (i) _____ by perception and the passing of time when she indicated that incidences such as the Boston Massacre and the Tonypandy Riots in Wales did not occur as (ii) _____.

Blank (i)
a. amalgamated
b. obscured
c. featured

Blank (ii)
d. widely inspected
e. generally accepted
f. fully appreciated

16. Although the history of the Knights Templar is filled with (i) _____ and intrigue, the founding of the order is far from mysterious or even dubious. In the year 1119, French Crusader Hugues de Payens created an order, to be known as the Knights Templar, to protect pilgrims to the Holy Land. Over the years the Knights Templar grew in wealth and (ii) _____ powerful connections with both church and state. Eventually, the Templars faced persecution for their acquired privilege, and in the 14th century the order was largely disbanded and lost power. Many since then have claimed a relationship between the modern-day Masons and the Templars of old, due to the Mason habit of (iii) _____ Templar imagery, but the idea is heavily rejected among authorities of both groups.

Blank (i)	Blank (ii)	Blank (iii)
a. deceit	d. forged	g. adopting
b. symbolism	e. manipulated	h. alienating
c. enigma	f. severed	i. approving

Directions – Questions 17-20: Select the *two* answer choices that, when used to complete the sentence, fit the meaning of the sentence as a whole *and* produce completed sentences that are alike in meaning.

---

17. When the victim did not prove as _____ as expected, the blackmailer decided to resort to a more intense method of motivation.

    a. sycophantic
    b. patronizing
    c. indolent
    d. tractable
    e. sardonic
    f. amenable

18. The industrious third grade teacher was given a classroom full of _____ students, but by the end of the year they all received awards for good behavior.

    a. flagrant
    b. obstreperous
    c. boorish
    d. officious
    e. unruly
    f. sagacious

19. Sugar tends to weaken the immune system and will only _____ a problem, so patients recovering from illness are advised to stay away from sweets until fully recovered.

    a. belie
    b. ratify
    c. compound
    d. substantiate
    e. exacerbate
    f. opine

20. While the clergyman was extremely popular in the parish, the allegations of inappropriate behavior forced the leadership to _____ him of his position and send him to a purely administrative job.

    a. deliberate
    b. divest
    c. demolish
    d. decimate
    e. disconnect
    f. dispossess

Section 5: Quantitative Reasoning

Time – 40 minutes

QUANTITATIVE COMPARISON

Directions: Compare Quantity A and Quantity B, using additional information centered above the two quantities if such information is given, and select one of the following four answer choices:

1.

$$10^x = 10\ 000\ 000\ 000$$

Quantity A	**Quantity B**
x	12

a. Quantity A is greater
b. Quantity B is greater
c. The two quantities are equal
d. The relationship cannot be determined from the information given

2.

Line A is represented by the following equation:

$$10y + 20x = 50$$

Quantity A	**Quantity B**
The y-intercept of Line A	The slope of line A

a. Quantity A is greater
b. Quantity B is greater
c. The two quantities are equal
d. The relationship cannot be determined from the information given

3.

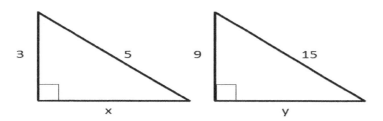

Figure is not drawn to scale

Quantity A	**Quantity B**
$\dfrac{y}{x}$	3

a. Quantity A is greater
b. Quantity B is greater
c. The two quantities are equal
d. The relationship cannot be determined from the information given

4. The following table displays the income Jane's business earned and the percentage of that income she paid in taxes for the first half of the year.

Month	Income earned ($)	Percentage paid in taxes (%)
January	10,000	10
February	50,000	30
March	20,000	20
April	10,000	10
May	30,000	20
June	90,000	40

Quantity A	**Quantity B**
The average of the income tax Jane paid	22% of Jane's average income

    a.   Quantity A is greater
    b.   Quantity B is greater
    c.   The two quantities are equal
    d.   The relationship cannot be determined from the information given

MULTIPLE-CHOICE – SELECT ONLY ONE ANSWER CHOICE

5. If q is the smallest composite number greater than 2 and p is the smallest prime number less than 10, what is $\frac{p}{q}$?

    a.   0.5
    b.   1
    c.   2
    d.   4

Question 6 pertains to the following:

$$\frac{1}{25^n} > 1$$

6. For which value of n is the above statement true?

    a. $n = 1$
    b. $n = \sqrt{2}$
    c. $n = \frac{1}{2}$
    d. $n = -\frac{1}{2}$

Questions 7 – 9 pertain to the following diagram:

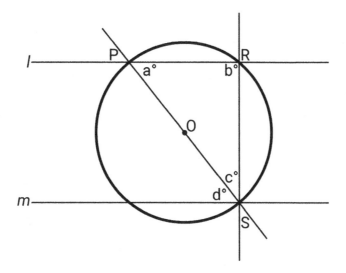

Figure **NOT** drawn to scale

Lines *l* and *m* are parallel. O is the center of the circle. The measure of angle d is 45°. The length of line RS is $\frac{\sqrt{2}}{2}$. Line RS forms a right angle with line *m*.

7. What is the measure of angle a?

    a. 30°
    b. 45°
    c. 60°
    d. 90°

8. What is the length of line PR?

    a. $\frac{\sqrt{2}}{2}$
    b. $\sqrt{2}$
    c. $2\sqrt{2}$
    d. 1

9. What is the diameter of circle O?

    a. 1
    b. $1\sqrt{2}$
    c. $2\sqrt{2}$
    d. $\frac{\sqrt{2}}{2}$

MULTIPLE-CHOICE – SELECT ONE OR MORE ANSWER CHOICES

Directions: If the question specifies how many answer choices to select, select exactly that number of choices. If the question does not specify how many answer choices to select, select all that apply.

- The correct answer may be just one of the choices or may be as many as all of the choices
- No credit is given unless you select all of the correct choices and no others

10. Which two lines are parallel?

    a. $y - 4x - 3 = 0$
    b. $y - 2x - 3 = 0$
    c. $4y - 12x - 16 = 0$
    d. $3y - 9x + 18 = 0$

Question 11 pertains to the following equation:

$$\sqrt{x^2 + y^2} = 5$$

$$x^2 - y^2 = -7$$

11. If x and y satisfy the above system of equations, then which of the following are possible values for $x^3 + y^3$?

    a. 21
    b. 25
    c. 37
    d. 91

12. A square has vertices at the following four points: (0,0), (P,0), (0,P), and (P,P). Which of the following answers necessarily represent the perimeter of the square?

    a. P^2
    b. $P + P + P + P$
    c. $(P)(P)$
    d. $4P$

Questions 13 – 15 pertain to the following diagram:

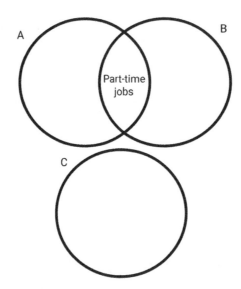

Figure **NOT** drawn to scale

Circle A represents students who major in liberal arts at a certain university. Circle B represents students who major in the life sciences at that university, and circle C represents engineering majors at the same university.

13. What does $A \cup B$ represent?

    a. Only the subset of liberal arts and life science double-majors
    b. All liberal arts and life science students
    c. Only liberal arts students
    d. Only life science students

14. What does $A \cap B$ represent?

    a. The subset of liberal arts and life science double-majors
    b. All liberal arts and life science students
    c. Only liberal arts students
    d. Only life science students

15. Why is circle C a disjoint set? Select all correct answers.

    a. No engineering students are also liberal arts majors
    b. No engineering students are also life science majors
    c. No engineering students have part-time jobs
    d. A small subset of engineering students double majored in liberal arts or life sciences

NUMERIC ENTRY

Directions:

Enter your answer as an integer or a decimal if there is a single answer box OR as a fraction if there are two separate boxes—one for the numerator and one for the denominator.

Equivalent forms of the correct answer, such as 2.5 and 2.50, are all correct. Fractions do not need to be reduced to lowest terms, though you may need to reduce your fraction to fit in the boxes.

Enter the exact answer unless the question asks you to round your answer.

Questions 16 – 20 pertain to the following:

John and Jane bought a house for $300,000. They put 20% down and took on a 30 year mortgage for the balance. The following graph represents the amount they paid towards the principal, interest, and taxes throughout the life of the loan. Use this information to answer questions 16 – 20.

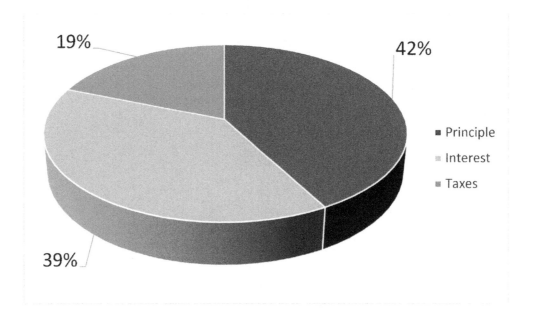

Figure: Breakdown of mortgage payments

16. What was the original amount of the loan?

17. What is the total amount John and Jane will pay the bank at the end of their 30-year mortgage? Round your answer to the nearest dollar.

18. By the end of their 30-year mortgage, what percentage of the original loan amount did they pay in interest? Round your answer to the nearest tenth of a percent.

19. What was their average annual interest rate? Round your answer to the nearest tenth of a percent.

20. How much did they pay in taxes by the end of the 30-year mortgage? Round your answer to the nearest dollar.

Section 6: Quantitative Reasoning

Time – 40 minutes

QUANTITATIVE COMPARISON

Directions: Compare Quantity A and Quantity B, using additional information centered above the two quantities if such information is given, and select one of the following four answer choices:

1.

$$A\Psi B = (AB)^2 + (A + B)^2$$

Quantity A	**Quantity B**
$2\Psi5$	150

a. Quantity A is greater
b. Quantity B is greater
c. The two quantities are equal
d. The relationship cannot be determined from the information given

2. The electrical engineering department at a certain graduate school in the United States (US) has a total of 36 students. The department has twice as many male students as female students and three times as many international students as students who are US citizens.

Quantity A	**Quantity B**
The number of students who are US citizens	The number of female students

a. Quantity A is greater
b. Quantity B is greater
c. The two quantities are equal
d. The relationship cannot be determined from the information given

3.

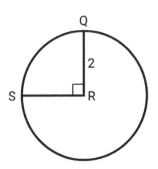

R is the center of the circle above:
Figure NOT drawn to scale

Quantity A	**Quantity B**
Half the circumference of the circle	The area of triangle QRS

a. Quantity A is greater
b. Quantity B is greater
c. The two quantities are equal
d. The relationship cannot be determined from the information given

298

4. The graph below shows the gross domestic product (GDP) in trillions of US dollars for four countries between 2000 and 2008.

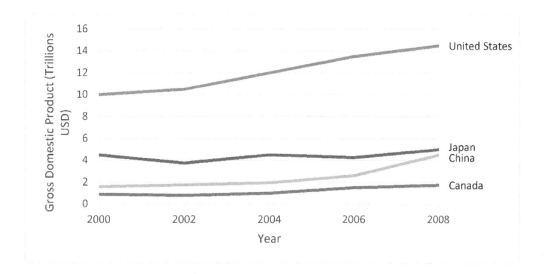

Quantity A
The combined GDP of Japan, China, and Canada in 2008

Quantity B
The GDP of the US in 2008

a. Quantity A is greater
b. Quantity B is greater
c. The two quantities are equal
d. The relationship cannot be determined from the information given

MULTIPLE-CHOICE – SELECT ONLY ONE ANSWER CHOICE

5. The graduating class at a certain university has 100 students. Within that class, 60% of the students are male. 30% of the class will attend graduate school in computer science in the fall. Of the students who will attend graduate school in computer science, the ratio of males to females is 2:1. What percentage of the female students in the graduating class will attend graduate school in computer science?

a. 10%
b. 20%
c. 25%
d. 75%

Questions 6 pertains to the following equation:

The equation for Line Q is $5y - 100x - 75 = 0$.

6. **Which line below has a slope that is twice the slope of Line Q?**

a. Line A: $y - 20x - 15 = 0$
b. Line B: $y - 40x - 15 = 0$
c. Line C: $2y - 40x - 30 = 0$
d. Line D: $2y - 20x - 15 = 0$

Questions 7 – 10 pertain to the following table:

Table: May 2010 occupational wage estimates for California

Occupational category	Median hourly wage (US dollars)	Mean hourly wage (US dollars)	Mean annual wage (US dollars)
Management	50.67	57.44	119,480
Legal	47.22	57.27	119,120
Computers and mathematics	40.66	42.30	87,980
Education, training, and library	25.18	27.89	58,010
Food preparation and related services	9.28	10.57	21,990

7. If there were only four managers in the state of California, which list below could represent their hourly wages?

   a. $50.67, $50.67, $50.67, $50.67
   b. $57.44, $57.44, $57.44, $57.44
   c. $48.25, $50.57, $50.77, $80.18
   d. $50.67, $50.67, $57.44, $57.44

8. Which of these is the smallest percentage that the mean wage would have to increase for those who work in computers and mathematics to earn more on average annually than those who work in management?

   a. 32%
   b. 33%
   c. 35%
   d. 36%

9. Assume a short order cook earns the mean hourly wage for his standard shift and when working overtime. How many hours of weekly overtime must he work to earn approximately the mean annual salary of a librarian? The standard work schedule is 40 hours per week, 52 weeks per year.

   a. 106
   b. 66
   c. 46
   d. 40

10. A junior associate lawyer at a top law firm currently earns the mean annual income for working 40 hours per week, 52 weeks per year. In addition to her annual salary, she also earns the mean hourly wage for each hour of the ten overtime hours she averages weekly. She was recently offered a promotion to senior associate, a position that comes with a 25% increase in annual salary but which offers no overtime compensation. Considering that senior associates typically work 55 hours per week, would the promotion be to the lawyer's financial advantage?

   a. Yes
   b. No
   c. Not enough information

MULTIPLE-CHOICE – SELECT ONE OR MORE ANSWER CHOICES

If the question specifies how many answer choices to select, select exactly that number of choices.

If the question does not specify how many answer choices to select, select all that apply.

- The correct answer may be just one of the choices or may be as many as all of the choices.
- No credit is given unless you select all of the correct choices and no others.

11. Which two numbers have a product of A^{11} and a possible quotient of A^7?

   a. A^2
   b. A^3
   c. A^6
   d. A^9

Questions 12 – 13 pertain to the following figure:

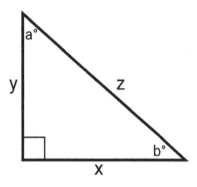

Figure **NOT** drawn to scale

12. If z = 3, indicate all answers that could be the length of x.

   a. 1
   b. 2
   c. 3
   d. 4

13. If $\frac{b}{a} = 2$ and x = 1, then what are possible values for z?

   a. 1
   b. 2
   c. 3
   d. 4

14. Jack, Jill, and John are siblings. Jack is twice as old as Jill and half as old as John. If the ages of all three siblings are contained within the answer choices, how old could Jill be?

   a. 2
   b. 4
   c. 8
   d. 16

15. A triangle has vertices at points (0,0), (0,3), and (4,0). Which of the following are lengths of the triangle's sides?

    a. 2
    b. 3
    c. 5
    d. 7

NUMERIC ENTRY

Directions:

Enter your answer as an integer or a decimal if there is a single answer box OR as a fraction if there are two separate boxes—one for the numerator and one for the denominator.

Equivalent forms of the correct answer, such as 2.5 and 2.50, are all correct. Fractions do not need to be reduced to lowest terms, though you may need to reduce your fraction to fit in the boxes.

Enter the exact answer unless the question asks you to round your answer.

Questions 16 – 20 pertain to the following figure:

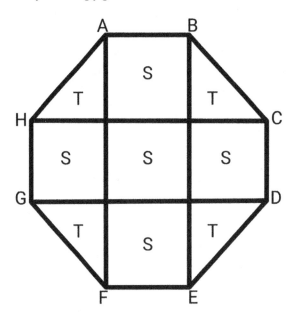

Figure **NOT** drawn to scale

Octagon ABCDEFGH contains five squares (S) and four triangles (T). The length of side AB is 6.

16. What is the sum of the areas the five squares S?

17. What is the length of side BC? Round your answer to nearest tenth.

18. What is the area of a single triangle T?

19. What is the perimeter of octagon ABCDEFGH? Round your answer to nearest tenth.

20. What is the area of octagon ABCDEFGH?

Answer Key and Explanations for Test #1

Section 3: Verbal Reasoning

1. C: In the first sentence, the author notes the following: "It might be surprising to discover that Europe's first republic pre-dated the turn of the 11th century, long before Europe would see the rise of another such system." This statement clearly indicates that Iceland's republic came well before another in Europe, so indeed it was "many years" before another republic emerged in Europe. The author of the passage mentions a monarchy in Norway and Denmark, but this mention alone is not enough to assume that monarchy was the more common system–based only on the information in the passage. The information in answer choices B and D focuses solely on the republic in Iceland, and this counters the question with its focus on the development of republics in Europe. Additionally, the author mentions that Iceland is currently a republic, but this mention alone is not enough to comment on modern republics in Europe or on the level of "sophistication" that defines them.

2. C: The last two statements in the passage state the following: "This system, and Iceland's identity as a republic, remained in place until 1262, when the decision of the Althing agreed to the Old Covenant and placed Iceland under the authority of the king of Norway. Iceland would not become a self-governing republic again until 1944, when the people of Iceland voted to end their political relationship with the kingdom of Denmark." As Norway and Denmark are definitely different nations, the author fails to explain how (and when) Iceland came to be part of Denmark; the lack of information creates confusion for the reader. Answers choice A and B contain information that, while potentially interesting, offer nothing of substantial value to the topic of the passage. It is not necessary to know when Iceland converted to Christianity, and there is little use in digging deeper to find out why settlers left Norway and went to Iceland in the first place.

3. B: It stands to reason that if the 13th century agreement became known as the Old Covenant, there must have been a later covenant to follow. However, the question specifically asks for implication of mentioning the Althing in relation to the Old Covenant, so the information about a later covenant ultimately is irrelevant to the question. At the same time, the mention of the Althing indicates that the freemen of Iceland, who did have a voice in their government, were involved in the decision in some fashion. Answer choice C creates the potential for a correct option, but it contains information that cannot be inferred clearly from the passage: the free men of Iceland might have had some say in the decision of the Old Covenant, but it is impossible to determine from the passage if they ultimately resisted the union.

4. D: The Althing was largely a legislative body with a degree of judicial authority. The role of the Lawspeaker was to oversee the Althing, read the laws, moderate disputes, and oversee the assembly. This role is ultimately similar to the role of the Speaker of the House within the U.S. House of Representatives, who oversees the activities of the House and moderates when necessary. The Lawspeaker had a much lesser role than that of the President or of a Lieutenant Governor (who acts in a role similar to the Vice President, but within a state instead of at the federal level). The President of the Senate oversees the Senate and casts the occasional tie-breaking vote but has nowhere near the same presence or the role as the Speaker of the House. The Secretary of State is largely a bureaucratic position with political responsibilities, but it does not offer a comparative position to the Lawspeaker.

5. A: The author notes that the purpose of the Althing was "to discuss and determine legal issues." In addition, the first sentence points out that the Althing "represented an important development in making the people of a nation an active part of the system that governed them." This statement clearly matches the information in answer choice A, that the Althing's purpose was to "determine the laws of Iceland and to provide the free men with a role in their government." While the Althing might have contributed to creating a stable government in Iceland, that is not its purpose as noted in the passage. The author points out that the Althing called together the leaders from each community, but nothing in the passage suggests that the Althing developed leaders or attempted to make the communities self-governing. Additionally, the author of the passage says nothing about uniting the citizenry against foreign powers. And while it might be inferred that the Althing contributed to developing consistent application of the laws, this answer choice does not offer as good a summary as the information in answer choice A.

6. E: Early in the passage, the author says, "Most grains contain phytic acid, which can prevent proper mineral absorption. For instance, phytic acid can block the body's ability to absorb iron from foods and thus raise the potential over time for anemia." This statement matches the information in answer choice E. The author says nothing about phytic acid binding with the minerals; instead, the author explains that phytic acid blocks mineral absorption. The author does not discuss the amount of phytic acid within other foods; as the passage only discusses phytic acid within grains, there is no way to determine if the amount in grains is higher than in other foods (or if phytic acid is found in other foods at all). The passage mentions both phytic acid and gluten, and the author points out that reducing the phytic acid can make glutinous grains easier to digest for those persons with gluten-intolerance; but this assertion is not enough to make the leap that phytic acid attaches itself to gluten. Finally, the passage makes no claim about phytic acid attacking the body's digestive system; rather, it seems that the harm is more passive.

7. A, C: The author provides a two-part reason for soaking grains: soaking the grains reduces the amount of phytic acid within them and thus makes them easier for the body to digest. The author makes no mention about whether or not soaking grains removes the gluten, so answer choice B cannot be a correct option.

8. B: Food science is mentioned without definition within the passage, but the information provided about phytic acid and the comments from food scientists regarding the soaking of grains provide enough detail for inference. Based on the information in the passage, it can safely be said that a food scientist considers the chemicals in food and analyzes the properties of those chemicals. The passage does not offer enough information to indicate that food science is related solely to food preparation, particularly since phytic acid is an ingredient in grains prior to their preparation. The passage is based primarily on a chemical within grains, but the claim that food science is limited entirely to grains is too narrow. If this were the case, the field would likely be called grain science, instead of food science. The passage mentions people preparing their grains at home, but it mentions nothing about the commercial preparation of food, so it cannot be said that food science is limited to domestic food preparation. The author makes no mention of the use of modern technology, so answer choice D cannot be inferred from the passage.

9. B: The Spanish cannot attack a colony if they are unaware of its location. Historical documents indicating that the Spanish government had not yet discovered the location of Roanoke would certainly lend credence to the claims of historians "who argue conflicting evidence" regarding the theory of Spanish attack. Colonies can be attacked by more ways than just gunfire, so the idea that archeologists cannot find ammunition represents weak evidence against a Spanish attack. Answer choice C offers an option that does more to support the idea of Spanish attack rather than offering evidence to conflict with it. Answer choice D combines ideas in the paragraph but also confuses them; the author notes that Chief Powhatan "claimed responsibility for their deaths, because the colonists allied themselves with a tribe that did not support him." It makes little sense then for him to claim to have killed the Roanoke colonists if he was working to forge a treaty that would protect them. The author of the passage clearly negates the theory about a cannibal attack, so answer choice E cannot be correct.

10. D: The first sentence of the passage provides a strong clue about the substance of the passage: "The mystery of Roanoke Colony has never been solved to any satisfaction, although a number of theories have arisen over the years." In other words, there are many theories about what happened at Roanoke Colony, but not enough evidence exists to prove the validity of any of them. The author mentions the information in answer choice A as one of the theories but does not claim it as the best or most likely. The information in the passage would suggest a measure of disagreement among historians, but "complete disagreement" cannot be inferred; furthermore, this hardly can be described as the main point of the passage. Answer choice C offers an alternative not provided, or implied, within the passage and as a result cannot represent a summary of the main point. Answer choice E takes details from the passage and remixes them to some extent, but this information cannot be inferred and clearly is not the main point of the passage.

11. B, F: The correct answer is choice B (address) and choice F (intricacies).

12. A, D: The correct answer is choice A (fabricated) and choice D (refute).

13. C: Answers (A) and (E) are incorrect because they suggest the disarray was minor; the opposite of the meaning suggested by the rest of the sentence. Answers (B) and (D) are incorrect because they offer information about the disarray that is not relevant to the rest of the sentence.

14. B, F: The correct answer is choice B (boisterous) and choice F (overwhelm).

15. B, D, H: The tone of the passage is one of contrast, primarily the contrast in the friendship between the young Prince Hal and the man who becomes King Henry V. The first part of the sentence should indicate the strength of the friendship, while the second part should indicate both Falstaff's failure to grow up as Hal does and the subsequent results of Falstaff's failure. Answer choice A (preferred) indicates an option for the first blank, but it does not provide the sense of importance about the relationship. Falstaff's friendship was not just preferred; rather, it was cherished. The second blank has to indicate the disparity between Falstaff and Hal as the latter grows into King Henry, and the best contrast to the phrase "youthful antics" is to describe the new king as "maturing." Finally, the last blank has to suggest that the differences between them have led to a breach in friendship. Nothing in the passage suggests that Hal/Henry tries to reform his friend, and as a result the passage seems to imply that the former friendship cannot be restored.

Thus, the correct answers are choice B (cherished), choice D (maturing), and choice H (renounce).

16. A, E, I: Determining the correct answers to question 2 requires reading the entire passage and appreciating all of its suggestions before attempting to fill in any of the blanks. For the first blank, two answer choices can be eliminated immediately. Answer choice B (utterly detestable) is largely an opinion statement with no support within the passage, while answer choice C faces contrast from the later portions of the passage. (If King Richard III is not actually guilty of the crime, then he can hardly be described as "consistently suspicious.") He can, however, be described as "popularly malevolent," if his guilt has always been presumed among the general population. For the second blank, the best option will indicate that a theory has been proposed, and the closest word to this is "propounded." What is more, neither of the other answer choices makes any sense. Finally, the third blank should indicate correctly that King Richard III's successor King Henry VII went back in time, so to speak, to give the impression that his predecessor committed the crime. The best answer choice for this blank is "retrospectively." No doubt Henry also did these things eagerly and intentionally, but the former word is impossible to determine within the context of the sentence, and the second word feels redundant without adding anything to the sentence.

Thus, the correct answers are choice A (popularly malevolent), choice E (propounded), and choice I (retrospectively).

17. B, E: The sentence implies that the student is unprepared for the information in the course; a prerequisite is a course required or encouraged before another course is taken. A prerequisite tends to offer the information a student needs to be prepared for increasingly complex information in the course that follows. This would suggest that, without the information, the student does not know how to appreciate the shades of meaning within the poetry.

Thus, the correct answer choices are choice B (nuance) and choice E (subtlety). The words *counterfeit*, *presumption*, and *pariah* make little sense within the context of the sentence. The word *resonance* can be applied to poetry, but it does not fit the suggestion that the student lacks the necessary background to understand the complexity of the information being presented.

18. A, F: If the couple plans to live within a budget, then likely the couple plans to reduce any unnecessary spending and focus only on their basic needs. The implication is that extra spending–spending that is excessive or not essential to their absolute requirements–will end. This indicates that they are eliminating superfluous or irrelevant expenditures.

Thus, the correct answer choices are choice A (superfluous) and choice F (irrelevant). Something that is indispensable is necessary, so answer choice B expresses the very opposite of the implied meaning. The word *unequivocal* means definite, so this word does not fit the meaning of the sentence. Additionally, the words *indifferent* and *paramount* offer little to the meaning of the sentence.

19. C, D: The sentence seems to suggest that the vehicle manufacturer had advertised a very large trunk, but the reality proved to be the opposite of this claim. Additionally, the opening word *although* provides a sense of contrast between the small trunk space and the expectation of something larger. The correct answer choice options will indicate great size or a large amount of space. As a result, the only possible correct answers are *capacious* and *commodious*.

Thus, the correct answers are choice C (capacious) and choice D (commodious). Something ostentatious is flamboyant or showy, and while such words can describe some vehicles, these words hardly offer a solid contrast to the reality of the trunk size. The words *inadvertent*, *palatable*, and *analogous* make no sense in the context of the sentence or in contrast to the small size of the trunk.

20. B, D: The context of the sentence indicates that the woman represents the man's perfect image of beauty. There is a further indication of contrast between this image he has carried in his head and the reality of the changes in her over the years. As a result, the answers must present her as his highest ideal from years before. She is not merely a pretty girl he remembers; instead, she represents the highest standard of beauty upon which all others are judged.

Thus, the correct answers are choice B (exemplar) and choice D (archetype). The word *conjecture*, meaning guess, makes no sense in the context of the sentence. The word *precedent* suggests a previously established example. While she is the precedent for his standard, she is more of a

paradigm than a mere precedent. The words *malefactor* and *dilettante* have no place in the sentence.

Section 4: Verbal Reasoning

1. D: In the first paragraph, the author notes that the expression *et filioque* "was widely rebuked by the Eastern churches as lacking theological foundation." This statement corresponds with the answer choice claiming that the Eastern Church believed that the expression altered the acknowledged understanding of scripture and was thus unacceptable to them. Answer choice A, claiming that the church in the East rejected the inclusion of a Latin phrase has no justification in the passage, because the author makes no comment about standard liturgical languages among the different churches. Answer choice B is irrelevant, because it discusses the request by the pope to be named supreme head of the Church, instead of the *et filioque* dispute. Answer choice C includes information that cannot be inferred from the passage; there is not enough detail in the passage to claim that the addition of *et filioque* reflected theological understanding of the day. Answer choice E simply summarizes the issue as explained in the first paragraph but does not effectively explain *why*.

2. B, C: In the second paragraph, the author notes the following: "The Eastern Orthodox Church, which operated under a recognizably fallible patriarch and a more regional system of bishops, rejected this outright." This statement suggests two things. First, the church in the East operated under its own (long-accepted) traditions, with the move by the pope thus placing the church in the East under the church in the West and undermining these traditions. Additionally, it implies that the church in the East, which believed its primary leader (the patriarch) to be fallible, would not be able to acknowledge infallibility in the pope. The author of the passage says nothing about a move by the patriarch to be named supreme head; furthermore, this actually takes away from the statement about the traditions in the East, so it cannot be correct.

3. A, B: The author makes the following statements in the second paragraph: "The church was the center of life and governed most aspects of it. Kings and emperors turned to the church for guidance. They ruled with the support of the church, and the church had only to remove that support to create a foundational weakness in the ruler's power." Of the answer choices, two can be derived from this statement. On the one hand, the church offered the people of medieval Europe guidance for everyday life. On the other hand, the church gave moral direction to leaders and influenced their decisions. The author does suggest that the church's influence could be extended to making or breaking kings, but there is not enough information in the passage to make the claim that the church governed *through* leaders. (In many cases, this statement was more or less true, but the passage does not go this far, so answer choice C cannot be correct.)

4. C: The author states, "The Eastern Orthodox Church, which operated under a recognizably fallible patriarch and a more regional system of bishops, rejected this outright. In breaking communion with the West, the East also broke the sense of accountability that each church had traditionally held toward the other." This statement suggests that the communion between the churches offered a degree of accountability, even though the pope was seen as infallible in the West. (The fact that he was not seen this way in the East would necessarily undermine the idea to some degree and maintain an ongoing sense of accountability between the churches.) When the pope asked that the East accept him as the infallible head of the church, the accountability that head developed over the centuries would more or less vanish, and the church in the East would find itself operating under the church in the West instead of working alongside it. Answer choice A might have truth in it, particularly since the author does note that the Eastern Church did not recognize infallibility in its patriarch, but this is not as strong an answer choice as choice C. It takes a more simplistic look at the issue but fails to acknowledge the broader implication of accepting infallibility in the pope. Similarly, answer choice B likely is true, but it fails to consider the larger issue of accountability that the author mentions clearly in the passage. The question that should follow answer choice B is *why* the East might object to this, and the correct answer choice will, not surprisingly, answer questions instead of raise them. Answer choice D offers details not contained within the passage, so it cannot be correct. (This is in fact true: the patriarch excommunicated the pope, and the pope returned the favor. But the author does not mention this, so the information is irrelevant as an answer choice.) Answer choice E also brings up information not within the passage; the author does not indicate in any place that the churches defined "fallible/infallible" a certain way, so this answer choice cannot be correct.

5. A: The first sentence of the first paragraph reads as follows: "The divide between the Christian churches of the East and those of the West went beyond a mere theological break and had broad social, political, and cultural effects." This statement summarizes the overall thrust of the passage, and answer choice A offers a clear restatement of this. Answer choice B summarizes the last sentence of the paragraph but fails to include the information about the broader effects of the Great Schism (with regards to social, political, and cultural effects). Answer choice C offers a more skeletal version of answer choice A, but it is not as strong an option and feels vague in focus. It also focuses only on the cultural differences and fails to take into account the social and political effects that the author mentions. Answer choice D infers information not necessarily stated in the passage; the author does not claim that the Great Schism was inevitable, so it is impossible to read this as a summary of the passage. Additionally, answer choice E mentions excommunication, which the author does not mention, so it too fails as a solid summary of the passage.

6. A: The author notes within the passage that scientists have questioned the theory of greenhouse gas emissions as contributing to global warming on two counts: (1) periods of warming might be part of natural temperature cycles on the earth, and (2) scientists cannot agree if humans can produce enough greenhouse gases to exert such a massive effect on global temperature. The first of these options is not among the answer choices; the second is, so that is the only correct answer choice. Answer choice B is connected to the idea of a period of global warming, but it infers too much with the claim that scientists believe this; in fact, the author only notes that scientists have pointed out the possibility. The author says nothing about scientists believing that the causes of global climate change are too complex for human involvement, so answer choice C cannot be correct.

7. C: Question 20 asks for the "purpose" of the parenthetical comment in the passage. Taken in context, there really is just one purpose: to explain that periods of widespread climate change do occur and have occurred in earth's history. The mention of heavy clothing and gloves in the Elizabethan period is more of a point of interest but in reality, has little to do with the main point of the passage; it certainly does not explain the purpose of the parenthetical comment within the passage. The author does not go so far as to say that the information about "mini ice ages" conflicts with the theory espoused by scientific journals. It might, but it also might be that the scientific journals have taken this into account. Without further information, answer choice B cannot describe the purpose of the parenthetical comment.

8. C: The final sentence of the passage states the following: "These doubts aside, the consensus among scientific journals supports the theory of global warming from greenhouse gas emissions." In other words, for now the official statement among scientific journals accepts the theory of global warming as a result of greenhouse gas emissions. Science is an evolving field, and scientists are always studying data and offering updates where appropriate. It is not surprising that some scientists have questions about this official theory, but it is also not surprising that scientific journals currently present the theory as official. Until solid evidence suggests otherwise, the official theory will hold. Answer choice A indicates part of the information in the passage, but it leans too far in inferring details from the author. The author suggests scientists continue to study this matter; the author says nothing about an increasing number doubting the official theory. The author says nowhere that scientific journals refuse to acknowledge the questions that scientists have, so answer choice B also infers too much. The final sentence indicates that scientific journals, for now, are confident about their claims. This might indicate that the authors of these journals believe in strong evidence to support the official theory and a lack of evidence to support alternative theories. The problem with this statement, however, is its inference based on the final sentence, rather than a summary of the final sentence. So, answer choice D is not a good option. Nowhere in the passage does the author mention political policy, least of all in the final sentence, so answer choice E cannot be correct.

9. B: The second sentence of the passage notes the following: "Unlike the earlier schism, though, this Western Schism resulted from political disputes among the factions within the church." This statement clearly indicates that the primary difference was the result of internal conflict and political disagreements. The author mentions that the church moved from Rome to Avignon due to a "period of crisis." This is not part of the author's statement about the differences between the East-West split and the Western Schism, however. Additionally, the author mentions that the cardinals viewed their selection of Pope Urban VI as a bad idea, but this falls under the idea of internal conflict and even political disagreements. Furthermore, it is an incidental part of the larger problem(s) that arose. The question is looking for information about the larger problem(s)–as this is what distinguishes the two splits–so answer choice C is too narrow in focus.

10. E: The final sentence reads as follows: "Order returned with the election of Pope Martin V in 1417, although Avignon continued a feeble resistance until 1429." This statement indicates that the appointment of Pope Martin V was widely accepted in Europe and not disputed among the cardinals, but that Avignon resisted by retaining a different claimant until 1429. Answer choice A explains the first part of the sentence but fails to explain the second part about the "feeble resistance" in Avignon. Answer choice B attempts to reconcile what appears an inconsistency in the passage. But the information in the passage would indicate that historians correctly recognize that the Western Schism ended in 1417, even though Avignon continued to do its own thing for a few years. Apparently, the appointment of Pope Martin V was enough to provide an acceptable conclusion to the split for most parties involved. The author makes no attempt to explain *why* Pope Martin V was generally acceptable, and given that Avignon did continue to resist for a few more years it would stand to reason that he did not have connections here. Answer choice D reiterates information from the passage but fails entirely to answer the question.

11 C, E: The correct answer is choice C (ambition) and choice E (pursue).

12. B, D: The correct answer is choice B (relevant) and choice D (topical).

13. B: The correct answer is (B) prescient, which means able to anticipate the course of events. Choice (A) means early in development and is incorrect. Choice (C) means preceding in time and is incorrect. Choice (D) means related to a preface or located in front and is incorrect. Choice (E) means showing preference and is incorrect.

14. B, D: The correct answer is choice B (dispersed) and choice D (with ease).

15. B, E: The first blank of this sentence should indicate the changes that can occur with the understanding of events in history. The author of the passage mentions the ideas of "perception" and "passage of time," both of which suggest that the truth can be difficult (or even impossible) to see clearly. The best option, then, is the word "obscured." It is worth mentioning that neither answer choice A nor answer choice C makes much sense in the context. For the second blank, the best answer choice will suggest the perception noted in the first part of the sentence, that is, the perception of the way that events occurred. This perception correctly could be described as "generally accepted." The phrase "fully appreciated" has potential, but it does not quite work with the statement about truth being obscured; something can hardly be appreciated in full if the information about it is not entirely correct. The phrase "widely inspected," on the other hand, offers nothing of value to the sentence and can be eliminated immediately.

Thus, the correct answers are choice B (obscured) and choice E (generally accepted).

16. C, D, G: Although the test-taker would be well advised to read the entire passage before attempting to fill in the blank, this question does not necessarily require such an action. The sentence can be completed blank by blank, without any of the meaning being lost. In the first blank, it is essential to sense the contrast between the first part of the sentence and the second. The word in the blank is set alongside the word "intrigue" and then contrasted with the words "mysterious or even dubious." Since the nature of intrigue tends to be questionable (and thus dubious), this would suggest that the first blank should encapsulate the idea of mystery. The best option then is "enigma." The word "deceit" functions as a synonym for "intrigue" and is thus redundant. The word "symbolism" offers nothing to the contrast. For the second blank, it is necessary to decide which verb makes the most sense in explaining the Templars and their connections. Based on the context, the Templars expanded in both wealth and connections, so the verb should be positive in this sense. The best choice, therefore, is "forged." There is not enough information in the passage to suggest–in this specific case–that the Templars "manipulated" connections (nor does this make a great deal of sense in the context), and the word "severed" suggests exactly the opposite of what is implied in the sentence. The final blank should offer some explanation for why a connection has been assumed between Masons and Templars. It makes no sense for Masons to "alienate" imagery, and there is not enough in the idea of "approving" it to justify this answer choice. The best option then is "adopting." The use of Templar imagery adopted into Masonic ritual would certainly lead some people to believe in a potential connection.

Thus, the correct answers are choice C (enigma), choice D (forged), and choice G (adopting).

17. D, F: The sentence suggests that the blackmailer had expected the victim to be easier to work with and more malleable to his plans. There is a hint of contrast between the expectations and the reality, so the correct answer(s) will indicate the prospect of a pliable victim and the result of someone who requires more encouragement from the blackmailer.

Thus, the correct answers are choice D (tractable) and choice F (amenable). The word *sycophantic* indicates a fawning submissiveness that is not entirely implied in the relationship between a blackmailer and the victim. It makes a remote option and not a very good one. The word *patronizing*, with its implication of demeaning behavior, suggests more of the blackmailer's role than the victim's. The word *indolent* indicates laziness, and while a lazy person often needs motivation it is difficult to apply this to the context of the sentence–with the blackmailer's victim being more stubborn against the demands than purely lazy in responding to them. The word *sardonic* makes no sense in the context of the sentence.

18. B, E: The correct answer choices will reflect the contrast between the beginning of the school year and the end of the school year, between the behavior of the children at the beginning of the year and the behavior of the children at the end of the year. Since the sentence indicates that the students all received awards for good behavior at the end of the school year, it stands to reason that their behavior was significantly worse when the school year began. Additionally, the teacher is described as being industrious, or hard-working and productive, so this indicates effort and results on her part.

Thus, the correct answers are choice B (obstreperous) and choice E (unruly). These words indicate a very challenging group of children that required the industrious teacher to roll up her sleeves and work hard. The word *flagrant* might describe the unruly nature of the children–in that they were flagrant in their poor behavior–but it does not make a good description for their actual behavior, as called for in the sentence. The word *boorish* suggests behavior that is rude or impolite, but this is not quite strong enough to offer a solid option. (It also fails to describe third grade children effectively; at the age of 8/9, children are more likely to be described as obstreperous or unruly– that is, out of control due to bad training–than boorish, which has a larger indication of being uncouth simply for the sake of it.) The words *officious* and *sagacious* make no sense in the sentence.

19. C, E: The sentence states that sugar weakens the immune system, particularly during illness, and that it contributes to negative results. As a result, the best answer choices will encompass the suggestion of increasing to the point of making something worse.

Thus, the correct answers are choice C (compound) and choice E (exacerbate). The word *substantiate* does suggest the idea of giving support to something and could be interpreted to mean adding sugar supports the ongoing illness. But this is a round-about way of reading the sentence, and the word *substantiate* does not offer a very good option. The words *belie*, *ratify*, and *opine* offer nothing except confusion to the meaning of the sentence.

20. B, F: The meaning within the sentence is that despite the clergyman's popularity, the leadership feels the need to remove him from his job and place him in a different role. The correct answer choices will suggest this removal, this stripping of a position with the implication of force. The array of words starting with the letter "d" provides a range of possibilities, and several of them with potential, but only two offer the clear sense of removing or stripping away.

Thus, the correct answers are choice B (divest) and choice F (dispossess). The word *deliberate* only applies to the activities of those persons in leadership, as they decide what to do. The words *decimate* and *demolish* suggest destruction, which may describe the clergyman's feelings, but these words do not express the clear activity of removing him from the job. The word *disconnect* does suggest removal or a broken connection between two items; nonetheless, this word does not suggest the further indication of stripping away. The correct answers will have a somewhat negative connotation: to divest or dispossess is to remove with the element of force or with negative results. To disconnect is simply to detach. Cable can be disconnected. A computer can be disconnected. But these meanings lack the intensity suggested in the sentence and fail to indicate the same element of forced removal that the words *divest* and *dispossess* offer.

Section 5: Quantitative Reasoning

1. B: To determine the value of x, write 10 000 000 000 in scientific notation. Because the number has 10 zeros, it can be written as 10^{10}. Therefore, $10^{10} = 10\ 000\ 000\ 000$ and $x = 10$. Since 12 is greater than 10, quantity B is greater.

2. A: Write the equation for Line A in slope-intercept form: $y = mx + b$ where m is the slope and b is the y-intercept.

$$10y + 20x = 50$$
$$10y = -20x + 50$$
$$y = -2x + 5$$

Therefore, the slope of Line A is -2 and the y-intercept of Line A is 5. Hence quantity A is greater.

3. C: The ratio of the sides of both triangles is 3:4:5. Therefore, $x = 4$ and $y = 12$. Since $\frac{y}{x} = 3$, both quantities are equal.

4. A: Calculate the income tax Jane paid each month by multiplying the percentage paid in taxes by the monthly income earned.

Month	Income earned ($)	Percentage paid in taxes (%)	Income tax
January	10,000	10	1,000
February	50,000	30	15,000
March	20,000	20	4,000
April	10,000	10	1,000
May	30,000	20	6,000
June	90,000	40	36,000

Jane's average income tax is $\frac{1,000+15,000+4,000+1,000+6,000+36,000}{6} = \$10,500$.

Jane's average income is $\frac{10,000+50,000+20,000+10,000+30,000+90,000}{6} = \$35,000$, and 22% of $35,000 = $7,700. Therefore, quantity A is greater.

5. A: A prime number is a positive integer that is divisible by exactly two numbers: 1 and itself. A composite number is a positive integer that is divisible by more than just 1 and itself. The number 1 is neither prime nor composite. The smallest composite number greater than 2 is 4, and the smallest prime number less than 10 is 2. Therefore,

$$p = 2, q = 4, and\ \frac{p}{q} = \frac{1}{2} = 0.5$$

6. D: This problem can be solved by the process of elimination. If n is 1, then $\frac{1}{25}$ is less than 1. Similarly, if $n = \sqrt{2}$ or if $n = \frac{1}{2}$, then $\frac{1}{25^{\sqrt{2}}}$ and $\frac{1}{25^{\frac{1}{2}}}$ are both less than 1. However, if $n = -\frac{1}{2}$, then $\frac{1}{25^{-\frac{1}{2}}} = 25^{\frac{1}{2}} = \sqrt{25} = 5$, which is greater than 1.

7. B: Angles a and d are alternate interior angles of parallel lines and are therefore congruent. Since angle d measures 45°, angle a measures 45° as well.

8. A: Since RS forms a right angle with line m and angle d measures 45°, angle c measures 45° as well. The measure of angle a is also 45°, making triangle PRS a 45°-45°-90° triangle. Hence, both sides of the triangle are equal. Line RS measures $\frac{\sqrt{2}}{2}$ units longTherefore, line PR is also $\frac{\sqrt{2}}{2}$ units long.

9. A: Triangle PRS is a 45°-45°-90° triangle with sides equal to $\frac{\sqrt{2}}{2}$. Therefore, the hypotenuse of triangle PRS is 1. The hypotenuse of triangle PRS is also the diameter of circle O. Hence, the diameter of circle O is 1.

10. C, D: Write each equation in slope-intercept form: $y = mx + b$, where m is the slope.

$$4y - 12x - 16 = 0$$
$$4y = 12x + 16$$
$$y = 3x + 4$$

and

$$3y - 9x + 18 = 0$$
$$3y = 9x - 18$$
$$y = 3x - 6$$

Both of the equations for choices C and D have slopes of 3. Parallel lines have the same slope.

11. C, D: First, solve the system of equations for x and y. Begin by solving the first equation for x^2.

$$\sqrt{x^2 + y^2} = 5$$
$$x^2 + y^2 = 25$$
$$x^2 = 25 - y^2$$

Next, substitute the equation for x^2 into the second equation.

$$x^2 - y^2 = -7$$
$$25 - y^2 - y^2 = -7$$
$$-2y^2 = -32$$
$$y^2 = 16$$
$$y = 4, -4$$

Substitute either value for y into the second equation:

$$x^2 - y^2 = -7$$
$$x^2 - 16 = -7$$
$$x^2 = 9$$
$$x = 3, -3$$

Since there are two possible values each for x and y, $x^3 + y^3$ has four possible values:

$$(3)^3 + (4)^3 = 27 + 64 = 91$$
$$(-3)^3 + (4)^3 = -27 + 64 = 37$$
$$(3)^3 + (-4)^3 = 27 - 64 = -37$$
$$(-3)^3 + (-4)^3 = -27 - 64 = -91$$

The first two values are choices C and D.

12. B, D: Based on the coordinate pairs, the length of each side of the square is *P*. The perimeter of the square is the sum of the lengths of the sides. The sum of four sides of length *P* is $P + P + P + P = 4P$. If *P* happens to equal 4, then all 4 answers are correct, but only B and D are necessarily correct.

13. B: $A \cup B$ is the union of A and B. The union of two sets is all elements that are in either A or B or both. Therefore, $A \cup B$ is the set of all liberal arts and life science students.

14. A: $A \cap B$ is the intersection of A and B. The intersection of two sets is the set of all elements that are in both A and B. Therefore, $A \cap B$ represents the subset of liberal arts and life science double-majors. According to the diagram, this intersection also represents students who have part-time jobs, but this is not included among the answer choices

15. A, C: Set C is disjoint because it has no elements in common with sets A or B. Therefore, no engineering students also major in liberal arts or life science or both. Also, no engineering students have part-time jobs.

16. $240,000. The value of the house was $300,000, and John and Jane put 20% down. So the down payment was $(0.2)(\$300,000) = \$60,000$. Therefore, the original loan amount was $\$300,000 - \$60,000 = \$240,000$.

17. $571,429. The original loan amount of $240,000 represents the principle of the loan According to the graph, the principle was 42% of the total amount they paid throughout the life of the loan. Therefore, the total they paid is $\frac{\$240,000}{0.42} = \$571,429$.

18. 92.9%. The total amount they paid was $571,429. They paid 39% of this total in interest. So, the amount of money they paid in interest was $(0.39)(\$571,429) = \$222,857$. The original loan amount was $240,000. The percentage of the original loan amount they paid in interest was $\frac{\$222,857}{\$240,000} \cdot 100\% = 92.9\%$.

19. 3.1%. The total interest they paid over 30 years was 92.9% of the original loan amount. Therefore, their average annual interest rate was $\frac{92.9}{30} = 3.1\%$.

20. $108,572. According to the graph, John and Jane paid 19% of the total amount in taxes. The total amount was $571,429.

$$(0.19)(\$571,429) = \$108,572$$

Section 6: Quantitative Reasoning

1. B: First calculate $2\Psi5$.

$$2\Psi 5 = [(2)(5)]^2 + (2+5)^2$$
$$2\Psi 5 = 10^2 + 7^2$$
$$2\Psi 5 = 100 + 49$$
$$2\Psi 5 = 149$$

Since 149 is less than 150, quantity B is greater.

2. B: Let x represent the number of female students and let y represent the number of students who are US citizens. Because the department has 36 students and twice as many male as female students

$$x + 2x = 36$$
$$3x = 36$$
$$x = 12.$$

Hence, the department has 12 female students. Because the department has three times as many international students as US citizens

$$y + 3y = 36$$
$$4y = 36$$
$$y = 9.$$

The department has 9 students who are US citizens. Hence, quantity B is greater.

3. A: The circumference of a circle is $C = 2\pi r$, where r is the radius of the circle. Since R is the center of the circle, the radius of the circle is r = 2, and the circumference is C = (2)(π)(2) = 4π. Hence, half the circumference is 2π. The area of a triangle is $0.5bh$, where b and h are the base and height of the triangle, respectively. Segment SR represents the base of the triangle and segment QR represents the height. Both the base and height are radii of the circle. So, $b = h = 2$. Therefore, the area of the triangle, $A = (0.5)(2)(2) = 2$. Since 2π is greater than 2, quantity A is greater.

4. B: One can roughly estimate the 2008 GDP of Canada, Japan, and China to be $2, $5, and $5 trillion, which totals $12 trillion. The 2008 GDP of the US is greater than $14 trillion. Therefore, quantity B is greater.

5. C: The class has 100 students, and 60% of the students are male; therefore, the class has 60 male students and 40 female students. 30% of the class, i.e. 30 students, will attend graduate school in computer science. Of the students who will attend graduate school in computer science, the ratio of males to females is 2:1. So, 20 males and 10 females will attend graduate school in computer science. Therefore, 10 of the 40 female students will attend graduate school in computer science. This is 25% of the female students.

6. B: Write the equation for Line Q in slope-intercept form: $y = mx + b$, where m is the slope of the line.

$$5y - 100x - 75 = 0$$
$$5y = 100x + 75$$
$$y = 20x + 15$$

Therefore, the slope of Line Q is 20, and twice the slope is 40. Line B is the only line which has a slope of 40. The slope of Line A and Line C is 20. The slope of Line D is 10.

7. C: According to the table, the list that could represent their hourly wages must have a median of $50.67 and a mean of $57.44. The median is the middle value in a set of numbers arranged in increasing order. Because the set of numbers in this problem has four values, the median is the average of the middle two values. The average of the middle two values for choice C is $50.67. The mean is the average of a set of numbers, and the average wage in choice C is $57.44. Visual inspection of the wages in choice A reveal the mean is not $57.44. Visual inspection of wages in choice B show the median is not $50.67. Both the median and mean are incorrect for the wages in choice D.

8. D: The inequality which represents the given scenario is $87,980 + 87980x > 119,480$, where x is the decimal representation of the percent increase in annual salary. Solve the inequality for x:

$$87,980 + 87980x > 119,480$$
$$87,980(1 + x) > 119,480$$
$$1 + x > 1.358036$$
$$x > 0.358036$$

Therefore, the mean annual salary for those working in the fields of computers and mathematics must be raised by more than 35.8% to exceed the mean annual salary earned by those in management.

9. B: Set up and solve an equation to determine how many hours a week the cook must work to earn an annual salary of $58,000: $(\$10.57)(x)(52) = \$58,000$, where x represents the number of hours the cook must work each of the 52 weeks of the year. Since x is approximately equal to 106 and since a 40-hour work week is standard, the cook must work $106 - 40 = 66$ additional hours each week in order to earn the same annual wage as a librarian.

10. B: As a junior associate, the lawyer currently earns an annual salary of $119,120 plus overtime pay equivalent to 25% of her 40 hour salary (10/40 = 25%). Therefore, her total annual compensation for working 50 hours per week is $(1.25)(\$119,120) = \$148,900$. As a senior associate with a 25% raise, she would earn the same annual salary ($148,900) but would be working 15 hours of overtime every week instead of 10. Therefore, this promotion is not in her best financial interest.

11. A, D:

$$(A^2)(A^9) = A^{2+9} = A^{11}.$$

$$\frac{A^9}{A^2} = A^{9-2} = A^7.$$

12. A, B: Side z is the hypotenuse of a right triangle, and the hypotenuse is the longest side. Therefore, the other two sides can hold any value less than the hypotenuse as long as the Pythagorean Theorem is satisfied.

13. B: Since $\frac{b}{a} = 2$, $b = 60°$ and $a = 30°$. Therefore, this is a 30°-60°-90° triangle. Since $x = 1$, $y = \sqrt{3}$ and $z = 2$.

14. A, B: If the ages of all three siblings are contained within the choices given, then the siblings' ages are either $(2, 4, 8)$ or $(4, 8, 16)$. Since Jill is the youngest of the three, she could only be 2 or 4.

15. B, C: The distance between points $(0,0)$ and $(0,3)$ is 3 units along the y-axis. The distance between points $(0,0)$ and $(4,0)$ is 4 units along the x-axis. The triangle described is a right triangle with a hypotenuse 5 units long.

16. 180. The area of a single square is $A = s^2$ where s is the length of one side of the square. In this case, the length of one side of a single square is 6. Therefore, the area of a single square is $6^2 = 36$. The sum of the areas of the five squares is $5A = (5)(36) = 180$.

17. 8.5. Side BC is the hypotenuse of a right triangle, it can be found by using the Pythagorean Theorem: $a^2 + b^2 = c^2$, where a and b are sides of the triangle and c is the hypotenuse. The length of both sides of the triangle is 6. Hence,

$$6^2 + 6^2 = c^2$$
$$36 + 36 = c^2$$
$$\sqrt{36 + 36} = c$$
$$\sqrt{72} = c$$
$$8.5 = c$$

18. 18. The area of a triangle is $A = \frac{1}{2}bh$ where b and h are the lengths of the triangle's base and height, respectively. In this case, both b and h are sides of square S. Therefore,

$b = h = 6$, and the area of the triangle is $\frac{1}{2}(6)(6) = 18$.

19. 58.0. The perimeter of the octagon is the sum of the lengths of its sides. The lengths of sides $AB = CD = EF = GH = 6$, and the lengths of sides $BC = DE = FG = AH = 8.5$. (See explanation for question 17.) Therefore, the sum of the lengths is $(4)(6) + (4)(8.5) = 24 + 34 = 58$.

20. 252. The area of the octagon is the sum of the areas of the five squares and four triangles. The area of a single square is 36. (See the explanation for question 16.) The area of a single triangle is 18. (See the explanation for question 18.) Therefore, the area of the octagon is $A = (5)(36) + (4)(18) = 180 + 72 = 252$.

GRE Practice Test #2

Section 1: Analytical Writing

Time – 30 minutes

ANALYZE AN ISSUE

You will have a choice between two Issue topics. Each topic will appear as a <u>brief quotation that</u> states or implies an issue of general interest. Read each topic carefully; then decide on which topic you could write a more effective and well-reasoned response. You will have 45 minutes to plan and compose a response that presents your perspective on the topic you select. A response on any other topic will receive a zero. You are free to accept, reject, or qualify the claim made in the topic you selected, as long as the ideas you present are clearly relevant to the topic. Support your views with reasons and examples drawn from such areas as your reading, experience, observations, or academic studies.

GRE readers, who are college and university faculty, will read your response and evaluate its overall quality, based on how well you do the following:

- consider the <u>complexities</u> and <u>implications</u> of the issue
- organize, develop, and express your ideas on the issue
- support your ideas with relevant reasons and examples
- <u>control the elements of standard written English</u>

nocliors

You may want to take a few minutes to think about the issue and to plan a response before you begin writing. Because the space for writing your response is limited, use the next page to plan your response. Be sure to develop your ideas fully and organize them coherently, but leave time to reread what you have written and make any revisions that you think are necessary.

> History is an important topic of study primarily because human and societal interactions have remained relatively consistent over time.

Write a short essay discussing whether you agree or disagree with this statement. Your essay should include the degree to which you agree or disagree as well as your reasoning for taking this position. In addition, you must include specific examples of human interactions and societal conditions and explain how these examples impact your position.

Section 2: Analytical Writing

Time – 30 minutes

ANALYZE AN ARGUMENT

You will have 30 minutes to plan and write a critique of an argument presented in the form of a short passage. A critique of any other argument will receive a score of zero. Analyze the line of reasoning in the argument. Be sure to consider what, if any, questionable assumptions underlie the thinking and, if evidence is cited, how well it supports the conclusion. You can also discuss what sort of evidence would strengthen or refute the argument, what changes in the argument would make it more logically sound, and what additional information might help you better evaluate its conclusion. *Note that you are NOT being asked to present your views on the subject.*

GRE readers, who are college and university faculty, will read your critique and evaluate its overall quality, based on how well you

- identify and analyze important features of the argument
- organize, develop, and express your critique of the argument
- support your critique with relevant reasons and examples
- control the elements of standard written English

Before you begin writing, you may want to take a few minutes to evaluate the argument and plan a response. Because the space for writing your response is limited, use the next page to plan your response. Be sure to develop your ideas fully and organize them coherently, but leave time to reread what you have written and make any revisions that you think are necessary.

Researchers recently conducted a study on professional weightlifters to determine the importance of protein in post-workout routines. Consequently, the researchers discovered that protein was most effective at promoting muscle growth when consumed within one hour of a workout. However, the amount of protein consumed needed to be at least 25 grams for it to positively impact muscle mass. A high school football team is currently looking at ways to improve their performance. Given the results of the researchers' study, the coach should instruct his players to drink a protein shake when they get home from practice.

outside

implied

Write a short essay describing the argument's explicit and implicit assumptions. In your essay, explain whether the argument depends on any of these assumptions. In addition, evaluate the reasonableness of the assumptions as well as the likely consequences for the argument if the assumptions prove false.

Section 3: Verbal Reasoning

Time – 30 Minutes

20 Questions

Directions – Questions 1-10: Each passage in this group is followed by questions based on its content. After reading a passage, choose the best answer to each question. Answer all the questions following a passage on the basis of what is stated or *implied* in that passage.

Questions 1–5 are based on the following passage:

In the tide of emigration which impetuously rolled from the confines of China to those of Germany, the most powerful and populous tribes may commonly be found on the verge of the Roman provinces. The accumulated weight was sustained for a while by artificial barriers; and the easy condescension of the emperors invited, without satisfying, the insolent demands of the Barbarians, who had acquired an eager appetite for the luxuries of civilized life. The Hungarians, who ambitiously insert the name of Attila among their native kings, may affirm with truth that the hordes, which were subject to his uncle Roas, or Rugilas, had formed their encampments within the limits of modern Hungary, in a fertile country, which liberally supplied the wants of a nation of hunters and shepherds. In this advantageous situation, Rugilas, and his valiant brothers, who continually added to their power and reputation, commanded the alternative of peace or war with the two empires. His alliance with the Romans of the West was cemented by his personal friendship for the great Ætius; who was always secure of finding, in the Barbarian camp, a hospitable reception and a powerful support. At his solicitation, and in the name of John the usurper, sixty thousand Huns advanced to the confines of Italy; their march and their retreat were alike expensive to the state; and the grateful policy of Ætius abandoned the possession of Pannonia to his faithful confederates. The Romans of the East were not less apprehensive of the arms of Rugilas, which threatened the provinces, or even the capital. Some ecclesiastical historians have destroyed the Barbarians with lightning and pestilence; but Theodosius was reduced to the more humble expedient of stipulating an annual payment of three hundred and fifty pounds of gold, and of disguising this dishonorable tribute by the title of general, which the king of the Huns condescended to accept.

Adapted from *History of the Decline and Fall of the Roman Empire* by Edward Gibbon, revised by Henry Hart Milman, 1845.

4/2

1. The passage expressly discusses which of the following topics? Consider each of the three choices separately, and select all that apply.

a. The passage focuses on how the Barbarians exacerbated the rivalry between the Western and Eastern Romans.
b. The passage discusses how the Huns threatened the Roman Empire and entrenched themselves within Rome's sphere of influence.
c. The passage provides an account of how Rugilas seized power and acquired an official title from the Romans.

2. What does the author mean when describing how Rugilas "condescended to accept" the title of general?

    a. Rugilas believed the title would be incredibly valuable, but he was uncomfortable purchasing it with tribute. X

    b. Rugilas wanted to penetrate Rome's high society, and he had hoped to receive a higher rank.

    c. Rugilas viewed the title as a betrayal of his people, but he felt it was necessary to prevent further violence.

    d. Rugilas wanted to annex Pannonia and rule independently without having to rely on his official Roman title.

    (e.) Rugilas felt belittled by the title because he was an accomplished conqueror and king.

X **3. Select the sentence that most accurately summarizes the author's attitude toward the Huns.**

    (a.) The Romans of the East were not less apprehensive of the arms of Rugilas, which threatened the provinces, or even the capital.

    b. His alliance with the Romans of the West was cemented by his personal friendship for the great Ætius; who was always secure of finding, in the Barbarian camp, a hospitable reception and a powerful support.

    c. In this advantageous situation, Rugilas, and his valiant brothers, who continually added to their power and reputation, commanded the alternative of peace or war with the two empires.

    (d.) The accumulated weight was sustained for a while by artificial barriers; and the easy condescension of the emperors invited, without satisfying, the insolent demands of the Barbarians, who had acquired an eager appetite for the luxuries of civilized life.

    e. In the tide of emigration which impetuously rolled from the confines of China to those of Germany, the most powerful and populous tribes may commonly be found on the verge of the Roman provinces.

X **4. Based on the passage, which of the following can be concluded about ecclesiastical historians?**

    a. Ecclesiastical historians did not view diplomacy as a legitimate conflict resolution method.

    b. Ecclesiastical historians took artistic license to promote their religion and downplay Roman secularism.

    (c.) Ecclesiastical historians' biases sometimes resulted in inaccurate accounts of factual events.

    (d.) Ecclesiastical historians wanted to protect the legacy of Theodosius.

    e. Ecclesiastical historians disavowed Rugilas as a rightful Roman general.

5. Which of the following is the passage's main point about Rugilas?

    a. Rugilas ultimately seized Pannonia from the Romans.

    b. Rugilas reluctantly paid tribute to the Romans.

    c. Rugilas first gained power in an area located in modern-day Hungary.

    (d.) Rugilas held immense power over Rome's fate.

    e. Rugilas benefited greatly from his close friendship with Ætius.

Questions 6–10 are based on the following passage:

> The dream creates a form of psychical release for the wish which is either suppressed or formed by the aid of repression, inasmuch as it presents it as realized. The other procedure is also satisfied since the continuance of the sleep is assured. Our ego here gladly behaves like a child; it makes the dream pictures believable,

saying, as it were, "Quite right, but let me sleep." The contempt which, once awakened, we bear the dream, and which rests upon the absurdity and apparent illogicality of the dream, is probably nothing but the reasoning of our sleeping ego on the feelings about what was repressed; with greater right it should rest upon the incompetency of this disturber of our sleep. In sleep we are now and then aware of this contempt; the dream content transcends the censorship rather too much, we think, "It's only a dream," and sleep on.

It is no objection to this view if there are borderlines for the dream where its function, to preserve sleep from interruption, can no longer be maintained—as in the dreams of impending dread. It is here changed for another function—to suspend the sleep at the proper time. It acts like a conscientious night-watchman, who first does his duty by quelling disturbances so as not to waken the citizen, but equally does his duty quite properly when he awakens the street should the causes of the trouble seem to him serious and himself unable to cope with them alone.

Adapted from *Dream Psychology: Psychoanalysis for Beginners* by Sigmund Freud, translated by David Eder, 1920.

6. Which of the following best describes the relationship between the first and second paragraphs?
   a. The first paragraph presents an argument, and the second paragraph serves as the conclusion.
   b. The first paragraph provides generalized information, and the second paragraph narrows the discussion.
   c. The first paragraph features a topic sentence, and the second paragraph functions as the thesis.
   d. The second paragraph addresses a possible counterpoint to the reasoning contained in the first paragraph.
   e. The second paragraph includes a metaphor to summarize the first paragraph's main points.

7. Select the sentence(s) that best describes a purpose of dreams as expressed in the passage.
   a. The dream creates a form of psychical release for the wish which is either suppressed or formed by the aid of repression, inasmuch as it presents it as realized.
   b. It is no objection to this view if there are borderlines for the dream where its function, to preserve sleep from interruption, can no longer be maintained—as in the dreams of impending dread. It is here changed for another function—to suspend the sleep at the proper time.
   c. Our ego here gladly behaves like a child; it makes the dream pictures believable, saying, as it were, "Quite right, but let me sleep."
   d. The contempt which, once awakened, we bear the dream, and which rests upon the absurdity and apparent illogicality of the dream, is probably nothing but the reasoning of our sleeping ego on the feelings about what was repressed; with greater right it should rest upon the incompetency of this disturber of our sleep.
   e. In sleep we are now and then aware of this contempt; the dream content transcends the censorship rather too much, we think, "It's only a dream," and sleep on.

8. The author mentions a "conscientious night-watchman" for which of the following reasons?

  a. The author is demonstrating why bad dreams are useful.
  b. The author is evaluating the different causes of bad dreams.
  c. The author is explaining the sleeping ego through a metaphor.
  d. The author is describing how dreams provide psychical release.
  e. The author is elaborating on why people hold dreams in contempt.

9. The passage's reasoning depends on which of the following assumptions?

  a. Dreams are not a purely arbitrary and random phenomenon.
  b. People always remember the details of their dreams.
  c. Dreams constitute a source of subconscious and unconscious advice.
  d. The purpose of dreams is multifaceted and complementary.
  e. Dreams of impending dread interrupt sleep at important times.

10. The author would most likely draw which of the following conclusions about someone suffering from a nightmare? Consider each of the three choices separately, and select all that apply.

  a. The nightmare mirrors and represents a phobia.
  b. The nightmare failed to function as a conscientious night-watchman.
  c. The nightmare occurred for the purpose of interrupting sleep.

Directions - Questions 11-15: For each blank select one entry from the corresponding column of choices. Fill all blanks in the way that best completes the text.

11. Arianna made her son an appointment for a speech therapist after he suddenly became (i) _____. After several months of regular sessions, her son's (ii) _____ personality returned.

Blank (i)
a. auspicious
b. capricious
c. taciturn

Blank (ii)
d. belligerent
e. loquacious
f. sanguine

12. Ever since she was a puppy, Lucy always barked when she needed to go to the bathroom. So, when she started to have accidents in the house, her owners were concerned with this _____ behavior.

a. aberrant
b. adept
c. antithetical
d. arduous
e. audacious

13. Alexandra almost always scored the highest in her class on tests, so she was secure in her elite standing atop the (i) _____ of the school's scholars. However, Alexandra was also incredibly (ii) _____, and she believed a classmate when he told her an upcoming test was canceled. As a result, Alexandra failed the test and felt (iii) _____.

Blank (i)
a. abyss
b. hierarchy
c. vestige

Blank (ii)
d. abreast
e. naive
f. sublime

Blank (iii)
g. ambivalent
h. mortified
i. vapid

14. The politician was (i) _____, having refused to even enter negotiations on a proposed budget cut. Although her colleagues found her (ii) _____ incredibly irritating, her constituents (iii) _____ her commitment to fully funding education and health care.

Blank (i)
a. artless
b. intransigent
c. surly

Blank (ii)
d. abasement
e. gambit
f. obstinacy

Blank (iii)
g. coalesced
h. endowed
i. hailed

15. The government generally seeks to (i) _____ extremist groups as soon as they're formed because it's more efficient to take aggressive action during a group's (ii) _____ stage.

Blank (i)
a. extirpate
b. malign
c. polarize

Blank (ii)
d. aesthetic
e. nascent
f. ostentatious

Directions – Questions 16-20: Select the *two* answer choices that, when used to complete the sentence, fit the meaning of the sentence as a whole *and* produce completed sentences that are alike in meaning.

16. The _____ student spent all of his money on craft beer, gourmet snacks, and computer gadgets instead of buying the books he needed for the semester.

    a. bombastic
    b. erudite
    c. prodigal
    d. spendthrift
    e. subversive
    f. whimsical

17. A notorious and _____ fan of the local team went too far during the last game and was banned for throwing garbage on the field when the referees called a penalty on his favorite player.

    a. ardent
    b. benign
    c. fervent
    d. gullible
    e. prolific
    f. soporific

18. After he arrived late and missed an important meeting, the employee sought to _____ his boss and avoid being fired.

    a. bolster
    b. mitigate
    c. mollify
    d. placate
    e. rebut
    f. refute

19. The moment might have been _____, but Brian instantly knew he was in love with Janet.

    a. arbitrary
    b. ephemeral
    c. fortuitous
    d. salubrious
    e. transient
    f. unadorned

20. During halftime, the coach lambasted his players for their _____ performance.

    a. errant
    b. frenetic
    c. hapless
    d. immutable
    e. lethargic
    f. listless

Work on vocabulary

9/20

Section 4: Verbal Reasoning

Time – 30 Minutes

20 Questions

Directions – Questions 1-10: Each passage in this group is followed by questions based on its content. After reading a passage, choose the best answer to each question. Answer all the questions following a passage on the basis of what is stated or *implied* in that passage.

Questions 1–5 are based on the following passage:

Such being the reasons which make it imperative that human beings should be free to form opinions, and to express their opinions without reserve; and such the baneful consequences to the intellectual, and through that to the moral nature of man, unless this liberty is either conceded, or asserted in spite of prohibition; let us next examine whether the same reasons do not require that men should be free to act upon their opinions—to carry these out in their lives, without hindrance, either physical or moral, from their fellow-men, so long as it is at their own risk and peril. This last proviso is of course indispensable. No one pretends that actions should be as free as opinions. On the contrary, even opinions lose their immunity, when the circumstances in which they are expressed are such as to constitute their expression a positive instigation to some mischievous act. An opinion that corn-dealers are starvers of the poor, or that private property is robbery, ought to be unmolested when simply circulated through the press, but may justly incur punishment when delivered orally to an excited mob assembled before the house of a corn-dealer, or when handed about among the same mob in the form of a placard. Acts, of whatever kind, which, without justifiable cause, do harm to others, may be, and in the more important cases absolutely require to be, controlled by the unfavourable sentiments, and, when needful, by the active interference of mankind. The liberty of the individual must be thus far limited; he must not make himself a nuisance to other people. But if he refrains from molesting others in what concerns them, and merely acts according to his own inclination and judgment in things which concern himself, the same reasons which show that opinion should be free, prove also that he should be allowed, without molestation, to carry his opinions into practice at his own cost. That mankind are not infallible; that their truths, for the most part, are only half-truths; that unity of opinion, unless resulting from the fullest and freest comparison of opposite opinions, is not desirable, and diversity not an evil, but a good, until mankind are much more capable than at present of recognising all sides of the truth, are principles applicable to men's modes of action, not less than to their opinions.

Adapted from *On Liberty* by John Stuart Mill, 1859.

1. Select the sentence that best describes a limitation on the expression of opinions as expressed in the passage.

    a. No one pretends that actions should be as free as opinions.

    b. But if he refrains from molesting others in what concerns them, and merely acts according to his own inclination and judgment in things which concern himself, the same reasons which show that opinion should be free, prove also that he should be allowed, without molestation, to carry his opinions into practice at his own cost.

    c. That mankind are not infallible; that their truths, for the most part, are only half-truths; that unity of opinion, unless resulting from the fullest and freest comparison of opposite opinions, is not desirable, and diversity not an evil, but a good, until mankind are much more capable than at present of recognising all sides of the truth, are principles applicable to men's modes of action, not less than to their opinions.

    d. Such being the reasons which make it imperative that human beings should be free to form opinions, and to express their opinions without reserve; and such the baneful consequences to the intellectual, and through that to the moral nature of man, unless this liberty is either conceded, or asserted in spite of prohibition; let us next examine whether the same reasons do not require that men should be free to act upon their opinions—to carry these out in their lives, without hindrance, either physical or moral, from their fellow-men, so long as it is at their own risk and peril.

    (e.) On the contrary, even opinions lose their immunity, when the circumstances in which they are expressed are such as to constitute their expression a positive instigation to some mischievous act.

2. Which of the following can be inferred about the author's opinions about the nature of truth? Consider each of the three choices separately, and select all that apply.

    (a.) Truth is full of complications and can be easily corrupted by people's internal biases.

    (b.) Mankind will likely never be able to recognize full truths.

    c. Opinions typically reveal the truth more easily than actions unless the opinion is popular.

3. The passage primarily distinguishes between which of the following?

    (a.) The passage distinguishes between truths and opinions.

    (b.) The passage distinguishes between opinions based on their consequences.

    c. The passage distinguishes between the universal truths of mankind.

    d. The passage distinguishes between undesired opinions based on unfavorable sentiments.

    e. The passage distinguishes between mere nuisances and criminal actions.

4. How does the first sentence relate to the rest of the passage?

    a. The first sentence functions as the passage's topic sentence by summarizing the passage.

    b. The first sentence outlines the passage's ultimate conclusion.

    c. The first sentence provides an anecdote as a way to introduce a new topic.

    (d.) The first sentence summarizes an earlier point and leads into a discussion of a related topic.

    e. The first sentence compares and contrasts important concepts.

5. Which of the following best articulates the weakest aspect of the author's position?

    a. The nature of truth is entirely unrelated to opinions.

    (b.) Determining whether an opinion is likely to inspire a mischievous act is nebulous.

    c. Opinions are endowed with an inherent immunity.

    d. Mankind is fallible, and people have difficulty reconciling conflicting opinions.

    e. Opinions of any kind rarely ever lead to harm.

Questions 6–10 are based on the following passage:

There would be meat that had tumbled out on the floor, in the dirt and sawdust, where the workers had tramped and spit uncounted billions of consumption germs. There would be meat stored in great piles in rooms; and the water from leaky roofs would drip over it, and thousands of rats would race about on it. It was too dark in these storage places to see well, but a man could run his hand over these piles of meat and sweep off handfuls of the dried dung of rats. These rats were nuisances, and the packers would put poisoned bread out for them; they would die, and then rats, bread, and meat would go into the hoppers together. This is no fairy story and no joke; the meat would be shoveled into carts, and the man who did the shoveling would not trouble to lift out a rat even when he saw one—there were things that went into the sausage in comparison with which a poisoned rat was a tidbit. There was no place for the men to wash their hands before they ate their dinner, and so they made a practice of washing them in the water that was to be ladled into the sausage. There were the butt-ends of smoked meat, and the scraps of corned beef, and all the odds and ends of the waste of the plants, that would be dumped into old barrels in the cellar and left there. Under the system of rigid economy which the packers enforced, there were some jobs that it only paid to do once in a long time, and among these was the cleaning out of the waste barrels. Every spring they did it; and in the barrels would be dirt and rust and old nails and stale water—and cartload after cartload of it would be taken up and dumped into the hoppers with fresh meat, and sent out to the public's breakfast. Some of it they would make into "smoked" sausage—but as the smoking took time, and was therefore expensive, they would call upon their chemistry department, and preserve it with borax and color it with gelatine to make it brown. All of their sausage came out of the same bowl, but when they came to wrap it they would stamp some of it "special," and for this they would charge two cents more a pound.

Adapted from *The Jungle* by Upton Sinclair, 1906.

6. Which of the following is the passage's main point?
   a. Meat products often contained sawdust and rats.
   b. The meatpacking industry rarely abided by regulations, resulting in low-quality products.
   ⓒ Meatpacking was unsanitary, chaotic, and profit oriented.
   d. Sausage was often treated with chemicals and deceptively labeled.✗
   e. The owners of meatpacking factories were lackadaisical in supervising the packers.✗

7. The author most likely wrote the passage for which of the following reasons?
   a. The author hoped readers would buy fewer meat products.
   b. The author had a vendetta against the owners of the meatpacking factory.✓
   ⓒ The author wanted to shed light on the meatpacking industry.
   d. The author sought to reduce the profits of the meatpacking factory.✗
   e. The author supported the regulation of food product labels.✗

8. Which of the following can be properly inferred about the owners of the factories?

　　a. The owners focused more on maintaining the quality of corned beef than sausage.

　　b. The owners did not understand how to properly process smoked sausage.

　　c. The owners rarely visited their meatpacking factories and ignored the unsanitary conditions.

　　d. The owners failed to purchase an adequate number of hoppers to process the meat. ✓

　　(e) The owners prioritized making a profit significantly more than producing quality products.

9. Select the sentence that best describes the vast number of contaminants in the meat.

　　(a.) This is no fairy story and no joke; the meat would be shoveled into carts, and the man who did the shoveling would not trouble to lift out a rat even when he saw one—there were things that went into the sausage in comparison with which a poisoned rat was a tidbit.

　　b. It was too dark in these storage places to see well, but a man could run his hand over these piles of meat and sweep off handfuls of the dried dung of rats. ✗

　　c. Some of it they would make into "smoked" sausage—but as the smoking took time, and was therefore expensive, they would call upon their chemistry department, and preserve it with borax and color it with gelatine to make it brown. ✗

　　d. Under the system of rigid economy which the packers enforced, there were some jobs that it only paid to do once in a long time, and among these was the cleaning out of the waste barrels. ✗

　　e. There was no place for the men to wash their hands before they ate their dinner, and so they made a practice of washing them in the water that was to be ladled into the sausage.

10. Which of the following can be properly concluded about the author's opinions about the meatpacking industry? Consider each of the three choices separately, and select all that apply.

　　(a) The author was aghast at the industry's unethical practices.

　　(b) The author was opposed to the deceptive labeling of meat products.

　　(c) The author was disgusted by the lack of quality control.

Directions - Questions 11-15: For each blank select one entry from the corresponding column of choices. Fill all blanks in the way that best completes the text.

11. Some television shows have become increasingly (i) _____ as they seek to attract a massive audience. Despite this attempt to provide comforting and familiar content, many of these derivative shows have suffered a (ii) _____ drop in viewership.

Blank (i)
a. esoteric
b. fastidious
c. hackneyed

Blank (ii)
d. magnanimous
e. mercurial
f. precipitous

12. Some musicians seem to wield magical power in their ability to produce melodies that can miraculously _____ pain and distress.

a. assuage
b. desiccate
c. impugn
d. precipitate
e. winnow

13. The social media company (i) _____ navigated tricky and complex regulatory pitfalls in order to continue collecting their users' data. Although market forecasters assumed the company would eventually experience a vicious (ii) _____, the vast majority of users were surprisingly either totally unconcerned or (iii) _____, even after the practice became public knowledge.

Blank (i)	Blank (ii)	Blank (iii)
a. arduously	d. backlash	g. apathetic
b. deftly	e. dirge	h. desultory
c. insipidly	f. probity	i. polemical

14. Although she was too afraid to tell her mother outright lies, Madeline was a master at _____.

a. abjuring
b. inculpating
c. obviating
d. prevaricating
e. vacillating

15. The researcher was growing tired of discovering mere (i) _____ features of the recently discovered phenomenon. Rather than steadily achieving minor breakthroughs, she yearned to uncover the (ii) _____.

Blank (i)
a. banal
b. equivocal
c. peripheral

Blank (ii)
d. catalyst
e. omniscience
f. pith

Directions – Questions 16-20: Select the *two* answer choices that, when used to complete the sentence, fit the meaning of the sentence as a whole *and* produce completed sentences that are alike in meaning.

16. A _____ of resources triggered a wave of migration from outlying areas into the city.

    a. cacophony
    b. dearth
    c. milieu
    d. paucity
    e. plethora
    f. temperance

17. At the last team meeting, Walter _____ his staff for all the hard work they did in preparing for the product launch.

    a. extolled
    b. flouted
    c. galvanized
    d. goaded
    e. groused
    f. lauded

18. The teacher resisted admonishing a/an _____ student because he didn't want to interrupt the flow of the class discussion.

    a. florid
    b. garrulous
    c. homogeneous
    d. implacable
    e. nonplussed
    f. voluble

19. The lawyer trusted her client, but she still sought to find an eyewitness to _____ her client's testimony.

    a. corroborate
    b. delineate
    c. disseminate
    d. emulate
    e. substantiate
    f. venerate

20. The dismissal of a beloved coworker effectively _____ a rebellion against the managers, culminating in a mass walkout on Friday.

    a. deigned
    b. engendered
    c. fomented
    d. marred
    e. posited
    f. rued

Work on vocabulary

7/20

332

Section 5: Quantitative Reasoning

Time – 35 Minutes

20 Questions

QUANTITATIVE COMPARISON

Directions: Compare Quantity A and Quantity B, using additional information centered above the two quantities if such information is given, and select one of the following four answer choices:

1.

$$x + 2y = 12$$
$$y = x + 3$$

Quantity A	**Quantity B**
x	y

a. Quantity A is greater.
b. Quantity B is greater.
c. The two quantities are equal.
d. The relationship cannot be determined from the information given.

2. The original cost of a car is y dollars.

Quantity A	**Quantity B**
y	The cost of the car if it is first increased by 20% and then decreased by 20%.

a. Quantity A is greater.
b. Quantity B is greater.
c. The two quantities are equal.
d. The relationship cannot be determined from the information given.

3. A restaurant had x people waiting in line. During the next hour, half of those people were seated, but 30 more people entered the restaurant so that there were 45 people waiting in total.

Quantity A	**Quantity B**
x	40

a. Quantity A is greater.
b. Quantity B is greater.
c. The two quantities are equal.
d. The relationship cannot be determined from the information given.

4. In the following question, 5% of x is equal to 6% of y, where $x > 0$ and $y > 0$.

Quantity A	**Quantity B**
x	y

a. Quantity A is greater.
b. Quantity B is greater.
c. The two quantities are equal.
d. The relationship cannot be determined from the information given.

333

MULTIPLE-CHOICE – SELECT ONLY ONE ANSWER CHOICE

Directions: These questions have five answer choices. Select a single answer choice.

5. A ski resort charges $45 for equipment rental and $12.50 per hour for the chairlift. If you purchased both the rental package and used the chairlift for the day, how many hours did you pay for if your total charge was $120?

    a. 7
    b. 10
    c. 5
    d. 8
    e. 6

Handwritten: $120 = \$45 + 12.50(x)$; -45; $\dfrac{75}{12.50} = \dfrac{12.50(x)}{}$; $x = 6$

6. How many positive odd factors does 368 have?

    a. 0
    b. 1
    c. 2
    d. 3
    e. 4

7. At a school, the ratio of teachers to students is 3:41. If there are 342 more students than teachers, how many students are there?

    a. 345
    b. 359
    c. 369
    d. 375
    e. 400

8. Before yesterday's quiz, a student had scored an average of 93 in the quiz category in her class. After yesterday's quiz, she had an average of 96 in the quiz category. If she scored a 99 on yesterday's quiz, how many quizzes had she taken before yesterday's quiz?

    a. 1   *93 96 99*
    b. 2
    c. 3
    d. 4
    e. 5

MULTIPLE-CHOICE – SELECT ONE OR MORE ANSWER CHOICES

Directions: If the question specifies how many answer choices to select, select exactly that number of choices. If the question does not specify how many answer choices to select, select all that apply.

9. Which of the following numbers has only 2 distinct prime factors? Select all the answer choices that apply.

    a. 18   *9*
    b. 20   *4 5*
    c. 25   *5*
    d. 30   *6 5*

10. Which of the following are NOT in the domain of $f(x) = \frac{\sqrt{x-7}}{x-2}$? Select all the answer choices that apply.

$\frac{2-7\sqrt{-5}}{0}$

   a. 0
   b. 2
   c. 8
   d. 7

11. Find the next 3 numbers in the sequence: 5, 10, 17, 26, 37, ... Select all the 3 choices that apply.

   5   7   9   11 +13   15 +17

   a. 45
   b. 50
   c. 63
   d. 65
   e. 82
   f. 83

12. If $4x^3 - 20x^2 - 4x + 20 = 0$, which of the following are solutions for x? Select all the answer choices that apply.

$4x^3 - 20x^2 - 4x + 20 = 0$

$4(0)^3 - 20(0)^2 - 4(0) + 20$

   a. -5
   b. 5
   c. 1
   d. -1
   e. 0

NUMERIC ENTRY

Directions:

Enter your answer as an integer or a decimal if there is a single answer box OR as a fraction if there are two separate boxes—one for the numerator and one for the denominator.

Equivalent forms of the correct answer, such as 2.5 and 2.50, are all correct. Fractions do not need to be reduced to lowest terms, though you may need to reduce your fraction to fit in the boxes.

Enter the exact answer unless the question asks you to round your answer.

13. In a bag of marbles, 9 of the marbles are red, 7 are blue, and 5 are yellow. If a marble is chosen randomly from the bag, what is the probability that the marble is not blue? Simplify your answer.

9r   7b   5y $\frac{14}{21}$ $\frac{2}{3}$

$\boxed{\frac{2}{3}}$

14. Alex is 3 times as old as Carl. 6 years ago, he was 4 years older than Carl is right now. How old is Alex?

$\boxed{15}$ $6 - (x+4) = (x)3$

15. Rectangle R has a length of 15 cm and a width of 8 cm. Rectangle S has a length of 20 cm and a width of 12 cm. What value can you multiply the area of rectangle R by in order to get the area of rectangle S?

$$\boxed{2}$$

L = 15cm w = 8cm   L = 20cm w = 12cm

120   240

16. An experiment has 4 possibilities, which are mutually exclusive. Their probabilities are $m, \frac{m}{3}, 2m,$ and $\frac{m}{4}$. What is the value of m? Enter your response as a fraction.

$$\boxed{1}$$

$12/43$ m_1

DATA INTERPRETATION SETS

Questions 17–18 refer to the following graph.

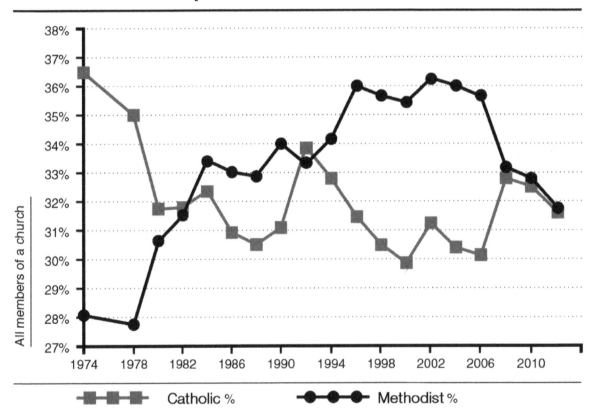

Church Memberships in Town X

✗ 17. Which time period saw the maximum percentage change in church membership for the Catholic church?

- (a.) 1978-1980 ✗
- b. 2000-2002 ✗
- c. 1990-1992
- (d.) 2006-2008
- e. 2010-2012 ✗

✗ 18. What was the approximate average percentage of membership for the Methodist church from 1980 to 2010?

- a. 28%
- (b.) 30%
- (c.) 34%
- d. 36%
- e. 40%

$31.5 + 33.5 + 33 + 33 + 34 + 33.5 + 34 + 36$

$+35.5 + 35.2 + 36.1 + 36 + 35.7 + 33 + 32.9$

$+$

32.9

Questions 19–20 refer to the following information:

Seven randomly selected grocery carts contain the following quantities of paper bags:

$$\frac{11, 5, 6, 9, 12, \cancel{10, 7}}{7} = 8.5$$

✗ 19. What is the interquartile range of the numbers?

- (a.) 9
- b. 6
- (c.) 5
- d. 3
- e. 5.5

✗ 20. If each cart had 2 fewer bags, what would be the interquartile range?

- a. 9
- (b.) 6
- (c) 5
- d. 3
- e. 5.5

9/20

Section 6: Quantitative Reasoning

Time – 35 Minutes

20 Questions

QUANTITATIVE COMPARISON

Directions: Compare Quantity A and Quantity B, using additional information centered above the two quantities if such information is given, and select one of the following four answer choices:

1.

Quantity A	**Quantity B**
The product of the positive factors of 10	The product of the positive factors of 11
25	1

a. Quantity A is greater.
b. Quantity B is greater.
c. The two quantities are equal.
d. The relationship cannot be determined from the information given.

(answer a circled)

2.

Quantity A	**Quantity B**
$\dfrac{\frac{\sqrt{3}}{3}}{\frac{5}{\sqrt{3}}}$ 0.577 / 2.88	$\dfrac{\frac{5}{\sqrt{2}}}{\frac{\sqrt{2}}{3}}$ 3.535 / 0.4714 1

a. Quantity A is greater.
b. Quantity B is greater.
c. The two quantities are equal.
d. The relationship cannot be determined from the information given.

(answer b circled)

3.

Quantity A	**Quantity B**
The sum of the coefficients in the expression $3z^2 + 7z - 8x$	The product of the constants in the expression $2 + 7x + 12 - 13z$
18	20

a. Quantity A is greater.
b. Quantity B is greater.
c. The two quantities are equal.
d. The relationship cannot be determined from the information given.

(answer b circled)

✗ 4.

	Quantity A	Quantity B
	$\dfrac{x^2}{3y-2}$	$\dfrac{x^2-4}{y}$

a. Quantity A is greater.
b. Quantity B is greater.
c. The two quantities are equal.
d. The relationship cannot be determined from the information given.

MULTIPLE-CHOICE – SELECT ONLY ONE ANSWER CHOICE

These questions have five answer choices. Select a single answer choice.

✗ 5. What are the first 5 prime numbers?

a. 2, 3, 5, 7, 11 ✗
b. 1, 2, 3, 5, 7
c. 1, 2, 3, 5, 11
d. 2, 3, 5, 7, 9 ✗
e. 1, 2, 3, 4, 5

6. Find the sum of $\frac{2}{3} + \frac{4}{5}$. $\frac{10}{15} + \frac{12}{15}$ $\frac{22}{15}$

a. $\frac{6}{8}$

b. $\frac{3}{4}$

c. $\frac{6}{15}$

d. $\frac{22}{15}$

e. $\frac{2}{5}$

7. Solve the following equation: $2x + 7 = -3$

a. $x = 5$
b. $x = -5$
c. $x = 2$
d. $x = -2$
e. $x = -10$

$\begin{array}{r} -7 \\ \hline 2x = -10 \\ \overline{2} \quad\; \overline{2} \\ x = -5 \end{array}$

8. A coffee shop increased its pay for workers by 15%. If the workers were making $11 an hour before the increase, how much more will they make per hour now?

a. $12.50 ✗
b. $0.15
c. $1.65
d. $1.15
e. $12.65 ✗

$\$11 \times 15\%$

MULTIPLE-CHOICE – SELECT ONE OR MORE ANSWER CHOICES

Directions: If the question specifies how many answer choices to select, select exactly that number of choices. If the question does not specify how many answer choices to select, select all that apply.

9. A runner takes the average of his top 3 times to qualify for the state match. If a runner's average for the 100-meter race is 28 seconds, choose the combination of times that would result in this average, using only the given numbers. Select all the answer choices that apply.

a. 29
b. 31
c. 25
d. 24
e. 22

$31 + 25 + 29 = 28.3$

10. Which of the following expressions results in a number between 0 and 1 when simplified? Select all the answer choices that apply.

a. 2^{-3} $= 0.125$
b. 3^2 $= 9$
c. 8×-2 $= -16$
d. -3^{-1} $= -0.33$
e. 5^{-1} $= 0.2$

11. A grocery bill comes out to be $250 before applying discounts. If a shopper has budgeted $175 for this grocery trip, which of the following price discounts will bring the price for the groceries within budget? Select all the answer choices that apply.

a. 30%
b. 20%
c. 18%
d. 25%
e. 10%

$250 \times 30\% = 250 \times 0.30 = 75$
$250 \times 20\% = 50$

12. Which of the following is a factored form of the expression $4x^4 - 2x^2 + 6x$? Select all the answer choices that apply.

a. $2x(2x^3 - x + 3)$
b. $x(4x^3 - x^2 + 6)$
c. $4x(x^3 - x + 1)$
d. $-x(-4x^3 + 2x - 6)$
e. $4x(x^3 - \frac{1}{2}x + \frac{3}{2})$

$2x(2x^3 - x + 3)$

NUMERIC ENTRY

> *Directions*:
>
> Enter your answer as an integer or a decimal if there is a single answer box OR as a fraction if there are two separate boxes: one for the numerator and one for the denominator.
>
> Equivalent forms of the correct answer, such as 2.5 and 2.50, are all correct. Fractions do not need to be reduced to lowest terms, though you may need to reduce your fraction to fit in the boxes.
>
> Enter the exact answer unless the question asks you to round your answer.

13. Circle A has a circumference of 10π. Circle B has a circumference of 40π. If the ratio of these measurements stays the same and the radius for Circle A is doubled, what will be the new value for the circumference for Circle B?

 π

A 10π $B = 40\pi$
      20π 80π

14. Lines k and m are parallel to each other. If $y - x = 120$, what is the measure of angle x?

30

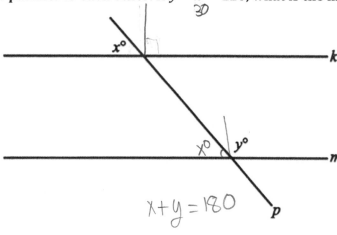

$x + y = 180$

30

$\boxed{45}$ degrees

15. A car dealership sold 35 cars and 26 trucks in January. In February, they sold 27 cars and 22 trucks. March sales were slower, with 15 trucks and 19 cars sold. In April, the dealership sold 24 cars and 19 trucks. What is the ratio of cars to trucks sold for the first three months of the year?

$\boxed{9}$: $\boxed{7}$

27   21

35c   26t
27c   22t
19c   15t
24c   19t

16. The ratio of third-grade students that chose virtual classes to those that chose in-person classes was 2 to 3. If there were 32 students who chose virtual classes in third grade, how many students chose in-person classes?

33 | 48
Students

32 : 33

DATA INTERPRETATION SETS

Questions 17–20 are based on the following chart.

Survey results of students who attended an engineering outreach event:

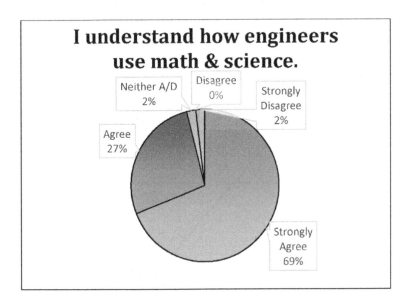

17. If there were 125 students who participated in the survey, how many of them agreed or strongly agreed with the statement?

86.25 strong agree
33.75 agre

a. 86
b. 34 ✗
c. 120
d. 5 ✗
e. 89

18. Based on the rounded percentage data in the chart, which of the following statements is definitely FALSE?

a. The number of students who strongly disagreed was 3.
b. The number of students who neither agreed nor disagreed was 3.
c. The number of students who agreed was 34. ✓
d. The number of students who strongly agreed was 86. ✓
e. None of these.

19. If 10 of the 125 students changed their answer from strongly agree to agree, what would be the new percentage of students who agree with the statement?

a. 35%
b. 61% ✗
c. 37%
d. 59%
e. 10% ✗

20. Prior to the event, an identical pre-survey was given. The percentage of students who strongly agreed with this statement on the pre-survey was 25 percentage points lower than the percentage who strongly agreed with this statement on the post-survey. How many students strongly agreed with this statement in the pre-survey?

a. 44
b. 55
c. 69
d. 25
e. None of the above

25% ✓

13/20

Answer Key and Explanations for Test #2

Section 3: Verbal Reasoning

1. B, C: The passage primarily discusses the relationship between the Huns and Romans. According to the passage, the Huns threatened to engulf the Romans in war, but they ultimately accepted tribute and integrated themselves into Roman power structures. The passage also describes how Rugilas seized power from the Romans throughout the passage, and it specifically describes how he received tribute in exchange for taking the title of general. Therefore, Choices *B* and *C* are correct. Choice *A* is incorrect because although the passage briefly references the Western and Eastern Romans' approaches to dealing with the Huns, it doesn't discuss a rivalry between Western and Eastern Romans.

2. E: The expression "condescended to accept" means that the acceptance is belittling or demeaning. Because Rugilas was a king in his own right and had recently secured a major victory against the Romans, accepting the title of general in his former enemy's army constituted a demotion despite its political benefits. Thus, Choice *E* is the correct answer. Choice *A* is incorrect because Rugilas received tribute in exchange for accepting the title; he wasn't giving tribute. The title likely would have helped Rugilas enter Rome's high society, but there's no support in the passage for Rugilas wanting a higher rank. If anything, Rugilas likely would've preferred not to join the Roman power structure. As such, Choice *B* is incorrect. The Romans were the ones looking to avoid further violence, not Rugilas, because the Huns were the aggressor. Therefore, Choice *C* is incorrect. Rugilas likely wanted to conquer all of the Roman territory and rule independently; however, this overarching goal wasn't directly related to why he considered the new title demeaning. So, Choice *D* is incorrect.

3. D: The passage reflects the author's disdain for the Huns, especially in terms of culture. Choice *D* reflects this disgust by characterizing the Huns as insolent and uncivilized barbarians. Choice *A* is incorrect because it is a factual statement about how the Huns' military might threaten the Romans. Choice *B* is incorrect because it describes an important alliance rather than characterizing the behavior of the Huns. Choice *C* is incorrect because it constitutes one of the few relatively positive assessments of the Huns contained in the passage. Choice *E* is incorrect because the description of the Huns as "impetuously rolling" into Roman territory does not provide a complete summary of the author's feelings toward the Huns.

4. C: At the end of the passage, the author describes ecclesiastical historians who claimed that a divine intervention defeated the Huns with lightning and pestilence. However, according to the passage, the Romans absorbed the Huns into their political system. This factual discrepancy reflects the ecclesiastical historians' bias toward religion. Therefore, Choice *C* is the correct answer. Bias better explains the historians' account than an opposition to diplomacy, which isn't supported in the passage. As such, Choice *A* is incorrect. The historians did take an artistic license to promote religion, but the passage is unclear about their motivations and doesn't state whether Rome was secular. So, Choice *B* is incorrect. Although the ecclesiastical historians' account would've benefited Theodosius, he wasn't specifically included in their historical account, so this inference lacks sufficient support. Therefore, Choice *D* is incorrect. The ecclesiastical historians likely disdained Rugilas, but their alternative explanation is broader than his title. So, Choice *E* is incorrect.

5. D: The passage characterizes Rugilas as a highly skilled military commander and political operative. At one point, the author describes how Rugilas controlled whether the societies would be

344

at war or peace. Overall, the passage's main point is that Rugilas wielded immense power in regard to the future of Rome; therefore, Choice *D* is correct. Choice *A* is incorrect because the capture of Pannonia was only an example of Rugilas' power. Choice *B* is incorrect because Rugilas was the recipient of the tribute. The passage doesn't state where Rugilas came to power, and the discussion of the encampments in Hungary is a minor point. So, Choice *C* is incorrect. Rugilas definitely benefited from his relationship with Ætius, but this was only part of why he was such an influential figure in Roman history. Therefore, Choice *E* is incorrect.

6. D: The first paragraph explains how dreams primarily serve to prevent the interruption of sleep, and the second paragraph qualifies this claim by addressing a possible counterpoint about nightmares. According to the second paragraph, dreams have the secondary function of suspending sleep at an appropriate time. The first paragraph can be properly characterized as an argument, but the second paragraph is more like a qualification or elaboration than a conclusion. As such, Choice *A* is incorrect. Choice *B* is incorrect because both paragraphs have a comparable level of specificity. The first paragraph does include a topic sentence, but the second paragraph doesn't function as the thesis because it doesn't revolve around the passage's main point. So, Choice *C* is incorrect. The second paragraph heavily features a metaphor, but it is used to illustrate dreams' secondary function, which isn't mentioned in the first paragraph. Therefore, Choice *E* is incorrect.

7. B: Choice B expresses how the function of dreams is to preserve sleep. In this context, function is synonymous with *purpose*. Choice *A* provides a general description of dreams, so it is incorrect. Choice *C* presents a metaphor to illustrate the ego's role in dreams and is therefore incorrect. Choice *D* is incorrect because it explains why people hold their dreams in contempt rather than articulating the purpose of dreams. Choice *E* is incorrect because although it references the purpose of dreams while describing the relationship between dream content and censorship, Choice *B* provides a much more explicit description.

8. A: The conscientious night-watchman is the central figure in the metaphor found in the second paragraph, representing how dreams both serve to preserve and interrupt sleep. In that metaphor, the author claims that bad dreams serve as a wake-up call, like a watchman awakening the street, which is undoubtedly useful. Thus, Choice *A* is the correct answer. Choice *B* is incorrect because the author never delves into the various causes of bad dreams. The sleeping ego is briefly referenced in the first paragraph, but it isn't directly incorporated in the metaphor. As such, Choice *C* is incorrect. The author does claim that dreams provide a form of psychical release, but the metaphor primarily serves to explain the dual function of dreams. Therefore, Choice *D* is incorrect. The author's discussion of contempt for dreams is about self-censorship and entirely unrelated to the night-watchman metaphor, so Choice *E* is incorrect.

9. A: The passage's reasoning hinges on dreams not being arbitrary and random. If dreams were arbitrary and random, they wouldn't be able to fulfill the function articulated in the passage due to lack of a connection between the sleeping ego and dreams. Therefore, Choice *A* is correct. The author characterizes dreams as part of the subconscious, so the argument doesn't depend on people remembering anything. Therefore, Choice *B* is incorrect. Although the passage discusses the subconscious, it never claims that dreams are a source of advice. As a result, Choice *C* is incorrect. Choice *D* is incorrect because it states the passage's conclusion. Similarly, Choice *E* is incorrect because it states a critical premise in the passage's argument.

10. C: A nightmare is a dream of impending dread, and the author claims the function of these dreams is to interrupt sleep and awaken the dreamer. Thus, Choice *C* is the correct answer. The passage doesn't mention phobias or their relationship to dreams, so Choice *A* is incorrect. According to the passage, nightmares are part of dreams' dual function, which is represented by the night-watchman. As such, the nightmare was appropriately functioning as the metaphorical conscientious night-watchman, so Choice *B* is incorrect.

11. C, E: *Taciturn* and *loquacious*: Blank (1) must be a characteristic or trait that concerned Arianna enough to take her son to a speech therapist. *Taciturn* means to be reserved or silent, so a speech therapist would likely be helpful for a taciturn child. *Auspicious* means something looks promising or favorable; therefore, it is incorrect. To be *capricious* is to be unpredictable or fickle. Blank (2) is describing the son's personality, and it can be inferred that the speech therapy worked. So, the correct answer is likely the opposite of *taciturn*. *Loquacious* is synonymous with *talkative,* so it is the correct choice. *Belligerent* denotes aggression or hostility and is incorrect. *Sanguine* is synonymous with *cheerful* and *optimistic* and is incorrect.

12. A: *Aberrant*: The sentences describe a dog that's having accidents for the first time in many years. Something aberrant is shocking and/or contrary to an existing pattern. If the dog has been well trained for years, the accidents could reasonably be characterized as aberrant behavior. Thus, *aberrant* is the correct answer. *Adept* means proficient or skilled. *Antithetical* means to be directly opposed. *Arduous* means difficult, but the sentence is describing the dog's behavior, not the situation facing Lucy's owners. *Audacious* is incorrect because it means bold or impudent.

13. B, E, H: *Hierarchy, naive,* and *mortified*: Blank (1) characterizes Alexandra as an elite student who stands at the top of something related to the school's scholars. A *hierarchy* is a top-down arrangement of things based on status or power, and the group with the highest status or most power is positioned at the top of the hierarchy. Within the hierarchy of the school's scholars, Alexandra would be at the top based on her test scores. An *abyss* is a deep chasm or bottomless hole. Standing atop an abyss metaphorically means to be in danger. As such, *abyss* is incorrect. *Vestige* is incorrect because a vestige is a trace of something that's outdated or historic. Blank (2) characterizes Alexandra, and the next clause describes how her classmate tricked her. To be *naive* is to be overly innocent, credulous, and/or easy to fool, so *naive* is incorrect. *Abreast* means to stand next to someone in a line or to be aware of current events and is therefore incorrect. *Sublime* is incorrect because *sublime* denotes something that's exalted or awe inspiring. Blank (3) describes how Alexandra felt after realizing she was tricked, which caused her to fail the test. *Mortified* means to be extremely embarrassed, ashamed, or humiliated. To be *ambivalent* is to be uncertain and unsure, so *ambivalent* is incorrect. *Vapid* is incorrect because *vapid* describes something that's uninteresting or uninspired.

14. B, F, I: *Intransigent, obstinacy,* and *hailed*: Blank (1) describes a politician who is refusing to negotiate over budget cuts. *Intransigent* is synonymous with *uncompromising* and *inflexible*. *Artless* can either mean to do something without deception, effort, or skill; therefore, it is incorrect. *Surly* is incorrect because *surly* means to be unfriendly. Blank (2) also describes the politician's refusal to negotiate. *Obstinacy* is a stubborn refusal to change one's decision, like the politician continuing to refuse to negotiate even when it irritated her colleagues, so it is incorrect. *Abasement* is synonymous with *humiliation* or *degradation,* so it is incorrect. A *gambit* is incorrect because a gambit is an opening move, typically one that accepts a degree of risk to gain an advantage. Blank (3) describes how the politician's constituents viewed her refusal to negotiate, and based on the sentence's structure, it can be inferred that they supported her refusal. *Hailed* means to enthusiastically welcome and acclaim, which matches how the sentence contrasts the politician's popularity with constituents as opposed to her colleagues. *Coalesced* is incorrect because *coalesced* means to gather together or combine parts into a whole. *Endowed* means to be equipped with a quality or ability, so it is incorrect.

15. A, E: *Extirpate* and *nascent*: Based on the sentence's context, it can be inferred that Blank (1) must be an action the government is taking to undermine or destroy the extremist group. *Extirpate* means to annihilate or utterly destroy. Thus, it is the correct choice. When used as a verb, *malign* means to slander, defame, or libel. Although maligning the group would undermine it, *extirpate* better matches the sentence's characterization of the action as aggressive. *Polarize* means to create separation between groups, typically by inflaming or underscoring their differences. As such, it is incorrect. Blank (2) describes an early stage of the extremist group. *Nascent* is correct because it refers to something that's only recently come to exist and/or begun to show potential. As an adjective, *aesthetic* denotes appreciating or being concerned with beauty and therefore is incorrect. *Ostentatious* is incorrect because *ostentatious* is synonymous with *pretentious*.

16. C, D: The sentence is describing a student who seems to be wastefully spending money on unnecessary items while neglecting his responsibilities. *Prodigal* and *spendthrift* both mean to spend money in a lavish, reckless, and/or wasteful manner. *Bombastic* means to be pompous and indicates a lack of substance, so Choice *A* is incorrect. Choice *B* is incorrect because *erudite* is synonymous with being *scholarly*, which is the opposite of the student in question. To be *subversive* is to undermine authority and/or violate norms, which could fit the sentence, but there's no equivalent adjective in the answer choices. So, Choice *E* is incorrect. Choice *F* is incorrect because *whimsical* means fanciful or playful.

17. A, C: The sentence is describing a notorious fan who threw garbage on the field in a misguided effort to support his favorite player. *Ardent* and *fervent* both denote extreme passion, which would explain the fan's over-the-top reaction. *Benign* means gentle or kindly, which the rowdy fan definitely is not. As such, Choice *B* is incorrect. *Gullible* is synonymous with *credulous,* and it indicates that someone can be easily persuaded to do something. The fan could've thrown the garbage because they gullibly believed a friend claiming it would make a difference; however, there's no equivalent adjective in the answer choices. As such, Choice *D* is incorrect. Choice *E* is incorrect because *prolific* indicates that something is abundant or plentiful. *Soporific* is synonymous with *sleepiness,* so Choice *F* is incorrect.

18. C, D: The sentence is describing an employee who made a mistake and fears being fired over it. *Mollify* and *placate* both mean to make someone less angry. So, if the employee successfully mollifies or placates his boss, they'd be less likely to fire him. To *bolster* is to strengthen or reinforce something, so Choice *A* is incorrect. *Mitigate* means to alleviate or diminish harm, but it would make more sense if it was directed at the problem rather than the boss. For example, the employee mitigating his late arrival would fit much better than mitigating his boss. As such, Choice *B* is incorrect. *Rebut* and *refute* are alike in meaning, but they don't fit the context of the sentence. They both mean to disprove something, and the employee is not attempting to claim that his boss is in the wrong. So, Choice *E* and Choice *F* are both incorrect.

19. B, E: The sentence references an instantaneous connection Brian feels toward Janet, and the blank is describing the moment he felt the connection. *Ephemeral* and *transient* both mean something is short lived or fleeting. This fits well with the sentence's structure and Brian's claim of an instant connection. *Arbitrary* denotes randomness or capriciousness. Although *arbitrary* fits the sentence's context and content, there isn't an equivalent adjective in the answer choices. As such, Choice *A* is incorrect. Likewise, *fortuitous* means unexpected, lucky, or fortunate. *Fortuitous* doesn't have an equivalent adjective among the answer choices; therefore, Choice *C* is incorrect. Choice *D* is incorrect because *salubrious* denotes healthiness. *Unadorned* indicates plainness and a lack of ornamentation, so Choice *F* is incorrect.

20. E, F: The sentence describes a coach lambasting his team, so it can be inferred that the coach is upset by their performance. *Lethargic* and *listless* both denote a state of low energy and/or enthusiasm. If the team performed lethargically or listlessly, it makes sense why the coach is upset. *Errant* refers to an error or misdirection, so Choice *A* is incorrect. *Frenetic* denotes a fast pace and/or recklessness. Although this fits the sentence, there is no equivalent adjective in the answer choices. Therefore, Choice *B* is incorrect. *Hapless* means unlucky or unfortunate, so Choice *C* is incorrect. Choice *D* is incorrect because to be *immutable* is to be unchanging or unyielding.

Section 4: Verbal Reasoning

1. E: Choice *E* describes how opinions lose their immunity when they are likely to lead to a mischievous act. Based on context, immunity references how most opinions should be freely expressed, so the mischievousness component is functioning as an exception and limitation. Choice *A* is incorrect because it serves to introduce a discussion of how opinions can lead to actions, and it doesn't address a limitation on expressing opinions. Choice *B* is incorrect because it tangentially references the limitation, but this sentence primarily serves to explain the general rule about why opinions should be expressed freely. Choice *C* is incorrect because it concerns the nature of truth, which is unrelated to the limitations on opinions. Choice *D* is incorrect because it is the passage's topic sentence, which merely announces the possibility of a limitation on expressing opinions.

2. A, B: The author discusses the nature of the truth at the end of the passage and asserts that most people only speak half-truths and cannot understand all sides of the truth due to their internal biases. In addition, the author contends that mankind cannot recognize truth because people are fallible. So, it can be inferred that people will only recognize full truths when mankind becomes infallible, which is unlikely to happen. Therefore, Choices *A* and *B* are correct. Choice *C* is incorrect because the passage doesn't compare actions and opinions in terms of their truthfulness, and it's unlikely the author would find opinions more truthful than actions.

3. B: The passage distinguishes between opinions based on their consequences in order to argue for the protection of free speech, and the author repeatedly compares merely unpopular opinions with those likely to lead to harmful actions. Thus, Choice *B* is the correct answer. Choice *A* is incorrect because the author only mentions truth as part of a broader philosophical discussion. The passage distinguishes between half-truths and the potential existence of a universal truth; however, the passage doesn't name or compare universal truths. As such, Choice *C* is incorrect. The passage doesn't distinguish between unpopular opinions based on their sentiments; rather, the distinction is based on outcomes. So, Choice *D* is incorrect. The passage indirectly distinguishes between nuisances and criminal actions; however, this is a part of the primary distinction between opinions based on their consequences. Therefore, Choice *E* is incorrect.

4. D: The passage's first sentence is summarizing an earlier point about the importance of free speech and then launches into a discussion of the limits to free speech. In the middle of the sentence, "let us next examine" signals to the reader that what came before is a summary and what follows is a fresh discussion. Therefore, Choice *D* is the correct answer. The first sentence functions as a topic sentence, but it doesn't summarize the passage. So, Choice *A* is incorrect. The sentence references the conclusion's main topic, but it doesn't outline the conclusion about distinguishing between opinions based on consequences. As such, Choice *B* is incorrect. Choice *C* is incorrect because it doesn't contain an anecdote, which is an illustrative example. Similarly, the sentence introduces, but doesn't compare, important concepts. Therefore, Choice *E* is incorrect.

5. B: The author's conclusion is that people should be free to share their opinions unless doing so would directly cause harm. If it were difficult to predict whether an opinion would directly cause harm, the passage's reasoning and conclusion would largely become irrelevant, so Choice *B* is correct. The author agrees that mankind's opinions only contain partial truths, so Choice *A* is incorrect. The author also supports the notion that opinions have an inherent immunity except he contends that immunity is lost when they directly cause harm. So, Choice *C* is incorrect because it doesn't impact the author's exception. Choice *D* is incorrect because it is a restatement of premises found at the end of the passage. Choice *E* is incorrect because it doesn't directly impact the author's conclusion. Additionally, if speech rarely led to consequences, it would somewhat strengthen the author's argument for more free speech.

6. C: The passage provides a litany of details about the unsanitary and disgusting practices in a meatpacking factory. In addition, the author repeatedly alludes to a lack of regulatory protocols and describes how the meatpackers cut corners and deceived their customers to boost profits. Therefore, Choice *C* is correct. According to the passage, meat products contained sawdust and rats; however, this is only part of the picture. The meat products also contained dangerous chemicals, dirt, workers' germs, waste, and old scraps of meat. In addition, the author focuses on how the packers increased their profit margin in an underhanded manner. Therefore, Choice *A* is incorrect. The passage doesn't mention regulations, so it's unclear whether the regulations were being ignored or didn't exist. As a result, Choice *B* is incorrect. Choice *D* is incorrect because the factory's issues went far beyond sausage production; therefore, chemical treatments and deceptive labeling is a relatively minor point to the overall lack of sanitation. Choice *E* is incorrect because it's unclear whether the owners were lackadaisical or intentionally indifferent. In addition, the issues with the packers are also a relatively minor point.

7. C: The author doesn't spare any details in his description of the horrific conditions at the meatpacking factory. Based on the extensive amount of detail, it can be inferred that the author wants to raise awareness about the meatpacking industry, Choice *C*, likely for the purpose of sparking a public outcry and condemnation. Choice *A* is incorrect because the passage overwhelmingly focuses on issues associated with meatpacking rather than the consumption of meat. The author likely doesn't care for the owners based on what he witnessed, but there's no indication that he's biased from the outset. As such, Choice *B* is incorrect. The author is critical of how the factory is profit oriented, but the passage seems much more concerned with increasing sanitation than reducing profits. So, Choice *D* is incorrect. The author certainly would support more regulation of food product labels, but the passage has a much broader focus. Therefore, Choice *E* is incorrect.

8. E: The passage repeatedly mentions how the meatpacking factory lacked supervision and regulation, opted for cheap solutions, and deceived its customers. So, although the passage doesn't mention the factory's owners, it can be properly inferred that they cared more about profits than producing a safe, sanitary, and tasty product, making Choice *E* the correct answer. Based on how the factory produced sausage, it seems very unlikely that corned beef production was any better. As a result, Choice *A* is incorrect. The author characterizes the labeling of smoked sausage as deceptive rather than ignorant, so Choice *B* is incorrect. Choice *C* is incorrect because it's unclear whether the owners visited the factory or if the operation was going as planned. The author criticizes what's going into the hoppers more than the number of hoppers; therefore, Choice *D* is incorrect.

9. A: Choice *A* describes how workers wouldn't bother to pick a poisoned rat out of the carts because they viewed the rat as merely a tidbit. A tidbit is a tiny piece of something, which implies there was already a vast number of contaminants in the sausage. Choice *B* is incorrect because although it describes rat dung in the meat, it doesn't provide information about the amount of contamination. Choice *C* describes a cost-cutting and deceptive business practice, not the number of contaminants, so it is incorrect. Likewise, Choice *D* is incorrect because it only describes a cost-

349

cutting and unsanitary business practice. Choice *E* provides information about an unsanitary practice, but dirty hands were only one of many contaminants, so it is incorrect.

10. A, B, C: The author characterizes the meatpacking industry as highly unpleasant. *Aghast* means full of shock and horror, which likely describes the author's attitude toward the unsanitary conditions. The author also critically examines the production of "smoked" and "special" sausage at the end of the passage, and it's strongly implied that he opposes these deceptive business practices. Finally, *quality control* refers to the maintenance of consistent quality during production, and the author provides numerous examples of unsanitary conditions negatively impacting the quality of the meat product. Therefore, Choices *A*, *B*, and *C* are all correct.

11. C, F: *Hackneyed* and *precipitous*: Blank (1) is a characteristic describing television shows, and it can be inferred based on the second sentence that the characteristic is likely negative. *Hackneyed* means something is cliché and unoriginal. Therefore, it is correct. Something *esoteric* is obscure and only understood by a limited number of people. As such, it is incorrect. *Fastidious* is incorrect because *fastidious* means paying attention to the accuracy of small details. Blank (2) is describing a drop in television viewership, and *precipitous* is synonymous with *steep* and is therefore correct. To be *magnanimous* is to be humble, generous, and/or gentle; therefore, it is incorrect. *Mercurial* denotes rapid and unpredictable change, but it is most often used to describe a mood, temperament, or behavior.

12. A: *Assuage*: The sentence is describing a positive quality of music, so the correct answer likely diminishes pain and distress. To *assuage* a feeling is to make it less intense, so it is the correct choice. *Desiccate* is incorrect because *desiccate* refers to removing moisture. To *impugn* something is to challenge or call it into question, so it is incorrect. *Precipitate* means to cause something to happen suddenly or prematurely; therefore, it is incorrect. *Winnow* is incorrect because *winnow* means to reduce a quantity to a desired amount.

13. B, D, G: *Deftly, backlash,* and *apathetic*: Blank (1) describes the company's ability to avoid regulations. *Deftly* means skillfully or cleverly and is therefore correct. *Arduously* is incorrect because although it means something requires a tremendous amount of effort or labor, skill and cleverness were the implied requirements. *Insipidly* is incorrect because *insipidly* describes something with a lack of flavor, interest, or stimulation. Blank (2) is something negative that market forecasters believed the company would suffer. A *backlash* occurs when a mass of people has an adverse reaction to something, which is a reasonable prediction as to how users might respond to a company stealing data. *Dirge* is incorrect because a *dirge* is an elegy or funeral lament. *Probity* is synonymous with *honesty* and *integrity*; therefore, it is incorrect. Blank (3) describes how users were surprisingly unconcerned about the company's data collection. *Apathetic* denotes a lack of interest or enthusiasm, so it is the correct answer choice. Something that's *desultory* lacks a plan, purpose, or structure, so it is incorrect. *Polemical* is incorrect because *polemical* refers to something that's aggressively controversial or critical.

14. D: *Prevaricating*: Based on the structure of the sentence, it can be inferred that Madeline is talented at something similar to lying. Because *prevaricate* means to be evasive or deceptive, it is the correct answer. *Abjure* means to renounce or reject something, typically in a solemn or serious manner. As such, it is incorrect. *Inculpate* is incorrect because *inculpate* means to accuse, blame, or incriminate. *Obviating* means to remove an obstacle or avoid something difficult, so it is incorrect. *Vacillate* means to waver or be indecisive; therefore, it is also incorrect.

15. C, F: *Peripheral* and *pith*: Blank (1) is describing features of a phenomenon that only lead to minor breakthroughs. Something *peripheral* is on the outskirts of something. So, if the researcher is only discovering peripheral features, their frustration makes sense. *Banal* means unoriginal or hackneyed; therefore, it is incorrect. To be *equivocal* is to be ambiguous or uncertain, so it is incorrect. Blank (2) is the opposite of a peripheral feature. *Pith* refers to the core essence of something, so if the researcher uncovered the pith, she'd likely achieve a major breakthrough. A *catalyst* is something that triggers a rapid change, so it is incorrect. *Omniscience* means an all-knowing state of being. As such, it is incorrect.

16. B, D: Based on context, it can be inferred that there's a problem with the resources because it triggered a refugee crisis. *Dearth* and *paucity* both denote extreme scarcity, and if resources are scarce in an area, it makes sense why people would flee. Choice *A* is incorrect because a *cacophony* is an unpleasant and discordant mixture of harsh sounds. *Milieu* refers to something's background, environment, or context. As such, Choice *C* is incorrect. *Plethora* is synonymous with *abundance* or *excess,* which is the polar opposite of the sentence's meaning. As such, Choice *E* is incorrect. *Temperance* denotes a state of moderation or restraint; therefore, Choice *F* is incorrect.

17. A, F: The sentence is describing how Walter is pleased with his staff because they worked hard. *Extolled* and *lauded* both match the sentence's positivity because they mean to lavish with praise. Choice *B* is incorrect because *flouted* means to blatantly ignore someone and/or undermine their authority. *Galvanized* could possibly fit the context of a team meeting because it means to encourage, inspire, and/or unite; however, *extolled* and *lauded* create more equivalent sentences than *galvanize* does when paired with any other answer choice. As such, Choice *C* is incorrect. *Goaded* means to prod or trick someone into taking an action they otherwise wouldn't do; so, Choice *D* is incorrect. *Groused* means to complain in a petty or grumpy manner, so Choice *E* is incorrect.

18. B, F: The sentence describes a student who is doing something the teacher doesn't usually tolerate except in the context of a class discussion. *Garrulous* and *voluble* both mean to be overly talkative, which appropriately describes a characteristic the teacher would otherwise admonish if not for the ongoing discussion. *Florid* can either refer to something incredibly intricate or a flushed complexion, but either way, Choice *A* is incorrect. *Homogenous* is synonymous with *uniformity*, so Choice *C* is incorrect. Something that's *implacable* is unwavering and relentless; therefore, Choice *D* is incorrect. To be *nonplussed* is to be shocked into bewilderment or confusion, so Choice *E* is incorrect.

19. A, E: Based on the structure of the sentence's clauses, it can be inferred that the lawyer is trying to support or strengthen her client's testimony. *Corroborate* and *substantiate* both involve supplying validation, which perfectly matches the lawyer's goal. *Delineate* means to portray something in a precise manner. As such, Choice *B* is incorrect. *Disseminate* means to spread something, usually information or knowledge, so Choice *C* is incorrect. To *emulate* something is to mimic it; therefore, Choice *D* is incorrect. *Venerate* means to highly revere or respect something, so Choice *F* is incorrect.

20. B, C: The sentence connects the firing of a coworker to a rebellion, so the missing verb most likely denotes a causal relationship. *Engendered* and *fomented* both mean to cause or instigate an event, which matches how the firing triggered a rebellion. Choice *A* is incorrect because *deigned* means to do something demeaning or in violation of their dignity. *Marred* means to contaminate or ruin, so Choice *D* is incorrect. Choice *E* is incorrect because *posit* means to assert or assume something is true while making a point. *Rued* denotes extreme regret; therefore, Choice *F* is incorrect.

Section 5: Quantitative Reasoning

QUANTITATIVE COMPARISON

1. B: In order to solve the system, plug the second equation in for y in the first equation to obtain $x + 2(x + 3) = 12$. This simplifies to $3x + 6 = 12$, or $x = 2$. Therefore, from the second equation, $y = 2 + 3 = 5$. In conclusion, y is greater than x.

2. A: Pick an amount for the car. If it cost $20,000 and the price was increased by 20%, the new price would be $20,000(1.2) = $24,000. Then, if the price were reduced by 20%, the final price would be $24,000(0.8) = $19,200. This amount is less than the original price.

3. B: Because we are told how many people end up in the line, we can work backwards to determine how many people were in the line originally. There are 45 people in line after an influx of 30 people into the restaurant, which means there were $45 - 30 = 15$ people in the line after half of those originally in the line were seated. We can then double this to determine the original number of people in the line. Thus, $x = 15 \times 2 = 30$. This means that Quantity B is greater than Quantity A.

4. A: From the given statement we have $.05x = .06y$. Therefore, $x = 1.2y$. This equation states that 1.2 times y is equal to x. Therefore, Quantity A is larger.

MULTIPLE-CHOICE – SELECT ONLY ONE ANSWER CHOICE

5. E: If h represents the number of hours that you used the chair lift, the following expression represents the total amount paid to the ski resort: $12.5h + 45$. Setting this equal to $120 and solving for h results in $h = 6$. Therefore, 6 hours on the lift were paid for.

6. B: The number 368 is broken down into prime factors. As a result, $368 = 2 \times 2 \times 2 \times 2 \times 23$. The number 23 is the only odd factor, so the correct answer is 1.

7. C: If x represents the number of teachers, then there are $x + 342$ students. We can set up the following proportion:

$$\frac{3}{41} = \frac{x}{x + 342}.$$

Cross multiplying gives us $3(x + 342) = 41x$, or $3x + 1026 = 41x$. This has a solution of $x = 27$. Therefore, there are 27 teachers and $27 + 342 = 369$ students.

8. A: We can solve this algebraically. Let q represent the number of quizzes she had taken previously. Therefore, from the definition of average,

$$96 = \frac{93q + 99}{q + 1}$$

Solving this, we obtain $96(q + 1) = 93q + 99$. This has a solution of $q = 1$, so there was one quiz prior to yesterday's quiz.

MULTIPLE-CHOICE – SELECT ONE OR MORE ANSWER CHOICES

9. A, B: We break down each number into prime factors to determine the correct answer. $18 = 3 \times 3 \times 2, 20 = 2 \times 2 \times 5, 25 = 5 \times 5, 30 = 2 \times 3 \times 5$. Therefore, 18 and 20 have exactly 2 distinct prime factors.

10. A, B: Because the numerator is a square root function, the radicand must be greater than or equal to 0. Therefore, $x \geq 7$. Also, the denominator cannot be equal to 2 since it cannot be equal to 0. Therefore, any value can be plugged into the function that is not equal to 2 and greater than or equal to 7. Only 7 and 8 can be plugged into the function.

11. B, D, E: The sequence is equal to the sum of perfect squares and 1. For instance, the first term is $2^2 + 1$ and the second term is $3^2 + 1$. Therefore, the next three terms are $7^2 + 1 = 50, 8^2 + 1 = 65$, and $9^2 + 1 = 82$.

12. B, C, D: The polynomial on the left side can be factored by grouping as:

$$4x^2(x - 5) - 4(x - 5) = 4(x^2 - 1)(x - 5) = 0.$$

Setting each factor equal to 0, we see that there are 3 solutions: -1, 1, and 5.

NUMERIC ENTRY

13. $\frac{2}{3}$: The probability is equal to the number of desired outcomes divided by the number of possible outcomes. There are 21 total marbles in the bag, so the number of possible outcomes is 21. Of all the marbles, 14 are not blue, so 14 is the number of desired outcomes. Therefore, the probability is $\frac{14}{21}$, which is simplified into $\frac{2}{3}$.

14. 15: Let A represent Alex's age and C represent Carl's age. The problem gives us the following two equations:

$$A = 3C$$

$$A - 6 = 4 + C$$

Substituting the first equation into the second, we have $3C - 6 = 4 + C$. Solving this for C, we have $C = 5$. Therefore, $A = 3(5) = 15$. Alex is 15 years old.

15. 2: The area of rectangle R is $15(8) = 120$ square centimeters. The area of rectangle S is $20(12) = 240$ square centimeters. The area of rectangle R can be multiplied times 2 in order to obtain the area of rectangle S.

16. $\frac{12}{43}$: Because there are 4 possibilities, the sum of them equals 1:

$$m + \frac{m}{3} + 2m + \frac{m}{4} = 1$$

Writing over common denominators, the result is:

$$\frac{12m + 4m + 24m + 3m}{12} = 1$$

This is equivalent to $\frac{43m}{12} = 1$, or $m = \frac{12}{43}$.

DATA INTERPRETATION SETS

17. A: The largest percentage change of the blue line, which represents Catholics, occurred between 1978 and 1980. The percentage decreased over 3%. This amount can be seen by referring to the vertical axis, which represents percentage. The other options had changes that were less than 3%.

18. C: The red line, which represents Methodists, shows that from 1980 to 2010 most of the data points lie around the 34% range. Any amount equal to or below 30% would not be a good estimation, as those represent the lower end of the range. Also, any amount equal to or above 36% would not be a good estimation, as those represent the higher end of the range.

19. C: There is an odd number of values, so the median is the middle value when the numbers are placed in order. In numerical order, we have 5, 6, 7, 9, 10, 11, 12. The median is 9. The first quartile Q_1 is the median of the lower half of the data, not including the median of the complete set. This is 6. The third quartile Q_3 is the median of the upper half of the data, not including the median of the complete set. This is 11. The interquartile range is the difference between Q_3 and Q_1, which is $11 - 6 = 5$.

20. C: Subtracting 2 from each number, we have the following amounts of grocery bags: 3, 4, 5, 7, 8, 9, 10. The median is 7. The first quartile Q_1 is the median of the lower half of the data but does not include the median of the complete set. This is 4. The third quartile Q_3 is the median of the upper half of the data but does not include the median of the complete set. This is 9. The interquartile range is the difference between Q_3 and Q_1, which is $9 - 4 = 5$. The interquartile range stays the same because the distances between the data values do not change.

Section 6: Quantitative Reasoning

QUANTITATIVE COMPARISON

1. A: Choice A is correct because the positive factors of 10 are 1, 2, 5, 10. These numbers multiplied together give a product of 100. The positive factors of 11 are 1 and 11, which give a product of 11. The first product of 100 is greater than 11.

2. B: Choice B is the correct answer because Quantity B is greater. Rewriting the expression in Quantity A makes it $\frac{\sqrt{3}}{3} \times \frac{\sqrt{3}}{5}$ because we multiplied by the reciprocal. The new product is $\frac{3}{15}$, once the fractions are multiplied, which simplifies to $\frac{1}{5}$. Quantity B becomes $\frac{5}{\sqrt{2}} \times \frac{3}{\sqrt{2}}$, after the expression is rewritten by multiplying by the reciprocal. Simplifying this expression leads to a product of $\frac{15}{2}$, which becomes 7.5. This value is greater than $\frac{1}{5}$, so Quantity B is greater than Quantity A.

3. B: Choice B is correct because Quantity B is greater. The coefficients in an expression are those numbers that lie in front of variables. For Quantity A, the coefficients are 3, 7, and -8. Adding these numbers together yields a sum of 2. The constants in an expression are the numbers that do not have a variable attached to them. The constants in Quantity B are 2 and 12. Multiplying these numbers gives a product of 24, which is greater than 2.

4. D: Choice D is correct because the relationship cannot be determined from the information given. There are two expressions with two unknowns. The guess and check method can be used to compare the two quantities. If $x = 1$ and $y = 2$, the first expression becomes $\frac{1^2}{3(2)-2} = \frac{1}{4}$. The second expression becomes $\frac{1^2-4}{2} = \frac{-3}{2}$. For these values of x and y, Quantity A is greater. If these values are changed to $x = -3$ and $y = 2$, then the first expression becomes $\frac{(-3)^2}{3(2)-2} = \frac{9}{4}$. The expression for

Quantity B becomes $\frac{(-3)^2-4}{2} = \frac{5}{2}$. For these values of x and y, Quantity B is greater. These examples show that the relationship cannot be determined based on the information given.

Multiple-Choice – Select Only One Answer Choice

5. A: Choice A is the correct answer because it lists the first five prime numbers. A prime number is an integer greater than one that only has factors of one and itself. Choices B, C, and E are not correct because they list 1 in the list of prime numbers. Choice D is not correct because it lists 9 as a prime number, and it has factors of 1, 3, and itself.

6. D: Choice D is the correct answer for the sum of the fractions. When adding fractions, the first step is to create a common denominator. For these fractions, the denominators are 3 and 5. The lowest common multiple of these numbers is 15. Multiplying the first fraction by $\frac{5}{5}$ gives the new fraction $\frac{10}{15}$. The second fraction becomes $\frac{12}{15}$, after it is multiplied by $\frac{3}{3}$. Adding these fractions, gives the sum $\frac{22}{15}$. Choice A is incorrect because it simply adds the numerators and the denominators. Choice B is incorrect because it adds in the same way as Choice A and simplifies the fraction. Choice C is incorrect because it creates a common denominator and does not change the numerators. Choice E is incorrect because it is only the simplified version of Choice C.

7. B: Choice B is the correct answer because it makes a true statement when plugged into the given equation. The equation is solved by first subtracting 7 from both sides. The resulting equation is $2x = -10$. From this equation, both sides are divided by 2, giving the answer of $x = -5$. Choice A is incorrect because it does not consider the negative sign on the numbers. Choice C is incorrect because it results from solving the equation by adding the 7 to both sides, instead of subtracting. Choice D is incorrect because it does not consider the negative, and it also results from solving the equation by adding the 7 to both sides. Choice E is incorrect because it leaves out a step in solving the equation, subtracting the 7, but not dividing by 2.

8. C: Choice C is correct because $1.65 is 15% of $11. Choice A is incorrect because it gives a total amount that the worker would make and increases the pay by $1.50 instead of $1.65. Choice B is incorrect because it uses $0.15, instead of 15% of the hourly pay. Choice D is incorrect because it uses the 15 as the cents and adds a dollar to the pay instead of using 15 as a percentage of the pay. Choice E is incorrect because the question asks *how much more* they will make, not the total pay per hour.

Multiple-Choice – Select One or More Answer Choices

9. A, B, D: Choices A, B, and D are the possible values that yield an average of 28 seconds for the runner's fastest times in the 100-meter race. Average is found by adding up the values and dividing by 3.

10. A, E: When simplified, the values of Choices A and E fall between 0 and 1. Choice A has a value of $\frac{1}{8}$, and Choice E has a value of $\frac{1}{5}$. These values are found by moving the numbers to the denominator to make a simplified fraction. The value of Choice B is $3^2 = 9$. The value of Choice C is $8 \times -2 = -16$. The value of Choice D is $-3^{-1} = \frac{1}{-3}$. None of these three values fall between zero and one.

11. A: Choice *A* gives the only discount percentage that will yield a grocery bill less than or equal to $175. With a discount of 30%, the grocery bill would be $175, found by the equation $0.7 \times 250 = 175$. This also means that Choices *B*, *C*, *D*, and *E* are all less than the discount needed to come in under budget because the discounts for each of these are smaller.

12. A, D, E: Factored forms of an expression are those that break down the expression into multiple expressions that when multiplied together give the original expression. Choice *A* gives a factored form because $2x$ is factored out to the front. When multiplied back together, it yields the original expression. Choices *D* and *E* give the correct factored form as they multiply together to give a final expression equal to the original. Choice *B* is not a correct answer because the middle term does not equal the original expression; it becomes $4x^4 - x^3 + 6x$. Choice *C* gives an incorrect expression as well, yielding a final answer of $4x^4 - 4x^2 + 4x$. In this expression, the second and third terms are not equal to the given expression.

NUMERIC ENTRY

13. 80π: The ratio of the values of the circumference between the circles is 1 to 4. If the value of the radius for Circle A is doubled, then the circumference is doubled. This makes the new circumference 20π. If the ratio stays the same, then the circumference for Circle B would be 80π.

14. 30 degrees: Using the properties of transversals, notice that angles x and y are supplementary: $x + y = 180°$. The question also indicates that $y - x = 120$. This equation can be rearranged to give $y = 120 + x$ and then substituted into the first equation:

$$x + (120 + x) = 180$$

Solve this equation for x:

$$2x + 120 = 180$$

$$2x = 60$$

$$x = 30$$

15. 9:7 : The first quarter of the year includes January through March. In the first three months, there were 81 cars and 63 trucks sold. The ratio of cars to trucks sold is 81 to 63. That ratio can be reduced to 9 to 7. Any fraction equivalent to this ratio will be accepted.

16. 48: The ratio of 2 to 3 can be written as a fraction, $\frac{2}{3}$. This fraction can be set equal to the fraction that represents the given number of students who chose virtual school, 32. The equation becomes $\frac{2}{3} = \frac{32}{x}$. Solving by cross-multiplication, the equation becomes $2x = 3 \times 32$. Multiplying 3 by 32, then dividing by 2, the answer is $x = 48$. There would be 48 students who chose in-person classes in the third grade.

DATA INTERPRETATION SETS

17. C: The sum of the percentages for those that chose "agree" or "strongly agree" is $69 + 27 = 96$. Taking 96% of the total number of students yields a population of 120 students that chose "agree" or "strongly agree."

18. E: Because the percentage data is rounded to the nearest whole number, the exact number of students who responded with strong disagreement or neither agreement nor disagreement cannot be determined. Each student's response carries a weight of 0.8% in the survey results. Thus, the weight of 2 student responses is 1.6% (which rounds to 2%), and the weight of 3 student responses is 2.4% (which also rounds to 2%). One of the groups contains 2 students and the other contains 3 students, but it is impossible to determine from the chart which is which.

19. A: The most straightforward way to approach this problem is to determine what percentage of the whole these 10 students constitute:

$$\frac{10}{125} = 0.08 = 8\%$$

If 10 more students are added to the number of those who agreed with the statement, it will be an addition of 8%:

$$27\% + 8\% = 35\%$$

20. B: The percentage of students that strongly agreed with the statement in the post-survey is 69%. If this value is up 25 percentage points from the pre-survey, then there were $69\% - 25\% = 44\%$ who strongly agreed in the pre-survey.

$$125 \times 44\% = 55$$

GRE Practice Test #3

Section 1: Analytical Writing

Time – 30 minutes

ANALYZE AN ISSUE

You will have a choice between two Issue topics. Each topic will appear as a brief quotation that states or implies an issue of general interest. Read each topic carefully; then decide on which topic you could write a more effective and well-reasoned response. You will have 45 minutes to plan and compose a response that presents your perspective on the topic you select. A response on any other topic will receive a zero. You are free to accept, reject, or qualify the claim made in the topic you selected, as long as the ideas you present are clearly relevant to the topic. Support your views with reasons and examples drawn from such areas as your reading, experience, observations, or academic studies.

GRE readers, who are college and university faculty, will read your response and evaluate its overall quality, based on how well you do the following:

- consider the complexities and implications of the issue
- organize, develop, and express your ideas on the issue
- support your ideas with relevant reasons and examples
- control the elements of standard written English

You may want to take a few minutes to think about the issue and to plan a response before you begin writing. Because the space for writing your response is limited, use the next page to plan your response. Be sure to develop your ideas fully and organize them coherently, but leave time to reread what you have written and make any revisions that you think are necessary.

> Students receiving financial aid from the government should only be able to apply that aid to coursework that leads directly to their intended degree.

Write a response in which you discuss the extent to which you agree or disagree with whether or not students should be able to spend financial aid dollars on whatever coursework they choose. Then, explain your reasoning for the position you take. In developing and supporting your position, describe specific circumstances in which adopting or rejecting the recommendation would or would not be advantageous, and explain how these examples shape your position.

Section 2: Analytical Writing

Time – 30 minutes

ANALYZE AN ARGUMENT

You will have 30 minutes to plan and write a critique of an argument presented in the form of a short passage. A critique of any other argument will receive a score of zero. Analyze the line of reasoning in the argument. Be sure to consider what, if any, questionable assumptions underlie the thinking and, if evidence is cited, how well it supports the conclusion. You can also discuss what sort of evidence would strengthen or refute the argument, what changes in the argument would make it more logically sound, and what additional information might help you better evaluate its conclusion. *Note that you are NOT being asked to present your views on the subject.*

GRE readers, who are college and university faculty, will read your critique and evaluate its overall quality, based on how well you

- identify and analyze important features of the argument
- organize, develop, and express your critique of the argument
- support your critique with relevant reasons and examples
- control the elements of standard written English

Before you begin writing, you may want to take a few minutes to evaluate the argument and plan a response. Because the space for writing your response is limited, use the next page to plan your response. Be sure to develop your ideas fully and organize them coherently, but leave time to reread what you have written and make any revisions that you think are necessary.

> Pedestrian deaths are a significant issue in just about every city in the United States. In several major European cities, however, pedestrians use a shared street concept that means pedestrians, bikes, and cars all use the same space with no curbs, no lights, and no traffic signs. The argument is that everyone is forced to be more alert, and the shared space forces cooperation rather than any one group claiming ownership of the space (as cars in America do now). This model has been quite successful in decreasing accidents among all groups. Most American models suggest that we should simply build more sidewalks instead. Areas with sidewalks on both sides of the street have been opposed, however, due to presentation concerns (maintaining a rural versus urban feel) and safety (tripping) hazards for residents. Everyone agrees that reducing pedestrian crashes and deaths is a goal in our communities, and the European model appeases those who oppose sidewalks in their communities while still meeting the objective.

Write a response in which you discuss what specific evidence is needed to evaluate whether the shared street concept is viable in the United States, and explain how the evidence would weaken or strengthen the argument.

Section 3: Verbal Reasoning

Time – 30 Minutes

20 Questions

Directions – Questions 1-10: Each passage in this group is followed by questions based on its content. After reading a passage, choose the best answer to each question. Answer all the questions following a passage on the basis of what is stated or *implied* in that passage.

Questions 1–3 are based on the following passage:

School buses transport more than 25 million American students every day, and they provide the safest transportation for children to get to and from school. However, many older school buses emit harmful diesel exhaust that directly affects children. The U.S. Environmental Protection Agency (EPA) is ensuring that all new buses meet tighter standards developed to reduce diesel emissions and improve safety. Today's new buses are cleaner—60 times cleaner than buses built before 1990—and feature additional emergency exits, improved mirror systems, and pedestrian safety devices. But replacing America's school bus fleet will take time because diesel school buses can operate for 20 to 30 years. Clean School Bus USA is a national, innovative program designed to help communities reduce emissions from diesel school buses. It provides resources and assistance to fleet owners and operators as well as educators, transportation officials, and community partners committed to improving school bus fleets and protecting children's health.

Adapted from the EPA's National Clean Diesel Campaign educational material.

1. The passage above suggests which of the following about school buses?

   a. Older buses lack emergency exits and other safety mechanisms.
   b. Replacement of outdated school buses will happen over the next 20 to 30 years.
   c. No diesel buses have been made since 1990.
   d. Fleet owners are more concerned with longevity than safety.
   e. Buses built after 1990 are safer for both transport and emissions than those built before 1990

2. Based on the passage above, one could conclude which of the following?

   a. Although there are programs to assist with replacing fleets, schools still cannot afford it.
   b. Students who walk to school or travel in a car are more likely to experience an accident.
   c. The new bus fleets likely include electric or hybrid buses.
   d. Prior to 1990, no one was concerned about school bus emissions.
   e. As part of stricter standards, the EPA will require schools to replace their fleets with safer buses.

3. From the passage, select the sentence that best explains why modern buses are safer.

a. The U.S. Environmental Protection Agency (EPA) is ensuring that all new buses meet tighter standards developed to reduce diesel emissions and improve safety.

b. School buses transport more than 25 million American students every day, and they provide the safest transportation for children to get to and from school.

c. Clean School Bus USA is a national, innovative program designed to help communities reduce emissions from diesel school buses.

d. Today's new buses are cleaner—60 times cleaner than buses built before 1990—and feature additional emergency exits, improved mirror systems, and pedestrian safety devices.

e. It provides resources and assistance to fleet owners and operators as well as educators, transportation officials, and community partners committed to improving school bus fleets and protecting children's health.

Questions 4–6 are based on the following passage:

The impacts of invasive species are second only to habitat destruction as a cause of global biodiversity loss. In fact, introduced species are a greater threat to native biodiversity than pollution, harvest, and disease combined. Aquatic Nuisance Species (ANS) cause severe and permanent damage to the habitats they invade by reducing the abundance of native species and altering ecosystem processes. They impact native species by preying upon them, competing with them for food and space, interbreeding with them, or introducing harmful pathogens and parasites. ANS may also alter normal functioning of the ecosystem by altering fire regimes, hydrology, nutrient cycling, and productivity.

ANS are increasingly seen as a threat not only to biodiversity and ecosystem functioning, but also to economic development. They reduce production of agricultural crops, forests, and fisheries, decrease water availability, block transport routes, choke irrigation canals, foul industrial pipelines impeding hydroelectric facilities, degrade water quality and fish and wildlife habitat, accelerate filling of lakes and reservoirs, and decrease property values. The costs to control and eradicate invasive species in the U.S. alone amount to more than $137 billion annually. This number is likely an underestimate as it does not consider ecosystem health or the aesthetic value of nature, which can influence tourism and recreational revenue. Estimating the economic impacts associated with ANS is further confounded as monetary values cannot be given to extinction of species, loss in biodiversity, and loss of ecosystem services.

Adapted from the Fish and Wildlife Service's Aquatic Nuisance Species educational material.

4. The passage suggests which of the following is true? Consider each of the three choices separately, and select all that apply.

a. There is a greater threat to global biodiversity than invasive species.

b. Invasive species can be beneficial to the environments where they are introduced.

c. ANS can have significant impacts beyond environmental devastation.

5. Based on the passage, one could conclude that the cost of eradicating ANS

    a. is likely close to $140 billion.

    b. should include a comprehensive focus on prevention.

    c. isn't as important as the nonfinancial impacts.

    d. is more expensive than other environmental disasters.

    e. should be borne by the individuals responsible for introducing them.

6. Select the sentence that best explains why we may never know the cost of ANS.

    a. ANS are increasingly seen as a threat not only to biodiversity and ecosystem functioning, but also to economic development.

    b. The costs to control and eradicate invasive species in the U.S. alone amount to more than $137 billion annually.

    c. They reduce production of agricultural crops, forests and fisheries, decrease water availability, block transport routes, choke irrigation canals, foul industrial pipelines impeding hydroelectric facilities, degrade water quality and fish and wildlife habitat, accelerate filling of lakes and reservoirs, and decrease property values.

    d. Estimating the economic impacts associated with ANS is further confounded because monetary values cannot be given to extinction of species, loss in biodiversity, and loss of ecosystem services.

Questions 7–10 are based on the following passage:

In October 2018, CDC and the U.S. Department of Agriculture's Food Safety and Inspection Service were investigating a large outbreak of *Salmonella* Newport infections linked to ground beef. When NARMS scientists used Whole Genome Sequencing (WGS) to predict antibiotic resistance, they noticed that although most strains were susceptible to antibiotics, some were resistant to multiple antibiotics. This tipped off epidemiologists that two outbreaks were occurring simultaneously and led to the investigation of a distinct outbreak of multidrug-resistant *Salmonella* Newport with decreased susceptibility to azithromycin. Azithromycin is a recommended antibiotic for treatment of severe *Salmonella* infections. *Salmonella* with decreased susceptibility to azithromycin is a rare finding and occurs in fewer than 1 percent of *Salmonella* infections. State public health officials asked patients about recent food, animal, and travel exposures to find a common link for their infections. Illnesses were linked to beef consumed in the United States and Mexico and to soft cheese from Mexico—findings that suggested that cattle in both countries could be a source of this multidrug-resistant *Salmonella*. From June 2018 through March 2019, 255 people in 32 U.S. states became ill from this strain of *Salmonella*.

NARMS scientists can use WGS to predict antibiotic resistance in *Salmonella* and other pathogens much faster than with traditional methods. Combining this detailed genetic information with epidemiologic information helps scientists more precisely link illnesses to food or animal sources. In fact, every U.S. public health department is supported by CDC's Antibiotic Resistance Solutions Initiative to perform WGS on the enteric germs that NARMS tracks, including *Salmonella*, to rapidly identify and stop outbreaks of antibiotic-resistant infections.

Beyond its contributions to outbreak response, WGS helps scientists understand transmission, including how resistant strains get into the food supply. WGS strengthens the fight against the global health threat of antibiotic resistance.

Adapted from CDC informational material.

7. The passage addresses which of the following issues related to antibiotic resistance?
   a. *Salmonella* is often found in beef.
   b. Whole genome sequencing will lead to a cure.
   c. Azithromycin-resistant *Salmonella* is rare.
   d. Multiantibiotic resistance is common.
   e. Tracking food, animal, and travel exposure to *Salmonella* is difficult.

8. The passage suggests that WGS is successful in which of the following? Consider each of the three choices separately, and select all that apply.
   a. identifying exposure source
   b. predicting antibiotic resistance
   c. preventing multiantibiotic resistance

9. Based on the passage, one could conclude that
   a. scientists will be able to stop *Salmonella* outbreaks.
   b. multidrug-resistant *Salmonella* is a growing concern.
   c. other antibiotics will have to be used to treat *Salmonella*.
   d. multiple outbreaks of *Salmonella* often happen simultaneously.
   e. beef is often the source of *Salmonella* outbreaks.

10. Select the sentence that best explains the source of the outbreak as determined by scientists.
   a. State public health officials asked patients about recent food, animal, and travel exposures to find a common link for their infections.
   b. This tipped off epidemiologists that two outbreaks were occurring simultaneously and led to the investigation of a distinct outbreak of multidrug-resistant *Salmonella* Newport with decreased susceptibility to azithromycin.
   c. Combining this detailed genetic information with epidemiologic information helps scientists more precisely link illnesses to food or animal sources.
   d. Illnesses were linked to beef consumed in the United States and Mexico and to soft cheese from Mexico—findings that suggested that cattle in both countries could be a source of this multidrug-resistant *Salmonella*.

Directions - Questions 11-15: For each blank select one entry from the corresponding column of choices. Fill all blanks in the way that best completes the text.

11. It may seem (i) _____, but your average citizen can claim riches under the sea if they discover a shipwreck. (ii) _____ law, or the law of admiralty, is what dictates who has rights to discovered treasures such as (ii) _____.

Blank (i)
a. incontrovertible
b. incomprehensible
c. inconsequential

Blank (ii)
d. Maritime
e. Seafaring
f. Captain's

Blank (iii)
g. bouillon
h. bullion
i. Boolean

12. The Middle Ages are defined as the period between the (i) _____ of the Roman Empire and the start of the Renaissance period of great (ii) _____ and growth.

Blank (i)
a. collapse
b. emergence
c. revitalization

Blank (ii)
d. abatement
e. decadence
f. enlightenment

13. Elite athletes spend (i) _____ amounts of time on conditioning for both strength and cardiovascular (ii) _____.

Blank (i)
a. paltry
b. copious
c. scant

Blank (ii)
d. endurance
e. inefficacy
f. deficiencies

14. Although some curriculums have (i) _____ courses such as art history as (ii) _____, they provide a connection between the human experience of the past and present.

Blank (i)
a. abolished
b. devised
c. deemed

Blank (ii)
d. critical
e. superfluous
f. preposterous

15. The art of (i) _____ likely began on cave walls, expanding to two-dimensional paper maps and, eventually, three-dimensional (ii) _____ maps.

Blank (i)
a. macramé
b. drafting
c. cartography

Blank (ii)
d. topographical
e. street
f. heat

Directions – Questions 16-20: Select the *two* answer choices that, when used to complete the sentence, fit the meaning of the sentence as a whole *and* produce completed sentences that are alike in meaning.

16. Civil engineers argue that the city storm sewer system is ill-equipped to handle the storm surge, and residents will need to be prepared to _____ the damage caused by rising water.

    a. mitigate
    b. escalate
    c. aggravate
    d. extenuate
    e. alleviate
    f. satisfy

17. Researchers _____ multiple tests to determine the cause of the inflammation.

    a. circulated
    b. postured
    c. conducted
    d. revoked
    e. performed
    f. radiated

18. Multiple theories were _____ during the meeting, any one of which could influence the opinion of the board.

    a. controverted
    b. undisclosed
    c. capitulated
    d. voiced
    e. suppressed
    f. espoused

19. A significant number of his followers found their faith _____ when they learned their donations were spent on luxuries rather than charities.

    a. rejuvenated
    b. obliterated
    c. extirpated
    d. stimulated
    e. entrenched
    f. aggrandized

20. In response to protests, administrators announced plans to _____ diversity on campus.

    a. promote
    b. quell
    c. attenuate
    d. cultivate
    e. depress
    f. impede

Section 4: Verbal Reasoning

Time – 30 Minutes

20 Questions

Directions – Questions 1-10: Each passage in this group is followed by questions based on its content. After reading a passage, choose the best answer to each question. Answer all the questions following a passage on the basis of what is stated or *implied* in that passage.

Questions 1–4 are based on the following passage:

The Journal of Pediatrics published a study that looks at the different types of treatment received by U.S. children, aged 4-17 years, diagnosed with attention-deficit/hyperactivity disorder (ADHD). Experts recommend using both medication and behavior therapy for children over 6 years of age and using behavior therapy as the first line of treatment for children under 6 years of age. CDC researchers found the most common treatment for ADHD is medication, and the majority of children have not received any type of behavior therapy.

Based on the best available evidence, effective strategies include treating ADHD with medication, parent-delivered behavior therapy, and teacher-delivered behavior therapy. The American Academy of Pediatrics (AAP) recommends that children 6 years or older be treated with medication or behavior therapy, preferably in combination. Parent-delivered behavior therapy is used as the first-line treatment for children younger than 6 years. The AAP also recommends that schools participate in any ADHD treatment plan, including support and accommodations, such as preferred seating and modified exams, homework, or school assignments.

Researchers have previously reviewed the treatments for ADHD, looking at whether different types of psychosocial treatments for ADHD were effective. They found that behavioral peer intervention, which is a form of behavior therapy where teachers train other students to support a child's positive behaviors, could be effective. The information on using dietary supplements or neurofeedback for treatment was too limited to determine whether they were effective. Social skills training, alone, which focuses on children's ability to interact and communicate with others, was not found to be effective.

Adapted from CDC informational material.

1. Select the sentence that best explains ADHD treatment for children under 6.

    a. CDC researchers found the most common treatment for ADHD is medication, and the majority of children have not received any type of behavior therapy.

    b. Experts recommend using both medication and behavior therapy for children over 6 years of age and using behavior therapy as the first line of treatment for children under 6 years of age.

    c. The AAP also recommends that schools participate in any ADHD treatment plan, including support and accommodations, such as preferred seating and modified exams, homework, or school assignments.

    d. They found that behavioral peer intervention, which is a form of behavior therapy where teachers train other students to support a child's positive behaviors, could be effective.

2. Based on the passage, what treatment is likely to be least effective?

    a. Medication
    b. Parent-delivered behavior therapy
    c. Dietary supplements
    d. Social skills training
    e. Teacher-delivered behavior therapy

3. What have most children diagnosed with ADHD received? Consider each of the three choices separately, and select all that apply.

    a. Medication
    b. Behavior therapy
    c. Neurofeedback

4. Based on the passage, what does social skills training involve?

    a. Having peers encourage positive behavior
    b. Offering students their favorite place to sit in class
    c. Teaching children how to interact and communicate with people
    d. Having teachers train other students to intervene
    e. Having parents reinforce positive behaviors

Questions 5–7 are based on the following passage:

A report out today from the Centers for Disease Control and Prevention (CDC), in collaboration with the Food and Drug Administration (FDA), found that current tobacco product use declined among U.S. middle and high school students from 2019 to 2020—driven by decreases in e-cigarette, cigar, and smokeless tobacco use. However, the National Youth Tobacco Survey (NYTS) data analysis also found that about 1 in 6 (nearly 4.5 million) students were current users of some type of tobacco product in 2020.

The study found that nearly 1 in 4 high school students (3.65 million) were current users of any tobacco product in 2020, down about 25% from about 1 in 3 (4.7 million) in 2019. About 1 in 15 middle school students (800,000) were current users of any tobacco product in 2020, down nearly 50% from about 1 in 8 (1.5 million) in 2019. From 2019 to 2020, decreases among both middle and high school students also occurred in use of any combustible tobacco product, the use of 2 or more tobacco products, e-cigarettes, cigars, and smokeless tobacco. In contrast, no change occurred in current use of cigarettes, heated tobacco products, hookah, or pipe tobacco during 2019–2020.

For the 7th year in a row, e-cigarettes were the most commonly used tobacco product among both middle and high school students. Additionally, many youths used multiple tobacco products; among current tobacco product users, about 1 in 3 high school students (1.27 million) and about 2 in 5 middle school students (340,000) used two or more tobacco products in 2020.

"The decline in tobacco product use over the past year is a win for public health," said CDC Director Robert R. Redfield, MD. "Yet, our work is far from done. Nearly 4.5 million U.S. youths still use tobacco products, putting a new generation at risk for nicotine addiction and other health risks."

"These findings demonstrate success in reducing youth use of tobacco overall, while also revealing changes in use patterns that will inform policymakers," said FDA Commissioner Stephen M. Hahn, M.D. "We remain very concerned about the overall tobacco use rates for young people, including the nearly 3.6 million youth who currently use e-cigarettes. FDA will continue to monitor the marketplace, expand our public education efforts, and use our regulatory authority to further ensure all tobacco products, and e-cigarettes in particular, are not marketed to, sold to, or used by kids."

The comprehensive and sustained implementation of evidence-based tobacco control strategies, combined with tobacco product regulation by FDA, is warranted for continuing progress toward reducing and preventing all types of tobacco product use among U.S. youths. Additionally, as the tobacco product landscape continues to diversify, surveillance of youth tobacco product use, including novel products, is important to inform public health policy and practice at national, state, and local levels.

Adapted from CDC informational material.

5. Based on the passage, although tobacco use has declined among U.S. teens, which of the following is true? Consider each of the three choices separately, and select all that apply.

   a. E-cigarettes still remain common.
   b. Students often use two or more tobacco products.
   c. Smokeless tobacco use is increasing.

6. Based on the passage, the overall decline in tobacco use is positive, but experts are concerned with

   a. increased tobacco use among middle schoolers.
   b. failed regulatory practices.
   c. a resurgence in combustible smoking products.
   d. marketing targeted toward teens.
   e. changing patterns in tobacco product usage.

7. Select the sentence that best expresses the continued threat to youth smoking rates.

   a. "FDA will continue to monitor the marketplace, expand our public education efforts, and use our regulatory authority to further ensure all tobacco products, and e-cigarettes in particular, are not marketed to, sold to, or used by kids."
   b. Additionally, as the tobacco product landscape continues to diversify, surveillance of youth tobacco product use, including novel products, is important to inform public health policy and practice at national, state, and local levels.
   c. "These findings demonstrate success in reducing youth use of tobacco overall, while also revealing changes in use patterns that will inform policymakers," said FDA Commissioner Stephen M. Hahn, M.D.
   d. Nearly 4.5 million U.S. youths still use tobacco products, putting a new generation at risk for nicotine addiction and other health risks.

Questions 8–10 are based on the following passage:

Students are more likely to engage in healthy behaviors and succeed academically when they feel connected to school. The National Longitudinal Study of Adolescent Health looked at the impact of protective factors on adolescent health and well-being among more than 36,000 7th–12th grade students. The study found that family, school, and individual factors such as school connectedness, parent-family connectedness, high parental expectations for academic achievement, and the adolescent's level of involvement in religious activities and perceived importance of religion and prayer were protective against a range of adverse behaviors. School connectedness was found to be the strongest protective factor for both boys and girls to decrease substance use, school absenteeism, early sexual initiation, violence, and risk of unintentional injury (e.g., drinking and driving, not wearing seat belts). In this same study, school connectedness was second in importance, after family connectedness, as a protective factor against emotional distress, disordered eating, and suicidal ideation and attempts. Research has also demonstrated a strong relationship between school connectedness and educational outcomes, including school attendance; staying in school longer; and higher grades and classroom test scores. In turn, students who do well academically are less likely to engage in risky behaviors. Compared with students with low grades, students with higher grades are significantly less likely to carry a weapon, smoke cigarettes, drink alcohol, and have sexual intercourse.

According to research by Blum and colleagues, children and adolescents' beliefs about themselves and their abilities are shaped by the extent to which they perceive that the adults in their lives care about them and are involved in their lives. Children and adolescents who feel supported by important adults in their lives are likely to be more engaged in school and learning. In the school setting, students feel supported and cared for when they see school staff dedicating their time, interest, attention, and emotional support to them. Students need to feel that adults care about them as individuals as well as about their academic achievement. Smaller schools may encourage more personal relationships among students and staff and allow for personalized learning. Schools can form schools-within-a-school or create multidisciplinary teams of teachers in which a small number of teachers know each student and can ensure that every student has an identified advisor.

Adapted from CDC informational material.

8. Based on the passage, why might students who have school connectedness have an extra advantage?

a. Students who feel connected to school are more likely to be connected to family.
b. Students who are connected at school are more likely to attend religious events.
c. Students who are connected at school are more likely to participate in after-school activities.
d. Students with higher grades are also less likely to engage in risky behaviors.
e. Students who are connected at school are more likely to attend smaller schools.

9. Based on the passage, *connectedness* matters to which of the following? Consider each of the three choices separately, and select all that apply.

    a. parents.

    b. school.

    c. peers.

10. School connectedness is determined to be the strongest protective factor for both boys and girls for a wide range of negative behaviors. Based on other information in the passage, what is one reason for this conclusion?

    a. Grades have a significant impact on the way students perceive themselves.

    b. More of the students in the study attended religious schools.

    c. Some of the students were homeschooled, and so there is a home-school connection.

    d. Testing provides a built-in process of validation and approval.

    e. There are more adults at school with whom they interact.

Directions – Questions 11-15: For each blank select one entry from the corresponding column of choices. Fill all blanks in the way that best completes the text.

---

11. Not everyone can chop down a tree. In fact, becoming a (i) _____ arborist requires quite a bit of work and study to earn one's (ii) _____.

Blank (i)	Blank (ii)
a. ersatz	d. credentials
b. specious	e. milieu
c. certified	f. collateral

12. For some time now, scientists have been observing the monarch butterfly (i) _____ from Mexico and California to other regions across the United States. The significant (ii) _____ of their population has scientists concerned about their extinction.

Blank (i)	Blank (ii)
a. caucuses	d. explosion
b. migration	e. propagation
c. population	f. decimation

13. Tidal flats, also called *mud flats,* are coastal wetlands where tides or rivers have (i) _____ sediment. They vary between two stages: submergence, when the water covers the area, and (ii) _____, when the water recedes.

Blank (i)	Blank (ii)
a. scoured	d. exposure
b. eroded	e. eradication
c. deposited	f. engulfed

14. Artists are often (i) _____ by other artists and their works of art. For example, one musician, so (ii) _____ by *1,001 Arabian Nights,* composed a/an (iii) _____ score to put the folktales to music.

Blank (i)	Blank (ii)	Blank (iii)
a. discouraged	d. confounded	g. elaborate
b. inspired	e. dispassionate	h. partial
c. dispirited	f. enthralled	i. discordant

15. The Seven Summits have summoned many a mountaineer who aimed to add their peaks to the climbing challenges they have _____.

a. surmounted
b. overlooked
c. succumbed to
d. dreaded
e. shunned

Directions – *Questions 16-20*: Select the *two* answer choices that, when used to complete the sentence, fit the meaning of the sentence as a whole *and* produce completed sentences that are alike in meaning.

16. The company offers drones with advanced AI, enabling them to fly _____ by locking on a target and tracking its path rather than being piloted remotely.
    a. expeditiously
    b. autonomously
    c. haphazardly
    d. erratically
    e. haltingly
    f. independently

17. The candidate went to every town hall and even door-to-door in the community to _____ support for her campaign.
    a. dissuade
    b. squelch
    c. hinder
    d. depreciate
    e. bolster
    f. buttress

18. Currently, many companies are _____ social values and social justice campaigns openly, both in store and online in an effort to align with consumers.
    a. advocating
    b. disputing
    c. suppressing
    d. endorsing
    e. rebuffing
    f. repudiating

19. One of the primary issues facing working families is the lack of _____ childcare.
    a. exorbitant
    b. dubious
    c. economical
    d. disreputable
    e. affordable
    f. inexpedient

20. In many ways, a scientist welcomes _____ because even they offer an opportunity to learn.
    a. contravention
    b. hardships
    c. compliance
    d. tribulations
    e. altercations
    f. remonstrances

Section 5: Quantitative Reasoning

Time – 35 minutes

20 Questions

QUANTITATIVE COMPARISON

Directions: Compare Quantity A and Quantity B, using additional information centered above the two quantities if such information is given, and select one of the following four answer choices:

1. $x > 1$

Quantity A	**Quantity B**
$\dfrac{x}{x-1}$	$\dfrac{-x}{-1+x}$

   a. Quantity A is greater.
   b. Quantity B is greater.
   c. The two quantities are equal.
   d. The relationship cannot be determined from the information given.

2. In the coordinate plane, the point $(2, 3)$ is on line m and the point $(3, 4)$ is on line n. Both lines have a negative slope.

Quantity A	**Quantity B**
The slope of line m	**The slope of line n**

   a. Quantity A is greater.
   b. Quantity B is greater.
   c. The two quantities are equal.
   d. The relationship cannot be determined from the information given.

3. m is a positive integer

Quantity A	**Quantity B**
The remainder when m is divided by 8	The remainder when m is divided by 16

   a. Quantity A is greater.
   b. Quantity B is greater.
   c. The two quantities are equal.
   d. The relationship cannot be determined from the information given.

4. A right circular cylinder with a radius of 5 centimeters has a volume of 25π cubic centimeters.

Quantity A	**Quantity B**
The height of the cylinder	1 centimeter

   a. Quantity A is greater.
   b. Quantity B is greater.
   c. The two quantities are equal.
   d. The relationship cannot be determined from the information given.

MULTIPLE-CHOICE – SELECT ONLY ONE ANSWER CHOICE

Directions: These questions have five answer choices. Select a single answer choice.

5. The outside of a ballpark has a circular path that has a radius of $\frac{8}{5\pi}$ km. If Katie starts at one point and walks continuously in one direction for a total of 4.8 km, how many times does she walk around the entire ballpark?

    a. 0.5
    b. 1
    c. 1.25
    d. 1.5
    e. 2

6. What is the average of $4x + 1, 8x - 3, 2x + 9, 6x - 4$?

    a. $5x + 1$
    b. $4x - 1$
    c. $5x - 0.75$
    d. $5x + 0.75$
    e. $3x + 0.75$

7. A fair, six-sided die is rolled once. What is the probability of it landing on a 1 or a 3? Round your answer to three decimal places.

    a. 0.333
    b. 0.033
    c. 0.598
    d. 0.167
    e. 0

8. If an integer is divisible by both 12 and 15, then the integer must also be divisible by which of the following integers?

    a. 60
    b. 48
    c. 24
    d. 40
    e. 50

MULTIPLE-CHOICE – SELECT ONE OR MORE ANSWER CHOICES

Directions: If the question specifies how many answer choices to select, select exactly that number of choices. If the question does not specify how many answer choices to select, select all that apply.

9. Which of the following are solutions of the equation $|5 + |x + 2|| = 16$? Select all the answer choices that apply.

    a. 9
    b. -9
    c. -13
    d. -23

10. A line passes through the point $(0, 6)$ and has slope $-\frac{1}{3}$. Which point or points does the line also pass through? Select all the answer choices that apply.

    a. $(6, 0)$
    b. $(-3, 5)$
    c. $(3, 5)$
    d. $(-6, 8)$

11. The average of all the consecutive integers from x to y inclusive is 67. Which of the following could be x and y? Select all the answer choices that apply.

    a. 33 and 101
    b. 33 and 103
    c. 67 and 73
    d. 55 and 87

12. If x and y are positive integers and $x = \sqrt{18y}$, which of the following are possible values of y? Select all the answer choices that apply.

    a. 0
    b. 2
    c. 3
    d. 8

NUMERIC ENTRY

Directions:

Enter your answer as an integer or a decimal if there is a single answer box OR as a fraction if there are two separate boxes—one for the numerator and one for the denominator.

Equivalent forms of the correct answer, such as 2.5 and 2.50, are all correct. Fractions do not need to be reduced to lowest terms, though you may need to reduce your fraction to fit in the boxes.

Enter the exact answer unless the question asks you to round your answer.

13. How many cubic inches of water are needed to fill a cylinder with a radius of 5 inches and a height of 8.5 inches? Write your answer in terms of π.

☐ π

14. What is the slope of a line with equation $3x + 10y - 4 = 56$?

☐

15. Next week, the probability that it will snow on any day of the week is $\frac{1}{10}$. What is the probability that it will snow on Wednesday but not on Saturday of next week?

☐

16. Two machines working simultaneously can produce 500 tin cans in 4 hours. If one machine can produce 150 cans in 3 hours, what is the rate of the other machine, in tin cans per hour?

DATA INTERPRETATION SETS

Question 17 refers to the following information:

Seven randomly selected grocery carts contain the following quantities of paper bags: 11, 5, 6, 9, 12, 10, and 7 paper bags.

17. If each grocery cart had 4 times as many bags, what would be the average?
    a. 36
    b. 8.57
    c. 35
    d. 34.286
    e. 33.245

Questions 18–20 refer to the following pie chart.

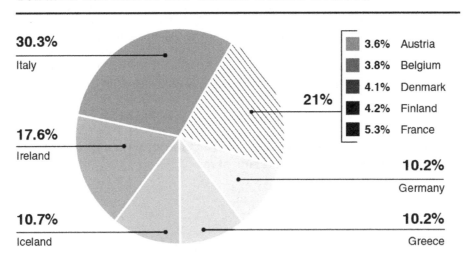

Percentage of students from European countries that studied abroad in the United States in 2018

- 30.3% Italy
- 17.6% Ireland
- 10.7% Iceland
- 21%
- 3.6% Austria
- 3.8% Belgium
- 4.1% Denmark
- 4.2% Finland
- 5.3% France
- 10.2% Germany
- 10.2% Greece

18. If 2,800 total students studied abroad in 2018, how many of them were from Iceland? Round to the nearest whole number.
    a. 29
    b. 30
    c. 11
    d. 300
    e. 299

19. If 2,800 total students studied abroad in 2018, and 40% of those from Italy were female, how many of the total students were Italian male students? Round to the nearest whole number.

    a. 509
    b. 510
    c. 339
    d. 340
    e. 848

20. If one student is randomly selected from the study abroad group in 2018, what is the probability that the student is NOT from Greece?

    a. 0.9
    b. 0.102
    c. 0.898
    d. 0.893
    e. 0.8

Section 6: Quantitative Reasoning

Time – 35 minutes

20 Questions

QUANTITATIVE COMPARISON

Directions: Compare Quantity A and Quantity B, using additional information centered above the two quantities if such information is given, and select one of the following four answer choices:

1.

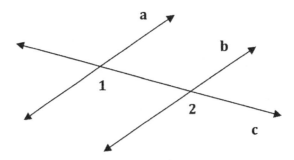

Lines *a* and *b* are parallel to one another.

Quantity A	**Quantity B**
Angle 1	Angle 2

a. Quantity A is greater.
b. Quantity B is greater.
c. The two quantities are equal.
d. The relationship cannot be determined from the information given.

2.

Quantity A	**Quantity B**

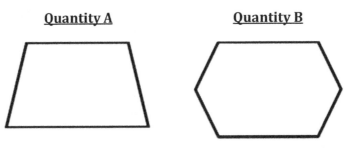

The sum of the measure of the interior angles.	The sum of the measure of the exterior angles.

a. Quantity A is greater.
b. Quantity B is greater.
c. The two quantities are equal.
d. The relationship cannot be determined from the information given.

3.

Test Scores	85	100	67	92	86

Quantity A
The mean of the given set of test scores

Quantity B
The median of the given set of test scores

a. Quantity A is greater.
b. Quantity B is greater.
c. The two quantities are equal.
d. The relationship cannot be determined from the information given.

4.

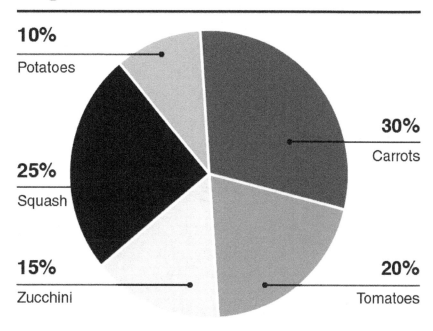

Vegetables

Quantity A
Percentage of vegetables that are carrots or tomatoes.

Quantity B
Percentage of vegetables that are zucchini, squash, or tomatoes.

a. Quantity A is greater.
b. Quantity B is greater.
c. The two quantities are equal.
d. The relationship cannot be determined from the information given.

MULTIPLE-CHOICE – SELECT ONLY ONE ANSWER CHOICE

Directions: These questions have five answer choices. Select a single answer choice.

5. Find the area of the shape.

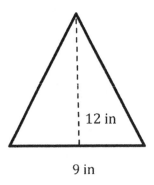

12 in

9 in

 a. 54 in^2
 b. 84 in^2
 c. 144 in^2
 d. 108 in^2
 e. 36 in^2

6. Find the surface area of the solid.

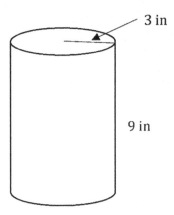

3 in

9 in

 a. 90 π
 b. 27 π
 c. 72 π
 d. 81 π
 e. 108 π

7. Choose the line that best fits the data below.

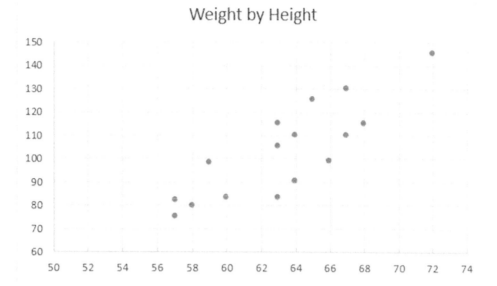

Weight by Height

a. $y = 5x - 210$
b. $y = 5x + 50$
c. $y = \frac{1}{5}x + 41$
d. $y = 4x + 300$
e. $y = 20x + 50$

8. What is the interquartile range for the following set of numbers?

$$2, 3, 4, 4, 5, 7, 8, 8, 11$$

a. 5
b. 4.5
c. 9
d. 5.8
e. 3

MULTIPLE-CHOICE – SELECT ONE OR MORE ANSWER CHOICES

Directions: If the question specifies how many answer choices to select, select exactly that number of choices. If the question does not specify how many answer choices to select, select all that apply.

9. Which number or numbers are prime factors of 320? Select all the answer choices that apply.

a. 5
b. 2
c. 3
d. 8
e. 10

10. The ratio of the number of apples to the total pieces of fruit in a fruit basket is 2 to 5. The other fruit in the basket is bananas. What is a possible ratio of fruit in the basket? Select all the answer choices that apply.

    a.   4 apples in a basket of 10 pieces of fruit
    b.   6 apples in a basket of 12 pieces of fruit
    c.   6 bananas in a basket of 10 pieces of fruit
    d.   5 apples in a basket of 11 pieces of fruit
    e.   9 bananas and 6 apples in the basket of fruit

11. What is a possible value of x that makes the inequality true? Select all the answer choices that apply.

$$2^{-3}\left(\frac{x}{2}\right) > 8^{-1}$$

    a.   16
    b.   12
    c.   3
    d.   6
    e.   -2

12. The ratio of the volume of Cylinder A (shown below) to the volume of Cylinder B (not shown) is 4:3. If the height of Cylinder B is a whole number, what are the possible values for the radius of Cylinder B? Select all the answer choices that apply.

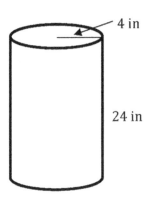

4 in

24 in

    a.   2
    b.   3
    c.   7
    d.   8
    e.   12

NUMERIC ENTRY

> *Directions*:
>
> Enter your answer as an integer or a decimal if there is a single answer box OR as a fraction if there are two separate boxes: one for the numerator and one for the denominator.
>
> Equivalent forms of the correct answer, such as 2.5 and 2.50, are all correct. Fractions do not need to be reduced to lowest terms, though you may need to reduce your fraction to fit in the boxes.
>
> Enter the exact answer unless the question asks you to round your answer.

13. The cost of groceries rose by a total of 12% from January to July. The Smith family spent $400 on groceries in January. If the month-to-month increase was linear, how much did the Smith family pay for their groceries in March?

$

14. A dessert company wants to package and sell its ice cream by the quart. The company picked containers that cost 73 cents each. The ice cream costs $2.07 per quart to make. How much should the company charge to turn a 30% profit?

$

15. Find the value of x. Enter your answer as a decimal number.

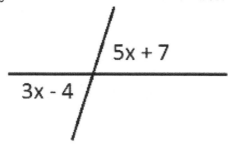

$5x + 7$

$3x - 4$

16. There are 12 students in a class. The teacher wants to choose 3 of them to be group leaders. How many different possible combinations of 3 students could be formed from this class of 12 students?

 combinations

DATA INTERPRETATION SETS

Questions 17–20 are based on the following data.

Population data for three cities is displayed below.

Martinville		Tradesville		Cratesville	
Year	Population	Year	Population	Year	Population
1980	72	1980	78	1980	107
1990	108	1990	120	1990	160
2000	162	2000	162	2000	213
2010	243	2010	204	2010	266

17. What is the percent increase in population in Martinville from 1980 to 1990?

   a. 150%

   b. 72%

   c. 50%

   d. 30%

   e. 15%

18. Which town or towns have a growth that shows an exponential pattern? List all that apply.

19. Which town or towns show a linear model of growth? Select all that apply.

   a. Martinville

   b. Tradesville

   c. Cratesville

   d. None of the above

20. Predict the population of Cratesville in 2050.

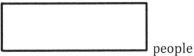 people

Answer Key and Explanations for Test #3

Section 3: Verbal Reasoning

1. E: Choice *E* is correct because the passage notes that not only do the buses made post-1990 feature reduced emission, but they also include more safety features such as mirrors and additional emergency exits. Choice *A* is not correct. Although older buses may not be built with as many safety features in mind, the passage does not suggest that those buses lack safety features. Choice *B* is also incorrect. Buses can be in use for 20 to 30 years, but there is no indication in the passage that replacements will occur within fleets in this time period. Choice *C* is incorrect. There is no data in this passage that suggests more modern buses have stopped using diesel. Instead, it suggests that emissions are a concern, not the type of fuel. Choice *D* is also incorrect. Although fleet owners are interested in using buses for as long as possible, it is not clear that longevity is prioritized over other concerns.

2. B: The passage states that travel by bus is the safest method for student transportation. Therefore, one can conclude that students who use other methods of transportation are, statistically, more likely to experience an accident. Therefore, Choice *B* is correct. Choice *A* is incorrect. The passage does discuss the Clean School Bus USA program, but it does not provide data that would lead to a conclusion that cost is the primary obstacle. Choice *C* is incorrect. Although new fleets are discussed and decreased emissions a priority, the mechanisms to achieve these goals (electric or hybrid options) are not discussed. Choice *D* is incorrect. Emissions are now a greater concern, but there is nothing in the passage to suggest there was no concern prior to 1990. Finally, Choice *E* is incorrect because although the EPA is developing stricter standards, the passage does not discuss enforcement of fleet replacement.

3. D: According to the passage, modern buses decrease emissions and include safety features and mechanisms that, in the past, have not been present. Based on these features and updates, modern buses are safer so Choice *D* is correct. Choice *A* is incorrect because it does not provide any evidence or support to explain how the EPA is ensuring safety. Choice *B* is incorrect because, again, simply stating that something is safe does not offer evidence or support. Although there is a fact in this sentence, it does not support the safety claim. Choice *C* is incorrect because it focuses on diesel emissions, but not safety, and doesn't offer evidence either. Choice *E* is incorrect. This option discusses the efforts and support aimed at improving school buses and health; however, it doesn't discuss safety in particular, nor does it offer any evidence.

4. A, C: The passage notes that habitat destruction is a greater threat than invasive species. In addition, the passage comments on the impact of ANS on tourism, recreational revenue, and property values, all of which extend beyond environmental devastation. Therefore, Choices *A* and *C* are correct. Choice *B* is incorrect because there are no benefits of invasive species discussed in this passage.

5. B: Choice *B* is correct. The passage discusses, in detail, the extensive costs of eradicating ANS, with a low-end estimate at $137 billion. Considering the known financial and nontangible costs, working to prevent cleanup and eradication would likely be more cost-effective than the cleanups required. Choice *A* is incorrect because the passage notes that one element alone is close to $140 billion, and therefore the costs are likely much more. Choice *C* is incorrect because the passage seems to indicate that the nonfinancial costs, such as extinction, are far more damaging. Choice *D* is incorrect because there is no data included here by which to make such a comparison or

385

conclusion. Choice *E* is incorrect because, logically, no single individual could possibly cover the costs of the consequences, even if one person could be identified.

6. D: This sentence clearly lays out the reasons (provides detailed evidence) why we may never know the cost; therefore, Choice *D* is the correct answer. Choice *A* is incorrect because it does not clearly discuss the cost, although it does reference an economic impact. Choice *B* is incorrect. Although it lays out the actual cost and provides details, it does not include a reason why the cost is so high. Choice *C* is incorrect; it is quite detailed about the impacts but not about why those impacts are so costly.

7. C: Choice *C* is the correct answer because the passage specifically discusses that azithromycin is used to treat *Salmonella,* so to find a strain that was resistant to that particular antibiotic was shocking. Choice *A* is incorrect because although beef was tied to this specific outbreak, it is not established in this passage that beef is often the culprit. Choice *B* is incorrect. WGS is expected to lead to quicker identification of strains and their origins; however, it will not cure the food poisoning that occurs with *Salmonella.* Choice *D* is incorrect because there is no concrete detailed discussion here of the prevalence of *Salmonella* that demonstrates multiantibiotic resistance. Finally, Choice *E* is incorrect because the passage clearly discusses how WGS can be used to track the origins of an outbreak.

8. A, B: WGS is discussed as a method to both predict the likelihood of an antibiotic-resistant strain as well as the ability to track the source. However, the passage does not discuss Choice *C* because WGS cannot help to prevent those strains.

9. B: The tone of the passage, particularly mentioning two separate outbreaks as well as the desire to be able to mitigate the risk and spread of these outbreaks, suggests that multiantibiotic-resistant strains are a growing concern. Therefore, Choice *B* is correct. Choice *A* is incorrect because there is no indication in the passage that scientists can stop *Salmonella,* but instead will have more success mitigating its spread by identifying risk and source. Choice *C* is incorrect because although there is discussion of azithromycin resistance occurring, it is noted to be rare. As such, it's not clear that other antibiotics should be explored. Choice *D* is incorrect because although multiple outbreaks happen simultaneously in this instance, there is no evidence or indication to suggest the frequency of simultaneous outbreaks. Choice *E* is incorrect. This outbreak was traced to beef; however, in part, it was also linked to cheese, which suggests, first, that beef is not the only source of *Salmonella,* and furthermore, there is no additional evidence in this passage that suggests it is typically the source for an outbreak.

10. D: Choice *D* is correct. Scientists discovered the source by linking the illness to beef and cheese consumed in the United States and Mexico. Choice *A* is incorrect because although it suggests methodology (how they tracked the evidence), it doesn't present the evidence gathered. Choice *B* is incorrect. It presents information about observations made by the scientists, but it doesn't suggest what they were able to track. Choice *C* is incorrect because although it discusses the methodology behind tracking and why it works, it doesn't isolate the evidence they were able to gather to draw their conclusion.

11. B, D, H: *Incomprehensible, Maritime,* and *bullion:* The textual clues and language such as "it may seem" and "average" mean Blank (1) is something akin to unbelievable. Blank (2) is the term for laws that apply to the sea, and Blank (3) is some kind of treasure. *Incontrovertible* means cannot be denied, and *inconsequential* means not important (being able to claim riches seems kind of important). *Seafaring* means ocean going but is informal and refers more to a vessel than a legal title. Similarly, a captain runs a specific ship rather than determining the laws of the oceans, so

Captain's doesn't fit. *Bouillon* is a type of broth, and *Boolean* is a language used by search engines, so neither of those is correct.

12. A, F: *Collapse* and *enlightenment:* The textual clue of "the start of the Renaissance" suggests that another time period ends first. Further, *great* and *growth* suggest something positive, so the best fit is *collapse* and *enlightenment. Abatement* means decline or stoppage, so it's not correct. Next, *emergence* suggests the Roman Empire is just starting rather than ending, and *decadence* means moral and cultural decline, so these answers suggest the opposite and are therefore incorrect. *Revitalization* suggests a new beginning and is also incorrect.

13. B, D: *Copious* and *endurance:* Contextual clues suggest that Blank (1) is filled by a word that means a lot, like *copious,* and Blank (2) is filled by a positive outcome related to building strength and cardio training, like *endurance.* Both *paltry* and *scant* mean little and therefore are not a good fit for Blank (1)'s meaning. Similarly, *inefficacy* and *deficiencies* are weaknesses and not something that someone builds toward, so both are incorrect.

14. C, E: *Deemed* and *superfluous:* The word "Although" at the start of the sentence should suggest to the reader that the sentence's meaning will provide a contradiction. So, Blank (1) should be a word that implies belief or thought and Blank (2) a word that contradicts the significance of the "connection between the human experience" of two time periods. Therefore, *deemed,* which means to call or name, and *superfluous,* which means extra, are the best fits. *Abolished* means to destroy or get rid of and is incorrect. *Critical* offers no contradiction in terms of the conditions of the sentence and isn't correct. *Devised,* which means to create or think up, isn't a great fit because the individuals implied in the sentence, who disagree with the course, wouldn't create it. Similarly, *preposterous* means utterly absurd and, in addition to being hyperbolic, doesn't match the conditions of the sentence.

15. C, D: *Cartography* and *topographical:* The contextual clues of the sentence reveal that we're looking for words that are related to maps, so when considering Blank (1), we'd look at the skill or art of mapmaking, which is called *cartography.* Similarly, for Blank (2), we'd be looking for a word that means a three-dimensional map, which is a *topographical* map. Although *macramé* is an art, it involves textiles and knots and is not related to maps. *Drafting* is too general a term and could apply to many different arts and therefore isn't the best fit here given the context clues. *Street maps* are not three-dimensional and is therefore incorrect. *Heat maps* exist as a way to measure temperature, usually related to contact or action in a specific location, but are not three-dimensional.

16. A, E: The sentence mentions the sewer system is ill-equipped and damage will occur, so one can infer that the correct words would be related to how to control the damage. Both *mitigate,* which means to limit, and *alleviate,* which means to make less severe, suggest how to handle potential damage. *Escalate* and *aggravate,* Choices *B* and *C,* suggest making the damage worse. *Extenuate,* Choice *D,* means to make it seem less serious. No doubt the damage will be serious, so it's incorrect. Finally, Choice *F* is incorrect because *satisfy* means to fulfill or meet expectations, and there is no implication here that there are expectations or demands to be fulfilled.

17. C, E: Based on the rest of the sentence, one can infer that tests were *conducted* and *performed* because the researchers were looking for answers. Choice *A* is incorrect because *circulated* means to pass around. Choice *B* is incorrect because *postured* means to act in a misleading way, and that's the antithesis to sound research. Choice *D* is incorrect because *revoked* means to take back rather than administer as one would a test. Finally, Choice *F* is incorrect because *radiated* means to emit energy.

18. D, F: One can infer from the sentence that theories were "brought up" or adopted by speakers. Both Choices *D* and *F*, *voiced* and *espoused*, mean to support and bring up. Choices *A*, *B*, and *E* are incorrect because *controverted*, *undisclosed*, and *suppressed* mean to deny or keep secret, all of which contradict the meaning of the sentence. Choice *C* is incorrect because *capitulated* means to surrender, which suggests, again, the opposite of voicing one's theory.

19. B, C: One can deduce, from the contrast at the end of the sentence, that the followers would be disappointed at best and their faith shaken. For that reason, Choice *B*, *obliterated*, and Choice *C*, *extirpated*, which mean destroyed, are the best answers. Choice *A* is incorrect because *rejuvenated* would mean their faith was renewed. Similarly, Choice *D* is incorrect because *stimulated* would mean they were invigorated by the betrayal. Choice *E*, *entrenched*, is incorrect because it suggests they would have "doubled down" on donations even with the betrayal. Finally, Choice *F* is incorrect because *aggrandized* also means to increase, and their faith likely would not have increased upon that discovery.

20. A, D: The word "protests" implies that change is being demanded, so the blank would best be filled by a word that would suggest increasing diversity. Choices *A* and *D*, *promote* and *cultivate*, both mean to improve and increase or to bolster, so they are the best choices. Choices *B*, *C*, *E*, and *F*, *quell, attenuate, depress,* and *impede*, all mean to stop, reduce, or impede and are therefore incorrect.

Section 4: Verbal Reasoning

1. B: Experts recommend medication and behavior therapy for children over 6 years of age and behavior therapy for children under 6 years of age, so Choice *B* is correct. Choice *A* is incorrect because although it mentions the types of therapy available, it discusses how they are currently applied rather than how and to whom they should be applied. Choice *C* is incorrect. It provides another avenue to aid in treatment; however, this is only one avenue, and often, children under 6 are not yet in school full-time, so it's not applicable. Choice *D* is incorrect because, much like Choice *C*, it is an avenue for treatment but may not be applicable to children under 6 and does not explain the full breadth of treatment.

2. D: Choice *D* is correct because the final paragraph of the passage states rather clearly that social skills training was not found to be an effective treatment method. Choice *A* is incorrect because medication is mentioned, repeatedly, as one of the most effective primary treatment options. Choices *B* and *E* are incorrect because it's noted that behavior therapy, delivered by parents or teachers, can be effective. Choice *C* is incorrect because the passage notes that dietary supplements and neurofeedback research has been inconclusive.

3. A: The passage notes that medication is the most common treatment method. Therefore, Choice *A* is the correct answer. Choice *B* is incorrect because the passage notes that most children have not had any behavior therapy. Choice *C* is incorrect because research involving neurofeedback has been inconclusive, and there's no mention here of the number of children who were studied.

4. C: Choice *C* is correct. The final sentence of the passage defines social skills training as teaching children with ADHD how to interact with others in social settings. Choice *A* is incorrect because peer behavior intervention is discussed, although that involves peers engaging with the student by praising positive behavior, whereas social skills training refers to peers interacting appropriately with one another without necessarily commenting on or praising their behavior. Choice *B* is incorrect because although it is mentioned as a modification schools could employ and may encourage socialization, it does not provide the guidance that social skills training would. Choice *D* is incorrect because, again, it is peer behavioral intervention instead. Choice *E* is incorrect because parental-based behavioral therapy is not the same as social skills training.

5. A, B: The passage notes that e-cigarettes are still used by 3.6 million young people, so Choice A is correct. Choice B is also correct because the passage notes that about 1 in 3 high school students and 2 in 5 middle school students used two or more tobacco products in 2020. Choice C is incorrect because the passage directly contradicts the idea that smokeless tobacco use is increasing.

6. E: In two separate sections, the passage notes that changing patterns and product diversity remain the biggest challenge in continuing the downward trend. Therefore, Choice *E* is correct. Choice *A* is incorrect because there is no indication that there is an increase in tobacco usage by middle school students (although they seem to be using more than high school students). Choice *B* is incorrect. In fact, continued regulatory practices are mentioned as a way to continue the decline. Choice *C* is incorrect because there was a decrease in combustible tobacco as with other methods. Choice *D* is also incorrect. Although marketing e-cigs is noted as a trend because it is on the decline as well, it's not the primary challenge noted.

7. B: Choice *B* is the correct answer because this sentence best details the threat through the diversification of the market and the introduction of new "novel" products, as e-cigs once were. Choice *A* is incorrect because it illustrates the method by which experts hope to continue the downward trend rather than illuminating continued risks. Choice *C* is incorrect because it suggests how data will help determine methods for continued mitigation but does not discuss the evolving threat. Choice *D* is incorrect because although it provides a significant statistic and the consequences of the threat (nicotine addiction), the greater threat is the method of nicotine delivery, such as e-cigs and novel methods that attract young smokers.

8. D: Choice D is correct because the overall goal of this connection is to prevent students from engaging in risky behaviors. Research found that not only did school connection do this, but it also raised grades, and students with higher grades were also less likely to engage in risky behaviors. This suggests the impacts might compound one another. Choice *A* is incorrect because there is no evidence in this passage that suggests connectedness to one institutional group correlates to connectedness in another. Choice *B* is incorrect because, again, there isn't evidence here to conclude that one connection helps foster another or that one connection means two connections must exist. Choice *C* is incorrect because there is no concrete evidence to suggest students with strong school ties also participate in after-school or extracurricular activities. Choice *E* is also incorrect because although the passage suggests that creating small groups within schools may help foster this school connectedness, there is no suggestion here that those with connection only attend small schools.

9. A, B: The passage discusses parental, school, and religious group connections specifically. However, Choice *C*, peer connection, is not discussed in this passage and is therefore incorrect.

10. E: The passage notes that the impact of connectedness is felt when adults in particular interact with and care about children. Further, the passage notes that, at school, students are likely to interact with multiple teachers and staff. One can then deduce that the multiple touchpoints, amount of time spent at school, and interactions with multiple adults would make school connection more powerful, so Choice *E* is the correct answer. Choice *A* is incorrect because although high grades and school focus may also decrease negative or risky behaviors, there's not enough data here to suggest that school connection is tied to high grades or that this would make school connection more powerful. In fact, students with poor grades may have strong school connections as well. Choices *B* and *C* are incorrect because there is no data to suggest that more of the students studied attended religious schools or that combining two elements, such as religious school and homeschooling, would amplify the impact. Choice *D* is incorrect because there is no data about the impact of testing and its effect on school or parental connections.

11. C, D: *Certified* and *credentials*: Contextual clues tell us the sentences are about tree professionals, and language clues tell us Blank (1) is an adjective that describes a type of arborist and Blank (2) is a noun that has a meaning related to something an individual could earn through studying. *Ersatz* means fake and is incorrect. Similarly, *specious* means misleading and is incorrect. *Milieu* simply means surroundings, and those aren't earned as much as being physically present in any space. *Collateral* is also incorrect because it is usually something (an asset) offered in exchange for a loan.

12. B, F: *Migration* and *decimation*: Language clues lead a reader to understand that Blank (1) is related to the movement of the butterflies and Blank (2) is filled with a word that suggests a diminishing population because it has led to concerns about extinction. The monarch *migration* sees the butterflies move from Mexico and California to across the United States, and *decimation* means to destroy. *Caucuses* is incorrect because it means to gather, and an *explosion* in population would contradict the concerns regarding extinction. Similarly, *population* doesn't suggest movement, and *propagation* means the population is growing rather than decreasing and is therefore also incorrect.

13. C, D: *Deposited* and *exposure*: Contextual clues regarding tidal flats or mud flats would clue a reader into the idea that sediment remains after the tide recedes, so Blank (1) is filled with a verb that likely means leave behind, such as *deposited*. Similarly, the receding waters expose the sediment, so *exposure* is the best fit for Blank (2). *Scoured* and *eroded* both mean to take away, so they do not work for Blank (1). *Eradicate* means to destroy, and if it were correct, tidal flats wouldn't exist at all. *Engulfed* means to cover, so the flats would never be exposed and would be underwater all the time (and thus just be referred to as part of the body of water).

14. B, F, G: *Inspired*, *enthralled*, and *elaborate*: Contextual clues here show that these sentences are about an artist who was moved to create something new after experiencing another piece of art. Therefore, in Blank (1), readers should expect a verb that expresses motivation, such as *inspired*. A *discouraged* or *dispirited* artist does not create, so those answers are incorrect. In Blank (2), there should be a word that describes the artist's incredibly positive reaction to the work (enough so that they would want to create), and Blank (3) should be an adjective that describes a score worthy of the words we find in Blanks (1) and (2) (meaning how the musician feels after experiencing a great work of art). For that reason, *enthralled* best expresses the passionate energy and excitement the artist feels to be so moved to create a new work. *Confounded* means confusion, and *dispassionate* means uninterested, neither of which inspires artistic response. Finally, an inspired artist does not create *partial* works because they are incomplete, and this doesn't fit with the rest of the meaning. *Discordant* means non-melodic and doesn't fit the meaning of the sentence in terms of artistic quality.

15. A: *Surmounted:* Contextual clues and language clues (such as *challenge*) suggest that Blank (1) will best be filled by a word that, by definition, means to overcome a challenge. *Surmounted* means both to overcome and to stand on top and is therefore an excellent fit. *Overlooked* means to have abandoned or ignored. *Succumbed to* means to fail; in other words, it would mean the mountaineers were conquered by the mountain and did not reach the summit. *Dreaded* means to fear, and that doesn't match the meaning of the sentence in terms of the subjects' desire to climb. Finally, *shunned* means to avoid or ignore and is also incorrect.

16. B, F: Several cues within the sentence suggest that the drone would be able to fly independent of an operator. As such, Choices *B* and *F, autonomously* and *independently,* are the best answers. Choice *A, expeditiously,* is incorrect because it suggests the drone would be able to fly quickly, and there aren't any indicators in the sentence that suggest this ability would impact speed. Choices *C, D,* and *E, haphazardly, erratically,* and *haltingly,* all suggest the drone would fly in an out-of-control manner; the words "target" and "track" within the sentence suggest precision, so those choices are incorrect.

17. E, F: The information in the sentence sets up a situation wherein a reader would understand that a door-to-door effort would be made to garner support. Therefore, Choices *E* and *F, bolster* and *buttress,* both of which mean to build or reinforce, would be the best answers. Choices *A, B,* and *C, dissuade, squelch,* and *hinder,* would all imply the effort was made to suppress support, so they are incorrect. Similarly, to *depreciate,* Choice *D,* means to belittle or diminish in value and would also be incorrect.

18. A, D: Several cues within the sentence, including the words "align" and "openly," suggest that companies would be building support. Therefore, *advocating* and *endorsing,* Choices *A* and *D,* which both mean to actively support, are the best choices. Choice *B, disputing,* which means to fight, is incorrect because, again, cues in the sentence suggest otherwise. Choice *C, suppressing,* would mean to hold back, and the word "openly" contradicts that. Choices *E* and *F, rebuffing* and *repudiating,* would be actively fighting against, and again, alignment with customers and the open effort suggests the opposite.

19. C, E: One of the biggest issues with childcare is its affordability. For that reason, Choices *C* and *E, economical* and *affordable,* which both mean cost-effective, are the best choices. Choice *A, exorbitant,* is incorrect because it means expensive. Choice *B, dubious,* is incorrect because it means questionable and, logically, no parent wants to leave their child at a questionable daycare. The same is true for Choice *D, disreputable,* which means having a bad reputation, which is also incorrect. And Choice *F, inexpedient,* means inconvenient and is therefore contradictory and incorrect.

20. B, D: The structure of the sentence suggests there is a contradiction happening—that the blank will be completed by something people don't normally want, but that offers opportunities, such as a challenge would. Therefore, Choices *B* and *D, hardships* and *tribulations,* which mean obstacles, are the best answers. Choice *A, contravention,* is incorrect because it means an illegal action, and that would create problems beyond an obstacle. Choice *C, compliance,* is also incorrect because it suggests things go well and smoothly and therefore contradicts the rest of the sentence structure. Choice *E, altercations,* means to fight. Although debate is healthy, *altercations* imply interactions that are a bit more intense than debate, perhaps physical, and is therefore incorrect. Choice *F, remonstrances,* suggest protests and significant pushback, and that is more forceful than a challenge or obstacle, so it is also not the best fit.

Section 5: Quantitative Reasoning

QUANTITATIVE COMPARISON

1. A: Given that $x > 1$, Quantity A is always going to be positive, and Quantity B will always be negative. Therefore, Quantity A is larger.

2. D: There is not enough information given. The slope is determined from 2 points on a line. Since only one point is given on each of the lines, other points need to be given to guarantee that the slope of each line is either larger than, smaller than, or equal to the other.

3. D: There is not enough information given. Either the two remainders will be equal, or the remainder when divided by 16 will be greater. For example, if the number is 156, the remainder when it is divided by 8 is 4, and the remainder when it is divided by 16 is 12. However, if the number is 214, the remainder when it is divided by 8 is 6, and the remainder when it is divided by 16 is also 6.

4. C: The height of a right circular cylinder is $V = \pi r^2 h$. In this case, $25\pi = \pi(5^2)h$, so $h = 1$ cm. The height of the cylinder is equal to 1 centimeter.

MULTIPLE-CHOICE – SELECT ONLY ONE ANSWER CHOICE

5. D: The circumference of the circle is equal to $2\pi r$, where r is the radius. Therefore, the radius of this circle is $2\pi\left(\frac{8}{5\pi}\right) = \frac{16}{5} = 3.2$ km. If Katie walked a total of 4.8 km, she walked $\frac{4.8}{3.2} = 1.5$ km around the arena.

6. D: The average is equal to $\frac{(4x+1)+(8x-3)+(2x+9)+(6x-4)}{4} = \frac{20x+3}{4} = 5x + 0.75$.

7. A: There are 6 outcomes on a six-sided die. There are 2 desired outcomes. Therefore, the probability is $\frac{2}{6} = \frac{1}{3} = 0.333$.

8. A: The number 12 factored into primes is $2 \times 2 \times 3$, and 15 factored into primes is 5×3. Therefore, the integer can be divisible by 60, which is $2 \times 2 \times 3 \times 5$.

MULTIPLE-CHOICE – SELECT ONE OR MORE ANSWER CHOICES

9. A, C: Solving the equation gives the following result:

$$5 + |x + 2| = 16 \text{ or } 5 + |x + 2| = -16$$

Therefore,

$$|x + 2| = 11 \text{ or } |x + 2| = -21$$

The second equation has no solution since the absolute value of an expression cannot be negative. The first equation gives us two possibilities:

$$x + 2 = 11; \ x + 2 = -11$$

Thus, the two solutions are 9 and -13.

10. C, D: Both the slope and the y-intercept of the line are given, so the equation of the line is $y = -\frac{1}{3}x + 6$. The two points $(3, 5)$ and $(-6, 8)$ are the only two ordered pairs that satisfy this equation.

11. A: The average of a group of consecutive integers can be found by averaging the smallest and largest numbers. Therefore, any pair of numbers whose average is 67 is an option. Therefore, their sum must be 134. The only choice with a pair of numbers whose sum is 134 is Choice A, 33 and 101.

12. B, D: Plugging 0 in for y results in $x = 0$, which is not a positive integer. Plugging 2 in for y results in $x = 6$, which is a positive integer. Plugging 3 in for y, the result is $x = \sqrt{54} = 3\sqrt{6}$, which is not a positive integer. Finally, plugging 8 in for y, the result is $x = \sqrt{144} = 12$, which is a positive integer.

NUMERIC ENTRY

13. 212.5π: Using the volume formula $V = \pi r^2 h$, where r represents the radius and h represents the height, we have $V = \pi(5^2)(8.5) = 212.5\pi$ cubic inches.

14. $-\frac{3}{10}$: We need to put the equation into slope-intercept form $y = mx + b$. Adding 4 to both sides and subtracting $3x$ from both sides, we have $10y = -3x + 60$. Then, dividing both sides by 10, we have $y = -\frac{3}{10}x + 6$. Therefore, $m = -\frac{3}{10}$.

15. $\frac{9}{100}$: We need to multiply the probability of each event. The probability of it snowing on Wednesday is $\frac{1}{10}$, and the probability of it not snowing on Saturday is $\frac{9}{10}$. Therefore, the probability of it snowing on Wednesday and not snowing on Saturday is $\frac{1}{10}\left(\frac{9}{10}\right) = \frac{9}{100}$.

16. 75: The combined rate of the two machines is 500 cans per 4 hours, which is equivalent to 125 cans per hour. The rate of the first machine is 150 cans per 3 hours, which is equivalent to 50 cans per hour. If x is equal to the rate of the second machine, then $50 + x = 125$ and $x = 75$. Therefore, the rate of the second machine is 75 cans per hour.

DATA INTERPRETATION SETS

17. D: If each number is multiplied by 4, the new grocery bag amounts are: 44, 20, 24, 36, 48, 40, and 28. The sum of these values is 240. Dividing by 7 results in the average 34.286.

18. D: The percentage corresponding to Iceland is 10.7%. We multiply .107 times 2,800 to obtain 299.6. Rounding to the nearest whole number, we know that 300 of the students in 2018 were from Iceland.

19. A: The percentage corresponding to Italy is 30.3%. Multiplying .303 by 2,800, we have 848.4. Because 40% were females, 60% were males. Therefore, .6(848.4) = 509.04. Rounding this value to the nearest integer shows that 509 students were male students from Italy.

20. C: The probability that the selected student was from Greece was 10.2%, or 0.102. Subtracting this value from 1, we have 1 – 0.102 = 0.898.

Section 6: Quantitative Reasoning

QUANTITATIVE COMPARISON

1. C: Choice C is correct because the two quantities are equal. Because lines a and b are parallel, corresponding angles are equal. Angles 1 and 2 are corresponding angles because they are in matching corners.

2. C: Choice C is correct because Quantity A and Quantity B are equal. The sum of the measure of the interior angles of a polygon is found by the expression $(n - 2) \times 180$. Using $n = 4$ because there are 4 sides to the polygon, Quantity A is $(4 - 2) \times 180 = 2 \times 180 = 360$. Quantity B is equal to 360 also because the measure of the sum of all exterior angles of a polygon is 360 degrees. These quantities are equal.

3. C: Choice C is correct because quantities A and B are equal. Quantity A is the mean, or average, of the given set of numbers. The average is found by adding all numbers together and dividing by the number of values. An expression to show this is $\frac{85+100+67+92+86}{5}$. The value of this mean is 86. The

393

median value of these test scores is found by placing them in ascending order and choosing the middle number. Putting them in ascending order gives the numbers 67, 85, 86, 92, 100. The middle of these numbers is 86. These two values are equal.

4. B: Choice B is correct because the percentage of those vegetables is larger. Quantity A is the sum of carrots and tomatoes, which is 30% and 20%. The percent of vegetables that are tomatoes or carrots is 50%. Quantity B is the sum of the vegetables that are zucchini (15%), squash (25%) or tomatoes (20%). These percentages add up to 60%. Therefore, quantity B is greater.

MULTIPLE-CHOICE – SELECT ONLY ONE ANSWER CHOICE

5. A: Choice A is correct because it uses the formula $A = \frac{1}{2}bh$ to calculate the area of the triangle. This formula becomes $A = \frac{1}{2} \times 9 \times 12 = 54$ in^2. Choice B is incorrect because it is the product of 12 times 7. Choice C is incorrect because it is the product of 12 multiplied by itself, not considering the base dimension. Choice D is incorrect because it is the product of 12 and 9. This answer would be the area for a rectangle with these dimensions, not a triangle. Choice E is incorrect because it is the product of $\frac{1}{3}$ of 9 and 12.

6. C: Choice C is correct because it takes the area of the top and bottom of the cylinder and adds it to the area of the side. The area of the top is found by the formula $A = \pi r^2$. For the top circle, the area is $A = \pi 3^2 = 9\pi$. The top and bottom are the same, so that area can be multiplied by 2. The area of the side is found by multiplying the height, 9, by the circumference, $C = 2\pi r = 2\pi(3) = 6\pi$, so $A = 9 \times 6\pi = 54\pi$. Adding the 2 together, the surface area is $A = 9\pi + 9\pi + 54\pi = 72\pi$. Choice A is incorrect because it takes the square of 9 and adds it to 9 to get 90 multiplied by π. Choice B is incorrect because it multiplies the two dimensions together, not considering the shapes or area formulas. Choice D is incorrect because it is the square of 9, not considering the top and bottom of the cylinder. Choice E is incorrect because it is the product of 9 and 12, not used in these dimensions.

7. A: Choice A is correct. A line of best fit is used with scatter plots to give a general pattern for the set of data. A line of best fit equation can be found by choosing two points that make a line that runs through the middle of the data. For this set, the points $(57, 75)$ and $(63, 105)$ were chosen. Writing a linear equation, the slope is found to be $\frac{105-75}{63-57} = \frac{30}{6} = 5$. Choosing one point and the slope, the missing y-intercept can be found by the equation: $75 = 5 \times 57 + b$. The value of b is -210. Writing the equation for the line of best fit yields $y = 5x - 210$.

8. B: Choice B is correct because it provides the interquartile range for the set of numbers. The interquartile range is found by first locating the median. The median of this set of numbers is 5. The Q1 value is the median of the lower half of numbers, which is 2, 3, 4, 4. These numbers have a median of 3.5. The Q3 value is the median of the upper half of numbers, which is 7, 8, 8, 11. The median is 8. The interquartile range is the different between the Q1 and Q3 values, which is $8 - 3.5 = 4.5$.

MULTIPLE-CHOICE – SELECT ONE OR MORE ANSWER CHOICES

9. A, B: Choices A and B give the two prime factors of 320. To find the prime factors of a number, the number must be broken down into smaller numbers that yield a product of 320. The prime factorization of 320 is $2^6 \times 5$. Since this is the prime factorization, there are only two numbers that are prime factors of 320. Choice C is incorrect because it is not a factor of 320. Choices D and E are not correct because they are not prime numbers.

10. A, C, E: Choice A gives a correct ratio of fruit because 4 to 10 can simplify to 2 to 5. Choice C gives a correct ratio of fruit because the original ratio of bananas to fruit is 3 to 5, which is a simplified form of 6 to 10. Choice E is correct because the ratio of bananas to apples is 3 to 2, which is a simplified form of 9 to 6. Choices B and D are incorrect because their ratios are not equal to those given in the original ratio of fruit.

11. A, B, C, D: Simplifying this inequality is the simplest way to solve this problem. When simplified, the inequality becomes $\frac{1}{8}\left(\frac{x}{2}\right) > \frac{1}{8}$. Solving for x gives a value of $x > 2$. Since the values in Choices A, B, C, and D are all greater than 2, they will all yield an inequality that is true. Choice E gives the inequality $\frac{1}{8}\left(-\frac{2}{2}\right) > \frac{1}{8}$. The final inequality becomes $-\frac{1}{8} > \frac{1}{8}$, which is not a true statement.

12. A, B, E: The volume of a cylinder is found by the formula $V = \pi r^2 h$. The volume of Cylinder A is found to be 384π. Since the ratio of the volumes of A to B is 4:3, the volume of the Cylinder B must have a value of $384\pi \times \frac{3}{4} = 288\pi$. Looking at the answer choices, the only numbers that have squares that are factors of 288 are 2, 3, and 12 (squares of 4, 9, and 144). These values for the radius would lead to a cylinder height of 72, 32, and 2. The other choices (7 and 8) have squares of 49 and 64. Since these values are not factors of 288, they would not allow for the height of the cylinder to be a whole number.

NUMERIC ENTRY

13. $416: If the cost of groceries rose linearly, the increase would be 2% of January's total per month. (This is found by taking the total increase of 12% and dividing it by the number of months from January to July.) March is the 2nd month after January, so the increase over January's total would be 2% × 2 = 4%. Thus, March's total would be $400 × 1.04 = $416.

14. $4.00: The first step to finding the answer is finding the total cost of materials per quart of ice cream. Adding the container price and the ice cream production cost, the total is $2.80. To find the price to charge based on cost of production and profit margin, one must use the formula Sales Price=Cost/(1-Profit Margin). For this problem, P=2.80/(1-.3), which simplifies to 2.8/.7, which is $4.00 even. This can be confirmed by dividing $2.80 by $4, which reduces to 70%, which confirms the 30% desired profit.

15. -5.5: The value of x can be found by setting the two expressions equal to each other, creating the equation $5x + 7 = 3x - 4$. This is a true statement because they are opposite angles, which makes them congruent. Solving the equation by subtracting $3x$ from both sides yields the equation $2x + 7 = -4$. Subtracting 7 from both sides, gives the equation $2x = -11$. Dividing both sides by 2, the value of x is found to be $x = -\frac{11}{2} = -5.5$.

16. 220 combinations: Since there are 12 students to choose from and the order does not matter, this problem can be solved using factorials. The formula needed for this problem is described as "12 choose 3" and is written as $\frac{12!}{3!(12-3)!}$. The value is calculated as follows:

$$\frac{12 \times 11 \times 10 \times 9 \times 8 \times 7 \times 6 \times 5 \times 4 \times 3 \times 2 \times 1}{(3 \times 2 \times 1) \times (9 \times 8 \times 7 \times 6 \times 5 \times 4 \times 3 \times 2 \times 1)} = \frac{12 \times 11 \times 10}{3 \times 2 \times 1} = \frac{1320}{6} = 220$$

Thus, there are 220 possible combinations for the 3 people chosen out of a group of 12 students.

DATA INTERPRETATION SETS

17. C: There was a 50% increase in the population of Martinville from 1980 to 1990. This increase is found by taking the population in 1990, 108 people, and dividing it by the population in 1980, 72 people. This yields 1.5, which is 150 percent. Finding the percent increase by taking 100 from this number, gives a final amount of 50%.

18. Martinville: Martinville has a population growth that is exponential. This is found by evaluating the changes in population over each of the ten-year periods. Each subsequent period can be found by increasing the previous period by 50%. By multiplying 72 by 1.5, the subsequent period's population is 108, $108 \times 1.5 = 162$, $162 \times 1.5 = 243$, and so on.

19. B, C: Tradesville shows a linear increase in population over the years given. This is confirmed by finding the slope of the line that passes through these points. The change in the years is consistently increasing by 10. The change in the population is consistently increasing by 42. These two numbers give a rate of change of 4.2 people per year. Cratesville shows a linear increase in population because it changes by 53 people over each of the ten-year periods. This constant change shows a linear relationship between population growth and time.

20. 478 people: The population of Cratesville in 2050 would be 478 people. This is found by using the linear relationship between population and time and predicting the next 40 years of growth. Since the rate of change is 53 people per 10 years, this same amount can be added for the next 40 years after 2010 to give a predicted population of 478 people.

How to Overcome Test Anxiety

Just the thought of taking a test is enough to make most people a little nervous. A test is an important event that can have a long-term impact on your future, so it's important to take it seriously and it's natural to feel anxious about performing well. But just because anxiety is normal, that doesn't mean that it's helpful in test taking, or that you should simply accept it as part of your life. Anxiety can have a variety of effects. These effects can be mild, like making you feel slightly nervous, or severe, like blocking your ability to focus or remember even a simple detail.

If you experience test anxiety—whether severe or mild—it's important to know how to beat it. To discover this, first you need to understand what causes test anxiety.

Causes of Test Anxiety

While we often think of anxiety as an uncontrollable emotional state, it can actually be caused by simple, practical things. One of the most common causes of test anxiety is that a person does not feel adequately prepared for their test. This feeling can be the result of many different issues such as poor study habits or lack of organization, but the most common culprit is time management. Starting to study too late, failing to organize your study time to cover all of the material, or being distracted while you study will mean that you're not well prepared for the test. This may lead to cramming the night before, which will cause you to be physically and mentally exhausted for the test. Poor time management also contributes to feelings of stress, fear, and hopelessness as you realize you are not well prepared but don't know what to do about it.

Other times, test anxiety is not related to your preparation for the test but comes from unresolved fear. This may be a past failure on a test, or poor performance on tests in general. It may come from comparing yourself to others who seem to be performing better or from the stress of living up to expectations. Anxiety may be driven by fears of the future—how failure on this test would affect your educational and career goals. These fears are often completely irrational, but they can still negatively impact your test performance.

Elements of Test Anxiety

As mentioned earlier, test anxiety is considered to be an emotional state, but it has physical and mental components as well. Sometimes you may not even realize that you are suffering from test anxiety until you notice the physical symptoms. These can include trembling hands, rapid heartbeat, sweating, nausea, and tense muscles. Extreme anxiety may lead to fainting or vomiting. Obviously, any of these symptoms can have a negative impact on testing. It is important to recognize them as soon as they begin to occur so that you can address the problem before it damages your performance.

The mental components of test anxiety include trouble focusing and inability to remember learned information. During a test, your mind is on high alert, which can help you recall information and stay focused for an extended period of time. However, anxiety interferes with your mind's natural processes, causing you to blank out, even on the questions you know well. The strain of testing during anxiety makes it difficult to stay focused, especially on a test that may take several hours. Extreme anxiety can take a huge mental toll, making it difficult not only to recall test information but even to understand the test questions or pull your thoughts together.

Effects of Test Anxiety

Test anxiety is like a disease—if left untreated, it will get progressively worse. Anxiety leads to poor performance, and this reinforces the feelings of fear and failure, which in turn lead to poor performances on subsequent tests. It can grow from a mild nervousness to a crippling condition. If allowed to progress, test anxiety can have a big impact on your schooling, and consequently on your future.

Test anxiety can spread to other parts of your life. Anxiety on tests can become anxiety in any stressful situation, and blanking on a test can turn into panicking in a job situation. But fortunately, you don't have to let anxiety rule your testing and determine your grades. There are a number of relatively simple steps you can take to move past anxiety and function normally on a test and in the rest of life.

Physical Steps for Beating Test Anxiety

While test anxiety is a serious problem, the good news is that it can be overcome. It doesn't have to control your ability to think and remember information. While it may take time, you can begin taking steps today to beat anxiety.

Just as your first hint that you may be struggling with anxiety comes from the physical symptoms, the first step to treating it is also physical. Rest is crucial for having a clear, strong mind. If you are tired, it is much easier to give in to anxiety. But if you establish good sleep habits, your body and mind will be ready to perform optimally, without the strain of exhaustion. Additionally, sleeping well helps you to retain information better, so you're more likely to recall the answers when you see the test questions.

Getting good sleep means more than going to bed on time. It's important to allow your brain time to relax. Take study breaks from time to time so it doesn't get overworked, and don't study right before bed. Take time to rest your mind before trying to rest your body, or you may find it difficult to fall asleep.

Along with sleep, other aspects of physical health are important in preparing for a test. Good nutrition is vital for good brain function. Sugary foods and drinks may give a burst of energy but this burst is followed by a crash, both physically and emotionally. Instead, fuel your body with protein and vitamin-rich foods.

Also, drink plenty of water. Dehydration can lead to headaches and exhaustion, especially if your brain is already under stress from the rigors of the test. Particularly if your test is a long one, drink water during the breaks. And if possible, take an energy-boosting snack to eat between sections.

Along with sleep and diet, a third important part of physical health is exercise. Maintaining a steady workout schedule is helpful, but even taking 5-minute study breaks to walk can help get your blood pumping faster and clear your head. Exercise also releases endorphins, which contribute to a positive feeling and can help combat test anxiety.

When you nurture your physical health, you are also contributing to your mental health. If your body is healthy, your mind is much more likely to be healthy as well. So take time to rest, nourish your body with healthy food and water, and get moving as much as possible. Taking these physical steps will make you stronger and more able to take the mental steps necessary to overcome test anxiety.

Mental Steps for Beating Test Anxiety

Working on the mental side of test anxiety can be more challenging, but as with the physical side, there are clear steps you can take to overcome it. As mentioned earlier, test anxiety often stems from lack of preparation, so the obvious solution is to prepare for the test. Effective studying may be the most important weapon you have for beating test anxiety, but you can and should employ several other mental tools to combat fear.

First, boost your confidence by reminding yourself of past success—tests or projects that you aced. If you're putting as much effort into preparing for this test as you did for those, there's no reason you should expect to fail here. Work hard to prepare; then trust your preparation.

Second, surround yourself with encouraging people. It can be helpful to find a study group, but be sure that the people you're around will encourage a positive attitude. If you spend time with others who are anxious or cynical, this will only contribute to your own anxiety. Look for others who are motivated to study hard from a desire to succeed, not from a fear of failure.

Third, reward yourself. A test is physically and mentally tiring, even without anxiety, and it can be helpful to have something to look forward to. Plan an activity following the test, regardless of the outcome, such as going to a movie or getting ice cream.

When you are taking the test, if you find yourself beginning to feel anxious, remind yourself that you know the material. Visualize successfully completing the test. Then take a few deep, relaxing breaths and return to it. Work through the questions carefully but with confidence, knowing that you are capable of succeeding.

Developing a healthy mental approach to test taking will also aid in other areas of life. Test anxiety affects more than just the actual test—it can be damaging to your mental health and even contribute to depression. It's important to beat test anxiety before it becomes a problem for more than testing.

Study Strategy

Being prepared for the test is necessary to combat anxiety, but what does being prepared look like? You may study for hours on end and still not feel prepared. What you need is a strategy for test prep. The next few pages outline our recommended steps to help you plan out and conquer the challenge of preparation.

STEP 1: SCOPE OUT THE TEST

Learn everything you can about the format (multiple choice, essay, etc.) and what will be on the test. Gather any study materials, course outlines, or sample exams that may be available. Not only will this help you to prepare, but knowing what to expect can help to alleviate test anxiety.

STEP 2: MAP OUT THE MATERIAL

Look through the textbook or study guide and make note of how many chapters or sections it has. Then divide these over the time you have. For example, if a book has 15 chapters and you have five days to study, you need to cover three chapters each day. Even better, if you have the time, leave an extra day at the end for overall review after you have gone through the material in depth.

If time is limited, you may need to prioritize the material. Look through it and make note of which sections you think you already have a good grasp on, and which need review. While you are studying, skim quickly through the familiar sections and take more time on the challenging parts.

Write out your plan so you don't get lost as you go. Having a written plan also helps you feel more in control of the study, so anxiety is less likely to arise from feeling overwhelmed at the amount to cover.

STEP 3: GATHER YOUR TOOLS

Decide what study method works best for you. Do you prefer to highlight in the book as you study and then go back over the highlighted portions? Or do you type out notes of the important information? Or is it helpful to make flashcards that you can carry with you? Assemble the pens, index cards, highlighters, post-it notes, and any other materials you may need so you won't be distracted by getting up to find things while you study.

If you're having a hard time retaining the information or organizing your notes, experiment with different methods. For example, try color-coding by subject with colored pens, highlighters, or post-it notes. If you learn better by hearing, try recording yourself reading your notes so you can listen while in the car, working out, or simply sitting at your desk. Ask a friend to quiz you from your flashcards, or try teaching someone the material to solidify it in your mind.

STEP 4: CREATE YOUR ENVIRONMENT

It's important to avoid distractions while you study. This includes both the obvious distractions like visitors and the subtle distractions like an uncomfortable chair (or a too-comfortable couch that makes you want to fall asleep). Set up the best study environment possible: good lighting and a comfortable work area. If background music helps you focus, you may want to turn it on, but otherwise keep the room quiet. If you are using a computer to take notes, be sure you don't have any other windows open, especially applications like social media, games, or anything else that could distract you. Silence your phone and turn off notifications. Be sure to keep water close by so you stay hydrated while you study (but avoid unhealthy drinks and snacks).

Also, take into account the best time of day to study. Are you freshest first thing in the morning? Try to set aside some time then to work through the material. Is your mind clearer in the afternoon or evening? Schedule your study session then. Another method is to study at the same time of day that you will take the test, so that your brain gets used to working on the material at that time and will be ready to focus at test time.

STEP 5: STUDY!

Once you have done all the study preparation, it's time to settle into the actual studying. Sit down, take a few moments to settle your mind so you can focus, and begin to follow your study plan. Don't give in to distractions or let yourself procrastinate. This is your time to prepare so you'll be ready to fearlessly approach the test. Make the most of the time and stay focused.

Of course, you don't want to burn out. If you study too long you may find that you're not retaining the information very well. Take regular study breaks. For example, taking five minutes out of every hour to walk briskly, breathing deeply and swinging your arms, can help your mind stay fresh.

As you get to the end of each chapter or section, it's a good idea to do a quick review. Remind yourself of what you learned and work on any difficult parts. When you feel that you've mastered the material, move on to the next part. At the end of your study session, briefly skim through your notes again.

But while review is helpful, cramming last minute is NOT. If at all possible, work ahead so that you won't need to fit all your study into the last day. Cramming overloads your brain with more information than it can process and retain, and your tired mind may struggle to recall even previously learned information when it is overwhelmed with last-minute study. Also, the urgent nature of cramming and the stress placed on your brain contribute to anxiety. You'll be more likely to go to the test feeling unprepared and having trouble thinking clearly.

So don't cram, and don't stay up late before the test, even just to review your notes at a leisurely pace. Your brain needs rest more than it needs to go over the information again. In fact, plan to finish your studies by noon or early afternoon the day before the test. Give your brain the rest of the day to relax or focus on other things, and get a good night's sleep. Then you will be fresh for the test and better able to recall what you've studied.

STEP 6: TAKE A PRACTICE TEST

Many courses offer sample tests, either online or in the study materials. This is an excellent resource to check whether you have mastered the material, as well as to prepare for the test format and environment.

Check the test format ahead of time: the number of questions, the type (multiple choice, free response, etc.), and the time limit. Then create a plan for working through them. For example, if you have 30 minutes to take a 60-question test, your limit is 30 seconds per question. Spend less time on the questions you know well so that you can take more time on the difficult ones.

If you have time to take several practice tests, take the first one open book, with no time limit. Work through the questions at your own pace and make sure you fully understand them. Gradually work up to taking a test under test conditions: sit at a desk with all study materials put away and set a timer. Pace yourself to make sure you finish the test with time to spare and go back to check your answers if you have time.

After each test, check your answers. On the questions you missed, be sure you understand why you missed them. Did you misread the question (tests can use tricky wording)? Did you forget the information? Or was it something you hadn't learned? Go back and study any shaky areas that the practice tests reveal.

Taking these tests not only helps with your grade, but also aids in combating test anxiety. If you're already used to the test conditions, you're less likely to worry about it, and working through tests until you're scoring well gives you a confidence boost. Go through the practice tests until you feel comfortable, and then you can go into the test knowing that you're ready for it.

Test Tips

On test day, you should be confident, knowing that you've prepared well and are ready to answer the questions. But aside from preparation, there are several test day strategies you can employ to maximize your performance.

First, as stated before, get a good night's sleep the night before the test (and for several nights before that, if possible). Go into the test with a fresh, alert mind rather than staying up late to study.

Try not to change too much about your normal routine on the day of the test. It's important to eat a nutritious breakfast, but if you normally don't eat breakfast at all, consider eating just a protein bar. If you're a coffee drinker, go ahead and have your normal coffee. Just make sure you time it so that the caffeine doesn't wear off right in the middle of your test. Avoid sugary beverages, and drink enough water to stay hydrated but not so much that you need a restroom break 10 minutes into the test. If your test isn't first thing in the morning, consider going for a walk or doing a light workout before the test to get your blood flowing.

Allow yourself enough time to get ready, and leave for the test with plenty of time to spare so you won't have the anxiety of scrambling to arrive in time. Another reason to be early is to select a good seat. It's helpful to sit away from doors and windows, which can be distracting. Find a good seat, get out your supplies, and settle your mind before the test begins.

When the test begins, start by going over the instructions carefully, even if you already know what to expect. Make sure you avoid any careless mistakes by following the directions.

Then begin working through the questions, pacing yourself as you've practiced. If you're not sure on an answer, don't spend too much time on it, and don't let it shake your confidence. Either skip it and come back later, or eliminate as many wrong answers as possible and guess among the remaining ones. Don't dwell on these questions as you continue—put them out of your mind and focus on what lies ahead.

Be sure to read all of the answer choices, even if you're sure the first one is the right answer. Sometimes you'll find a better one if you keep reading. But don't second-guess yourself if you do immediately know the answer. Your gut instinct is usually right. Don't let test anxiety rob you of the information you know.

If you have time at the end of the test (and if the test format allows), go back and review your answers. Be cautious about changing any, since your first instinct tends to be correct, but make sure you didn't misread any of the questions or accidentally mark the wrong answer choice. Look over any you skipped and make an educated guess.

At the end, leave the test feeling confident. You've done your best, so don't waste time worrying about your performance or wishing you could change anything. Instead, celebrate the successful completion of this test. And finally, use this test to learn how to deal with anxiety even better next time.

> **Review Video: Test Anxiety**
> Visit mometrix.com/academy and enter code: 100340

Important Qualification

Not all anxiety is created equal. If your test anxiety is causing major issues in your life beyond the classroom or testing center, or if you are experiencing troubling physical symptoms related to your anxiety, it may be a sign of a serious physiological or psychological condition. If this sounds like your situation, we strongly encourage you to seek professional help.

How to Overcome Your Fear of Math

Not again. You're sitting in math class, look down at your test, and immediately start to panic. Your stomach is in knots, your heart is racing, and you break out in a cold sweat. You're staring at the paper, but everything looks like it's written in a foreign language. Even though you studied, you're blanking out on how to begin solving these problems.

Does this sound familiar? If so, then you're not alone! You may be like millions of other people who experience math anxiety. Anxiety about performing well in math is a common experience for students of all ages. In this article, we'll discuss what math anxiety is, common misconceptions about learning math, and tips and strategies for overcoming math anxiety.

What Is Math Anxiety?

Psychologist Mark H. Ashcraft explains math anxiety as a feeling of tension, apprehension, or fear that interferes with math performance. Having math anxiety negatively impacts people's beliefs about themselves and what they can achieve. It hinders achievement within the math classroom and affects the successful application of mathematics in the real world.

SYMPTOMS AND SIGNS OF MATH ANXIETY

To overcome math anxiety, you must recognize its symptoms. Becoming aware of the signs of math anxiety is the first step in addressing and resolving these fears.

NEGATIVE SELF-TALK

If you have math anxiety, you've most likely said at least one of these statements to yourself:

- "I hate math."
- "I'm not good at math."
- "I'm not a math person."

The way we speak to ourselves and think about ourselves matters. Our thoughts become our words, our words become our actions, and our actions become our habits. Thinking negatively about math creates a self-fulfilling prophecy. In other words, if you take an idea as a fact, then it will come true because your behaviors will align to match it.

AVOIDANCE

Some people who are fearful or anxious about math will tend to avoid it altogether. Avoidance can manifest in the following ways:

- Lack of engagement with math content
- Not completing homework and other assignments
- Not asking for help when needed
- Skipping class
- Avoiding math-related courses and activities

Avoidance is one of the most harmful impacts of math anxiety. If you steer clear of math at all costs, then you can't set yourself up for the success you deserve.

LACK OF MOTIVATION

Students with math anxiety may experience a lack of motivation. They may struggle to find the incentive to get engaged with what they view as a frightening subject. These students are often overwhelmed, making it difficult for them to complete or even start math assignments.

PROCRASTINATION

Another symptom of math anxiety is procrastination. Students may voluntarily delay or postpone their classwork and assignments, even if they know there will be a negative consequence for doing so. Additionally, they may choose to wait until the last minute to start projects and homework, even when they know they need more time to put forth their best effort.

PHYSIOLOGICAL REACTIONS

Many people with a fear of math experience physiological side effects. These may include an increase in heart rate, sweatiness, shakiness, nausea, and irregular breathing. These symptoms make it difficult to focus on the math content, causing the student even more stress and fear.

STRONG EMOTIONAL RESPONSES

Math anxiety also affects people on an emotional level. Responding to math content with strong emotions such as panic, anger, or despair can be a sign of math anxiety.

LOW TEST SCORES AND PERFORMANCE

Low achievement can be both a symptom and a cause of math anxiety. When someone does not take the steps needed to perform well on tests and assessments, they are less likely to pass. The more they perform poorly, the more they accept this poor performance as a fact that can't be changed.

FEELING ALONE

People who experience math anxiety feel like they are the only ones struggling, even if the math they are working on is challenging to many people. Feeling isolated in what they perceive as failure can trigger tension or nervousness.

FEELING OF PERMANENCY

Math anxiety can feel very permanent. You may assume that you are naturally bad at math and always will be. Viewing math as a natural ability rather than a skill that can be learned causes people to believe that nothing will help them improve. They take their current math abilities as fact and assume that they can't be changed. As a result, they give up, stop trying to improve, and avoid engaging with math altogether.

LACK OF CONFIDENCE

People with low self-confidence in math tend to feel awkward and incompetent when asked to solve a math problem. They don't feel comfortable taking chances or risks when problem-solving because they second-guess themselves and assume they are incorrect. They don't trust in their ability to learn the content and solve problems correctly.

PANIC

A general sense of unexplained panic is also a sign of math anxiety. You may feel a sudden sense of fear that triggers physical reactions, even when there is no apparent reason for such a response.

CAUSES OF MATH ANXIETY

Math anxiety can start at a young age and may have one or more underlying causes. Common causes of math anxiety include the following:

THE ATTITUDE OF PARENTS OR GUARDIANS

Parents often put pressure on their children to perform well in school. Although their intentions are usually good, this pressure can lead to anxiety, especially if the student is struggling with a subject or class.

Perhaps your parents or others in your life hold negative predispositions about math based on their own experiences. For instance, if your mother once claimed she was not good at math, then you might have incorrectly interpreted this as a predisposed trait that was passed down to you.

TEACHER INFLUENCE

Students often pick up on their teachers' attitudes about the content being taught. If a teacher is happy and excited about math, students are more likely to mirror these emotions. However, if a teacher lacks enthusiasm or genuine interest, then students are more inclined to disengage.

Teachers have a responsibility to cultivate a welcoming classroom culture that is accepting of mistakes. When teachers blame students for not understanding a concept, they create a hostile classroom environment where mistakes are not tolerated. This tension increases student stress and anxiety, creating conditions that are not conducive to inquiry and learning. Instead, when teachers normalize mistakes as a natural part of the problem-solving process, they give their students the freedom to explore and grapple with the math content. In such an environment, students feel comfortable taking chances because they are not afraid of being wrong.

Students need teachers that can help when they're having problems understanding difficult concepts. In doing so, educators may need to change how they teach the content. Since different people have unique learning styles, it's the job of the teacher to adapt to the needs of each student. Additionally, teachers should encourage students to explore alternate problem-solving strategies, even if it's not the preferred method of the educator.

FEAR OF BEING WRONG

Embarrassing situations can be traumatic, especially for young children and adolescents. These experiences can stay with people through their adult lives. Those with math anxiety may experience a fear of being wrong, especially in front of a group of peers. This fear can be paralyzing, interfering with the student's concentration and ability to focus on the problem at hand.

TIMED ASSESSMENTS

Timed assessments can help improve math fluency, but they often create unnecessary pressure for students to complete an unrealistic number of problems within a specified timeframe. Many studies have shown that timed assessments often result in increased levels of anxiety, reducing a student's overall competence and ability to problem-solve.

Debunking Math Myths

There are lots of myths about math that are related to the causes and development of math-related anxiety. Although these myths have been proven to be false, many people take them as fact. Let's go over a few of the most common myths about learning math.

MYTH: MEN ARE BETTER AT MATH THAN WOMEN

Math has a reputation for being a male-dominant subject, but this doesn't mean that men are inherently better at math than women. Many famous mathematical discoveries have been made by women. Katherine Johnson, Dame Mary Lucy Cartwright, and Marjorie Lee Brown are just a few of the many famous women mathematicians. Expecting to be good or bad at math because of your gender sets you up for stress and confusion. Math is a skill that can be learned, just like cooking or riding a bike.

MYTH: THERE IS ONLY ONE GOOD WAY TO SOLVE MATH PROBLEMS

There are many ways to get the correct answer when it comes to math. No two people have the same brain, so everyone takes a slightly different approach to problem-solving. Moreover, there isn't one way of problem-solving that's superior to another. Your way of working through a problem might differ from someone else's, and that is okay. Math can be a highly individualized process, so the best method for you should be the one that makes you feel the most comfortable and makes the most sense to you.

MYTH: MATH REQUIRES A GOOD MEMORY

For many years, mathematics was taught through memorization. However, learning in such a way hinders the development of critical thinking and conceptual understanding. These skill sets are much more valuable than basic memorization. For instance, you might be great at memorizing mathematical formulas, but if you don't understand what they mean, then you can't apply them to different scenarios in the real world. When a student is working from memory, they are limited in the strategies available to them to problem-solve. In other words, they assume there is only one correct way to do the math, which is the method they memorized. Having a variety of problem-solving options can help students figure out which method works best for them. Additionally, it provides students with a better understanding of how and why certain mathematical strategies work. While memorization can be helpful in some instances, it is not an absolute requirement for mathematicians.

MYTH: MATH IS NOT CREATIVE

Math requires imagination and intuition. Contrary to popular belief, it is a highly creative field. Mathematical creativity can help in developing new ways to think about and solve problems. Many people incorrectly assume that all things are either creative or analytical. However, this black-and-white view is limiting because the field of mathematics involves both creativity and logic.

MYTH: MATH ISN'T SUPPOSED TO BE FUN

Whoever told you that math isn't supposed to be fun is a liar. There are tons of math-based activities and games that foster friendly competition and engagement. Math is often best learned through play, and lots of mobile apps and computer games exemplify this.

Additionally, math can be an exceptionally collaborative and social experience. Studying or working through problems with a friend often makes the process a lot more fun. The excitement and satisfaction of solving a difficult problem with others is quite rewarding. Math can be fun if you look for ways to make it more collaborative and enjoyable.

MYTH: NOT EVERYONE IS CAPABLE OF LEARNING MATH

There's no such thing as a "math person." Although many people think that you're either good at math or you're not, this is simply not true. Everyone is capable of learning and applying mathematics. However, not everyone learns the same way. Since each person has a different learning style, the trick is to find the strategies and learning tools that work best for you. Some people learn best through hands-on experiences, and others find success through the use of visual aids. Others are auditory learners and learn best by hearing and listening. When people are overwhelmed or feel that math is too hard, it's often because they haven't found the learning strategy that works best for them.

MYTH: GOOD MATHEMATICIANS WORK QUICKLY AND NEVER MAKE MISTAKES

There is no prize for finishing first in math. It's not a race, and speed isn't a measure of your ability. Good mathematicians take their time to ensure their work is accurate. As you gain more experience and practice, you will naturally become faster and more confident.

Additionally, everyone makes mistakes, including good mathematicians. Mistakes are a normal part of the problem-solving process, and they're not a bad thing. The important thing is that we take the time to learn from our mistakes, understand where our misconceptions are, and move forward.

MYTH: YOU DON'T NEED MATH IN THE REAL WORLD

Our day-to-day lives are so infused with mathematical concepts that we often don't even realize when we're using math in the real world. In fact, most people tend to underestimate how much we do math in our everyday lives. It's involved in an enormous variety of daily activities such as shopping, baking, finances, and gardening, as well as in many careers, including architecture, nursing, design, and sales.

Tips and Strategies for Overcoming Math Anxiety

If your anxiety is getting in the way of your level of mathematical engagement, then there are lots of steps you can take. Check out the strategies below to start building confidence in math today.

FOCUS ON UNDERSTANDING, NOT MEMORIZATION

Don't drive yourself crazy trying to memorize every single formula or mathematical process. Instead, shift your attention to understanding concepts. Those who prioritize memorization over conceptual understanding tend to have lower achievement levels in math. Students who memorize may be able to complete some math, but they don't understand the process well enough to apply it to different situations. Memorization comes with time and practice, but it won't help alleviate math anxiety. On the other hand, conceptual understanding will give you the building blocks of knowledge you need to build up your confidence.

REPLACE NEGATIVE SELF-TALK WITH POSITIVE SELF-TALK

Start to notice how you think about yourself. Whenever you catch yourself thinking something negative, try replacing that thought with a positive affirmation. Instead of continuing the negative thought, pause to reframe the situation. For ideas on how to get started, take a look at the table below:

Instead of thinking...	Try thinking...
"I can't do this math." "I'm not a math person."	"I'm up for the challenge, and I'm training my brain in math."
"This problem is too hard."	"This problem is hard, so this might take some time and effort. I know I can do this."
"I give up."	"What strategies can help me solve this problem?"
"I made a mistake, so I'm not good at this."	"Everyone makes mistakes. Mistakes help me to grow and understand."
"I'll never be smart enough."	"I can figure this out, and I am smart enough."

PRACTICE MINDFULNESS

Practicing mindfulness and focusing on your breathing can help alleviate some of the physical symptoms of math anxiety. By taking deep breaths, you can remind your nervous system that you are not in immediate danger. Doing so will reduce your heart rate and help with any irregular breathing or shakiness. Taking the edge off of the physiological effects of anxiety will clear your mind, allowing your brain to focus its energy on problem-solving.

DO SOME MATH EVERY DAY

Think about learning math as if you were learning a foreign language. If you don't use it, you lose it. If you don't practice your math skills regularly, you'll have a harder time achieving comprehension and fluency. Set some amount of time aside each day, even if it's just for a few minutes, to practice. It might take some discipline to build a habit around this, but doing so will help increase your mathematical self-assurance.

USE ALL OF YOUR RESOURCES

Everyone has a different learning style, and there are plenty of resources out there to support all learners. When you get stuck on a math problem, think about the tools you have access to, and use them when applicable. Such resources may include flashcards, graphic organizers, study guides, interactive notebooks, and peer study groups. All of these are great tools to accommodate your individual learning style. Finding the tools and resources that work for your learning style will give you the confidence you need to succeed.

REALIZE THAT YOU AREN'T ALONE

Remind yourself that lots of other people struggle with math anxiety, including teachers, nurses, and even successful mathematicians. You aren't the only one who panics when faced with a new or challenging problem. It's probably much more common than you think. Realizing that you aren't alone in your experience can help put some distance between yourself and the emotions you feel about math. It also helps to normalize the anxiety and shift your perspective.

ASK QUESTIONS

If there's a concept you don't understand and you've tried everything you can, then it's okay to ask for help! You can always ask your teacher or professor for help. If you're not learning math in a traditional classroom, you may want to join a study group, work with a tutor, or talk to your friends. More often than not, you aren't the only one of your peers who needs clarity on a mathematical concept. Seeking understanding is a great way to increase self-confidence in math.

REMEMBER THAT THERE'S MORE THAN ONE WAY TO SOLVE A PROBLEM

Since everyone learns differently, it's best to focus on understanding a math problem with an approach that makes sense to you. If the way it's being taught is confusing to you, don't give up. Instead, work to understand the problem using a different technique. There's almost always more than one problem-solving method when it comes to math. Don't get stressed if one of them doesn't make sense to you. Instead, shift your focus to what does make sense. Chances are high that you know more than you think you do.

VISUALIZATION

Visualization is the process of creating images in your mind's eye. Picture yourself as a successful, confident mathematician. Think about how you would feel and how you would behave. What would your work area look like? How would you organize your belongings? The more you focus on something, the more likely you are to achieve it. Visualizing teaches your brain that you can achieve whatever it is that you want. Thinking about success in mathematics will lead to acting like a successful mathematician. This, in turn, leads to actual success.

FOCUS ON THE EASIEST PROBLEMS FIRST

To increase your confidence when working on a math test or assignment, try solving the easiest problems first. Doing so will remind you that you are successful in math and that you do have what it takes. This process will increase your belief in yourself, giving you the confidence you need to tackle more complex problems.

FIND A SUPPORT GROUP

A study buddy, tutor, or peer group can go a long way in decreasing math-related anxiety. Such support systems offer lots of benefits, including a safe place to ask questions, additional practice with mathematical concepts, and an understanding of other problem-solving explanations that may work better for you. Equipping yourself with a support group is one of the fastest ways to eliminate math anxiety.

REWARD YOURSELF FOR WORKING HARD

Recognize the amount of effort you're putting in to overcome your math anxiety. It's not an easy task, so you deserve acknowledgement. Surround yourself with people who will provide you with the positive reinforcement you deserve.

Remember, You Can Do This!

Conquering a fear of math can be challenging, but there are lots of strategies that can help you out. Your own beliefs about your mathematical capabilities can limit your potential. Working toward a growth mindset can have a tremendous impact on decreasing math-related anxiety and building confidence. By knowing the symptoms of math anxiety and recognizing common misconceptions about learning math, you can develop a plan to address your fear of math. Utilizing the strategies discussed can help you overcome this anxiety and build the confidence you need to succeed.

Tell Us Your Story

We at Mometrix would like to extend our heartfelt thanks to you for letting us be a part of your journey. It is an honor to serve people from all walks of life, people like you, who are committed to building the best future they can for themselves.

We know that each person's situation is unique. But we also know that, whether you are a young student or a mother of four, you care about working to make your own life and the lives of those around you better.

That's why we want to hear your story.

We want to know why you're taking this test. We want to know about the trials you've gone through to get here. And we want to know about the successes you've experienced after taking and passing your test.

In addition to your story, which can be an inspiration both to us and to others, we value your feedback. We want to know both what you loved about our book and what you think we can improve on.

The team at Mometrix would be absolutely thrilled to hear from you! So please, send us an email at tellusyourstory@mometrix.com or visit us at mometrix.com/tellusyourstory.php and let's stay in touch.

Additional Bonus Material

Due to our efforts to try to keep this book to a manageable length, we've created a link that will give you access to all of your additional bonus material:

mometrix.com/bonus948/gre

Made in United States
Orlando, FL
29 April 2023

32605592R00233